THE REDISCOVERY OF JEWISH CHRISTIANITY

Society of Biblical Literature

History of Biblical Studies

Laurence L. Welborn, New Testament Editor

Number 5

THE REDISCOVERY OF JEWISH CHRISTIANITY
From Toland to Baur

THE REDISCOVERY OF
JEWISH CHRISTIANITY

FROM TOLAND TO BAUR

Edited by

F. Stanley Jones

Society of Biblical Literature
Atlanta

THE REDISCOVERY OF JEWISH CHRISTIANITY
From Toland to Baur

Copyright © 2012 by the Society of Biblical Literature

Library of Congress Cataloging-in-Publication Data

The rediscovery of Jewish Christianity : from Toland to Baur / F. Stanley Jones, editor.
    p. cm. — (Society of Biblical Literature history of biblical studies ; no. 5)
    Includes bibliographical references.
    ISBN 978-1-58983-646-4 (paper binding : alk. paper) — ISBN 978-1-58983-647-1 (electronic format)
    1. Messianic Judaism—History. 2. Jewish Christians—History. 3. Toland, John, 1670–1722. 4. Baur, Ferdinand Christian, 1792–1860. I. Jones, F. Stanley.
    BR158.R43 2012
    270.1072—dc23   2012006434

Printed on acid-free, recycled paper conforming to
ANSI/NISO Z39.48-1992 (R1997) and ISO 9706:1994
standards for paper permanence.

CONTENTS

Series Editor's Foreword vii
Preface
    F. Stanley Jones ix
Abbreviations xi

PART 1: BACKGROUND

"Christian Jews" and "Jewish Christians": The Jewish Origins
    of Christianity in English Literature from Elizabeth I to
    Toland's *Nazarenus*
    Matti Myllykoski 3

PART 2: JOHN TOLAND AND THE REDISCOVERY OF JEWISH CHRISTIANITY

John Toland's *Nazarenus* and the Original Plan of Christianity
    Pierre Lurbe 45

The Invention of Jewish Christianity in John Toland's *Nazarenus*
    Matt Jackson-McCabe 67

The Genesis, Purpose, and Significance of John Toland's *Nazarenus*
    F. Stanley Jones 91

PART 3: FROM TOLAND TO BAUR

"Jewish Christianity" and "Christian Deism" in Thomas Morgan's
    The Moral Philosopher
    Matt Jackson-McCabe 105

From Toland to Baur: Tracks of the History of Research into
    Jewish Christianity
    F. Stanley Jones 123

F. C. Baur's Place in the Study of Jewish Christianity
    David Lincicum 137

Nazarenus: Or, Jewish, Gentile, and Mahometan Christianity
    John Toland 167
    Preface 169
    Letter I 187

Contributors 243

Index of Modern Authors 245

SERIES EDITOR'S FOREWORD

When the plan was formulated for the SBL History of Biblical Studies, it was thought that the series would achieve its purpose by making available in English translation selected works of German and French scholarship that had established themselves as "classics" in the field of biblical studies. But the choice of Albert Eichhorn's provocative monograph on the Lord's Supper as the inaugural publication in the series (2007) already revealed the capacity (not fully anticipated by the series editor) of seminal scholarship to open new paths of research, when placed in the hands of a rising generation who appropriate the tradition in diverse cultural contexts.

Now the recovery and republication of a corrected text of John Toland's *Nazarenus* (1718) makes possible a startling, *alternative history* of the critical study of Christian origins. Working with new digital resources from the early modern period, F. Stanley Jones and his collaborators have shattered the foundations of one of the accepted truths of biblical studies, namely, that F. C. Baur inaugurated the critical investigation of early Christianity with his essay on the "Christ party" at Corinth in 1831. The contributors to the present volume demonstrate that the British Deists, and especially the Irishman John Toland, charted the path to the *terra nova* of a critical history of early Christianity and decisively influenced Johann Salomo Semler in Halle and then F. C. Baur and the members of his school in Tübingen. The chapters in this volume create the context for an informed reading of Toland's *Nazarenus*. Each chapter is a work of careful detection; the story unfolds with considerable suspense.

If a series editor may be permitted a proleptic evaluation, Matti Myllykoski's demonstration of the influence of John Selden (1584–1654), England's "chief rabbi," upon Toland's conception of early Christianity as a reform movement within Judaism may prove to be the most consequential moment in this revisionist history. Selden's justified claim that the first Christians were nothing but Jews gives point to Matt Jackson-McCabe's provocative question in the present volume: Why did Toland

and his German successors not ultimately formulate the category of their historical investigation as "Christian Judaism," rather than "Jewish Christianity"? The present volume answers this question by reconstructing the context of ecclesiastical politics and polemics in which Toland, Baur, and others were enmeshed. One cannot draw closed the net in which one is trapped. But for the rising generation of scholars and students, the question remains open. The arch of the revisionist history that Stanley Jones and his colleagues have begun to trace reaches from Selden to Boyarin and beckons us beyond.

L. L. Welborn
Professor of New Testament and Early Christianity
Fordham University

PREFACE

The following is a collective effort to lay the foundation for a revisionist history of the early critical study of Jewish Christianity. It grew out of the work of the Society of Biblical Literature's Consultation on Jewish Christianity, which has now become a Section.

That the Deists and the humanistic discussion of their time lie at the root of modern critical biblical studies has gained fairly general, though still not universal, recognition in historical accounts of the field. Anyone who has ever read Richard Bentley, for example, will be able to deny his primacy in the realm of New Testament textual criticism only with great difficulty. Further illumination of this British background of New Testament studies generally has proven a fruitful area of research over the last few decades; its relevance for the general intellectual revolution of the time has also attracted the attention of a noteworthy cadre of intellectual historians. The technological revolution of the Internet in combination with the digitalization of large collections of incunabula and other early publications has furthermore now made it possible for the modern scholar to research the early modern period with resources that exceed the individual holdings of even the world's greatest libraries. It is thus possible to rewrite the early history of biblical studies (not to speak of the intellectual history of the time) with greatly increased accuracy. This volume is such an exploration into one precise way in which the British Deists, in particular John Toland, set the table for later critical biblical studies. Combined, these studies explode the myth that F. C. Baur initiated the study of Jewish Christianity in 1831 and lay out the actual genesis of such inquiry over a century before Baur. This inquiry into Jewish Christianity has played, and still plays, no little role in the agenda of biblical and early Christian studies. Thus, examination of its genesis will shed some rarefied light on the study of Christian origins.

The book begins with a historical survey of English language usage of terms such as "Christian Jews" and "Jewish Christians" prior to John

Toland; it will be apparent here how Internet resources and digital collections with "search" capabilities have revolutionized the ability to trace in detail historical developments in early modern literature. Next, three studies seek to characterize Toland's accomplishment as reflected particularly in his book *Nazarenus* (1718), though also with attention to the context of this publication in Toland's career. A final section investigates the subsequent history of the study of Jewish Christianity and seeks to lift the veil on the mystery of how Toland's insights found their way to Germany and eventually to Ferdinand Christian Baur.

The contributions in this book do not explore why critical historical research into New Testament and ancient Christianity did not flourish further in England but instead found a way forward in Germany. That is a fascinating topic that the reader is encouraged to ponder and explore elsewhere.

Discussion of Toland would thus seem to be promising. Since, however, discussion cannot compete with actually reading Toland, a transcribed version of the most relevant parts of *Nazarenus* (title page, preface, and "first letter") is also included. This supplement should simultaneously enhance deliberation of the preceding studies and provide ready reference to *Nazarenus*. Corrections from a list of errata on the last page of *Nazarenus* have been silently inserted; other mistakes (mostly typographical, with the exception of a string of Greek transcriptional errors in note 33) Toland "left to the reader's candor." They are again left here as such, without the indication *sic*. In view of broken type and other printing imperfections, a number of copies of the second edition (also sometimes of the first edition) have been consulted. One day this transcription may provide a fairly accurate electronic version of the text. Archive.org currently has online an exceptional color pdf of the second edition from the library of Princeton Theological Seminary.

For consideration, acceptance, and encouragement of the project for the SBL History of Biblical Studies series, gratitude is extended particularly to Lawrence L. Welborn. Bob Buller has again earned thanks for implementation of his well-honed skills in turning a manuscript into a book.

Abbreviations

AANKG	*Archiv für alte und neue Kirchengeschichte*
AIHI	Archives internationales d'histoire des idées
AmSt.H	American University Studies Series, History
ANTZ	Arbeiten zur neutestamentlichen Theologie und Zeitgeschichte
APh	*Archiv für Philosophie*
BeRe	Beauchesne Religions
BHT	Beiträge zur historischen Theologie
CH	*Church History*
ExpTim	*Expository Times*
FKDG	Forschungen zur Kirchen- und Dogmengeschichte
Herm	*Hermathena*
HHS	Harvard Historical Studies
HTR	*Harvard Theological Review*
HUCA	*Hebrew Union College Annual*
JDTh	*Jahrbücher für deutsche Theologie*
JEH	*Journal of Ecclesiastical History*
JHI	*Journal of the History of Ideas*
JQR	*Jewish Quarterly Review*
JR	*Journal of Religion*
JTC	*Journal for Theology and the Church*
LCL	Loeb Classical Library
NTG	New Testament Guides
NTS	*New Testament Studies*
PrM	*Protestantische Monatshefte*
RAC	*Reallexikon für Antike und Christentum: Sachwörterbuch zur Auseinandersetzung des Christentums mit der antiken Welt.* Edited by Theodor Klauser et al. Stuttgart: Hiersemann, 1950–.
REJ	*Revue des études juives*

RESt	*Review of English Studies*
RSIt	*Rivista storica italiana*
SBLSymS	Society of Biblical Literature Symposium Series
SecCent	*Second Century*
ThJb(T)	*Theologische Jahrbücher (Tübingen)*
TRE	*Theologische Realenzyklopädie.* Edited by Gerhard Krause and Gerhard Müller. 36 vols. Berlin: de Gruyter, 1976–2004.
TZTh	*Tübinger Zeitschrift für Theologie*
VC	*Vigiliae christianae*
WUNT	Wissenschaftliche Untersuchungen zum Neuen Testament
ZKG	*Zeitschrift für Kirchengeschichte*
ZWT	*Zeitschrift für wissenschaftliche Theologie*

PART 1
BACKGROUND

"Christian Jews" and "Jewish Christians": The Jewish Origins of Christianity in English Literature from Elizabeth I to Toland's *Nazarenus*

Matti Myllykoski

The terms *Jewish Christian* and *Jewish Christianity* are often linked with the work of Ferdinand Christian Baur and the discussion of his ideas. However, it is generally known that these terms were used, at the beginning of the eighteenth century, by some British Deists, notably John Toland and Thomas Morgan.[1] As far as I know, no one has tried to look beyond that time and trace the roots and earliest use of this terminology in English literature. The following survey is an initial effort to penetrate into this unexplored area.[2] This study is limited to the specific terminology that characterizes Christian Jews and Jewish Christians (called here "JC terminology"). Therefore, it does not take into consideration all works on the origins of Christianity.

There is some justification for this narrow and focused approach. The English theologians knew Latin expressions such as *credentes ex circumcisione* and *credentes ex Judaeis* from quotations of the Church Fathers and medieval authors, but they did not try to translate and use them in

---

1. See, in particular, Hella Lemke, *Judenchristentum—Zwischen Ausgrenzung und Integration: Zur Geschichte eines exegetischen Begriffes* (Hamburger theologische Studien 25; Münster: Lit Verlag, 2001).

2. The present study is based on the data of Early English Books Online (EEBO: http://eebo.chadwyck.com/home), which—according to the introduction on the home page—"contains digital facsimile page images of virtually every work printed in England, Ireland, Scotland, Wales and British North America and works in English printed elsewhere from 1473–1700."

their English works. In turn, JC terminology is specifically employed in the exegetical discussion on the New Testament and early Christianity and sometimes also used to characterize contemporary Jews who had embraced Christian faith—but very seldom to portray Christians who had integrated Jewish customs in their religious practice. The terms *Christian Jew(s)* and *Jewish Christian(s)* were used throughout the seventeenth century, but the term *Jewish Christianity* was, as far as I can see, introduced later—perhaps first by John Toland in his *Nazarenus* (1718). The discussion of the Ebionites as the first and original Christians, in turn, starts with the debate on Unitarian (or Socinian) Christological views in the latter half of the seventeenth century. To be sure, this discussion, together with Toland's original contribution, can be regarded as the starting point for critical historical study of Jewish Christianity.

The terms *Christian Jew(s)* and *Jewish Christian(s)* were not used in the mission among the Jews. After the Puritan revolution in England, there were some Christians who were interested in the Jewish roots of Christianity, willing to admit that earliest Christianity was nothing else than reformed Judaism. Most of these individuals wanted both to advance the toleration of the Jews in England and to use their theological and political program to convert Jews to Christianity.[3] As far as I can see, in their written sources these protagonists do not characterize their potential converts or their ancient predecessors as Jewish Christians or Christian Jews.

In the written sources available to us, the use of JC terminology begins already at the end of the sixteenth century, and its earliest traces are clearly related to the general political and religious development of the country. The convocation of Queen Elizabeth (1558–1603) in 1563 stabilized the English reformation after the Catholic rule of Queen Mary (1553–1558); the moderate traditionalists and reformers were on the winning side, while the Catholics and the forefathers of the Puritans lost their case.[4] The anti-Catholic atmosphere among many Englishmen found expression in texts whose authors—among other peculiarities—regarded Catholic and Jewish practices as essentially similar. Therefore, the Catholics also resembled

---

3. For examples, see Richard Popkin, "Christian Jews and Jewish Christians in the 17th Century," in *Jewish Christians and Christian Jews from the Renaissance to the Enlightenment* (ed. Richard H. Popkin and Gordon M. Weiner; AIHI 138; Dordrecht: Kluwer, 1994), 60–61.

4. William P. Haugaard, *Elizabeth and the English Reformation: The Struggle for a Stable Settlement of Religion* (Cambridge: Cambridge University Press, 1968), 12–19.

Jewish Christians and Christian Jews of the early church. Protestant theology and its anti-Catholicism also strengthened the role of the Bible in the English reformation, particularly among the emerging party of the Puritans and especially during the Civil War. In his thorough treatment of the subject, Katz even says that the era of the English Civil War was "the high-water mark in bibliolatry in the Protestant world before the emergence of Fundamentalism in our own time."[5] Understandably enough, confessional polemics and self-serving readings of the biblical texts also called for more balanced, historically oriented, and context-related interpretations, which in turn contributed to the birth of modern biblical criticism. Through these developments, the use of JC terminology in the discussion on the beliefs and practices of early Christians grows notably after 1640. Statistically viewed, the terminology is particularly often present in the extensive exegetical works of Henry Hammond (1605–1660) and becomes more common in the latter half of the seventeenth century.

In this survey, we start with references to contemporary Christian Jews / Jewish Christians and then move on to discover how these designations were employed in studies of early Christianity. Since the use of the terms *Christian Jews* and *Jewish Christians* reveals interesting basic differences, we will explore their introduction to the written documents separately up to 1640. As for the later evidence, our study will focus on the use of the JC terminology in historically oriented confessional apology and the independent historical study of early Christian documents. The latter was particularly influenced by the Unitarian, or Socinian, debate in the 1690s.

"Christian Jews" and "Jewish Christians" of the Sixteenth and Seventeenth Centuries

Among the numerous references to individual contemporary Jewish converts to Christianity, these men and women are sometimes characterized as Christian Jews or Jewish Christians. In some late sixteenth- and early seventeenth-century English books, there are stories about Christian Jews. In his extensive—and heavily disputed—work on Protestant martyrs, John Foxe (1516–1587) tells "[t]he story of a christian Iew in

---

5. David S. Katz, *God's Last Words: Reading the English Bible from the Reformation to Fundamentalism* (New Haven: Yale University Press, 2004), 40.

Constantinople martyred by the Turkes" in 1528.[6] When this man was baptized and "became a good Christian," the "Turkes ... were vehemently exasperated agaynste hym, that he forsaking his Iewishnes, should bee regenerate to the faith of Christ." Foxe relates how they killed him for transgressing "theyr Mahometicall lawe" and left his corpse unburied. Also John Emmanuel Tremelius (1510–1580), born of Jewish parents in Ferrara and active as a Calvinist translator and teacher in Cambridge, was characterized as a "Christian Iew." In his work on speeches of dying Christians, the Puritan minister of Ipswich Samuel Ward (1577–1640) has a brief note about him: "Tremelius, a Christian Iew, Let Christ live, and Barrabas perish."[7] In his voluminous travel accounts from Africa and Asia, Samuel Purchas (1577?–1626) tells an exotic story about the Christians living in Goa, India, who are as superstitious as their Gentile countrymen in order to convert them into Christianity. Among them there are exchangers of money, called Xaraffos, "which are all Christian Iewes," experts of their trade who circulate the money and, unlike others, immediately recognize the counterfeit.[8]

In one instance, a Jew converted to Christianity and baptized into the contemporary English Church is called a "Cristian Jew." In an exhaustive doctrinal treatise, the Puritan theologian Edward Leigh (1602–1671) argues, among many other things, against celebrating sacraments in private houses. In this context, he refers to an individual Christian Jew who "desperately sick of the Palsie ... was with his bed carried to the place of Baptism."[9]

Beside these positive and neutral references, there are also negative ones. The term *Christian Jew* was also used of converted Jews who, despite their new identity, kept up their Jewish customs. In his anti-Semitic treatise, William Prynne (1600–1669), a Puritan lawyer and pamphleteer, complains that these Jews have even "converted Christian Jews to renounce

---

6. John Foxe, *Actes and Monuments of Matters Most Speciall and Memorable, Happenyng in the Church with an Vniuersall History of the Same* (London: Iohn Daye, 1583), 972.

7. Samuel Ward, *The Life of Faith in Death: Exemplified in the Liuing Speeches of Dying Christians* (London: Iohn Marriot and Iohn Grismand, 1622), 37.

8. Samuel Purchas, *Purchas His Pilgrimes* (London: Henry Fetherstone, 1625), 1760.

9. Edward Leigh, *A Systeme or Body of Divinity Consisting of Ten Books* (London: William Lee, 1654), 704.

their Christianity, and apostatise to their former Jewish Errors which they had quite renounced."[10] A Christian Jew is, in the theater and anecdotes, sometimes treated as a comical figure. In an anecdotal collection, Anthony Copley (1567–1609?), who can be characterized as a moderate Catholic loyalist during the reign of Queen Elizabeth, tells the following story, in which a Jewish Christian is treated as a hypocritical Jew in disguise:

> A drunken Christian, and a Iewish Christian being at tearms of brab-ble, the Drunkard call'd the counterfeit, a drunken companion, and the counterfeit call'd him a Iew: The next day they met again, & the Drunk-ard then said vnto the Iew: Sirrha, take thy Iew to thy selfe, and restore mee my Drunkard again.[11]

In his play *The wonder of a kingdome*, Thomas Dekker (ca. 1572–1632) portrays a "lame-legged souldier" who has been maltreated by a Christian Jew:[12] "More then my limbs losse; in one weeke he eate my wife up, and three children, this christian Iew did; Ha's a long lane of hellish Tenements, built all with pawnes."

All these texts refer to contemporary Jews converted to Christian-ity and use *Christian Jew* and *Jewish Christian* as an ethnic category. The former term seems to have been in common use in the time of Elizabeth I, but we know about the use of the latter only through negatively colored anecdotes by Anthony Copley. Furthermore, all these passages indicate that Christian Jews lived as members of Christian communities. Chris-tians who imitated Jewish customs, however, were much more likely to form communities of their own. In an interesting piece from the time after

---

10. William Prynne, *A Short Demurrer to the Jewes Long Discontinued Barred Remitter into England* (London: Edward Thomas, 1656), 6.

11. Anthony Copley, *Wits, Fittes, and Fancies* (London: Richard Iohnes, 1595), 106. Copley also tells another story of similar kind: "A Iewish Christian being at a banquet in a wood among many Ladies and Gent. a Gammon of Bacon was seru'd to the boord, and he to auoid suspition of Iudaisme, tasted therof: But when the banquet was done, he sorted himselfe alone into the thickest of the wood, & behind a tree forc'd vp all the Bacon againe with a fether out of his stomacke: Which being seene by one or two of the companie, they all jested at him therfore, and call'd him Iew: Wherunto he answered: No Iew (Gentlewomen) but thus: Assoone as euer the Deuilles saw, or smelt so good a relicke as Bacon within my body, they straight flue out at my mouth in vomit" (109).

12. Thomas Dekker, *The Wonder of a Kingdome* (London: Nicholas Vavasour, 1636), 4.1.

Cromwell's rule, Edward Brown (1644–1708) relates about a community of English men and women who lived in Heidelberg on the Rhine and called themselves Christian Jews:

> While I was at Heidelberg, two English men came kindly to me, Mr. Villers, and Timothy Middleton, belonging to Lobensfeldt Cloister, a Convent formerly of the Jesuites, but since let out to about an hundred English, who left their Country 1661. came up the Rhine, and by the permission of the Elector, settled themselves a few Miles from hence, living all together, Men, Women, and Children, in one house; and having a Community of many things: They are of a peculiar Religion, calling themselves Christian Jews; and one Mr. Poole, formerly living at Norwich, is their Head. They cut not their Beards, and observe many other Ceremonies and Duties, which they either think themselves obliged to from some Expressions in the old Testament, or from some New Exposition of their Leaders.[13]

To be sure, there were also some other Christian groups that imitated Jewish practices, but there is no evidence that they called themselves Christian Jews. The communities of Jewish believers in Jesus, in turn, originate in early nineteenth-century England, while the movement of the so-called messianic Jews developed only in the early 1970s.[14] Correspondingly, in seventeenth- and eighteenth-century English literature available through Early English Books Online (EEBO) and Eighteenth Century Collections Online (ECCO), the designation *messianic Jews* is still unknown. Even the word *messianic* seems to pop up only later in the British literature.

To sum up, the designation *Christian Jew* goes back at least to the early 1580s, but it is likely to be older than that. Among the earliest cases attesting the use of JC terminology, the expression *Christian Jew* (and, more seldom, *Jewish Christian*) is used to indicate or hint at Jews converted into Christianity. These terms are used with both positive and negative conno-

---

13. Edward Brown, *A Brief Account of Some Travels in Divers Parts of Europe* (2nd ed.; London: Benj. Toole, 1685), 122. The original italics have been removed.

14. Dan Cohn-Sherbock, "Modern Hebrew Christianity and Messianic Judaism," in *The Image of the Judaeo-Christians in Ancient Jewish and Christian Literature: Papers Delivered at the Colloquium of the Institutum Judaicum, Brussels 18–19 November, 2001* (ed. P. J. Tomson and D. Lambers-Petry; WUNT 158; Tübingen: Mohr Siebeck, 2001), 287–92. Cohn-Sherbock also presents the history and theology of the movement as well as critical discussion on its place within the boundaries of contemporary Judaism.

tations, and they may, but do not necessarily, indicate that the individual Jews in question continued to practice Jewish customs. As far as I can see, there is only one instance in which JC terminology is applied to Gentile Christians who imitate Jewish ritual traditions and call themselves Christian Jews. There do not seem to be cases in which *outsiders* would have regarded contemporary Gentile "Judaizers" as Christian Jews or Jewish Christians.

"Christian Jews" in Biblical Interpretation to the End of the Seventeenth Century

In late sixteenth- and early seventeenth-century English literature, detailed exegesis of biblical passages can be found not only in commentaries and annotated editions of the Holy Scriptures but also in works treating various doctrinal and ecclesiastical topics, such as the doctrines of justification and of the sacraments, the relationship between the church and the state, the authority of the king and the bishops, paying tithes, and similar issues. In the doctrinal and ecclesiastical works, the writings of the New Testament and the history of early Christianity are explained to support the views of the author in the debated contemporary cause. These works also include discussions on the Jewish origins of Christianity and refer here and there to "Christian Jews" as a notable group among early Christians. A special form of such discussion is the controversy between Protestant and Catholic theologians on divine providence and the authority of their corresponding institutions. This kind of discussion, which paved the way to thoroughly historical exegesis, was developed in the latter half of the seventeenth century, and we will turn to it only later in this essay.

It is interesting to see that, in the earliest period in which JC terminology was used, the designation *Christian Jews* is common, while *Jewish Christians* is rather unusual. It is surprising to see that the latter term was not introduced into the discussion of early Christianity until the second third of the seventeenth century. In their study of the New Testament, English Christian authors of the late sixteenth and early seventeenth centuries employed the term *Christian Jews* to describe ethnic Jews who had converted to the early Christian movement. The first author to introduce this term in the literary documents seems to be Gregory Martin (1542?–1582), Roman Catholic priest and biblical translator and commentator. In his commentary on the whole New Testament, Martin follows the view known from the writings of Augustine (*Epistle 82*, 15) on the Jewish

believers in the early Church. According to Augustine, the Jewish converts to Christ were allowed to follow the prescriptions of Mosaic law for
a certain time in order to ease away from them. During this transitional
period, they were neither to be despised by the Gentile converts nor were
they to criticize their fellow Christians for not obeying the law.[15] In his
introductory comment on Acts 11, Martin argues that the Christian Jews,
"like good Catholikes," yielded to Peter baptizing the Gentiles, and that
the mission of Barnabas and Paul in Antioch yielded Gentile converts,
"vvith perfite vnity betvvene them and the Church that vvas before them
atHierusalem."[16] During Paul's last visit to Jerusalem (Acts 21), Martin
says,[17] "he goeth about to satisfie the Christian Ievves there, vvho had been
misinformed of him as if he had taught it to be vnlawful for the Iewes to
keepe Moyses Lavv." While Paul does this "for feare of scandalizing the
vveake of that nation, nevvly conuerted or prone to receiue the faith, the
Apostles by Gods suggestion did thinke it good to obserue them as occasion required."[18] In a brief introduction to Romans 14, Martin further
observes about Paul's argument here:

> Like a moderator and peacemaker betvvene the firme Christians (vvho
> vvere the Gentils) and the infirme (vvho vvere the Christian Ievves,
> hauing yet a scruple to cease from keeping the ceremonial meates and
> daies of Moyses Lavv) he exhorteth the Ievv not to condemne the Gentil
> vsing his libertie: and the Gentil againe, not to condemne the scrupulous

---

15. To be sure, this basic view was developed before Augustine, but in view of the
influence of his debate with Jerome, it may be conveniently called the Augustinian
view. This view was characterized by a combination of an orthodox view of salvation
history and a moderate degree of goodwill and understanding toward Jewish believers in Jesus; cf. William Penn, *The Invalidity of John Faldo's Vindication of His Book,
Called, Quakerism No Christianity: Being a Rejoynder in Defence of the Answer, Intituled, Quakerism a New Nick-Name for Old Christianity* (n.p., 1673): "It is not bright
Day as soon as it is Day-break; *Shadows vanish gradually;* and Customs (especially if
grateful, as were Signs and Ceremonies to *Jewish-Christians)* are not easily left" (263).

16. Gregory Martin, *The Nevv Testament of Iesus Christ* (Rhemes: Iohn Fogny,
1582), 321 (original italics removed).

17. Ibid., 353.

18. Ibid., 356. It is interesting to note that some hundred years later, Samuel
Grascome (1641–1708?), in his work *An Historical Account of the Antiquity and Unity
of the Britanick Churches* (London: W. Whitwood, 1692), assumes that Paul was told
to go to the temple, not to calm down the Christian Jews but in order that "he might
Appear according to the Opinion of the Jews" (32).

Iew: but rather to abstaine from vsing his libertie, and then offending the Ievv, to be an occasion vnto him of aposting.[19]

In his comment on Gal 4:10, Martin says that, after all, "the Idolotrical obseruation" of Gentiles also "the Iudaical festiuities" have been "ended and abrogated, vnto vvhich notvvithstanding certaine Christian Ievves vvould haue reduced the Galatians against the Apostles doctrine."[20] He notes that all this "the Heretikes of our time falsely and deceitfully interprete against the Christian holidaies."

Martin also documents the traditional view when he says that specific New Testament letters were written to the Christian Jews. Paul wrote to the Hebrews, but Peter, whom "Christ designed" and made "his vicar," "executed that office after Christes departure, plating the Church first among the Ievves in Hierusalem and in al that countrey and coastes about, as Christ also him self before had preached to the Ievves alone."[21] Coming to Rome, Peter then preached to the Gentiles there, but he wrote his letters to "his Christian Ievves ... that vvere dispersed in Pontus, Galatia, Cappadocia, and Bithynia."[22] After Martin, other Christian authors also explained Peter's career in terms of his initial leadership of the Christian Jews and his later activity as apostle of the Gentiles and the leader of the church of Rome.[23]

At the end of the sixteenth century, the term *Christian Jews* was still variously used in discussions of early Christianity and New Testament texts. In his extensive work defending the constitution of the Church of England, John Bridges (d. 1618) once mentions how Paul, "to auoyde the offensiue opinion, that the multitude of the christian Iewes had conceyued of him," conformed "himselfe vnto theyr weakenesse."[24] In his marginal notes on "the Popish Testament," George Wither (1540–1605) once refers, in comments on Phil 3, to "the carnall Christian Iewes, that yet boasted in the circumcision of the flesh."[25] Both notes are in agree-

---

19. Martin, *Nevv Testament*, 416 (original italics removed).

20. Ibid., 507.

21. Ibid., 654 (original italics removed).

22. Ibid. (original italics removed).

23. Thus, e.g., Samuel Daniel, *Archiepiscopal Priority Instituted by Christ, Proved by Plaine Testimonies of Scripture* (London: Samuel Daniel, 1642), 17–18.

24. John Bridges, *A Defence of the Government Established in the Church of Englande for Ecclesiasticall Matters* (London: Thomas Chard, 1587), 1207.

25. George Wither, *A View of the Marginal Notes of the Popish Testament, Trans-*

ment with the Augustinian interpretation of Jewish believers: in the time of the apostles, the "Christian Jews" were still captivated by their customs, unable to embrace Christian freedom from the Law. This view sometimes leads to tensions that the theologians were reluctant to contemplate. The pious conformist William Perkins (1558–1602), in his commentary on Galatians, treats the Christian Jews as a comprehensive ethnical group that naturally includes Peter the Apostle;[26] in contrast, commenting on Gal. 2:21, he states theologically that "Paul here speakes against Christian Iewes, who ioyned the law and the Gospel."[27]

In his treatise *Of the Lavves of Ecclesiasticall Politie* (1604), the great Anglican Richard Hooker (1553?–1600) basically repeats the Augustinian view and does it more clearly and systematically than Martin. According to Hooker, the Apostles "did not so teach the abrogation" of the Law so "that euen the Iewes being Christian might for a time continue in them."[28] Hooker uses the term *Christian Jews* comprehensively when he notes that the "Christian Iewes did thinke at the first not onely themselues, but the Christian Gentiles also bound, and that necessarily, to obserue the whole lawe." After the apostolic council, Paul continued "still teaching the Gentiles, not onely that they were not bound to obserue the lawes of *Moses*, but that the obseruation of those lawes which were necessarily to be abrogated, was in them altogether vnlawfull." This, in turn, caused that in that point "his doctrine was misreported." On the basis of Paul's last visit to Jerusalem as portrayed in Acts 21, Hooker concludes that "[i]n some thinges therefore wee see the Apostles did teach, that there ought not to be conformitie betweene the Christian Iewes and Gentiles." After pointing out the various views on the "Iewish lawe" in the "Church of Christ," Hooker draws a line for the final abrogation of the law among Christians: "No, as long as the glory of the temple continued, and till the time of that finall desolation was accomplished, the very Christian Iewes did continue with their sacrifices and other parts of legall seruice."[29] The reason for Christian Jews to remain

---

lated into English by the English Fugitiue Papists Resiant at Rhemes in France* (London: Thomas Woodcocke, 1588), 213.

26. William Perkins, *A Commentarie or Exposition, vpon the Fiue First Chapters of the Epistle to the Galatians* (Cambridge: Rafe Cudworth, 1604) 152.

27. Ibid., 154–55.

28. Richard Hooker, *Of the Lavves of Ecclesiasticall Politie, Eight Bookes* (London: Iohn Windet, 1604) 188–89 (original italics removed).

29. Ibid., 191 (original italics removed).

loyal to the Mosaic law was for Hooker, as for numerous other Christian authors, to be sought in their "weaknesse."[30] Correspondingly, the anti-papal Calvinist Andrew Willet (1562–1621) emphasizes that the Christian Jews did not have a false, but a weak, faith.[31] Thus, most Christian authors who used the term *Christian Jews* in the course of the seventeenth century represented more or less clearly the Augustinian view. These authors also treated some particular problems with the Mosaic law, especially the tension between circumcision and baptism. For example, the royalist clergyman Jeremy Taylor (1613–1667) argues that in the times of the apostles, the Christian Jews were both circumcised and baptized, with the following rationale: "And indeed if the Christian Jews, whose children are circumcised, and made partakers of the same Promises and Title, and Inheritance and Sacraments, which themselves had at their conversion to the faith of Christ, had seen their children now shut out from these new Sacraments, it is not to be doubted but they would have raised a storm, greater then could easily have been suppressed."[32] Later, in *Antiquitates Christianae*, he points out the overlap of these practices: "The first Bishops of Jerusalem and all the Christian Jews for many years retained Circumcision together with Baptism; and Christ himself, who was circumcised, was also baptized; and therefore it is not so proper to call Circumcision a Type of Baptism: it was rather a Seal and Sign of the same Covenant to Abraham and the Fathers and to all Israel, as Baptism is to all Ages of the Christian Church."[33] Correspondingly, John Wallis (1616–1703) who is known as a mathematician, concludes in his "defense of the Christian Sabbath": "Those who thought themselves obliged to be Baptized, and to be Circumcised also, thought themselves in like manner obliged to observe the Lords day and also the Jewish Sabbath."[34]

---

30. Ibid., 196.

31. Andrew Willet, *Hexapla, That Is, a Six-fold Commentarie vpon the Most Diuine Epistle of the Holy Apostle S. Paul to the Romanes* (University of Cambridge, 1611), 626; similarly John Aucher, *The Arraignment of Rebellion: Or, The Irresistibility of Sovereign Powers Vindicated and Maintain'd* (London: William Abington, 1684), 14–15.

32. Jeremy Taylor, *A Discourse of Baptisme, Its Institution and Efficacy upon All Believers* (London: R. Royston, 1652), 49.

33. Jeremy Taylor, *Antiquitates Christianae: Or, The History of the Life and Death of the Holy Jesus as Also the Lives, Acts and Martyrdoms of His Apostles* (London: R. Royston, 1675), 117 (original italics removed).

34. John Wallis, *A Defense of the Christian Sabbath: In Answer to a Treatise of Mr. Tho. Bampfield Pleading for Saturday-Sabbath* (Oxford: Chr. Coningsby, 1692), 79

Furthermore, the presence of the Christian Jews in the early Church could explain the fulfilment of some traditional Old Testament prophecies. Sir Henry Finch (d. 1625) in his politically fatal book *The Worlds Great Restauration*, reads Dan 12:44 in allegorical terms: "One, his first declining vpon the Iewes of the East and North countries, conuerted to the Christian faith. Which must needs terribly affright him, being then beset before with vs Christians of the West, and behinde by the new Christian Iewes."[35] Samuel Purchas offers an "allegoricall and anagogicall sense or application of Solomon's Ophirian Nauigation" (1 Kgs 9:27–28): "Solomon seemes to signifie Christ, his Nauy the Church.... The Seruants of Hiram, the Doctors chosen out of the Gentiles, with the learned Christian Iewes (the seruants of Solomon) imployed ioyntly in this Ophirian Discouery."[36] Thomas Wilson (1563–1622), in *A Complete Christian Dictionary*, argues that Jerusalem "shou'd be re-inhabited by *Jews* again, viz. the *Christian Jews*."[37]

The use of the term *Christian Jews* in the period before 1700 is surprisingly coherent. In biblical scholarship, it characterizes the ethnic Jews who joined the Jesus movement and who for a time continued to observe the Mosaic law. Some authors say that the fall of the temple brought about the final abrogation of the law among the Christians and consequently turned all Christian Jews still following it into heretics.[38] In the light of the basic Augustinian view, the apostles are very seldom designated as Christian Jews and portrayed as keeping the Mosaic law, which was abrogated by the gospel. For these householders of the divine plan, all the (other) Christian Jews were a problem. In general statements, some authors are inclined to characterize these believers negatively; for example Arthur Lake (1569–1626), bishop of Bath and Wells, talks about the observation of "the cere-

(original italics removed); see also his work *A Defense of Infant-Baptism in Answer to a Letter (Here Recited) from an Anti-Paedo-Baptist* (Oxford: Henry Clements, 1697), 5.

35. Henry Finch, *The Worlds Great Restauration: Or, The Calling of the Ievves and (with Them) of All the Nations and Kingdomes of the Earth, to the Faith of Christ* (London: William Bladen, 1621), 57.

36. Purchas, *Purchas His Pilgrimes*, 3 (original italics removed).

37. Thomas Wilson, *A Complete Christian Dictionary Wherein the Significations and Several Acceptations of All the Words Mentioned in the Holy Scriptures of the Old and New Testament Are Fully Opened, Expressed, Explained* (London: Thomas Williams, 1661), 259 (article on "dispersion of Gentiles"; italics in the original).

38. Thus, e.g., Peter Heylyn, *The History of the Sabbath: In Two Books* (London: Henry Seile, 1636), 21.

monies whereunto the christian Jewes were pertinaciously addicted."[39] On the other hand, it was easy to imagine on the basis of Acts 15:1 that there were not so many misguided Christian Jews who stubbornly and incurably insisted on the circumcision of the Gentile Christians. Most commentators assume that the apostles acted rather pastorally in awkward situations, such as those described in Acts 21 and Gal 2:11–14, and took the weakness or zeal of some Christian Jews into consideration.

Despite these problems, the Christian Jews were basically seen as good followers of orthodox Christian doctrine. In his book *A Triall of our church-forsakers*, the puritan theologian Robert Abbot (1588?–1662?) contrasts the weaknesses of the Christian Jews with the spiritual Corinthian Christians, who "were more perfectly instructed in the mysteries of faith and charity." The "Iewes," in turn, "were Christians but in working: for the best of them (even the Apostles) were dreggish in *faith* and *life*: In faith about the death and resurrection of Christ, and about a temporall Kingdome doted upon. In life, when they too full of revenge in drawing the sword as *Peter,* or for calling down fire fró heaven upon the Samaritans."[40]

In 1661, the above-mentioned William Prynne published a tract in which he gives a thoroughly Augustinian answer to an exegetical problem:

> What was then the difference that made the practise of Paul lawfull in using the Ceremonies at Jerusalem, and the practice of Peter unlawfull in using the same Ceremonies among the Gentiles at Antioch. I answer; The difference was this: Though that corrupt opinion of the necessity of the Ceremonies prevailed alike in both places; yet the Ceremonies themselves had not the like warrant in both places. In Ierusalem they were known to have been the Commandements of God, and were not yet known to the Christian Jewes to have been abrogated, and therefore at Jerusalem they had warrant from God to use them, to avoid the offence of the weak Jew there; But at Antioch and all other Churches of the Gentile, they were (at best) but things Indifferent, as having never

---

39. Doctor Lake, bishop of Bath, and Wells, "Theses de Sabbato," 35, published as an appendix of William Twisse, *Of the Morality of the Fourth Commandement as Still in Force to Binde Christians* (London: Iohn Rothwell, 1641).

40. Robert Abbot, *A Triall of our Church-Forsakers: Or, A Meditation Tending to Still the Passions of Unquiet Brownists, upon Heb.10.25* (London: Philemon Stephens and Christopher Meredith, 1639), 143 (italics in the original).

been commanded of God there; Whence it was, that Peter saw his Liberty to forbear them there at his first comming.[41]

In the English literature of the seventeenth century, the term *Christian Jews* is seldom used for anti-Catholic polemics. As far as I can see, only one rather harmless example can be mentioned. In an extensive work from 1626, the anti-Catholic bishop Thomas Morton (1564–1659) relates Jerome's "dislike of the Clergie of Rome" with expressions that would make Catholics call him a schismatic and a Protestant. Morton points to the fact that Jerome "quit Rome, as a Land of Bondage, that he might inioy his libertie in Iudaea, among the Christian Iewes."[42]

On a few occasions the practices of the original "Christian Jews" were discussed in polemics against those who drew upon Jewish practices and rejected the tradition of the Church. John Traske (1583?–1636) was a Puritan who came to London in 1616, started to preach the observance of Sabbath instead of Sunday, and got some followers. He was accused of "Judaizing" and was put behind bars for three years.[43] John Falconer, in a lengthy pamphlet, refutes Traske's observance of the Sabbath with a typically Augustinian argument:

> many Christian Iewes did obserue their old Sabaoth as before, vntill the destruction of Ierusalem: yet can it not thence also be inferred, that such Christians obserued it in like manner afterwards, when they had seene the perfidious cruelty of their whole nation against Christ, so examplarly punished, their citty sacked, their Preists slaughtered, and Temple subuerted, neuer againe, by Christs speaches, to be restored, which could not but be taken by faithfull people as certaine signes of that law and religion wholy abrogated by Christ and ended, the cheifest exercises whereof consisted in prayers made in the Temple togeather with misterious rites and sacrifices therein only performed.[44]

---

41. William Prynne, *A Brief, Pithy Discourse upon I Corinthians 14. 40* (London: Edward Thomas, 1661), 12 (original italics removed).

42. Thomas Morton, *The Grand Imposture of the (Now) Church Of Rome: Manifested in This One Article of the New Romane Creede* (London: Mylbourne, 1626), 186 (original italics removed).

43. For Traske's own views, see Traske, *A Treatise of Libertie from Iudaisme, Or An Acknowledgement of True Christian Libertie* (London: N. Butter 1620).

44. John Falconer, *A Briefe Refutation of Iohn Traskes Iudaical and Nouel Fancyes* (Saint-Omer: English College Press, 1618) 39–40.

Sometimes Christians Jews and Gentile Christians are presented together as witnesses for the original practices of the early church against later ecclesiastical politics, particularly after the restoration of the monarchy and the victory of the Church of England over Puritanism. Some, for instance, argued against the practice of taking oaths. In his small treatise on the subject, John Gauden (1605–1662) takes up—after a reference to Jesus' saying in Matt 5:33–37—James and Christian Jews as witnesses for his case: "Agreeable to the same end and scope, and almost in the same words, Saint Iames writes to the dispersed Christian Iewes, who still retained that evil Custome of ordinary Swearing by the Creatures, as Heaven and Earth, and other such like Oathes, without any conscience of the manner or matter, or making good in effect such Oaths."[45] George Fox, arguing against tithes in a one-page pamphlet published in 1663, asks more than sceptically: "Did Christ give any such Command either among the Christian Jews, or Christian Gentiles, that they should receive or pay Tythes? or was there any mention of Tythes among the Christians for several hundred years after Christ?"[46] Thirteen years later, in a forty-three page treatise against baptism of the infants, Thomas Grantham (1634–1692) portrays a debate between a Baptist and a Presbyterian in which the Presbyterian develops an argument from the practice of the Christian Jews:

> Were not the Infants of the *Christian Jews* the day before their Conversion Members of the *Jewish* Church, and of Gods universal Church, of which the *Jews* were but a part? and doth it not sound strengely, that such Infants as were the day before Members of the *Jewish* Church, and of Gods universal Church, should be put out of the *Jewish* and the whole visible Church, by the faith of their Parents, or without unbelief? Either it was a Mercy to be a Member, of the Church, or not: If it was no mercy, then will it not follow, that the unbelieving Jews lost nothing by being broken off? If it was a mercy, how did the *Christians* Children forfeit it?[47]

---

45. John Gauden, *A Discourse concerning Publick Oaths, and the Lawfulness of Swearing in Judicial Proceedings* (London: R. Royston, 1662), 30 (original italics removed).

46. George Fox, *Queries concerning Tythes to the Priests and Bishops* (n.p., 1663).

47. Thomas Grantham, *The Quaeries Examined: Or, Fifty Anti-queries Seriously Propounded to the People Called Presbyterians* (London, 1676), 18 (emphasis in the original). In his answer, the Baptist separates the "Jewish Church," including the "Christian Jews" before their conversion, strictly from the "Gospel Church." Accord-

To sum up, despite some negative comments, the English authors also praise the faith and steadfastness of the "Christian Jews" and see among them continuity between the earliest followers of the Mosaic law and the later believers who were ready to leave the law behind.[48] Correspondingly, a thoroughly negative image of believers characterized as Christian Jews is simply missing from the English literature of this era. The term *Christian Jews* remains, up to the end of the seventeenth century, strongly tied to the Augustianian view of Jewish converts among first-century Christians and void of particular anti-Jewish or anti-Semitic characteristics. These attributes, in turn, enter in with the term *Jewish Christians*, which was coined notably later.

"JEWISH CHRISTIANS" AS A TERM FOR RELIGIOUS POLEMIC

In the literary sources available to us, the first appearances of the term *Jewish Christians* come from a different kind of discussion than the simple characterization *Christian Jews*. In texts of the seventeenth century, the former term does not replace the latter but rather enables Christian authors to characterize and discuss the earliest Jewish converts to Christianity from a different point of view, as if they were a group clearly separate from Jesus and his apostles. With the term *Jewish Christians*, the ethnic aspect of *Christian Jews* is placed in the background, and the Jewish converts to "Christianity" are basically portrayed as "Christians." The new term raises the question, What kind of Christians were these Jews? The common answer written on and between the lines: by their belief, practice, and ethos these early Jewish Christians were too "Jewish" to be identified as true Christians. They were a group apart.

The English translation of Celio Secondo Curione's (1503–1569) anti-Catholic work *Pasquine in a traunce* was published in two editions. One of them appeared in 1584, and the other was published *sine anno* but is dated by experts to 1566.[49] This edition includes an English introduction

---

ing to this point of view, the former was in fact "no Church at all," while the latter alone is "Gods universal Church."

48. See, e.g., William Chibald, *A Tryall of Faith: By the Touch-Stone of the Gospel, the Word of Faith. Whereby Christians May Discerne Whether or No, They Have a Saving Faith* (London: Iohn Teage, 1622), 344–45 (with a reference to Jas 2:5): "Christian Iewes, who are said to bee rich in faith."

49. Celio Secondo Curione, *Pasquine in a Traunce: A Christian and Learned Dia-*

about Curione's work and its intentions, which, on its very first page, refers to those who wish "secretly to walke with *Nichodemus* by night for feare of Iewish Christians." In this context, "Iewish Christians" means the leaders of the Church of Rome who later in the introduction are accused of "sophistrie, all their whole peste and trumperie, as meritorious Masses, fayned miracles, superstitious obseruances, hypocriticall fastings, paynted holiness, Sodomitical chastitie" and so on. If the date of 1566 is correct, this passage is the very first example of JC terminology that we have in the whole corpus of English literature. However, on the basis of other anti-Catholic, polemically colored references, this dating of the edition may be false. If it is correct, the reference to "Jewish Christians" must be an unparalleled ad hoc creation of the English author of the introduction.

Talk about "judaizers" and "judaizing Christians" was not very common in Protestant anti-Catholic polemic before the rise of Puritanism in the first half of the seventeenth century. However, there is some evidence of the use of these terms in the time of Queen Elizabeth. As far as I can see, the dialogue published by John Rainoldes (1549–1607) provides the earliest example. The two men mentioned in the title take up the Roman policy of cursing the Protestants, and Rainoldes states: "For as the Iewes, when they could not iustifie their wilful withstanding of the Sonne of God, agreed, that *if any man confessed him to be Christ, he should be excommunicated*: so by like reason your *Iudaizers* of *Rome* doo banne and curse vs, when they cannot iustifie their impudent customes and corruptions against vs."[50]

The term *Jewish Christians* was indeed seldom used in the first third of the seventeenth century, and the rare hits in the sources reveal the strongly negative view it was meant to convey. The above-mentioned Samuel Purchas says that among Christians, no "nationall calling" was possible after Jesus' resurrection.[51] The Jewish converts are "neither good Israelites which neglected the Temple and legall Rites; nor are good Christians to admit so many of them. Yet is it likely, that some *Iew*, or *Iewish Christians*

---

logue, *(Containing Wonderfull and Most Strange Newes, out of Heauen, Purgatorie and Hell).... Turned but Lately out of the Italian into This Tongue, by W. P.* (London: Wylliam Seres, 1566?); original italics removed.

50. John Rainoldes, *The Summe of the Conference betwene Iohn Rainoldes and Iohn Hart Touching the Head and the Faith of the Church* (London: Geor. Bishop, 1584), 575 (italics in the original).

51. Purchas, *Purchas His Pilgrimes*, 1112.

haue corrupted their *Christianitie* by continuance of Circumcision, which the *Ethiopians* and *Arabians* haue so many Ages before and since *Christ* vsed." This statement discards the Augustinian view of a certain period of time provided for Jewish converts to give up the observation of the Mosaic law. Instead, it presents the Christians of Jewish origins as heretics who "corrupted their Christianity." Purchas thus follows the classical view of Jerome, who found it impossible to think that true Christians would have observed the Law and confessed Jesus Christ at any time after Jesus' resurrection (*Epistle 112*, 13–17).

It is perplexing to see that some of the early references have nothing at all to do with the ethnic Jews among the first Christians. The negative statement of Purchas gives an indication of the way in which many Christian authors from 1640s on were about to use the term *Jewish Christians*. The introduction of this term into English theological literature in the 1640s is indeed strongly connected to the political debate of that period. In the 1630s, the Arminian bishops favored by Charles I had enraged the Puritans by decorating the interiors of churches and by introducing sacramental and ceremonial elements into the liturgy of the Church. This theological conflict was one of the main causes of the ensuing civil war and Puritan revolution. In the confused political and religious climate of the 1640s and 1650s, the ruling Puritans, fighting against the threat of Catholicism, introduced simplified versions of the ceremonies of the Common Book of Prayer.[52] In some works published in these decades, their Puritan authors point out the ceremonial, assumedly external, superstitious, and hypocritical character of the Catholic mass by calling those fond of all this Jewish Christians.

In the middle of the Civil War, William Gouge (1578–1653), an influential Puritan pastor at Blackfriars Church in London, published a lengthy sermon in which he attacked "the Popish rites." He refers to those "who on too great admiration of those externall glorious types, which were under the Law, doe wish the continuance of them still: as such a Temple as Solomon built, such Cherubims, such Altars, such Tables, such Candle-sticks, such Lavers, such Priestly vestments, and other such vessels and instruments."[53] He also finds a proper name for these people: "Some,

---

52. Susan Doran and Christopher Dunston, *Princes, Pastors and People: The Church and Religion in England 1529–1689* (London: Routledge, 1991), 28–32.

53. William Gouge, *The Progresse of Divine Providence* (London: William Gouge, 1645), 22–23 (original italics removed).

whom we may well stile *Jewish Christians*, so farre manifest their folly in this kinde, as they doe not only wish those former times, but also actually conform themselves to that servile pedagogy."[54] Thus, in Gouge's view, Catholics and "Jewish Christians" belong to the same *massa perditionis* whose "rites and ordinances" God reckons among "doctrines of devils." In a later work, an extensive commentary on the Hebrews, Gouge asks why priesthood was ordained and answers that it was ordained "for a meanes to draw men on to Christ."[55] However, the following groups cannot be included into this kind of priesthood: (1) "the superstitious Jewes," (2) "Christian Jewes, or Jewish Christians who conform themselves to the Jewish ceremonies," and (3) "Papists who do directly establish another Priest-hood." The second point of the list remains unclear, and Gouge does not make this group easier to identify when he rhetorically asks about them: "do they not advance the Leviticall Priest-hood against Christ, and make Christs Priest-hood imperfect?"[56]

It is reasonable to claim that the Civil War strengthened, particularly among the Puritans, the negative characterization of the "Jewish Christians." When George Wither (1588–1667) in a spiritual writing prays "for the Calling and Conversion of Jews, Turks, Heathens, and for all Heathenish and Jewish Christians in Gods time and mode," his readers knew what kind of Christians he had in mind.[57]

---

54. Ibid., 23.

55. William Gouge, *A Learned and Very Useful Commentary on the Whole Epistle to the Hebrews* (London: William Gouge, 1655), 164–65 of the new page numbering that starts at ch. 6.

56. In a confessional Catholic work entitled *Exomologesis Or, A Faithfull Narration of the Occaision and Motives of the Conversion unto Catholick Unity* (Paris: Chez Jean Billaine, 1653), Serenus Cressy (1605–1674), a Benedictine priest in French exile, also separates the Jewish Christians from the Jewish origin of Christianity, lumps them together with other Jews, and looks upon them as nonbelievers who have rejected the gospel. Explaining the priority given to S. Matthew among the evangelists, Cressy states: "because he having written his Gospel in Hebrew for the use of the Jewes and Jewish Christians to whom Christ commanded his Gospel should first be preached, and upon their refusall, to the Gentiles, even for that reason alone his Gospel might be thought to have deserved the first place, the rest following in the order as they were written" (107).

57. George Wither, *Meditations upon The Lords Prayer with a Preparatory Preamble to the Right Understanding, and True Use of This Pattern* (London: n.p., 1665), 36.

"Jewish Christians" in Historical
Study and Ecclesiastical Politics

In the time of the Reformation, Martin Luther, Ulrich Zwingli, Jéan Calvin, Thomas More, and others occasionally used of the congregation and institutions of the Old Testament Jews an overlapping term *ecclesia iudaeorum* ("the church of the Jews"), in contrast with *ecclesia gentium* ("the church of the Gentiles"). This term is sometimes used to point out a salvation-historical continuity, sometimes with the intention of comparing the stubborn people of the old covenant with the spiritual people of the new one. However, sometimes the terms *ecclesia iudaeorum* and *ecclesia gentium* are used to characterize the unity of the early Christian church that consisted of both Jews and Gentiles. Some Protestant authors also hint at "the church of the Jews in Jerusalem" as evidence against the idea of papacy. In his anti-papal work known in England in translation, Bernardino Ochino (1487–1564) argues that Peter cannot have been the first pope, because James the Just, called "the bishop of the bishops," was the first to rule, not only over "the churche of the Iewes at Hierusalem" but also over other churches.[58] This view is repeated by John Jewel (1522–1571), the bishop of Salisbury, in his lengthy treatise against "the weake, and vnstable groundes of the Romaine religion."[59]

In two early seventeenth-century works, we find a reference to the "Jewish Christian church." In English literature, the first known literary user of this term is Pierre Du Moulin (1568–1658), who aimed to expose the Pope and the Roman Catholic Church as evil powers of the end of times at hand. In his interpretation of the female figure in Rev 12, Du Moulin coins for the first time in written English documents the term *Iewish-Christian church* to describe the church of the "faithfull Iewes" after the ascension of Jesus, in order to separate them from "the Iewes that were the enimies of the gospell."[60] Du Moulin also explains Ezek 4:6

---

58. Bernardino Ochino, *A Tragoedie: Or, Dialoge of the Vniuste Vsurped Primacie of the Bishop of Rome, and of All the Iust Abolishyng of the Same* (London: Gwalter Lynne, 1549), 64v.

59. John Jewel, *A Replie vnto M. Hardinges Ansvveare by Perusinge Whereof the Discrete, and Diligent Reader May Easily See, the Weake, and Vnstable Groundes of the Romaine Religion, Whiche of Late Hath Beene Accompted Catholique* (London: Henry Wykes, 1565), 300.

60. Pierre Du Moulin, *The Accomplishment of the Prophecies: Or, The Third Booke*

and Num 14:34 as prophecies and takes up the "Iewish-christian Church" persecuted by the "heathenish Roman Empire" as parallel to the "Christian Church" persecuted by the "Papall Roman Empire."[61] According to Sir Henry Finch (d. 1625), Isa 24:23 portrays how Jews will again assume rule in Zion and Jerusalem, "not to set vp the legall ceremonies, but to institute the true spirituall worship and seruice of God."[62] In Isa 27:1 this theme is taken up again; the verse refers to "the flourishing felicite of the Iewish Christian Church."[63] Despite some scattered references, the expression *Jewish Christian Church* did not become popular. The basic division of the first Christians into Jewish and Gentile Christians is related to the dogmatic strife between Catholic and Protestant theologians. Both sides had an ardent desire to prove the truth of their own inherited ideas as well as the fallibility of the other party. Protestant apologists sought to present rational arguments for the independent historical truth of the Scriptures, while Catholic ones emphasized the insufficiency of the Bible alone and defended the infallibility of the oral tradition. This intense and manifold debate thus led to the quest for historical certainty concerning the practice and belief of the early church.[64]

One of the debaters was Henry Hammond (1605–1660), a moderate Puritan loyal to the crown.[65] Hammond uses the terms *Christian Jews* and *Jewish Christians* relatively interchangeably, through Augustinian lenses. He often uses both of them quite neutrally to designate the Jews of the Jerusalem church and Jews converted by them, without any reference to heresy. But he also employs these terms to indicate the internal schism among Jewish believers as well as those Jewish believers who wanted to bind the Gentile converts to the Mosaic law. Even when recalling the obstinate ones among the Christian Jews, Hammond wants to look at the problem from both sides. When talking about their "heresy," he also may refer,

---

in Defence of the Catholicke Faith Contained in the Booke of the High and Mighty King Iames I (trans. I Heath; Oxford: Iohn Barnes, 1613), 198 (italics in the original).

61. Ibid., 249.

62. Finch, *The Worlds Great Restauration*, 102.

63. Ibid., 135.

64. Beverley C. Southgate, "Blackloism and Tradition: From Theological Certainty to Historiographical Doubt," *JHI* 61 (2000): 97–114.

65. The "Puritanism" of Hammond has remained disputed. For a cautious view of Hammond as a moderate Puritan, see Michael McGiffert, "Henry Hammond and Covenant Theology," *CH* 74 (2005): 265–67.

as he does in his comment on the verb *skandalizein* in Matt 10:6,[66] to "the Gentile converts" who despise "the scrupulous Jewes." On several occasions, in order to designate some particular Jewish Christian "hereticks," he identifies "Judaizers" and "Gnosticks" who were followers of Simon Magus, describing them as converted Gentiles turned into Jews.[67] As far as I can see, Hammond is the first English author to use the term *Judaizing Gnosticks*, counting them particularly among Paul's opponents in Rome.[68] These distinctions are based on specific reasons related to the Catholic–Protestant debate concerning the distinctive groups of Jewish Christians and Gentile Christians.

In the documents of this debate, the question of Jewish Christians does not surface often, but it has a specific *Sitz im Leben*: the disagreement on the role and authority of Peter among the first Christians. The Catholic debaters argue that the supremacy of the pope is based on the donation made by Jesus Christ to Peter, the first bishop of Rome. Against this claim, Henry Hammond repeats in various writings the same basic line of reasoning. He reads the story about the election of the substitute for Judas Iscariot (Acts 1:12–26) in terms of commissioning each of the apostles and sending them to their own fields of mission. According to Hammond, "the Apostles distributed their great Province, the whole world, into severall lesser Provinces, one, or possibly more than one to go one way, the other another."[69] Since all these men were commissioned by Christ to have their own portion of apostolicity in their proper places—for example, Timothy as the bishop of Ephesus and the whole of Asia, and James as the bishop of Jerusalem and Judea, "[a]nd even of Syria and Cilicia also"

---

66. Henry Hammond, *A Paraphrase and Annotations upon All the Books of the New Testament Briefly Explaining all the Difficult Places Thereof* (London: Richard Davis, 1659), 61.

67. Hammond (*Paraphrase and Annotations,* 112) refers to Justin Martyr's statement (*Dial.* 122.2) about Gentile proselytes to Judaism who "doe, doubly to what the Jewes doe, blaspheme the name of Christ, and kill and reproach us, who doe believe." He continues: "The truth of this was very observable in the Gnosticks, who being Gentiles first, then Christians, at last in appearance turn'd Jewes, and then became the most bitter persecutors of the Orthodox Christians."

68. Hammond, *Paraphrase and Annotations,* 439, 448, 460. He refers to Rom 1:16–18; 2:17; 5:1. See also "Gnostick-Judaizers" (450).

69. Henry Hammond, *A Reply to the Catholick Gentlemans Answer to the Most Materiall Parts of the Booke of Schisme* (London: R. Royston, 1654), 50 (original italics removed).

(Acts 15:23)[70]—Peter had no special authority over them. Furthermore, since Peter was called to be the apostle exclusively to the circumcised and Paul exclusively to the Gentiles (Gal 2:7), Hammond says that it was by a special vision that Peter "was once commanded to preach to Cornelius a Gentile" (Acts 10).[71] Correspondingly, he explains Paul's preaching to the Jews, so often reported in Acts, by claiming that Paul always had to follow the divine economy of salvation and preach the gospel to the Jews in cities in which no other apostle had proclaimed the good news before him. But, in principle, when Peter and Paul "met in the same city (as at Antioch certainly they did, and at Rome also I make no question) then the one should constantly apply himself to the Iewes, receive disciples, form them into a Church, leave them to be governed by a Bishop of his assignation, and the other should doe in like manner to the Gentiles."[72] Here Hammond leans on a pseudo-Petrine passage in the *Apostolic Constitutions* (7.46.4, 6): "Of Antioch, Euodius, ordained by me Peter; and Ignatius by Paul.... Of the Church of Rome, Linus the son of Claudia was the first, ordained by Paul; and Clemens, after Linus's death, the second, ordained by me Peter." Thus, for Hammond, there were two different bishops and, correspondingly, two different communities in Antioch and Rome.[73]

John Sergeant (1622–1707), an Anglican apostate and a Roman Catholic controversialist and philosopher who first studied and then taught his new faith in Lisbon (1643–1655), became active in religious debates when he returned to England and later settled in London. He soon wrote two polemical treatises against Hammond's theory.[74] In his defense of Jesus' donation to Peter and Peter's primacy as the first bishop of Rome, Sergeant claims against Hammond that no apostle did anything that restrained the "illimited commission" given by Christ "to particular sorts of men"; in the

70. Henry Hammond, *Of Schisme: A Defence of the Church of England, against the Exceptions of the Romanists* (London: R. Royston, 1653), 44–45, 71. He further claims that James "hath the Principal place in the Councel at Jerusalem, where S. Peter is present" (72; original italics removed).

71. Hammond, *Reply,* 56 (original italics removed).

72. Ibid., 57 (original italics removed).

73. Ibid., 62–65; and Hammond, *Of Schisme.* 75–76. At Antioch, Peter ordained Euodius bishop of the Jewish Christians, while Paul ordained Ignatius to rule over the Gentile Christians. In Rome, Peter was followed by Clement and Paul by Linus.

74. John Sergeant, *Schism Dis-Arm'd of the Defensive Weapons, Lent It by Doctor Hammond, and the Bishop of Derry* (Paris: M. Blageart, 1655); *Schism Dispach't: Or, A Rejoynder to the Replies of Dr. Hammond and the Ld of Derry* (n.p., 1657).

commission of Christ, there simply was no division of jurisdictions or places among the apostles.[75] On the contrary: "the Apostles distributing themselves into several Provinces was done a long time after the coming of the Holy Ghost."[76] The election of Matthias as the substitute for Judas is a bad argument for the distribution theory, to say the least.[77] Sergeant further denies that the Jews were particularly "St. Peter's Province" and that his authority would have been limited to them.[78] He finds it obvious that all the Apostles were active in unlimited areas and considers it impossible to take literally that Peter went to the Jews and Paul to the Gentiles. He therefore asks Hammond, "What becomes of the rest of the Apostles? Must they stand by, and look on while St. Paul converts *all the Gentiles*, and St. Peter *all the Jews*?"[79] As for James's leading role in the apostolic council (Acts 15), Sergeant finds it unfounded to play his authority against that of Peter, since they held the same opinion on the Gentile believers.[80] Most importantly for Sergeant, Hammond's theory of two separate missions in cities with both Jewish and Gentile believers is absurd. The idea of Jews and Gentiles completely avoiding the company of each other, based on Peter's words in Acts 10:28, is "altogether destitute of any shadow of proof."[81] As for the evidence drawn from the passage in *Apostolic Constitutions*, Sergeant emphasizes that it merely relates that the bishops of Antioch and of Rome were ordained by Peter and Paul, thus offering no support at all for conclusions drawn by Hammond.[82]

For Catholics, then, it was vital to claim that the church was one in the time of the apostles, while Protestant authors pointed out the existence of parties (cf. 1 Cor 1:11–12) and emphasized that the first Christians were divided into two distinct camps, the Jewish Christians and Gentile Christians. Some Protestant debaters underlined this difference by stating that

---

75. Ibid., 44.

76. Ibid., 47.

77. Ibid., 48 (original italics removed): "So as now the Doctor hath found Iudas a Diocess amongst the Devils; and by his blasphemous interpretation would have St. Matthias succeed him."

78. Ibid., 52.

79. Ibid., 56 (italics in the original).

80. Ibid., 59.

81. Ibid., 317. With his theory, Hammond makes the Jewish Christians "perfectly Schismaticks & S. Peter their Ring-leader" (original italics removed).

82. Ibid., 320.

there were two distinct churches, the Gentile Christian Church and the Jewish Christian Church.[83]

Unitarianism, which was commonly called Socinianism, was promoted in England particularly by John Biddle (1615–1662) who wrote several tracts against the traditional Christian doctrine of the divinity of Jesus and the Holy Spirit.[84] His activities and publications were important for later Unitarian writings that emerged in the late 1680s and early 1690s. In the first of these tracts, *A Brief History Of The Unitarians*, Stephen Nye (1648–1719) seeks to deepen the Unitarian argumentation with historical and biblical exegesis that refers to the Jewish origins of the early Christianity.[85] He traces the so-called Socinians back to "Nazarens" and groups that were "also in those first times called Ebionites, Mineans, Artemonites, Theodotians, Symmachians, Paulinists, Samosatenians, Photinians, and Monarchians."[86] On another occasion, Nye asks:

For if the Trinity were indeed taught in the Old Testament, how came the Jewish Church in all Ages to be so wholly ignorant of it, that (as all confess) they had not the least Suspicion, that God is more than one Person? And if in this they had erred, 'tis not to be doubted our Saviour would have reproved their Heresy, and carefully set them right, as he did in the

---

83. See, e.g., the statement of the staunch anti-Catholic Anthony Burgess: "And if that opinion of some be true, That in most Cities converted to the Faith, there were two Churches, the *Gentile* Christian Church, and the *Jewish* Christian Church, then this might foment the division more; howsoever the Popish Interpreter laboureth under this difficulty, how they could be guilty of sinfull factions, who advanced *Peter:* but they build upon a rotten foundation" (*The Scripture Directory for Church-Officers and People* [London: Thomas Underhill *et alii*, 1659], 58 [italics in the original]).

84. Among these are, e.g., *Twelve Arguments Drawn Out of the Scripture, Wherein the Commonly Received Opinion Touching the Deity of the Holy Spirit, Is Clearly and Fully Refuted* (n.p., 1647) and *The Apostolical and True Opinion concerning the Holy Trinity, Revived and Asserted; Partly by Twelve Arguments Levyed against the Traditional and False Opinion about the Godhead of the Holy Spirit* (London: n.p., 1653).

85. Stephen Nye, *A Brief History of the Unitarians, Called Also Socinians in Four Letters, Written to a Friend* (n.p., 1687).

86. Ibid., 26 (original italics removed). Nye further states that "[T]he Writings of these Ancients are all lost, being destroyed by the *Arians* and Catholicks: Notwithstanding they had (I find) some very considerable Men among them" (italics in the original).

matter of the Resurrection. But doth our Lord any where charge them
with Heresy, for believing that God is only one Person[?][87]

The standard answer of the orthodox theologians was naturally that the
Apostles preached the pure Christian doctrine they had received from
Christ himself and that Jews and heretics fell over and over again into
errors that were there right from the beginning of Christianity.[88]

The basic Unitarian view was in some writings supplemented with
evaluation of particular early Christian authors. Hegesippus who wrote his
extensive but unfortunately lost work *Hypomnemata* about 180 C.E., was
an attractive figure for Unitarians. In his tract directed against the Nicene
creed, Thomas Smalbroke (1585–1649) claimed that the Nazareans were

> those Christian Jews that were gathered into churches in Jerusalem and
> Palestine, by the ministry of the Apostles themselves: Origen (who lived
> among them) witnesses, that all Jews who were Christians, were named
> Ebionites or the poor ones, partly from the poor Opinion they had on
> our Saviour's Person, partly because they adhered still to the beggarly
> Principles and Rites of the Mosaick Law: it unavoidably follows, that the
> Nazarens were Ebionites in this sense; that they held that the Lord Christ
> was a Man only, and observed the Law together with the Gospel.[89]

One particular line of his argumentation, that concerning Hegesippus,
may be taken up here. According to Smalbroke, "Hegesippus was himself
a Jewish Christian as Eusebius (Hist. l. 4 c. 22) witnesses: but all Jewish
Christians, saith Origen, (who lived and flourish'd above 100 years before
Eusebius) were Ebionites, that is, denied the Divinity of Christ."[90] However,
none of Eusebius's passages from the *Hypomnemata* of Hippolytus, written ca. 180 C.E., directly supports this claim (*Hist. eccl.* 2.23; 3.19–20; 4.8,

87. Nye, *A Brief History*, 68 (original italics removed).

88. Thus, e.g., Pierre Allix, *The Judgement of the Ancient Jewish Church, against the Unitarians in the Controversy upon the Holy Trinity, and the Divinity of Our Blessed Saviour* (London: Ri. Chiswell, 1699), xvii.

89. Thomas Smalbroke, *The Judgment of the Fathers concerning the Doctrine of the Trinity Opposed to Dr. G. Bull's Defence of the Nicene Faith: Part I. The Doctrine of the Catholick Church, During the First 150 Years of Christianity, and the Explication of the Unity of God (in a Trinity of Divine Persons) by Some of the Following Fathers, Consid-ered* (London, 1695), 35 (original italics removed).

90. Ibid., 41 (original italics removed).

22), even though Eusebius does say that Hippolytus was versed in Hebrew and borrowed from the Gospel of the Hebrews as well as "unwritten tradition of the Jews" (4.22).[91] Smalbroke further pays attention to the fact that Hegesippus, who gives a list of "Hereticks that were against Christ," does not count the Ebionites and Cerinthians among them.[92]

One of the foremost critics of the Unitarian writings was Edward Stillingfleet (1635–1699), the bishop of Worcester, who attacked Socinian reasoning with theological, philosophical, and historical counterarguments. Arguing against Smalbroke's general theory and his reasoning on Hegesippus, Stillingfleet leaves open whether Hegesippus was a Jewish Christian, but he asks whether really "all the Iewish Christians were at that time Ebionites or Cerinthians."[93] He takes it for granted that the piece of information stemming from Origen is correct but says, "as to his own time, it is not improbable that those who then made up the separate Body of Jewish Christians were *Ebionites*. But what is this to the *first Christians* of the Church of *Ierusalem*?"[94] Stillingfleet further notes that "the title of *Nazarens* did not always signifie the same thing," since "[i]t was at first used for *all Christians*" (Acts 24:5); then that name "was taken for the *Christians* who stay'd at *Pella* and setled at *Decapolis* and thereabouts" (Epiphanius, *Pan.* 29.7), and these believers "kept the name of *Nazarens,* and never were united with the Gentile Christians, but kept up their old Jewish customs, as to their Synagogues." Stillingfleet concludes, "Now these Nazarens might be all *Ebionites*, and yet those of the *Church of Ierusalem* not so at all."[95] He refers to Eusebius (*Hist. eccl.* 4.6) and says that "when the Iews were banished their Country by Hadrian's Edict, that then the Church of Ierusalem

---

91. Ibid. (original italics removed): "Hegesippus made use of St. Matthew's Hebrew Gospel, which was used only by the Ebionites, and Unitarian Christians." As for Origen, Smalbroke obviously has in mind those negative passages that speak of Jews who believe in Jesus (*Comm. Matt.* 16.12; *Hom. Gen.* 3.5; *Cels.* 2.1; 5.61).

92. Smalbroke, *Judgment*, 41.

93. Edward Stillingfleet, *A Discourse in Vindication of the Doctrine of the Trinity with an Answer to the Late Socinian Objections against It from Scripture, Antiquity and Reason* (London: Henry Mortlock, 1697), 19 (original italics removed).

94. Ibid., 20 (original italics removed). He also notes that Ebionites and Cerinthians "were opposite to each other" because the Cerinthians had a strikingly different Christology than the Ebionites (19). Stillingfleet admits that Hegesippus does not claim these groups to be heretics, but he finds no evidence that Hegesippus himself was an Ebionite or a Cerinthian.

95. Stillingfleet, *Discourse*, 20–21 (italics in the original).

was made up of Gentiles." Yet he concedes that there may have been some Jewish Christians in the second-century Christian community in Jerusalem, but its bishops were definitely of Gentile origin—which conclusively proves that there were no Ebionites at all in that community.[96]

The exegetical theses of the Unitarians discussion evoked a special interest in the Jewish origins of Christianity. In their view, the Ebionite character of the first Christians was related to the denial of Jesus' divine status. When John Toland's *Christianity Not Mysterious* was published in 1696, Toland was accused of Socinianism.[97] After the heresy hunt raised against him, Toland devoted more and more time to the question of the Jewish—or Ebionite—origin of Christianity. His work *Nazarenus* (1718), which was about to open a new chapter in historical study of early Christianity, was influenced not only by the Unitarian strife in the 1690s but also by a learned man who had died a generation earlier. John Toland respected the work of John Selden (1584–1654) and profited from it. Before moving on to Toland's work, it is appropriate to have a look at Selden's special view on the Jewish origin of Christianity.

The Completely Jewish Origin of Christianity: From Selden to Toland

John Selden was a statesman and legal adviser of the wealthy as well as an unequaled expert on oriental languages, laws, and religious customs. Since Selden has often been applauded for his notable works on the history of laws and British institutions, his writings on ancient religions in general and on Judaism in particular have often been passed over with only brief reference. According to Jason P. Rosenblatt, an American Jewish scholar specializing in this era, Selden was "the most learned person in England in the seventeenth century."[98] The exceptionally informative, well argued, and wide-ranging publications of Selden demonstrate that Rosenblatt has

96. Ibid., 22. After this, Stillingfleet moves on to defend the original Hebrew text behind the canonical Gospel of Matthew against the Unitarian assumption of an original Ebionite text that did not include the story of Jesus' birth by the virgin Mary (23–27).

97. Gerard Reedy, "Socinians, John Toland, and the Anglican Rationalists," *HT* 70 (1977): 294–98.

98. Jason P. Rosenblatt, *Renaissance England's Chief Rabbi: John Selden* (Oxford: Oxford University Press, 2006), 3.

not exaggerated. In spite of—or rather because of—his political interests for freedom, human dignity, and common sense, Selden studied a wide spectrum of biblical, rabbinic and other oriental sources in their original languages—Hebrew, Aramaic, Syriac, Arabic—and original contexts in order to produce strong and well founded contributions to a neglected field of scholarship as well as to contemporary political debates. A general presentation of Selden's works, which have now been made more easily accessible by the extensive study of G. J. Toomer (two volumes, 977 pages),[99] points out where his scholarly passion lies. Since only Selden's works related to Judaism and Christianity are relevant here, some general remarks on their character will suffice before moving on to the question of Jewish origins of Christianity in Selden's works.

De Diis Syris (On Syrian deities) is the first of Selden's major works on religion.[100] In this study, which was perhaps the most appreciated of his works in the eyes of his contemporaries but completely outdated for modern scholarship, he discusses the origins and development of pagan deities, or "idolatry." He offers several explanations for various deities, including misinterpretation of Biblical texts and deification of the forces of nature or demonical figures. Implicitly and on the general level, Selden makes a case against superstition and credulity among laypeople and theologians and argues for natural and historical explanations. In his *History of Tythes* (1618), Selden studies the origin of tithes in the Old Testament, the early church, and later Christianity. He finds no biblical evidence for collecting tithes to support the clergy and concludes after a survey of early Christian evidence that "[t]ill towards the end of the first foure hundred, no *Paiment* of [tithes] can be proved to have been in use."[101] Selden does not see the divine authority for the practice of collecting tithes, even though he conceded the legal right of the Church of England to do so.

In the last twenty years before his death in 1654, Selden worked and wrote intensively on the Talmud and its exegesis. After his earliest writings on the Jewish law (*De Successionibus in Bona Defuncti* [On the succession

---

99. G. J. Toomer, *John Selden: A Life in Scholarship* (Oxford: Oxford University Press, 2009).

100. John Selden, *De dis Syris Syntagmata II: Aduersaria nempè de Numinibus commentitijs in Vetere Instrumento memoratis. accedunt quae sunt reliqua Syrorum* (2nd ed.; London: Guilielmus Stansbeius, 1617).

101. John Selden, *The Historie of Tithes* (n.p., 1618), 35; cf. Toomer, *John Selden*, 270–71.

of the goods of the dead], 1631; *De Successione in Pontificatum* [On the succession of the high priests], 1636), Selden published his extensive work on natural law and the law concerning the Gentiles in Judaism.[102] This work is of vital importance here. Inspired by the studies of Hugo Grotius on natural law, Selden discussed at length—for almost nine hundred pages—natural law among the Jews. According to Jewish teaching, natural law—which should be valid for all people in all times—consists of the seven prohibitions of the so-called Noachide precepts.

In book 1, Selden presents his own theory of natural law. He thinks that natural law is given to all mankind as a natural faculty rather than as commandments first announced by God's voice and then handed down as tradition. In the following books, Selden proceeds to treat the concrete precepts in Jewish laws and traditions as well as their application concerning the relations of the Jews to the Gentiles: idolatry and blasphemy (book 2), positive duties of all men toward God (book 3; Selden's expansion to the list of Noachide commandments), murder and homicide (book 4), illicit sexual relations (book 5), theft (book 6), courts of justice and eating living animals (book 7; Selden has reversed the order of these two commandments). It is essential for Selden that the Mosaic law, including the Ten Commandments, was given to Jews alone while the Noachide precepts alone formed God's original code of law for all humans. (With his reserved stance on the Ten Commandments, he clearly took sides against the common trend of the Reformation and Biblicism.) Behind his detailed discussion, Selden has a theological agenda. He takes up the view of some prominent Jewish teachers who think that the pious Gentiles have a portion in the world to come. In his *Table Talk*, which was collected and published posthumously several times and which includes brief statements on several interesting items, Selden himself correspondingly suggests that righteous non-Christians will be saved.[103]

In his later works, Selden focused more and more on Judaism and the Jewish origins of Christianity. He published the edition, Latin translation, and commentary of "stringing of the Jewels" by Eutychius, the patriarch of Alexandria (933–940)—a work that was preserved only in

---

102. John Selden, *De Iure Naturali et Gentium, Iuxta Disciplinam Ebraeorum, Libri Septem* (London: Richardus Bishopius, 1640).

103. John Selden, *Table-Talk, Being Discourses of John Seldon, Esq: Or, His Sense of Various Matters of Weight and High Consequence, Relating Especially to Religion and State* (London: Jacob Tonson and Awnsham and John Churchill, 1696), 164–65.

Arabic.[104] Against many of his Protestant and Catholic contemporaries, Selden wished to demonstrate that Christian practices related to episcopal succession were of Jewish origin and that good scholarly knowledge of this background would not lead to self-interested claims about ecclesiastical leadership and its legitimation. In his *Uxor Ebraica* (1646), Selden discusses the Jewish law and practice concerning marriage and demonstrates how much the Christian church also here owes to its Jewish roots.[105] *De Synedriis*, in turn, is the last of Selden's large works; it was published in three parts, the last of them posthumously (1650, 1653, 1655).[106] Selden originally designed the first book to treat the administration of justice in the period before the Mosaic law, but in the course of time the main bulk of the volume came to treat excommunication—a hot issue in the British debate in the 1640s and 1650s, during the bitter strife between political and confessional parties. Selden wanted to prove that excommunication in both Judaism and early Christianity was a completely human practice that had no basis in the divine law. Furthermore, Selden argued that Jews excommunicated by their community in biblical times were separated neither from the temple and the absolution guaranteed by the Day of Atonement nor from any public service.[107] The Christian practice of excommunication was based on Jewish law and did not originate in divine law. In the second book of *De Synedriis*, Selden explores the role of the Sanhedrin after the giving of the Law at Sinai, while the third volume focuses on the competence of the Sanhedrin.With his detailed discussion of ancient Jewish documents, Selden implicitly and sometimes explicitly raises the claim that no one who is not able to master this field can either properly interpret the Bible or understand Christian origins. While thoroughly explaining various Jewish institutions and practices in their historical context, Selden here and there comments on the debated

---

104. John Selden, *Eutychii Agyptii, Patriarchae Orthodoxorum Alexandrini Scriptoris ut in Oriente admodum Vetusti ac Illustris ita in Occidente tum paucissimis Visi tum perraro Auditi, Ecclesiae suae origins* (London: Richardus Bishopus, 1642).

105. John Selden, *Uxor Ebraica, seu, De Nuptiis et Divortiis ex Iure Civili id est, Divino et Talmudico, Veterum Ebraeorum, libri tres* (London: Richard Bishop, 1646).

106. John Selden, *De Synedriis et Praefecturis Iuridicis Veterum Ebraeorum Liber primus* (London: Cornelius Bee, 1650); *Liber secundus* (London: Cornelius Bee, 1653); *Liber tertius et ultimus* (London: Cornelius Bee, 1655).

107. Selden, *De synedriis*, 1:189–90.

biblical issues of his time, particularly by criticizing the legitimization of ecclesiastical or worldly power with the word of God.

On several occasions, Selden draws attention to specific early Christian beliefs and practices that clearly originated in Judaism. In the first book of *De Synedriis*, however, he makes a fundamental statement about the Jewish origin of Christianity. While discussing the question of excommunication, Selden states that in the first years the early Christians were nothing but Jews. Proselytes converted into Judaism and Gentiles came to believe in Jesus only later, as the conversions of the Ethiopian eunuch (Acts 8:26–40) and Cornelius the centurion (10:1–11:18) clearly prove.[108] Selden further states that around 41 C.E., when the name *Christians* was first used in Antioch (Acts 11:26), most Christians were Jews or proselytes. He also points out that this name was notably uncommon in early Christian writings (Acts 26:28; 1 Pet 4:16). Both the apostolic decree (Acts 15) as well as the presence among Christians of heretics such as the Cerinthians, the Nazareans, and the Ebionites further demonstrate the Jewish roots of Christianity.[109] In these days and later, Christianity—with its thoroughly Jewish baptismal rite—was nothing else than new or reformed Judaism.[110] Furthermore, since Claudius expelled the Jews from Rome in 49 C.E. (Suetonius, *Claud.* 25.11) and Priscilla and Aquila were among these Jews (Acts 18:2), it is clear that Christians were even then officially regarded as Jews. In the light of this evidence, the Christians in Rome quite naturally observed Jewish rites and customs, without forming a separate group.[111] Only in the time of Nero does the separation of the Christians from the Jews in Rome become visible, since this Caesar persecuted only Christians and not Jews.[112]

As far as I can see, Selden never characterized the first Christians as "Christian Jews" or "Jewish Christians." This may partly be due to the fact that he mostly wrote in Latin. However, in the light of all evidence presented above, it is almost inevitable to assume that he knew JC terminology but did not employ it because he did not find it adequate or appropriate.

---

108. Ibid., 1:224–26.
109. Ibid., 1:226–27.
110. Ibid., 1:229 (*Judaismus novus seu reformatus*).
111. Ibid., 1:230–31.
112. Ibid., 1:241.

In the light of the seventeenth-century discussion on the Jewish origins of Christianity, it is difficult to overestimate the impact of John Toland's *Nazarenus*, published in 1718.[113] Since the present volume includes thorough discussion of Toland's contribution to the question of Jewish Christianity, there is no need to address that question here. Even though John Selden was not the only predecessor, it is useful to note that Toland, inspired by both John Selden and the views of the Unitarians,[114] completely rejected the mainstream Augustinian view on the early Jewish Christians that dominates the seventeenth-century discussion documented above. For Toland it was, among other things, essential to emphasize that the Jewish converts to Christianity were not forced to give up their obedience to the Mosaic law. Against the defenders of the Augustinian view, Toland points out, "in the Apostolic decree no accommodation is hinted in the least, no time is limited either unto the one for quitting the old Law, or unto the other for neglecting the four Precepts: as is positively taught in all our Systems or Catechisms."[115]

As for JC terminology, Toland prefers the term *Jewish Christians*.[116] However, he also once employs the term *Christian Jews*.[117] It is obvious that for Toland the former term is not loaded with the negative connotations that it had for many Christian authors of the seventeenth century. Even though Toland clearly follows Selden in defining earliest Christianity only as a reform movement within Judaism,[118] he—starting with the subtitle of his book, *Jewish, Gentile, and Mahometan Christianity*—treats "Christianity" as an overarching concept that refers to both early Jewish and early Gentile believers in Jesus. As far as I can see, the subtitle of his book is the first piece of evidence for the term *Jewish Christianity* in the English literature, even though Toland does not often use it later in his book.[119] The key idea is that Jewish Christianity, represented by Jesus, Ebionites, and Nazareans, all obedient to the Mosaic Law, was "THE TRUE

---

113. John Toland, *Nazarenus: Or, Jewish, Gentile, and Mahometan Christianity* (2nd ed.; London: J. Brotherton, 1718).

114. See especially ibid., 25–30 (ch. 9).

115. Ibid., 43.

116. Ibid., 28, 36, 44, 49, 50, 57, 63, 65 passim.

117. Ibid., 42.

118. Toland claims that Selden is not "the only person, that, in later times, has asserted CHRISTIANITY to be no more than REFORMED JUDAISM" (ibid., 30; original italics removed). However, he does not mention anybody else here.

119. Ibid., 4.

AND ORIGINAL PLAN OF CHRISTIANITY," or "the true and genuine Christianity."[120]

The basic outline of Toland's book reads like a thorough historical-critical defense of the Unitarian view on the earliest Christology and the role of the Mosaic law among the first Christians. At the same time, it was to become a pioneering study for the problem of so-called Jewish Christianity as a historical phenomenon. In the wake of the Unitarian pamphleteers, Toland challenged the conventional views held by most scholars and clergymen in England. However, while coining *Jewish Christianity* as a novel term, Toland leaned on traditional terminology: the terms *Christian Jew(s)* and *Jewish Christian(s)* had been in use for some one hundred fifty years before he made the Jewish origin of Christianity a debated issue for the British public. Even though later scholars of "Jewish Christianity" stood much closer to Thomas Morgan's anti-Semitic *Moral Philosopher* (1738)[121] than to Toland's interpretation, *Nazarenus* is finally receiving the credit it deserved almost three hundred years ago.

BIBLIOGRAPHY

Full bibliographies of the Old English books discussed here can be found in Early English Books Online (http://eebo.chadwyck.com). This bibliography includes short titles as well as references to the locations of printing and the publishers for whom works were printed.

Abbot, Robert. *A Triall of Our Church-Forsakers: Or, A Meditation Tending to Still the Passions of Unquiet Brownists, upon Heb.10.25.* London: Philemon Stephens and Christopher Meredith, 1639.

Allix, Pierre. *The Judgement of the Ancient Jewish Church, against the Unitarians in the Controversy upon the Holy Trinity, and the Divinity of Our Blessed Saviour.* London: Ri. Chiswell, 1699.

Aucher, John. *The Arraignment of Rebellion: Or, The Irresistibility of Sovereign Powers Vindicated and Maintain'd.* London: William Abington, 1684.

Augustine. *Epistulae mutuae.* Translated and introduced by Alfons Fürst. Fontes Christiani 41.2. Turnhout: Brepols, 2002.

---

120. Ibid., 33 (original italics removed). Cf. also "And, if the truth may be freely spoken, there remains very little on record, very little that's any way certain authentic, concerning *the originals of Christianity*, from the beginning of NERO to the end of TRAJAN or HARDIAN" (ibid., 60; emphasis original).

121. On Morgan's book, see Lemke, *Judenchristentum*, 148–67.

Biddle, John. *Twelve Arguments Drawn Out of the Scripture, Wherein the Commonly Received Opinion Touching the Deity of the Holy Spirit, Is Clearly and Fully Refuted.* N.p., 1647.

———. *The Apostolical and True Opinion concerning the Holy Trinity, Revived and Asserted; Partly by Twelve Arguments Levyed against the Traditional and False Opinion about the Godhead of the Holy Spirit.* London: n.p., 1653.

Bridges, John. *A Defence of the Government Established in the Church of Englande for Ecclesiasticall Matters.* London: Thomas Chard, 1587.

Brown, Edward. *A Brief Account of Some Travels in Divers Parts of Europe.* 2nd ed. London: Benj. Toole, 1685.

Burgess, Anthony. *The Scripture Directory for Church-Officers and People.* London: Thomas Underhill, 1659.

Chibald, William. *A Tryall of Faith: By the Touch-Stone of the Gospel, the Word of Faith. Whereby Christians May Discerne Whether or No, They Have a Saving Faith.* London: Iohn Teage, 1622.

Cohn-Sherbock, Dan. "Modern Hebrew Christianity and Messianic Judaism," Pages 287–98 in *The Image of the Judaeo-Christians in Ancient Jewish and Christian Literature: Papers Delivered at the Colloquium of the Institutum Judaicum, Brussels 18–19 November, 2001.* Edited by P. J. Tomson and D. Lambers-Petry. WUNT 158. Tübingen: Mohr Siebeck, 2001.

Copley, Anthony. *Wits, Fittes, and Fancies.* London: Richard Iohnes, 1595.

Cressy, Serenus. *Exomologesis: Or, A Faithfull Narration of the Occaision and Motives of the Conversion unto Catholick Unity.* Paris: Chez Jean Billaine, 1653.

Curione, Celio Secondo. *Pasquine in a Traunce: A Christian and Learned Dialogue (containing Wonderfull and Most Strange Newes, out of Heauen, Purgatorie and Hell).… Turned but Lately out of the Italian into This Tongue, by W. P.* London: Wylliam Seres, 1566?.

Daniel, Samuel. *Archiepiscopal Priority Instituted by Christ, Proved by plaine Testimonies of Scripture.* London: Samuel Daniel, 1642.

Dekker, Thomas. *The Wonder of a Kingdome.* London: Nicholas Vavasour, 1636.

Doran, Susan, and Christopher Dunston. *Princes, Pastors and People: The Church and Religion in England 1529–1689.* London: Routledge, 1991.

Du Moulin, Pierre. *The Accomplishment of the Prophecies: Or, The Third Booke In Defence of the Catholicke Faith Contained in the Booke of the High and Mighty King Iames I.* Translated by I. Heath. Oxford: Iohn Barnes, 1613.

Falconer, John. *A Briefe Refutation of Iohn Traskes Iudaical and Nouel Fancyes.* Saint-Omer: English College Press, 1618.

Finch, Henry. *The Worlds Great Restauration: Or, The Calling of the Ievves and (with Them) of All the Nations and Kingdomes of the Earth, to the Faith of Christ.* London: William Bladen, 1621.

Fox, George. *Queries concerning Tythes to the Priests and Bishops.* N.p., 1663.

Foxe, John. *Actes and Monuments of Matters Most Speciall and Memorable, Happenyng in the Church with an Vniuersall History of the Same.* 2 vols. London: Iohn Daye, 1583. Online: http://www.johnfoxe.org/.

Gauden, John. *A Discourse concerning Publick Oaths, and the Lawfulness of Swearing in Judicial Proceedings.* London: R. Royston, 1662.

Gouge, William. *The Progresse of Divine Providence.* London: William Gouge, 1645.

———. *A Learned and Very Useful Commentary on the Whole Epistle to the Hebrews.* London: William Gouge, 1655.

Grantham, Thomas. *The Quaeries Examined: Or, Fifty Anti-queries Seriously Propounded to the People Called Presbyterians.* London: n.p., 1676.

Grascome, Samuel. *An Historical Account of the Antiquity and Unity of the Britanick Churches.* London: W. Whitwood, 1692.

Hammond, Henry. *Of Schisme: A Defence of the Church of England, against the Exceptions of the Romanists.* London: R. Royston, 1653.

———. *A Reply to the Catholick Gentlemans Answer to the Most Materiall Parts of the Booke of Schisme.* London: R. Royston, 1654.

———. *A Paraphrase and Annotations upon All the Books of the New Testament Briefly Explaining All the Difficult Places Thereof.* London: Richard Davis, 1659.

Haugaard, William P. *Elizabeth and the English Reformation: The Struggle for a Stable Settlement of Religion.* Cambridge: Cambridge University Press, 1968.

Heylyn, Peter. *The History of the Sabbath: In Two Bookes.* London: Henry Seile, 1636.

Hooker, Richard. *Of the Lavves of Ecclesiasticall Politie, Eight Books.* London: Iohn Windet, 1604.

Jerome. *Epistulae mutuae.* Translated and introduced by Alfons Fürst. Fontes Christiani 41.2. Turnhout: Brepols, 2002.

Jewel, John. *A Replie vnto M. Hardinges Ansvveare by Perusinge Whereof the Discrete, and Diligent Reader May Easily See, the Weake, and Vnstable Groundes of the Romaine Religion, Whiche of Late Hath Beene Accompted Catholique.* London: Henry Wykes, 1565.

Katz, David S. *God's Last Words: Reading the English Bible from the Reformation to Fundamentalism.* New Haven: Yale University Press, 2004.

Leigh, Edward. *A Systeme or Body of Divinity: Consisting of Ten Books.* London: William Lee, 1654.

Lemke, Hella. *Judenchristentum—Zwischen Ausgrenzung und Integration: Zur Geschichte eines exegetischen Begriffes.* Hamburger theologische Studien 25. Münster: Lit Verlag, 2001.

Martin, Gregory. *The Nevv Testament of Iesus Christ.* Rhemes: Iohn Fogny, 1582.

McGiffert, Michael. "Henry Hammond and Covenant Theology." *CH* 74 (2005): 255–85.

McLachlan, Herbert. *Story of a Nonconformist Library.* Manchester: Manchester University Press 1923.

More, Thomas. *The Second Parte of the Co[n]futacion of Tyndals Answere in Whyche Is Also Confuted the Chyrche That Tyndale Deuyseth.* London: Wyllyam Rastell, 1533.

Morton, Thomas. *The Grand Imposture of the (now) Church Of Rome: Manifested in This One Article of the New Romane Creede.* London: Mylbourne, 1626.

Nye, Stephen. *A Brief History of the Unitarians, Called Also Socinians in Four Letters, Written to a Friend.* N.p., 1687.

————. *The Exceptions of Mr. Edwards in His Causes of Atheism against the Reasonableness of Christianity, as Deliver'd in the Scriptures, Examin'd and Found Unreasonable, Unscriptural, and Injurious Also It's Clearly Proved by Many Testimonies of Holy Scripture, That the God and Father of our Lord Jesus Christ Is the only God and Father of Christians.* London, 1695.

Ochino, Bernardino. *A Tragoedie: Or, Dialoge of the Vniuste Vsurped Primacie of the Bishop of Rome, and of All the Iust Abolishyng of the Same, Made by Master Barnardine Ochine an Italian, [and] Translated out of Latine into Englishe by Master Iohn Ponet Doctor of Diuinitie, Neuer Printed Before in Any Language.* London: Gwalter Lynne, 1549.

Parker, Samuel. *The Case of the Church of England, Briefly and Truly Stated.* London: Henry Faithorne and John Kersey, 1681.

Penn, William. *The Invalidity of John Faldo's Vindication of His Book, Called, Quakerism No Christianity: Being a Rejoynder in Defence of the Answer, Intituled, Quakerism a New Nick-Name for Old Christianity.* N.p., 1673.

Perkins, William. *A Commentarie or Exposition, vpon the Fiue First Chapters of the Epistle to the Galatians.* Cambridge: Rafe Cudworth, 1604.

Popkin, Richard. "Christian Jews and Jewish Christians in the 17th Century." Pages 57–72 in *Jewish Christians and Christian Jews from the Renaissance to the Enlightenment.* Edited by Richard H. Popkin and Gordon M. Weiner. AIHI 138. Dordrecht: Kluwer, 1994.

Prynne, William. *A Short Demurrer to the Jewes Long Discontinued Barred Remitter into England.* London: Edward Thomas, 1656.

————. *A Brief, Pithy Discourse upon I Corinthians 14. 40.* London: Edward Thomas, 1661.

Purchas, Samuel. *Purchas His Pilgrimes.* 5 vols. London: Henry Fetherstone, 1625.

Rainoldes, John. *The Summe of the Conference betwene Iohn Rainoldes and Iohn Hart Touching the Head and the Faith of the Church.* London: Geor. Bishop, 1584.

Reedy, Gerard. "Socinians, John Toland, and the Anglican Rationalists." *HTR* 70 (1977): 285–304.

Rosenblatt, Jason P. *Renaissance England's Chief Rabbi: John Selden.* Oxford: Oxford University Press, 2006.

Selden, John. *De dis Syris Syntagmata II. Aduersaria nempè de Numinibus commentitijs in Vetere Instrumento memoratis. accedunt quae sunt reliqua Syrorum.* 2nd ed. London: Guilielmus Stansbeius, 1617.

————. *De Iure Naturali et Gentium, Iuxta Disciplinam Ebraeorum, Libri Septem.* London: Richardus Bishopius, 1640.

————. *De synedriis et praefecturis iuridicis veterum Ebraeorum Liber primus.* London: Cornelius Bee, 1650; *Liber secundus.* London: Cornelius Bee, 1653; *Liber tertius et ultimus.* London: Cornelius Bee, 1655.

————. *Eutychii Agyptii, Patriarchae Orthodoxorum Alexandrini Scriptoris ut in Oriente admodum Vetusti ac Illustri ita in Occidente tum paucissimis Visi tum perraro Auditi, Ecclesiae suae origines.* London: Richardus Bishopus, 1642.

————. *The Historie of Tithes.* N.p., 1618.

————. *Uxor Ebraica, seu, De Nuptiis et Divortiis ex Iure Civili id est, Divino et Talmu-dico, Veterum Ebraeorum, libri tres.* London: Richard Bishop, 1646.

————. *Table-Talk, Being Discourses of John Seldon, Esq: Or, His Sense of Various Matters of Weight and High Consequence, Relating Especially to Religion and State.* London: Jacob Tonson and Awnsham and John Churchill, 1696.

Sergeant, John. *Schism Dis-arm'd of the Defensive Weapons, Lent It by Doctor Hammond, and the Bishop of Derry.* Paris: M. Blageart, 1655.

————. *Schism Dispach't: Or, a Rejoynder to the Replies of Dr. Hammond and the Ld of Derry.* N.p., 1657.

Smalbroke, Thomas. *The Judgment of the Fathers concerning the Doctrine of the Trinity Opposed to Dr. G. Bull's Defence of the Nicene Faith: Part I. The Doctrine of the Catholick Church, during the First 150 Years of Christianity, and the Explication of the Unity of God (in a Trinity of Divine Persons) by Some of the Following Fathers, Considered.* London: n.p., 1695.

Southgate, Beverley C. "Blackloism and Tradition: From Theological Certainty to Historiographical Doubt." *JHI* 61 (2000): 97–114.

Stephen, Leslie, ed. *The Dictionary of National Biography.* 63 vols, 3 suppl. vols. Oxford: Oxford University Press, 1885–1901.

Stillingfleet, Edward. *A Discourse in Vindication of the Doctrine of the Trinity with an Answer to the Late Socinian Objections against It from Scripture, Antiquity and Reason.* London: Henry Mortlock, 1697.

Taylor, Jeremy. *Antiquitates Christianae: Or, The History of the Life and Death of the Holy Jesus as Also the Lives, Acts and Martyrdoms of His Apostles.* London: R. Royston, 1675.

————. *A Discourse of Baptisme, Its Institution and Efficacy upon All Believers.* London: R. Royston, 1652.

Toland, John. *Nazarenus: Or, Jewish, Gentile, and Mahometan Christianity.* 2nd ed.. London: J. Brotherton, J. Roberts, and A. Dodd, 1718.

Toomer, G. J. *John Selden: A Life in Scholarship.* Oxford: Oxford University Press, 2009.

Traske, John. *A Treatise of Libertie from Iudaisme, Or An Acknowledgement of True Christian Libertie.* London: N. Butter, 1620.

Twisse, William. *Of the Morality of the Fourth Commandement as Still in Force to Binde Christians.* London: Iohn Rothwell, 1641.

Wallis, John. *A Defense Of Infant-Baptism in Answer to a Letter (Here Recited) from an Anti-Paedo-Baptist.* Oxford: Henry Clements, 1697.

————. *A Defense of the Christian Sabbath: In Answer to a Treatise of Mr. Tho. Bampfield Pleading for Saturday-Sabbath.* Oxford: Chr. Coningsby, 1692.

Ward, Samuel. *The Life of Faith in Death: Exemplified in the Liuing Speeches of Dying Christians.* London: Iohn Marriot and Iohn Grismand, 1622.

Willet, Andrew. *Hexapla, That Is, A Six-fold Commentarie vpon the Most Diuine Epistle of the Holy Apostle S. Paul to the Romanes.* University of Cambridge, 1611.

Wilson, Thomas. *A Complete Christian Dictionary Wherein the Significations and Several Acceptations of All the Words Mentioned in the Holy Scriptures of the Old and New Testament Are Fully Opened, Expressed, Explained.* London: Thomas Williams, 1661.

Wither, George. *A View of the Marginal Notes of the Popish Testament, Translated into English by the English Fugitiue Papists Resiant at Rhemes in France.* London: Thomas Woodcocke, 1588.

———. *Meditations upon the Lords Prayer with a Preparatory Preamble to the Right Understanding, and True Use of This Pattern.* London: n.p., 1665.

PART 2
JOHN TOLAND AND THE REDISCOVERY
OF JEWISH CHRISTIANITY

JOHN TOLAND'S *NAZARENUS*
AND THE ORIGINAL PLAN OF CHRISTIANITY

Pierre Lurbe

Although John Toland's *Nazarenus: Or, Jewish, Gentile, and Mahometan Christianity* was published in 1718,[1] barely four years before the author's untimely death at the age of fifty-two, it was yet another piece of evidence of the Irishman's lifelong concern with exegesis and scriptural criticism. The book was itself the English version of an earlier manuscript in French, entitled *Christianisme Judaïque et Mahométan*, written in 1710 as part of the *Dissertations diverses de Monsieur Tolandus*.[2] The *Dissertations* were dedicated to "Megalonymus," the pseudonym of Prince Eugene of Savoy, one of Toland's most powerful patrons and an avid collector of heterodox literature. Yet Toland's career as an intellectual maverick and challenger of orthodoxy had begun a dozen years before, with the publication of *Christianity Not Mysterious* in 1696, a book that made him famous, and even notorious, overnight. On account of what were perceived as its irreligious

---

1. There were two editions of the book in 1718, both made in London; see Giancarlo Carabelli, *Tolandiana: Materiali bibliografici per lo studio dell'opera et della fortuna di John Toland (1670–1722)* (Florence: La Nuova Italia Editrice, 1975), 210–11. Quotations from *Nazarenus* will be made from the second edition. Justin Champion's modern edition of *Nazarenus* is apparently based on the first edition (tip from Stanley Jones), although the "editorial conventions" state that the text reproduced was from the second edition. See Justin Champion, ed., *John Toland: Nazarenus* (British Deism and Free Thought 1; Oxford: Voltaire Foundation, 1999), 111.

2. The *Dissertations* are held under the shelfmark 10325 in the Österreichische Nationalbibliothek in Vienna. They have recently been published: Lia Mannarino, ed., *John Toland: Dissertations diverses* (Libre pensée et littérature clandestine 24; Paris: Honoré Champion, 2005). *Christianisme Judaïque et Mahométan* takes up pp. 61–99. The same dissertation is also available in the above-mentioned (see n. 1) modern edition of *Nazarenus*, 255–86.

and even heretical implications, the book was condemned to be burnt by the Irish Commons, which it duly was in September 1697. The author himself only escaped arrest and prosecution by hastily fleeing Ireland in the same month, never to return to his native country. Nor did the matter quite rest there, since the Lower House of Convocation tried to have him condemned in 1701. This attempt eventually came to nothing, but there is little doubt that Toland's prospects were to be marred for life by this act of juvenile indiscretion.

Not, however, that it seemed to matter all that much to him. Despite the self-justifications and disclaimers that followed the publication of *Christianity Not Mysterious* (*An Apology For Mr.* Toland, 1697; *A Defence of Mr. Toland*, 1697; *Vindicius Liberius*, 1702), Toland could never quite resist the lure and excitement of playing with fire, and of launching controversies on the most sensitive of issues. A mere three years after *Christianity Not Mysterious* was published, the Irishman launched a polemic that was to rumble on for a quarter of a century, and to continue sporadically even after his death.

In 1698, there appeared *A Complete Collection of the Historical, Political, and Miscellaneous Works of John Milton, Both English and Latin*. It is still uncertain whether Toland was the editor of Milton's works themselves, but it is beyond doubt that the "Life of Milton" that was prefixed to the *Works* was his. This "Life" was thought to be of sufficient interest in itself to warrant separate publication in 1699 (*The Life of John Milton, Containing, besides the History of His Works, Several Extraordinary Characters of Men and Books, Sects, Parties, and Opinions*, London, 1699). As the full title implies, the "Life of John Milton" interwove a narrative of Milton's life with a chronological account of his works, which included substantial extracts from the works themselves. When discussing *Eikonoklastes*—the book that exposed Charles I's *Eikon Basilike* as a forgery—Toland mused upon the easiness with which public opinion had been fooled into accepting as genuine a work that in fact was spurious. It is in the course of these musings that he made the following startling statement:

> When I seriously consider how all this happen'd among our selves within the compass of forty years, in a time of great Learning and Politeness, when both Parties so narrowly watch'd over one another's Actions, and what a great Revolution in Civil and Religious Affairs was partly occasion'd by the Credit of that Book, I cease to wonder any longer how so many suppositious pieces under the name of CHRIST, his Apostles,

and other great Persons, should be publish'd and approv'd in those primitive times, when it was of so much importance to have 'em believ'd; when
the Cheats were too many on all sides for them to reproach one another,
which yet they often did; when Commerce was not near so general as
now, and the whole Earth intirely overspread with the darkness of Superstition. I doubt rather the Spuriousness of several more such Books is yet
undiscover'd, thro the remoteness of those Ages, the death of the Persons
concern'd, and the decay of other Monuments which might give us true
Information; especially when we consider how dangerous it was always
for the weaker side to lay open the tricks of their Adversaries, though
never so gross: and that the prevailing Party did strictly order all those
Books which offended them to be burnt, or otherwise supprest, which
was accordingly perform'd, as well in obedience to the Laws by som, as
out of conscientious Obligations by others, which made the execution
more effectual than usually happens in cases of an ordinary nature.[3]

This passage was immediately interpreted as casting doubt on the authority of the existing canon of the New Testament—what could be the books
whose spuriousness was yet undiscovered, if not the canonical books
themselves?—while describing the process by which the canon was set up
as one of deliberate suppression of all those books that did not conform
to the views of the "prevailing party." This was history at its most concise,
allusive, and provocative. No wonder then, that in his sermon of January
30, 1699—the anniversary of the martyrdom of King Charles I—preached
before the House of Commons, Offspring Blackall, High Church cleric
and chaplain in ordinary to His Majesty, should have vigorously upbraided
Toland for casting aspersion simultaneously on the canonical book of the
Royalists, *Eikon Basilike*, and on the Christian canon, thereby underlining
the connection that the Irishman had made between a political forgery
and a religious one. Stung into replying and rebutting Blackall's charges,
Toland responded with *Amyntor* (1699), a hastily written but carefully
composed book in three parts:

> *Amyntor:* OR, A DEFENCE OF Milton's Life. CONTAINING I. A general
> Apology for all Writings of that kind. II. A Catalogue of Books attributed
> in the Primitive Times to JESUS CHRIST, his Apostles and other eminent

---

3. John Toland, *The Life of John Milton, Containing, Besides the History of His
Works, Several Extraordinary Characters of Men and Books, Sects, Parties, and Opinions* (London: John Darby, 1699), 91–92.

Persons: With several important Remarks and Observations relating to
the Canon of Scripture. III. A Complete History of the Book, Entitul'd,
Icon Basilike, proving Dr. GAUDEN, and not King CHARLES the First,
to be the Author of it: With an Answer to all the Facts alledg'd by Mr.
WAGSTAF to the contrary; and to the Exceptions made against my Lord
ANGLESEY's *Memorandum*, Dr. WALKER's Book, or Mrs. GAUDEN's Narrative, which last Piece is now for the first Time publish'd at large.

As so often with the Irishman, his answer was even more provocative
than the original, contentious passage from the "Life of Milton." The cen-
terpiece of the book was the "Catalogue of Books Attributed in the Primitive Times to Jesus Christ, His Apostles and Other Eminent Persons."
Although Toland claimed that this was merely a list of apocrypha that
did not impugn the authority of the New Testament, the poison was in
the tail—*in cauda venenum*—in the "Remarks and Observations Relating
to the Canon of Scripture" that followed the catalogue proper. Without
ever stating in blunt terms that the canon of Scripture was unreliable—
this would have entailed immediate prosecution—Toland left sufficient
room for doubt on the issue, through equivocal statements and sly questions, for the reader to be perplexed and puzzled. Hardly had the book
been published when retorts and answers began to appear,[4] representing
the entire spectrum of eighteenth-century English Protestantism.[5] Such
was the extent of the hostility that Toland's views aroused that, for once,
theologians who in the usual course of things were bitterly opposed to
one another found themselves forming a de facto united front against a
common enemy, the arch doubter John Toland. For what the Irishman
cast doubt on was the one thing these divines of all stripes unanimously
held sacred, beyond their differences and disagreements: the canon of the
New Testament. Not that the Irishman was in the least deterred by this

---

4. Samuel Clarke, *Some Reflections on That Part of a Book Called Amyntor: Or,
The Defence of Milton's Life, Which Relates to the Writings of the Primitive Fathers and
the Canon of the New Testament* (London: James Knapton, 1699); John Richardson,
*The Canon of the New Testament Vindicated: In Answer to the Objections of J. T. in
His Amyntor* (London: Richard Sare, 1700); Stephen Nye, *An Historical Account and
Defence of the Canon of the New Testament: In Answer to Amyntor* (London: J. Darby,
1700).

5. Church of England orthodoxy, of the High Church variety (Blackall); Unitarianism (Clarke); Socinianism (Nye); nonjurors (Richardson).

outcry: his later published works include *Origines Judaicae* (1709),[6] yet another provocative piece in which Toland gave more credit to Strabo's narrative of the Exodus than to the scriptural account of the same episode in the book by the same name, and *Nazarenus* (1718)—to which I shall soon be returning—as well as a collection of four dissertations, appositely entitled *Tetradymus* (1720),[7] of which the first one, *Hodegus*, provided a rational explanation of the pillar of cloud and fire that guided the Israelites in the wilderness, while the third one (*Mangoneutes*) was a defence of *Nazarenus*. Each of these books raised a storm of its own. In the meantime, Toland continued to expand his 1699 catalogue, until it became the (posthumous) "A Catalogue of Books Mention'd by the Fathers and Other Ancient Writers, as Truly or Falsely ascrib'd to Jesus Christ, His Apostles, and Other Eminent Persons," which was published for the first time in Pierre des Maizeaux's *A Collection of Several Pieces of Mr. John Toland*, in 1726.[8]

Even after Toland was dead, the task of rebutting his claims against the genuineness, and therefore the authority, of the canon of the New Testament, was far from over. It culminated in 1726–1727 in the substantial tomes (three octavo volumes) of Jeremiah Jones's *A New and Full Method of Settling the Canonical Authority of the New Testament*, a scholarly feat of such standing that it remained a textbook on the subject well into the nineteenth century.[9] Toland is by no means Jones's only target—he comprehensively rails against all the bugbears of orthodox Christianity, "Hobbes, Spinoza, Toland and the *club of Deists*, or *free-thinkers* (as they love to be called)"[10]—but his "celebrated catalogue"[11] is mentioned at the outset of the first volume, as a prime instance of impiety and devious

---

6. *Origines Judaicæ* was the second part of a larger work made of two dissertations of which it was the second: *Adeisidæmon, sive Titus Livius a superstitione vindicatus ... Annexae sunt ejusdem Origines Judaicæ* (Hagæ Comitatis: Thomam Johnson, 1709).

7. *Tetradymus: Containing I. Hodegus; Or, the Pillar of Cloud and Fire, That Guided the Israelites in the Wilderness, Not Miraculous* (London: J. Brotherton, 1720).

8. Pierre des Maizeaux, ed., *A Collection of Several Pieces of Mr. John Toland* (London: J. Peele, 1726), 1:350–403.

9. Champion, *John Toland: Nazarenus*, 93.

10. Jeremiah Jones, *A Vindication of the Former Part of St. Matthew's Gospel*, in *A New and Full Method of Settling the Canonical Authority of the New Testament* (3 vols.; Oxford: Clarendon, 1798), 3:8–9.

11. Jones, *A New and Full Method*, 1:4.

scholarship, while *Nazarenus,* although initially called "his [Toland's] late trifling book,"[12] comes for much harsher strictures a few pages down:

> Part of this fragment [by Epiphanius] is produced by Mr. Toland in his *Original Plan or Scheme of Christianity according to the Ebionites,* both in Greek and English; nor is it strange that a person of Mr. Toland's profession should grace his scheme with a passage so much to his purpose, I mean of abolishing the doctrines of Christianity, which are agreed upon by all Christians, and introducing his most ridiculous and impious scheme of Nazarene, or Jewish, or Ebionite, or Mahometan, or (which is the undoubted truth) of no Christianity at all.[13]

It is fitting indeed that two of John Toland's most controversial works—the catalogue drawn in his younger days and the much later *Nazarenus*—should be mentioned almost in the same breath in a book devoted to the authority of the New Testament, for this does provide the proper context for an understanding of the scope of *Nazarenus.* The 1718 book is part and parcel of its author's much larger drive to question the value of the scriptural canon, and to provide an alternative account of the origins of Christianity. In Toland's quest for what he viewed as "lost christianities,"[14] *Nazarenus* took pride of place.

Nazarenus: Or, Jewish, Gentile and Mahometan Christianity is made of two distinct letters, the first one concerning the Gospel of Barnabas, the second one being a relation of an Irish manuscript of the four Gospels. Most of the title page is devoted to an elaborate gloss of the contents of the first letter, which provides the focus for the entire book, while the second one is given much less editorial prominence (see page opposite).

Two telling epigraphs are placed at the bottom of the title page, in order both to give the reader a meaningful frame of interpretation to read the work that follows and to highlight the particular posture which the author has chosen to adopt. The first epigraph, which is taken from the *Letters of Pliny,* reads: "*Intacta & Nova? graves Offensae, levis Gratia.*"[15] The

---

12. Ibid., 1:162.

13. Ibid., 1:218.

14. To take up the title of Bart D. Ehrman's *Lost Christianities: The Battles for Scripture and the Faiths We Never Knew* (Oxford: Oxford University Press, 2003).

15. "Or shall I write of the past time, and those wherein no other author has gone before me? If so, I may probably give offence to many and please but few" (Pliny, *Letters* [Melmoth and Hutchinson, LCL], book 5, letter 8.403).

NAZARENUS:

O R,

Jewish, Gentile, and *Mahometan*

CHRISTIANITY.

CONTAINING

The hiftory of the antient GOSPEL OF BARNABAS, and the modern GOSPEL OF THE MAHOMETANS, attributed to the fame APOSTLE: this laft GOSPEL being now firft made known among CHRISTIANS.

ALSO,

The ORIGINAL PLAN OF CHRISTIANITY occafionally explain'd in the hiftory of the NAZARENS, wherby diverfe CONTROVERSIES about this divine (but highly perverted) INSTITUTION may be happily terminated.

WITH

The relation of an IRISH MANUSCRIPT of the FOUR GOSPELS, as likewife a Summary of the antient IRISH CHRISTIANITY, and the reality of the KELDEES (an order of Lay-religious) againft the two laft Bifhops of Worcefter.

By Mr. TOLAND.

Intacta & Nova? graves Offenfae, levis Gratia. Plin. lib. 5. Epift. 8.
Aft Ego Coelicolis gratum reor ire per omnes
Hoc opus, & Sacras populis notefcere Leges. Lucan. lib. 10. ver. 197.

The SECOND EDITION Revifed.

LONDON, Printed: And Sold by J. BROTHERTON at the Black Bull in Cornhill, J. ROBERTS in Warwick-Lane, and A. DODD at the Peacock without Temple-Bar. 1718.
[Price Two Shillings Stitch'd.]

second one, an extract from Lucan's *Pharsalia*, claims: "*Ast Ego Coelicolis gratum reor ire per omnes / Hoc opus, & Sacras populis notescere Leges.*"[16] The assertion that carefully kept secrets will at last be made public by a daring author who is prepared to challenge received opinion and to affront many in the process is typical of the Irishman's pose and not one of his most endearing features—as ever, Toland's *ego* looms large here.

The very large claim that Toland makes for himself in the preface to *Nazarenus* is that he has discovered a hitherto unknown Gospel,[17] a discovery of such moment that it should lead to a revision of the canon and to a new assessment of Christian origins. Whatever the actual importance of the text in question, it is undoubtedly true that John Toland was the first scholar to realize its potential significance. The manuscript of this supposed Mahometan Gospel was shown to the Irishman by Johann Jacob Cramer, Counsellor to the King of Prussia, who "had it out of the Library of a person of great name and authority in the said city [Amsterdam]; who, during his life, was often heard to put a high value on this piece" (*Nazarenus*, 15). According to Toland's description, the book, purporting to be the Gospel of Barnabas translated into Italian, "is written on Turkish paper delicately gumm'd and polish'd, and also bound after the Turkish manner. The ink is incomparably fine; and the orthography, as well as the character, plainly show it to be at least three hundred years old" (15). For Cramer, the manuscript was hardly more than a kind of *curio*, but Toland was quick to grasp that there might be much more to this piece than met the eye. It is through his agency that the book was sent to Prince Eugene, "*by the way of his Adjutant General the Baron de* HOHENDORF" (ii). Although we know that the first extensive discussion of the manuscript was penned by Toland in 1710, the first reference to it to appear in printed form was in Bertrand de la Monnoye's contribution to the *Menagiana* in 1715.[18] The manuscript Toland discussed in both *Christianisme Judaïque et Mahométan* and *Nazarenus* is still extant, and is held in the manuscript collections

---

16. "But I believe it the will of heaven that this fabric of theirs should be published abroad and that all mankind should learn their sacred laws" (Lucan, *The Civil War* [*Pharsalia*] [Duff, LCL], 10.197–198).

17. "I. IN *the first place you'll find the succinct history of a* NEW GOSPEL, *which I discovered at Amsterdam, in the year* 1709. *It is a* Mahometan Gospel, *never before publicly made known among Christians, tho they have much talkt about the Mahometans acknowledging the* Gospel" (*Nazarenus*, ii).

18. Vol. 4 of *Menagiana* (3rd ed.; Paris: Florentin Delaune, 1715), 202–14.

of the Österreichische Nationalbibliothek in Vienna (cod. 2662). It was published in facsimile form in the late 1970s, with a French translation and a substantial introduction by Luigi Cirillo and Michel Frémaux.[19] But before coming to these modern scholars' assessement of Toland's "Mahometan Gospel," we need to take a closer look at the Irishman's own view of the matter.

The first stage of Toland's demonstration is to remind the reader of the presumed existence of a Gospel of Barnabas. This is achieved by piling up authority upon authority, so as to prove the author's mastery of the relevant literature:

> AMONG the numerous *Gospels, Acts, Epistles,* and *Revelations,* which were handed about in the primitive Church, which since that time have been pronounc'd apocryphal by the majority of Christians, and wherof some remain entire to this day, as the *Gospel* of JAMES for example (tho we have only a few fragments of several others) among these, I say, there was a *Gospel* attributed to BARNABAS, as appears from the famous *Decree* of GELASIUS Bishop of *Rome,* who inserts it by name in his roll of apocryphal books. Yet GELASIUS, who only augmented and confirm'd it, is not generally allow'd to be the first author of this *Decree;* but DAMASUS before him, as it was augmented again by HORMISDAS after him. The *Gospel of* BARNABAS is likewise quoted in the *Index of the Scriptures,* which COTELERIUS has publish'd from the 1789th manuscript of the *French* King's library. Tis further mention'd in the 206th manuscript of the BAROCCIAN collection in the Bodleian library, and is follow'd by the *Gospel according to Matth:* which, to be sure, signifies MATTHIAS and not MATTHEW; since not only in some copies of the *Gelasian Decree* there is a *Gospel* attributed to MATTHIAS, but also by ORIGEN, EUSEBIUS, JEROM, and AMBROSE, as may be seen by the Catalogues of such as have written concerning the Apocryphal books of the *New Testament.* (*Nazarenus,* 6–8)

Even this long quotation does not quite give a full idea of Toland's method, since all the above assertions are backed up by an elaborate apparatus of footnotes, containing the relevant references and extensive quotations in Latin or Greek. Only true specialists of the field could make sense of this thick network of scholarly references, with names which meant nothing

---

19. Luigi Cirillo and Michel Frémaux, *Évangile de Barnabé: Recherches sur la composition et l'origine* (Paris: Beauchesne, 1977); a revised second edition was published in 1999: *Évangile de Barnabé. Fac-similé, traduction et notes* (BeRe; 2nd ed.; Paris: Beauchesne, 1999).

to the layman who was also Toland's target. What the layman would have missed in particular was the deliberate combination of canonical and apocryphal sources; nothing in the text signals the shift from one type of document to the other, since both are granted similar status as reliable authorities on early Christian history. For instance, Toland moves seamlessly from references taken from the canonical Acts of the Apostles, to the apocryphal Epistle of Peter to James.[20] Yet this was of course entirely in keeping with his view of the apocrypha, which he considered as valuable documents whose evidence had to be taken into account.

However, when it comes to connecting the ancient Gospel of Barnabas with the recently discovered Gospel of the Mahometans (or so the claim goes), Toland slips into what looks uncomfortably like an argument from authority:

> AFTER giving this account of the ancient *Gospel* of BARNABAS, or rather a bare proof that formerly there was such a *Gospel*, I come now to the *Gospel of the Mahometans*, which very probably is in great part the same book with that of BARNABAS; and so not yet extinct, as all Christian writers have hitherto imagin'd. (*Nazarenus*, 9)

This sentence hinges on the two adverbs "very probably," a flimsy logical link if any to connect the two Gospels in question. It is a fact that the book Toland was shown in Amsterdam does contain the claim that it is the Gospel of Barnabas,[21] but this bald, uncorroborated statement provides very shaky ground for the kind of conclusion Toland hastens to

---

20. Toland, *Nazarenus*, 23. As Justin Champion comments: "Here, without any indication that he is using an apocryphal source, Toland cites at length from the 'Clementine letters' of Peter to James, which prefaced the Clementine Homilies, a description of the travels of Clement of Rome in the East." *John Toland: Nazarenus*, 149 n. 13. This section is much indebted to Justin Champion's substantial introduction to his edition of *Nazarenus*, as well as to his illuminating article, "Apocrypha, Canon and Criticism from Samuel Fisher to John Toland, 1650–1718," in *Judaeo-Christian Intellectual Culture in the Seventeenth Century: A Celebration of the Library of Narcissus Marsh (1638–1713)* (AIHI 163; Dordrecht: Kluwer, 1999), 91–117.

21. "It is in the very first page attributed to BARNABAS, and the title of it runs in these words: *The true Gospel of* JESUS *called* CHRIST, *a new prophet sent by God to the world, according to the relation of* BARNABAS *his apostle*. Here you have not only a new *Gospel*, but also a true one, if you believe the Mahometans" (*Nazarenus*, 15).

draw. *Nazarenus*'s first critic, Thomas Mangey, Rector of St. Nicholas's in Guildford at the time, could justifiably argue that

> He [Toland] could not fancy the World so credulous, as to come readily into a new Gospel that was but a Translation into *Lingua Franca* not 300 Years old, without any other internal or external Evidence of its being genuine but his own bare Word; and that too when the subject Matter tended to prove our whole Christianity to be no other than a gross Blunder.[22]

What is more, Toland's scholarship was mercilessly faulted both by Mangey in his 1718 *Remarks upon Nazarenus* and by Jones in the 1726 *A New and Full Method*.[23]

Yet if the self-styled Gospel of Barnabas is not quite the authentic piece Toland claimed to have found, nor is it the mere forgery that his opponents suspected. Cirillo and Frémaux concluded in 1977 that, beyond the medieval accretions, the core of the text was a much older Gospel narrative, incorporating canonical material, apocryphal Judeo-Christian traditions and apocryphal Islamic traditions.[24] Furthermore, they suggested that the earliest stratum, on which the rest was built by accretion, was likely to be the Gospel attributed to Barnabas: the manuscript "contains discernible traces of an early text, in all likelihood the early Gospel placed under the name and authority of the apostle Barnabas."[25] Although this does not

---

22. Thomas Mangey, *Remarks upon Nazarenus* (London: William and John Innys, 1718), 3.

23. For a thorough discussion of this, see Champion, *John Toland: Nazarenus*, 92–94.

24. "Les observations faites sur le style, la méthode des citations, les contradictions internes, les idées christologiques et les traditions judéo-chrétiennes révèlent l'existence d'un niveau qui ne provient pas de l'auteur médiéval. Ce niveau représente, à notre avis, *un récit évangélique plus ancien* utilisé par l'auteur médiéval. Pour préciser davantage, nous pensons que le récit en question était *l'écrit de base* à partir duquel a été composé le volumineux texte transmis par le manuscrit de Vienne. Il semble que celui-ci était composé de: – citations canoniques remaniées, – traditions apocryphes judéo-chrétiennes, – traditions apocryphes d'origine islamique, surtout celles qui constituent la définition de l'Évangile" (Cirillo and Frémaux, *Évangile de Barnabé* [1977], 182–83).

25. "L'*EBV* contient des traces repérables d'un texte primitif, vraisemblablement l'*Évangile primitif placé sous le nom et l'autorité de l'apôtre Barnabé*" (Cirillo et Frémaux, *Évangile de Barnabé* [1977], 182).

mean that Toland was "right" in the strict sense of the word, this nevertheless shows that in spite of his often crude and faulty scholarship, his hunch concerning the connection between the "Mahometan Gospel" and the Gospel of Barnabas was not entirely misplaced.

In Toland's view, the major significance that attached to this recovered ancient Gospel was that it helped him to construct a narrative of the origins of Christianity that was entirely different from the orthodox one, by helping to shed new light on the relationship between "Jewish Christians" (or "Christian Jews")[26] and Gentile Christians. In this respect, the "Mahometan Gospel" is hardly more than the occasional cause of Toland's musings,[27] for the quotations he makes from it are in fact surprisingly few and far between. Thomas Mangey has reason to complain "that he neither gives his Author nor his Readers fair play in producing only a few Scraps, when the whole would have spoke better for it self."[28] This text is used by Toland as circumstantial evidence to confirm the evidence taken from Scripture, and to shore up his case in favour of what he calls from the outset the original plan of Christianity:

> FROM the history of the NAZARENS, and more particularly from the evident words of Scripture, I inferr in this discourse a distinction of two sorts of Christians, viz. those from among the Jews, and those from among the Gentiles: not onely that in fact there was such a distinction (which no body denies) but likewise that of right it ought to have been so (which every body denies) and that it was so design'd in THE ORIGINAL PLAN OF CHRISTIANITY. (Nazarenus, iv)

Toland's phrase "the original plan of Christianity" was his own, defiant equivalent of the canonical "Christian dispensation" of orthodox theology. On his reading of the scriptural evidence, the Church polity was meant to accommodate from the start both Jewish Christians and Gentile Christians, a distinction that was meant to persist across the ages to maintain

---

26. Toland favors the first form over the second most of the time in *Nazarenus* (it is used, for instance, on pp. v and 28), but he does use *Christian Jews* on one occasion (42).

27. "*I was naturally led by the* Gospel *of* BARNABAS *to resume some former considerations I had about the* NAZARENS; *as being the Primitive Christians most properly so call'd, and the onely Christians for some time*" (*Nazarenus*, iii).

28. Mangey, *Remarks upon Nazarenus*, 16.

a "union without uniformity"[29] between the two sorts of Christians. On the one hand, Jewish and Gentile Christians were to be united by their common faith in Christ:

> both of them were to be for ever after united into one body or fellowship, and in that part of Christianity particularly, which, better than all the preparative purgations of the Philosophers, requires the sanctification of the spirit, or the renovation of the inward man; and wherin alone the Jew and the Gentile, the Civiliz'd and the Barbarian, the Freeman and the Bondslave, are all one in CHRIST, however otherwise differing in their circumstances. (Nazarenus, v)

Yet on the other hand, complete uniformity was ruled out since the Jewish Christians were meant to remain faithful to the Levitical law to the end of time, while the Gentile Christians were free of any obligation to abide by the Jewish law:

> but JESUS and his Apostles made it manifest that the Gentile, who believ'd one God and the necessity of Regeneration, might, contrary to the notions of the degenerate Jews (who then plac'd all religion in outward practices) be justify'd by such his Faith, without being oblig'd to exercise the ceremonies of the Law, being things no way regarding him, either as to national origin or civil government; while the Jew, on the other hand, must, to the outward observance of his country Law by eternal covenant, add this inward Regeneration and the Faith of the Gospel, or the Levitical Law wou'd avail him nothing tho ever so strictly observ'd. (Nazarenus, 64)

This far-reaching claim is built on a threefold reassessment of the traditional view concerning the Christian dispensation.

First, from the linguistic and philological viewpoint, Toland is adamant that the scriptural terms used to refer to the eternal character of the Jewish law ought to be taken literally, and that *perpetuity* does mean perpetuity. According to him, these words cannot be interpreted as mere hyperbolic expressions, whose actual meaning is less than what it appears to be:

> But the present case is nothing at all to the matter, nor can there be any solution given of it (otherwise than on the foot of our scheme) that will

---

29. "*This Union without Uniformity, between Jew and Gentile, is the admirable Economy of the* Gospel" (Nazarenus, v).

not appear perfectly precarious, if not subject to several great inconveniences: as no other scheme can reconcile Christianity, and the promises of everlasting duration made in favor of the Jewish Law: which are poorly, I will not say sophistically, evaded, by making the words *eternal, everlasting, for ever, perpetual*, and *throout all generations*, to mean onely *a great while*; that the way of Christ's *accomplishing the Law*, was to *abolish it*; and that *till heaven and earth shall pass*, signify'd *till the reign of* TIBERIUS CESAR. (*Nazarenus*, 40–41)

It is no wonder that the Anglican divine Thomas Mangey should have rebutted this particular claim with an unequivocal reassertion of orthodox truth:

> The words eternal and everlasting, that are apply'd to the old Covenant, seem to contradict this temporary Reason of the Law. But this apparent Contradiction is owing to the mistaken sense of the Hebrew word, which doth not signify eternal, but only durable. The word is not, as *Nazarenus* suggests, *Sophistically evaded*, but truly and properly explained; one may guess from hence, what skill this Hypercritick hath in the Scriptures, that can be so impos'd upon by the letter of a Translation. I insist upon it, that the word (לעולם) [*leolam*] which we render everlasting, signifies only *for an Age*, according to its true meaning.[30]

Second, Toland's statements invite a thorough revision of the contents and meaning of the Apostolic Decree, implying that "the Jews believing on CHRIST may safely observe their own Law, provided they neither persuade nor force the Gentile Christians to do the same" (*Nazarenus*, 41), and that this provision was meant to be perpetual. This again ran contrary to the orthodox view of the Council of Jerusalem as expounded by Mangey in his *Remarks upon Nazarenus*.[31]

---

30. Mangey, *Remarks upon Nazarenus*, 91.

31. "The same Apostle [Peter], at the Council of *Jerusalem*, made the most forward Declaration against the Law, by calling it a Yoke which *neither they nor their Fathers were able to bear*: which shew'd that he did not only discharge the *Gentiles* but the *Jews* from observing it. The Question which gave occasion to that Council was not owing to the private Sentiment of any one Apostle, but to the Pride of some Pharisaical Christians; ... undoubtedly this their Decree, which set aside the Obligation of the *Jewish* Law, had the greater Sanction from their Numbers and Unanimity" (Mangey, *Remarks upon Nazarenus*, 67).

To back up this particular view of the history of apostolic times, Toland launches into an elaborate reinterpretation of the meaning of the supposed conflict between James and Paul over the respective importance of faith and works. The opposition is at its sharpest when Paul's statement that "*a man is justify'd by* FAITH *without the Works of the* LAW" (Rom 3:28, as quoted in *Nazarenus*, 65) is contrasted with James's view that "by Works a man is justify'd, and not by Faith onely" (Jas 2:24, as quoted in *Nazarenus*, xiii–xiv). On the face of it, these two passages cannot be reconciled, arguing as they do for two opposite definitions of justification. Yet, in order to solve this apparent contradiction, Toland argues that each apostle was in fact targeting a different audience: James's words were addressed to the Jewish Christians, to remind them that they were to remain observant of the Mosaic dispensation to the end of time; conversely, Paul's words were addressed to the Gentiles, to let them know that in their case, conversion to Christianity did not entail the observance of the Jewish law. The clinching argument for Toland is that the opposition between "Works" and "Faith" is built on a thorough misunderstanding of each of these terms, of which he proposes the following definitions to show that James and Paul can ultimately be reconciled:

> Besides the passage alledg'd before out of *the first Epistle to the Corinthians*, the following passage also out of that to the Romans, may serve for a perpetual key to this System of reconciling JAMES and PAUL, *viz.* that WORKS, as oppos'd to FAITH in their writings, signify the *opus operatum* of the Levitical Law, or the outward practice of it; and that FAITH signifies the belief of one God, a persuasion of the truth of CHRIST's doctrine, and the inward sanctification of the mind. (*Nazarenus*, 64)[32]

---

32. To counter what he viewed as yet another instance of Toland's disingenuousness, Mangey retorted: "There is therefore no need for this busy Intermedler to reconcile the two Apostles, whose Doctrines are very consistent with each other. St. *Paul* teacheth that Works of any kind, whether of the Ceremonial or Moral Law, were without Faith insufficient; and that therefore all the World, without the Merits of a Redeemer, was guilty before God. St. *James* finding this Doctrine misunderstood by some who join'd not their Practice to their Belief, shews what the Properties of this justifying Faith should be, that it should be active and lively, and exert it self eminently in good Works: that is, if Men truly believ'd in *Jesus Christ*, they would do readily what he had commanded, and take Care to make their Behaviour consistent with their Christian Profession. These are the Doctrines of the two Apostles, and, when so explain'd, are without the wicked Assistance of *Nazarenus*, reconcileable enough with each other" (Mangey, *Remarks upon Nazarenus*, 112).

With these arguments, the way is paved for the third stage of the reassessment of Christian doctrine, which is no less than a thorough rejection of supersessionism.[33] On this score, Toland is quite emphatic. As early as the preface to *Nazarenus*, he argues that the distinction of Jewish and Gentile Christians,

> and this distinction onely, ... makes the Gospels to agree with the Acts and the Epistles, and the Epistles with the Acts and one another: but, what is more than all, it shows a perfect accord between the Old Testament and the New; and proves that God did not give two Laws, wherof the one was to cancel the other, which is no small stumbling block to the opposers of Christianity, as the resolving of this difficulty is no sign, I hope, of my want of Religion. (*Nazarenus*, vii–viii)

In the course of the letter itself, he returns to the point by asking a pointed, rhetorical question to which he then provides his own, predictable answer:

> Is not this the onely method of according the Jews and the Gentiles? yea and of justifying God himself against those, who object the mutability or imperfection of giving one Law at one time, and another Law at another time? wheras there is no such abrogating or obrogating according to the ORIGINAL PLAN of CHRISTIANITY. The Religion that was true yesterday is not false to day; neither can it ever be false, if ever it was once true. (*Nazarenus*, 65)

The "Original Plan of Christianity" as expounded by Toland appears as a complete reworking of the Christian dispensation, dispensing as it does with supersessionism and aiming at "according the Jews and the Gentiles"— or more precisely the Jewish Christians and the Gentile Christians—in a

---

33. Here again, Thomas Mangey thought it his duty to reassert sound doctrine: "The last Stroke that was given to the observance of the *Jewish* Law, was the Destruction of *Jerusalem*, or to speak more accurately, the Expulsion of the *Jews* from thence by *Adrian*, which incident, as *Sulpitius Severus* informs us, was serviceable to the Church of God, as by the interposition of Providence it perfectly remov'd the Slavery of the Law by the Liberty of the Gospel.

"From that time there were no more Bishops of the Circumcision, and all distinction of *Jew* and *Gentile* was intirely taken away; those that afterwards added the observance of the Law to the Belief of the Gospel, were from that time deservedly reckon'd Hereticks, which was the Case of that Sect for which *Nazarenus* pleads" (Mangey, *Remarks upon Nazarenus,* 71).

unified, but not a uniform, church. Yet one can wonder how truly different
a prospect of this kind is from the orthodox churchmen's calls for the conversion of the Jews.[34] For the prospect that Toland seems to hold out is one
of eventual integration of the Jews into the Christian fold, an integration
made easier by allowing them to retain the Levitical law. On such reading,
Toland's plan would appear to be little better than a politic ploy, a cunning
device to obtain the return of the lost sheep to the "one fold under one shepherd, Jesus Christ our Lord," to take up the words of the Book of Common
Prayer. The sacrifice of uniformity would then be a comparatively small
price to pay for the rich rewards of unity, a line of interpretation to which
some of Toland's pronouncements do lend credibility:

> Here you see the antiquity of pressing *Uniformity*, and the effects of it
> too: and I am entirely satisfy 'd, that, were it not for this execrable treat-
> ment of them (so contrary to the practice of JESUS, and the doctrine of
> the *Gospel*) not a Jew, but, many ages since, had been likewise a Chris-
> tian; as it must be on this foot alone, that their conversion to Christianity
> can ever be reasonably expected. (*Nazarenus*, 56)

> And indeed the divine wisdom of the Christian Institution (the original,
> uncorrupted, easy, intelligible Institution; but not the fabulous systems,
> lucrative inventions, burthensom superstitions, and unintelligible jargon
> early substituted to it) is so apparent in enlightening the minds and
> regulating the conduct of men, in procuring their highest happiness in
> all respects, particularly in the admirable Economy of uniting the Jews
> and the Gentiles into one Family, and thus leading all the world to the
> knowledge of one God: that nothing, I am persuaded, but a perfect igno-
> rance of what it really is, or private interest, a worse enemy to truth than
> ignorance, cou'd keep any from cheerfully imbracing it. (*Nazarenus*, 70)

However tempting this line of interpretation might be, the available evidence is insufficient to buttress it.

---

34. In the 1662 Book of Common Prayer, the third collect for Good Friday reads,
"O merciful God, who hast made all men, and hatest nothing that thou hast made, nor
wouldest the death of a sinner, but rather that he should be converted and live: Have
mercy upon all Jews, Turks, Infidels, and Hereticks, and take from them all ignorance,
hardness of heart, and contempt of thy word; and so fetch them home, blessed Lord,
to thy flock, that they may be saved among the remnant of the true Israelites, and be
made one fold under one shepherd, Jesus Christ our Lord, who liveth and reigneth
with thee and the Holy Spirit, one God, world without end. *Amen.*"

For one thing, Toland does not in fact rule out the continuing existence of the Jews, as distinct from the "Jewish Christians" or "Christian Jews." As this is not central to his argument in *Nazarenus*, this point is not much in evidence but it is present all the same in this passage:

> *It follows indeed that* the JEWS, whether becoming CHRISTIANS or not, are for ever bound to the LAW OF MOSES, as now limited: *and he that thinks they were absolv'd from the observation of it by* JESUS, *or that tis a fault in them still to adhere to it, does err not knowing the* Scriptures. (*Nazarenus*, vi)

This very short, passing reference may seem somewhat flimsy to back up the claim that Toland was not looking for the conversion of the Jews on simplified terms, but much firmer evidence of this can in fact be found elsewhere. Four years before *Nazarenus* was published, John Toland had published a small pamphlet, *Reasons for Naturalizing the Jews in Great Britain and Ireland* (London: J. Roberts, 1714).[35] In this short book, the Irishman had called unambiguously for the full naturalization of the Jews residing in Britain and Ireland, without either calling for their prior conversion to Christianity or holding this out as a desirable prospect. Conversion was definitely not an ulterior motive of the Irishman's plea for the naturalization of the Jews; his "philosemitism"[36] was a noteworthy feature at a time when most of his Deist friends took a rather dim view of Jews and Judaism.

Furthermore, the brand of Christianity that Toland associated with the Jewish Christians, or Nazarenes,[37] was not of a kind to have allowed

---

35. *Reasons for Naturalizing the Jews* was not published again until the twentieth century, during which it went through several editions or translations: "Reasons for Naturalizing the Jews in Great Britain and Ireland," in *Pamphlets Relating to the Jews in England during the 17th and 18th Centuries* (ed. P. Radin; Occasional Papers, English Series 3; San Francisco: California State Library, Sutro Branch, 1939), 40–65; *Reasons for Naturalizing the Jews in Great Britain and Ireland* (facsimile of the 1714 edition; Jerusalem: Hebrew University of Jerusalem, 1963); *Gründe für die Einbürgerung der Juden* (ed. and trans. H. Mainusch; StDel 9; Stuttgart: Kohlhammer, 1965); *Raisons de naturaliser les Juifs* (ed. and trans. Pierre Lurbe; Fondements de la politique, Série Textes; Paris: Presses Universitaires de France, 1998); and *Ragioni per naturalizzare gli Ebrei* (ed. Paolo Bernardini; trans. Laura Orsi; Florence: Giuntina, 1998).

36. The word is used by Léon Poliakov, *Histoire de l'antisémitisme* (1955; Paris: Calmann-Lévy, 1981), 2:14.

37. Thomas Mangey is highly critical of Toland on this score too, arguing that the

their easy accommodation within the pale of orthodox Christianity. For him, the outstanding importance of the so-called Mahometan Gospel lay in the fact that it spelled out the unadulterated doctrine of the earliest Christians, those Jewish Christians whom he also indifferently calls Nazarenes or Ebionites. Since they were the earliest followers of Christ, they could therefore be relied on to provide the most accurate testimony concerning both the nature of Jesus, and the tenor of his doctrine. As he pointedly asks his readers:

> Since the Nazarens or Ebionites are by all Church-historians unanimously acknowledg'd to have been the first Christians, or those who believed in CHRIST among the Jews, with which his own people he liv'd and dy'd, they having been the witnesses of his actions, and of whom were all the Apostles: considering this, I say, how it was possible for them to be the first of all others (for they are made to be the first Heretics), who shou'd form wrong conceptions of the doctrine and designs of JESUS? and how came the Gentiles, who believ'd on him after his death, by the preaching of persons that never knew him, to have truer notions of these things; or whence they cou'd have their information, but from the believing Jews? (*Nazarenus*, 76)

As for the doctrine contained in the "Mahometan Gospel,"

> Tis, in short, the ancient Ebionite or Nazarene System, as to the making of JESUS a mere man (tho not with them the Son of JOSEPH, but divinely conceiv'd by the Virgin MARY) and agrees in every thing almost with the scheme of our modern Unitarians; excepting the history of his death and resurrection, about which a very different account is given from that in our *Gospels*: but perfectly conformable to the tradition of the Mahometans, who maintain that another was crucify'd in his stead; and that

---

Irishman had mixed the Nazarenes and the fourth century sect of the Nazaræans: "As the *Jews* have still retain'd the Name [Nazarenes] in their Books, and never meant any Sect of their own, but the whole Body of Christians; it appears from hence that they invented this falsehood to save themselves from just Prosecution. The *Nazaræan* Sect were not at that time considerable enough to be so especially mark'd, being very few at that time, as St. *Austin* tells us; and besides as it is certain from themselves that they did actually curse the Christian Church, it follows that if they likewise curs'd the *Nazaræan* Sect, they must have had two distinct Imprecations in their Prayers" (Mangey, *Remarks upon Nazarenus*, 8).

JESUS, slipping thro' the hands of the Jews, preach'd afterwards to his disciples, and then was taken up into heaven. (*Nazarenus*, 16–17)

At this point, Toland's reconstruction of early Christian history eerily echoes the concerns of his own countrymen in the early eighteenth century. The idea of a "union without uniformity" was bound to strike a chord at a time when the High Church, and its Tory allies, were still bent on imposing uniformity on the dissenters, and on preventing them from resorting to Occasional Conformity to bypass the stringency of the law. Seen in this light, *Nazarenus* can also be read as a pamphlet in favour of the rights of the nonconformists, and even of the Unitarians, whose denial of the Trinity exposed them to very harsh penalties[38] and whose situation was not entirely dissimilar to that of the Jewish Christians. This was certainly courting trouble (a posture long familiar to Toland), but this was also arguing for a policy of toleration towards modern Christian heretics, whose views, yet again, were not unlike those of the ancient Jewish Christians.

These few remarks are not meant to suggest that Toland's history of ancient Jewish Christianity is devoid of relevance and should only be read in terms of an elaborate analogy with the contemporary scene. But they do suggest that Toland could engage with contemporary debates in British society, while writing a genuinely innovative and provocative history of early Christianity.

At the time when he was writing *Nazarenus*, John Toland was all too aware that the kind of questions he was asking was bound to lead "the wooden Priests and Divinelings of all communions … to rail and raise a cry against those that do [ask questions], as profest Heretics or conceal'd Atheists" (*Nazarenus*, 75). Whether Toland was a deist, pantheist, or a "concealed atheist" is a moot point; that his scholarship was at times faulty is beyond doubt, and his conclusions cannot be taken for granted. Toland may have been better at asking questions—sometimes awkward or irrelevant ones—than at providing answers, but then this is what research is also about. What is of far more moment is that, through his unfailing interest in the apocrypha, of which *Nazarenus* is such a striking instance, he opened up entirely new vistas for biblical criticism by questioning the

---

38. The Blasphemy Act (1698) made it a serious offense to deny the Trinity. The act was passed to stem the tide of irreligion that was said (by Tory High Churchmen) to sweep the country in the wake of the publication of John Toland's *Christianity Not Mysterious* (1696).

demarcation line between canonical and apocryphal literature. In the same way, his focus on the Jewish roots of Christianity, and his daring stance against supersessionism, proved of seminal importance not only for later scholarship but also, though less directly, for the modern climate of mutual trust and friendship between Jews and Christians. On balance, this is no mean achievement: so let us give credit where credit is due, and render unto Toland the things that are Toland's.

BIBLIOGRAPHY

Carabelli, Giancarlo. *Tolandiana: Materiali bibliografici per lo studio dell'opera e della fortuna di John Toland (1670–1722)*. Florence: La Nuova Italia Editrice, 1975.

Champion, Justin. "Apocrypha, Canon and Criticism from Samuel Fisher to John Toland, 1650–1718." Pages 91–117 in *Judaeo-Christian Intellectual Culture in the Seventeenth Century: A Celebration of the Library of Narcissus Marsh (1638–1713)*. AIHI 163. Dordrecht: Kluwer, 1999.

Champion, Justin, ed. *John Toland: Nazarenus*. British Deism and Free Thought 1. Oxford: Voltaire Foundation, 1999.

Cirillo, Luigi, and Michel Frémaux. *Évangile de Barnabé. Fac-similé, traduction et notes*. 2nd ed. BeRe. Paris: Beauchesne, 1999.

———. *Évangile de Barnabé: Recherches sur la composition et l'origine*. BeRe. Paris: Beauchesne, 1977.

Clarke, Samuel. *Some Reflections on That Part of a Book Called Amyntor: Or, The Defence of Milton's Life, Which Relates to the Writings of the Primitive Fathers and the Canon of the New Testament*. London: James Knapton, 1699.

Ehrman, Bart D. *Lost Christianities: The Battles for Scripture and the Faiths We Never Knew*. Oxford: Oxford University Press, 2003.

Jones, Jeremiah. *A New And Full Method of Settling the Canonical Authority of the New Testament*. 3 vols. Oxford: Clarendon, 1798.

Lucan. *The Civil War (Pharsalia)*. Translated by J. D. Duff. LCL. Cambridge: Harvard University Press, 1962.

Maizeaux, Pierre des, ed. *A Collection of Several Pieces of Mr. John Toland*. 2 vols. London: J. Peele, 1726.

Mangey, Thomas. *Remarks upon Nazarenus*. London: William and John Innys, 1718.

Mannarino, Lia, ed. *John Toland: Dissertations diverses*. Libre pensée et littérature clandestine 24. Paris: Honoré Champion, 2005.

Monnoye, Bertrand de la. *Menagiana*. Vol. 4. 3rd ed. Paris: Florentin Delaune, 1715.

Nye, Stephen. *An Historical Account and Defence of the Canon of the New Testament: In Answer to Amyntor*. London: J. Darby, 1700.

Pliny. *Letters*. Translated by William Melmoth. Revised by W. M. L. Hutchinson. 2 vols. LCL. New York: Macmillan, 1931–1935.

Richardson, John. *The Canon of the New Testament Vindicated: In Answer to the Objections of J. T. in His Amyntor*. London: Richard Sare, 1700.

Toland, John. *Adeisidæmon, sive Titus Livius a superstitione vindicatus … Annexae sunt ejusdem Origines Judaicæ.* Hagæ Comitatis: Thomam Johnson, 1709.

———. *Amyntor: Or, A Defence of Milton's Life.* London: n.p., 1699.

———. *An Apology for Mr. Toland.* London: n.p., 1697.

———. *A Defence of Mr Toland.* London: E. Whitlock, 1697.

———. *Gründe für die Einbürgerung der Juden.* Edited and translated by Herbert Mainusch. StDel 9. Stuttgart: Kohlhammer, 1965.

———. *The Life of John Milton, Containing, Besides the History of His Works, Several Extraordinary Characters of Men and Books, Sects, Parties, and Opinions.* London: John Darby, 1699.

———. *Nazarenus: Or, Jewish, Gentile, and Mahometan Christianity.* 2nd ed. London: J. Brotherton, J. Roberts, and A. Dodd, 1718.

———. *Ragioni per naturalizzare gli Ebrei.* Edited by Paolo Bernardini. Translated by Laura Orsi. Florence: Giuntina, 1998.

———. *Raisons de naturaliser les Juifs.* Edited and translated by Pierre Lurbe. Fondements de la politique, Série Textes. Paris: Presses Universitaires de France, 1998.

———. *Reasons for Naturalizing the Jews in Great Britain and Ireland.* London: J. Roberts, 1714.

———. "Reasons for Naturalizing the Jews in Great Britain and Ireland." Pages 40–65 in *Pamphlets Relating to the Jews in England during the 17th and 18th Centuries.* Edited by P. Radin. Occasional Papers, English Series 3. San Francisco: California State Library, Sutro Branch, 1939.

———. *Reasons for Naturalizing the Jews in Great Britain and Ireland.* Jerusalem: Hebrew University of Jerusalem, 1963.

———. *Tetradymus. Containing I. Hodegus; Or, the Pillar of Cloud and Fire, That Guided the Israelites in the Wilderness, Not Miraculous.* London: J. Brotherton, 1720.

———. *Vindicius Liberius.* London: Bernard Lintott, 1702.

THE INVENTION OF JEWISH CHRISTIANITY IN JOHN TOLAND'S *NAZARENUS*

Matt Jackson-McCabe

I forsee that many of 'em … will say, that I advance a new Christianity,
tho I think it undoubtedly to be the old one.

—John Toland, *Nazarenus*[1]

The categories and taxonomies that scholars use to interpret and explain
religions, like religions themselves, are created in particular social-cultural contexts, evolve over time, and are sometimes abandoned. "Jewish
Christianity" is one such category. A staple of historical reconstructions of
early Christianity over much of the history of the critical study of the New
Testament, it has for good reason come increasingly under fire in recent
decades.[2] The history of the rise and incipient fall of this scholarly inven-

---

1. All citations of *Nazarenus* are taken from the second, revised edition, a facsimile of which is available on the Gallica digital library of the Bibliothéque Nationale de France (online: http://gallica.bnf.fr/ark:/12148/bpt6k67828g). Citations from
the earlier (1710) French version, titled *Christianisme Judaique et Mahometan*, are
taken from Claus-Michael Palmer's edition of *Nazarenus*, published as an appendix
in Gesine Palmer, *Ein Freispruch für Paulus: John Tolands Theorie des Judenchristentums mit einer Neuasgabe von Tolands 'Nazarenus' von Claus-Michael Palmer* (ANTZ
7; Berlin: Institut Kirche und Judentum, 1996). Following Palmer's conventions, I
abbreviate citations from *Nazarenus* as *N.* and those from the earlier French version
as *C.* I am very grateful to Stanley Jones for pointing out problems with the editions
of *N.* and *C.* provided in the otherwise indispensable study by Justin Champion, *John
Toland: Nazarenus* (British Deism and Free Thought 1; Oxford: Voltaire Foundation,
1999). I am also most grateful to Cleveland State University for funding that allowed
me to examine the still earlier draft of portions of *Nazarenus* in the British Library
Manuscripts collections.
2. For recent overviews of the problem, see my introduction and "What's in a
Name? The Problem of Jewish Christianity," in *Jewish Christianity Reconsidered:*

tion has yet to be fully written.[3] Even as its demise is still being negotiated,[4] its rise has not yet been adequately understood.

F. C. Baur is widely and rightly credited with making a dichotomy between "Jewish Christianity" and "Gentile Christianity" paradigmatic within the critical study of early Christianity. If, however, it was largely through Baur's immense influence that this dichotomy made its way into the standard vocabulary of the field, the distinction itself was not his own coinage.[5] More than a century before Baur began publishing his seminal works, the Irish-born John Toland had already placed the same dichotomy at the center of his own provocative reconstruction of early Christianity, published under the title *Nazarenus* in 1718. The ostensible occasion for Toland's study was his chance discovery of the Islamic Gospel of Barnabas—a text, he says, that "naturally" led him to "*resume some former considerations I had about the* NAZARENS; *as being the Primitive Christians most properly so call'd.*"[6] It was in the context of this study that the term

---

Rethinking Ancient Groups and Texts (ed. Matt Jackson-McCabe; Minneapolis: Fortress, 2007), 1–6, 7–38; Oskar Skarsaune, "Jewish Believers in Jesus in Antiquity: Problems of Definition, Method, and Sources," in *Jewish Believers in Jesus: The Early Centuries* (ed. Oskar Skarsaune and Reidar Hvalvik; Peabody, Mass.: Hendrickson, 2007), 3–21.

3. However, see most recently James Carleton Paget, "The Definition of the Terms *Jewish Christian* and *Jewish Christianity* in the History of Research," in Skarsaune and Hvalvik, *Jewish Believers in Jesus*, 22–52; also Gerd Luedemann, *Opposition to Paul in Jewish Christianity* (trans. M. Eugene Boring; Minneapolis: Fortress, 1980), 1–32; and A. F. J. Klijn, "The Study of Jewish Christianity," *NTS* 20 (1973–1974): 419–31.

4. Note that a number of scholars continue to advocate use of the category regardless of the criticism; e.g., Joseph Verheyden, "Jewish Christianity, A State of Affairs: Affinities and Differences with Respect to Matthew, James, and the Didache," in *Matthew, James, and Didache: Three Related Documents in Their Jewish and Christian Settings* (ed. Huub van de Sandt and Jürgen K. Zangenberg; SBLSymS 45; Atlanta: Society of Biblical Literature, 2008), 123–35; see also the essays by Craig Hill, Petri Luomanen, and F. Stanley Jones in *Jewish Christianity Reconsidered* (ed. Matt Jackson-McCabe; Minneapolis: Augsburg Fortress, 2007).

5. Observed already by David Patrick, "Two English Forerunners of the Tübingen School: Thomas Morgan and John Toland," *Theological Review* 14 (1877): 562–603. See further in the present volume F. Stanley Jones, "From Toland to Baur: Tracks of the History of Research into Jewish Christianity."

6. *N.*, iii. Throughout this essay, all use of italics, capitals, small capitals, and underlines in quotations from Toland's writings reflect the original text unless explicitly noted otherwise. It should be noted in this connection that where quotations from

Jewish Christianity, along with its inevitable mate *Gentile Christianity*, was apparently born.[7] What led Toland to invent these categories? How can we understand his decision to redescribe a group long known simply as Nazarenes in terms of "Jewish Christianity"?

For his part, Toland wished to present *Nazarenus* as being the work of someone who was "only a historian"—albeit one who might comment from time to time on the wider implications of his study.[8] His readers, however, have long recognized that there was something much more at stake here than merely an accurate description of the past. In fact, Toland composed *Nazarenus* not merely as an account of *early* Christianity but as an account of *true* Christianity.[9] Whether Toland participated in this ecclesiastical discourse sincerely, with a genuine interest in reforming the religion, or satirically, to subvert the whole project of ecclesiastical historiography itself, is a matter of debate.[10] What is plain at any rate is that the

---

the preface are concerned (evident by roman-numeral pagination), italic font is the norm, with roman font (with or without capitals) used for emphasis.

7. See below. For further confirmation, see in this volume Matti Myllykoski, " 'Christian Jews' and 'Jewish Christians': The Jewish Origins of Christianity in English Literature from Elizabeth I to Toland's *Nazarenus*." Myllykoski's research, while turning up multiple uses of *Jewish Christian* to describe individuals, yielded no instances of the substantive *Jewish Christianity*. The difference, as we shall see, is significant.

8. See *N.*, 5: "And tho for the most part I am only a historian, resolv'd to make no Reflections but what my facts will naturally suggest ... yet I am not wanting, when there's occasion for it, to chalk out the methods, whereby the errors of simple or designing men may be seasonably confuted."

9. E.g., *N.*, vi: "*These* [converts from the Gentiles] *did almost wholly subvert the TRUE CHRISTIANITY, which in the following Treatise I vindicate; drawing it out from under the rubbish of their endless divisions, and clearing it from the almost impenetrable mists of their sophistry.*"

10. The sincerity of Toland's Christian profession has been a matter of debate from his day to our own. Most recently, Justin Champion has argued forcefully for the genuineness of Toland's attempt to reform Christianity in a series of publications; see esp. "John Toland: The Politics of Pantheism," *Revue de synthese* 2–3 (1995): 259–80; *The Pillars of Priestcraft Shaken: The Church of England and Its Enemies, 1660–1730* (Cambridge Studies in Early Modern British History; Cambridge: Cambridge University Press, 1992); and *Republican Learning: John Toland and the Crisis of Christian Culture, 1696–1722* (New York: Manchester University Press, 2003). The most recent and perhaps most intriguing argument for the contrary position is that of Daniel C. Fouke, *Philosophy and Theology in a Burlesque Mode: John Toland and "The Way of Paradox"* (Amherst, N.Y.: Humanity Books, 2007). Fouke contends that Toland merely "*pretended* to engage in theology and to operate within its framework of assumptions,

category "Jewish Christianity," if supported by historical argumentation, was a byproduct of Toland's attempt to lay claim to the mythic source of Christian authority—Jesus and the apostles—for his own Enlightenment ethos of rationality, universal humanity, and tolerance. The concept of "Jewish Christianity," in other words, was an invention of ecclesiastical apologetic discourse and Christian myth.

TOLAND'S PROJECT

Toland's formulation of a new taxonomy of Christianity was emphasized boldly in the very title of his work: "*Nazarenus:* OR, *Jewish, Gentile,* and *Mahometan* CHRISTIANITY." If it is the first of these categories that is our chief interest here, the one that sounded most exotic to Toland's ears—and that his study would be particularly concerned to establish—was actually the third:

> and tho the very title of *Mahometan Christianity* may be apt to startle you (for *Jewish* or *Gentile Christianity* shou'd not sound quite so strange) yet I flatter my self, that, by perusing the following *Dissertation*, you'll be fully convinc'd there is a sense, wherin the Mahometans may not improperly be reckon'd and call'd a sort or sect of Christians. (*N.*, 4)[11]

In fact, when Toland first began to conceive of the project that would eventually be published as *Nazarenus*, the main title he gave it was simply "Mahometan Christianity."[12] The title evolved as the project did. By the

---

but constructed burlesques that exposed the inconsistencies and weaknesses of its framework" (25). "The whole thrust of his literary manner," in other words, "was to deconstruct the discourses of the establishment and to disrupt their ideological functions" (23). For Fouke's treatment of Toland's reconstruction of early Christianity in particular, see 215–68 in the same work.

11. Cf. the summarizing conclusion at the end of the analysis: "You perceive by this time … that what the Mahometans believe concerning CHRIST and his doctrine, were neither the inventions of MAHOMET, nor yet of those Monks who are said to have assisted him in the framing of his *Alcoran*; but that they are as old as the time of the Apostles, having been the sentiments of whole Sects or Churches" (*N.*, 84–85).

12. The full title as anticipated in BL 4465 f.64v is "Mahometan Christianity: or an Acco[un]t of ye ancient Gospel of Barnabas, and the modern Gospel of the Turks; with some reflections on the Contest between Peter and Paul about the observation of the Law of Moses by Christian Believers." I follow Champion's reading with respect to the words *Account* and *ye* (*Nazarenus*, 58), both of which are difficult to make out in the

time he produced a French version of the work in 1710, its title had been reformulated to highlight two categories: *Christianisme Judaique et Mahometan*.[13] When the published version finally appeared eight years later, the title was reworked again to emphasize three distinct categories—"*Jewish, Gentile,* and *Mahometan* CHRISTIANITY"—but with all this an alternate title to what was now called simply *Nazarenus*.[14]

It is plain both from Toland's sensitivity to the extent to which his categories might "startle" and from this repeated reworking of the title that the formulation of a new taxonomy of Christianity was a very conscious and deliberate dimension of the project that would eventually be published as *Nazarenus*.[15] If we wish to understand how Toland came to formulate the category "Jewish Christianity," then, we will do well to begin by contextualizing this move within Toland's larger taxonomic project.

The few extant portions of the initial draft of the work's introduction, apparently from the time when the project was still being called "Mahometan Christianity," are very helpful in this respect.[16] In a passage that

---

manuscript. What Champion transcribes as "contexts," however, seems to me to read "Contest"—a reading, moreover, that not only makes better grammatical sense, but also finds support in the subsequent French version of the title: "<u>Des Reflections</u> sur le *demelé* entre Pierre et Paul, touchant l'observation perpetuelle de La Loy de Moyse par les Chretiens d'entre les Juifs" (Palmer, *Freispruch*, appendix, 9; italics added).

13. Palmer, *Freispruch*, appendix, 9. Palmer gives the full title as "<u>Christianisme Judaique et Mahometan</u>. ou RELATION de l'ancien Evangile de Barnabas, et de l'Evangile moderne des Mahometans: avec <u>Des Reflections</u> sur le demelé entre Pierre et Paul, touchant l'observation perpetuelle de La Loy de Moyse par les Chretiens d'entre les Juifs, de meme que des preceptes Noachiques par les Chretiens d'entre les Gentiles; où l'on prouve que toutes les deux doivent etre d'obligation indispensable, selon le plan originel du Christianisme: comme aussi <u>Une Difficulté</u> proposeé touchant deux sortes de Christianisme, qui ont continué depuis le temps des Apotres jusqu'à nous; où l'on donne un veritable recit des Nazareens et Ebionites. Le tout dans une lettre à Megalonymus."

14. Note, however, that this tripartite scheme only makes explicit what was already implicit in the French title, where the "two sorts of Christianity" that existed from apostolic times are plainly "les Chretiens d'entre les Juifs" and "les Chretiens d'entre les Gentiles." See further Palmer, *Freispruch*, 45–46 (n. 90), 50.

15. This is also clear from the fact that Toland argued that this new classification scheme—particularly where Mahometan Christianity was concerned—should lead to sociopolitical changes in Christian Europe. See below.

16. All quotations from BL 4465 f63–64 represent my own reading of the manuscript unless otherwise noted; cf. the transcriptions in Champion, *Nazarenus*, 300–301. The date of the manuscript is something of a puzzle. The notation "1698" is given

would eventually evolve into the one quoted above, Toland can already be seen anticipating that his reader "might look on the title of the present dissertation [i.e., "Mahometan Christianity"] to be somwhat singular," and thus hoping to demonstrate precisely the point that "the Mahometans may not improperly be call'd and reckon'd a sort of Christians."[17] It is quite plain, then, that Toland had conceived this project from the very start as an attempt to establish and defend a new classification of Islam as "Mahometan Christianity." What led him to make this provocative taxonomic move?

In the same passage, though in a portion that would eventually be edited out of the published *Nazarenus*, Toland elaborates further on the context in which he is doing this. However "singular" his notion of "Mahometan Christianity" might seem, he was not, he says, "the first, who put <u>Christian</u> and <u>Mahometan</u> to'gether." He refers specifically in this connection to "a certain Doctor of Divinity"—namely, one Robert South—who had put the terms together precisely for the purpose of dismissing Toland himself as a "Mahometan Christian" based on the seemingly Unitarian vision of Christianity Toland had promulgated in *Christianity Not Mysterious* in 1696.[18] Notably, the question of Islam's relation to Christianity—and, more to the point, of Unitarian doctrine's relationship to Islam—had

---

at the top of f64r, but it was later, in pencil, struck through and replaced by "1718"— i.e., the publication date of *Nazarenus* itself. (Note that Toland's original numbering of these manuscript pages as 34 and 35 on f63r and 64r, respectively, was similarly struck through and replaced by their current folio designations in pencil. Whether this was all done by the same hand, however, is not immediately clear.) Champion, accordingly, appears to date them to 1698 (ibid., 56–57, 300). Such an early dating, however, does not seem to square with its references to the *Gospel of Barnabas*, which Toland elsewhere says he found only in 1709 (*N.*, ii). That these pieces of text in any case pre-date the French version of 1710 is clear from the fact that they assume a title of "Mahometan Christianity" in a passage that will be revised in the French version to account for the title, "Christianisme Judaique et Mahometan," and finally again in the published version to account for the tripartite subtitle, "*Jewish, Gentile*, and *Mahometan* CHRISTIANITY." Compare f63v (cf. Champion, *Nazarenus*, 300) with *C.*, 2, and *N.*, 4.

17. BL 4465 f63v (cf. Champion, *Nazarenus*, 300). It is plain from the manuscript page that the phrase "and reckon'd a sort of" was itself a secondary insertion into the sentence by Toland. The first draft of the line thus stated even more straightforwardly that "the Mahometans may not improperly be call'd Christians."

18. BL 4465 f64r and f63v (cf. Champion, *Nazarenus*, 300–301). The "Doctor" is identified by name in the corresponding passage in the French version (*C.*, 2); see further Champion, *Nazarenus*, 55–56.

become a regular topic in the Unitarian–Trinitarian debate flourishing in Toland's England.[19] Toland's "startling" formulation of the category "Mahometan Christianity," then, represented an ironic appropriation and reification of a term of slander directed against himself in the context of an ecclesiastical debate about true Christianity.

Toland's response to this charge is a study in ambiguity.[20] He initially characterized the intended slander ironically as a "complement," subsequently revised this to "odd complement," and in any event feigned not to understand its rationale. Compliment or not, he did not hesitate to hurl the characterization right back at his critic, and for reasons less than flattering either to South or to Islam.[21] He was in any case clearly perturbed by the charge—enough, indeed, to conceive of a full-blown treatise on "Mahometan Christianity" and to develop it over more than a decade into *Nazarenus*. And though he was quick to insist in his initial drafts that this sort of Christianity was by no means his own (f63v; cf. *C.*, 4), the aim of the treatise would be to show precisely that there was an ironic truth to South's intended slur: that Islam itself should be considered a form of Christianity—"*and not the worst sort neither, tho farr from being the best.*"[22] Indeed, he would press farther, arguing that this conclusion had immedi-

---

19. For a very helpful treatment of this wider context, see Champion, *Pillars*, esp. 99–132.

20. For a cogent treatment of ambiguity—an oft-noted aspect of Toland's writing in general—as rhetorical strategy for Toland, see Champion, "Politics of Pantheism," and further *Pillars*, 259–80.

21. BL 4465 f64r (cf. Champion, *Nazarenus*, 301): "The reason of this odd complement I am yet to learn, unless it be that I can't drink wine enough to pass for orthodox with some Doctors: for I am by no means for propagating Religion by force, in which respect the Doctor is a very good Mahometan, how ill a Christian soever he may be. Neither am I for passive obedience or nonresistance a fundamental article among the Turks, and what was formerly preach'd with the greatest warmth of any Disciple they have in England by the Doctor." (The insertion of the word *odd* is one of several secondary revisions evident in the manuscript.) The characterization of Islam on which Toland's critique depends was typical of the era; see Champion, *Pillars*, 99–132.

22. *N.*, iii, speaking of "Mahometan Christians." Cf. *Mangoneutes*, 157, where, following up on this comment, Toland says that they are "better than Idolatrous Christians, than tritheistical Christians, than persecuting Christians, than several other sorts of false Christians I cou'd easily specify." Cited from the Elibron Classics facsimile edition (Adamant Media, 2005) of the posthumously published collection *The Theological and Philological Works of the Late Mr. John Toland* (London: W. Mears, 1732).

ate sociopolitical implications for Christian Europe; "that consequently ...
[Muslims] might with as much reason and safety be tolerated at London
and Amsterdam, as the Christians of every kind are so at Constantinople
and thro-out all Turkey."[23] Toland's strategy for establishing these points
was to develop a second, more historically oriented thesis regarding the
relationship of Islam to the Ebionites and Nazarenes, and indeed to "the
original plan of Christianity" itself.

THE HISTORICAL ARGUMENT OF *NAZARENUS*

If Toland began ruminating about this project soon after the publication of *Christianity Not Mysterious*,[24] his chance discovery in 1709 of a
Muslim Gospel of Barnabas, previously unknown to Christian Europe,
provided an ideal occasion for him to make his historical case.[25] Though
he remained somewhat coy regarding the authenticity of this Gospel, he
argued that its discovery showed that the Islamic understanding of Jesus
did not come—as some, he says, have "rashly charg'd"—from forged or
"Apocryphal books" (*N.*, 20) but from this work, which was in all likelihood the very same Gospel of Barnabas known to Christian antiquity,
even if "not in its original purity" (*N.*, 21).[26] In any event, by examining

---

23. *N.*, 5. Cf. 61, where he says, even if Islam should be considered a Christian
heresy, "I still inferr, that, whether upon a prospect of advantaging Traffic, or of putting them in the way of conversion to a better Christianity, the Mahometans may be as
well allow'd Moschs in these parts of Europe, if they desire it, as any other Sectaries."

24. Champion, *Nazarenus*, 55–60.

25. Cf. *N.*, iii: "*therefore upon this occasion* [i.e., the discovery of the Gospel of
Barnabas] *I have given a clearer account, than is commonly to be met, of the Mahometan
sentiments with relation to* JESUS *and the* GOSPEL; *insomuch that it is not* (*I believe*)
*without sufficient ground, that I have represented them as a sort of Christians, and not
the worst sort neither, tho farr from being the best.*" And again, in section 2 (also iii):
"*I was naturally led by the* Gospel *of* BARNABAS *to resume some former considerations
I had about the* NAZARENS; *as being the Primitive Christians most properly so call'd,
and the onely Christians for some time.*"

26. Toland's amibiguity regarding the origins of the Gospel is intriguing. In line
with the remark quoted here, he repeatedly works to create a sense of its antiquity:
its opening is "Scripture-stile to a hair" (*N.*, 15); the fact that it is twice as long as the
known Christian Gospels is said to be at least *potentially* in favor of its authenticity
(*N.*, 16); Muslims are known for their special care in preserving texts (*N.*, 10–11);
etc. On the other hand, he does assume at the very least some Islamic redaction (e.g.,
N., 20, 61) and at one point even suggests that Acts 9:26–27 may have provided an

the views of this Gospel in light of the early Christian literature itself, he argued, "it manifestly appears from what source the Mahometans ... had their peculiar Christianity, if I be allow'd so to call it" (N., 61). Indeed, Toland's treatise would show that "some of the fundamental doctrines of Mahometanism ... have their rise ... from the earliest monuments of the Christian religion."[27]

By way of substantiating this claim, Toland showed that several distinctive aspects of the Gospel of Barnabas's understanding of Jesus and Paul were also to be found in early Christian reports about Nazarenes and Ebionites.[28] Their unitarianism represents a major case in point: "as to the

---

occasion for "Impostors" to write a Gospel critical of Paul in the name of Barnabas (N., 34). There is a similar ambivalence regarding its identification with the ancient Gospel of Barnabas; note in this connection the apparent distinction drawn between the "antient" and "modern" Gospels of this name in the subtitle of Nazarenus (see below, n. 46), and compare N., 20, where he makes the (rather sketchy) point that a saying attributed to Barnabas in the Barrocian manuscript, but otherwise unknown, is also found in the Gospel of Barnabas: "I found it almost in terms in this *Gospel*, and the sense is evidently there in more than one place; which naturally induces me to think, it may be the *Gospel* anciently attributed to BARNABAS, however since (as I said) interpolated." Standing in a certain amount of tension to this comment, however, is the rather less committed statement of the preface: "*I have shown by unexceptionable authorities, that Ecclesiastical writers did antiently attribute a* Gospel *to* BARNABAS, *whether there be any remains of it in this new-found* Gospel, *or not*" (N., ii–iii). His ambiguity on these matters was such that his critics, at any rate, took him to be claiming it was an authentic text, and thereby challenging the very canon itself. Champion (*Nazarenus*, 95) finds Toland's disavowal of the former charge in his subsequent rebuttal, *Mangoneutes*, to be "less than honest." It is hard to believe he is not at any rate being deliberately slippery. From the perspective of Fouke (*Philosophy and Theology*, 249–59), it represents another aspect of Toland's "burlesque" mockery of the whole project of ecclesiastical history writing.

27. N. 5, explicitly rejecting the view that such ideas can be traced to "SERGIUS the Nestorian monk"—a figure that seventeenth-century Christians had identified as Muhammad's collaborator in the composition of the Qur'an (cf. Champion, *Pillars*, 105, 115). Cf. the concluding summary, at the close of the discussion of this Gospel, in N., 84–85: "You perceive by this time ... that what the Mahometans believe concerning CHRIST and his doctrine, were neither the inventions of MAHOMET, nor yet of those Monks who are said to have assisted him in the framing of his *Alcoran*; but that they are as old as the time of the Apostles, having been the sentiments of whole sects or Churches: and that tho *the Gospel of the Hebrews* be in all probability lost, yet some of those things are founded on another *Gospel* anciently known, and still in some manner existing, attributed to BARNABAS."

28. Note that Toland considered Ebionites and Nazarenes to be essentially "the

making of JESUS a mere man," he says, the Gospel of Barnabas presents nothing other than "the ancient Ebionite or Nazaren System."[29] He notes further that even the Gospel's report that someone else had been cruci-fied in the place of Jesus was reported to have been taught already in the apostolic era by Cerinthus (N., 17–19)—the Cerinthians, in Toland's view, being themselves "a branch of the Ebionites" (N., 34). And if the Gospel of Barnabas singles out the apostle Paul as one who was later deceived into spreading false teachings about Jesus, this too only reflects an ancient Ebionite position:

> this notion of PAUL's having wholly metamorphos'd and perverted the true Christianity (as some of the Heretics have exprest it) and his being blam'd for so doing by the other Apostles, especially by JAMES and PETER, is neither an original invention of the Mahometans, nor any sign of the novelty of their *Gospel:* but rather a strong presumtion of its antiquity, at least as to some parts of it; since this was the constant language and profession of the most ancient Sects [i.e., the Ebionites and Nazarenes]. (N., 24)

It is this last point that receives the fullest elaboration. Toland seeks first to establish "beyond any room for doubt" (N., 24) that Nazarenes and Ebionites considered Paul "an intruder on the genuin Christianity" who "substitut[ed] his own pretended Revelations to the doctrines of those with whom CHRIST had [actually] convers'd" (N., 29). Having done this to his satisfaction (ch. 9), he proceeds to a consideration of Paul's relation-ship to the Jerusalem apostles as understood by the Ebionites and as told by Paul himself (ch. 10). Paul, Toland observes, not only did not deny the Ebionite charge that he did not get his Gospel from the Jerusalem apostles; he positively insists on it when recounting the history of his interaction with them in Gal 1–2 (N., 30).

---

same people" (N., 25). To be sure, the group was not entirely uniform: "There were diversities of opinion among 'em, no doubt, no less than among other societies" (28), but Toland does not seem to correlate such differences with the names *Ebionite* and *Nazarene*, which are thus for him basically interchangeable.

29. N., 16–17, noting that this "System" "agrees in every thing almost with the scheme of our modern Unitarians"; cf. N. 28, where Toland describes the patristic reports regarding the Nazarene and Ebionite understanding that Jesus was "a mere man" as being "just the Socinianism of our times."

At this point Toland's argument takes a critical turn. The focus shifts from simply proving that Islamic teaching about Jesus reflects ancient Nazarene teaching to establishing a more comprehensive theory regarding the origins of Christianity itself. "But we ought not," Toland says, "slightly to run over this passage, since from the history of the Nazarens we shall take occasion (and a very natural occasion it is) to set THE ORIGINAL PLAN OF CHRISTIANITY in its proper light" (*N.*, 32–33).[30] The heart of Toland's theory is that Jesus and the apostles had from the beginning envisioned a religion that Toland would sum up as a *"Union without Uniformity"* (*N.*, v), in which Christianity as practiced by Jews would necessarily and for all time be different from Christianity as practiced by Gentiles. Interestingly, however, Toland develops this point not in relation to christological doctrine but in relation to practice, specifically of Jewish law.[31] At this point the argument becomes essentially exegetical, based primarily on an interpretation of Gal 1–2 in light of Acts 15 and 21.

In discussing Gal 1–2, Toland highlights the fact that the Ebionites accused Paul of lying when he claimed that James, Peter, and John granted the legitimacy of his mission: for if James had acknowledged the legitimacy of Paul's gospel, he could scarcely himself have been—as Paul implies—the source of the subsequent conflict in Antioch (*N.*, 31–32).[32] Toland does not, however, side with this Ebionite position. The crucial point, rather, is this: "There's but one way in the world," he says, of "reconciling these things" (*N.*, 32; cf. 37): "Paul can never be otherwise defended against the

---

30. This, then, is the section that develops a second major thesis of *Nazarenus* as identified in its first chapter, namely, that concerning "THE TRUE AND ORIGINAL CHRISTIANITY," and specifically, the point "that JESUS did not, as tis universally believ'd, abolish the Law of MOSES (Sacrifices excepted) neither in whole nor in part, not in the letter no more than in the spirit" (*N.*, 5).

31. This is interesting not only because the intended slur *Mahometan Christian* arose precisely in connection with the Trinitarian–Unitarian debate but also because the Gospel of Barnabas, as Toland well knows, is critical of Paul specifically on the matter of Christology, especially with respect to the identification of Jesus as "Son of God"; see *Nazarenus*, ch. 8, esp. 22–23. Note also in this connection Palmer's observation regarding the diminished role of the issue in *Nazarenus* as compared to the early French version (*Freispruch*, 79–80, with n. 190).

32. According to Toland, it was precisely this reading of Paul's account that led to the composition of the letter from Peter to James preserved in the Pseudo-Clementine literature (*N.*, 32).

Ebionites" unless it was the case that his law-free gospel was understood by all the apostles to have been relevant for Gentiles only, not for Jews.[33]

Toland found ample support for this position in the canonical Acts.[34] Given Acts 21 and 25, he considers it an "incontestable matter of fact" that "all the Jews which became Christians were still Zealous for the Levitical Law" (N., 38). Insofar as this law was however particularly "expressive of the history of their peculiar nation," being in this sense "no less national and political, than religious and sacred," none but "a few private persons" among them considered Gentiles to be in any way bound by it.[35] This, Toland says, was not only the position of the apostles, but of Jesus as well.[36] What is more, he argued, Acts 21:26 shows "irrefragably" that Paul himself agreed.[37] To argue otherwise would be to accuse not only Paul, but the other apostles as well, of "dissembling":

> for if the matter was not so, how cou'd it be truly said [by James], *that those things were nothing*, with which he [i.e., Paul] was charg'd? namely, that he taught the Jews to forsake MOSES, and that they ought not to circumcise their children, neither to walk after the customs (N., 36).

In a remarkable anticipation of the so-called "new" reading of Paul advanced in recent decades by Lloyd Gaston, John Gager, and others, Toland thus argued that every negative word about the law in Paul's letters concerned only its relation to Gentiles, not Jews.[38] The apostolic decree, for its part, was instituted not out of any principled concern for Gentile

---

33. N., 38; further 36–37.

34. A work, he notes, the Ebionites rejected as spurious (N., 34–35).

35. See *Nazarenus*, ch. 12, here 38 (on the Jewish view of the law) and 42 (on those "few," as in Acts 15, who would compel Gentiles to be circumcised). Toland further contextualizes this understanding of the law by citing an analogous sentiment from Maimonides (N., 38–39).

36. E.g., N., 39–40; cf. the statement of this position as a general thesis of *Nazarenus* in N., 5. Apparently anticipating the counterargument that Peter ate with Gentiles according to Acts 10, Toland suggests that "it does not appear that he ate any thing prohibited by the Law" (N., 44).

37. It should be noted that Toland never does get around to explaining why this supposed agreement suddenly erupted in conflict in Antioch.

38. See esp. *Nazarenus*, ch. 16. For a brief account (and example) of the rise of this reading in our own era, see John G. Gager, *Reinventing Paul* (New York: Oxford University Press, 2000).

diet but simply for the pragmatic purpose of making social interaction possible between Jews and Gentiles in Judea.[39]

In short, Toland argued that "the original plan of Christianity" envisioned not one but in fact multiple ways that the religion was to be practiced, depending upon the ethnicity and geographical location of its practitioners. Jewish followers of Jesus were forever bound to practice their own ancestral laws. The Gentiles who lived among them in Judea were not to observe that law, but only the minimal dietary restrictions required to permit fellowship with Jews. Those Gentiles who lived outside of Judea, finally, did not need to bother with dietary restrictions at all. According to Toland, then, the difference between Jews and Gentiles in early Christianity was a matter not just of ethnic backgrounds but of distinct practices and even separate social institutions.[40] The distinction, in other words, was not simply between Jewish and Gentile *Christians*, but between Jewish and Gentile *Christianities*.[41]

Toland remains strangely vague as to how exactly Islam figures into this scheme.[42] But its general significance for his thesis, at least, he takes to be quite obvious:

---

39. The decree is discussed at length, esp. in chs. 12–13. Noting that it is precisely the matter of diet that "makes society so difficult a thing" between Jews and Gentiles (*N.*, 43), Toland argues that the decree serves the purely pragmatic purpose of facilitating social interaction. He argues further that, though it was to remain in force forever, it does not apply "out of Judea, or any place where the Jews and Gentiles don't cohabit in one society" (*N.*, 47–48).

40. On the social dimension, see e.g., *N.*, 59, where Toland mocks the "hotheaded raving monk" Jerome for his concern that Gentiles might adopt Jewish practices: "as if the Jews and Gentiles were not to have their Churches apart, and as if the former wou'd not perform their peculiar ceremonies in their own Churches."

41. Note in this connection his pointed comment regarding the subsequent fate of the Nazarenes, namely, that they were excluded on account "not only of their Judaism, but I may say of their Christianity too" (*N.*, 56).

42. As we have seen, Toland works primarily to correlate the Gospel of Barnabas with the Nazarenes. The fact that Muslims neither are Jews nor practice Jewish law, however, is never addressed. The implication would seem to be that "Mahometan Christianity" stems from Gentile Christianity as practiced in Judea (note esp. his emphasis on the relation of Islamic dietary practice to the apostolic decree in *N.*, 61). But if so, the point is never made explicitly, nor is the issue of the continued observance of dietary directives in the apostolic decree in places like Turkey (i.e., beyond Judea) addressed. On the latter point, note also that Toland does not idealize Islam but, as pointed out above, maintains a certain critical distance from it.

> Now, from all these things … it manifestly appears from what source the
> Mahometans (who always most religiously abstain from things strangl'd
> and from blood) had their peculiar Christianity, if I be allow'd so to call
> it; and that their *Gospel*, for ought I yet know, may in the main be the
> ancient *Gospel of* BARNABAS (*N.*, 61).

The Islamic understanding of Jesus and the apostles was not the creation of
Muhammad but is in fact "as old as the time of the Apostles" (*N.*, 84–85).
If different from the Gentile Christianity practiced in Europe, it is because
its roots lie in what was always meant to have been a distinctive form of the
religion, what was indeed at the beginning the *only* form of the religion:
Jewish Christianity.

"Jewish Christianity" as Apologetic Construct

Thus far, Toland's argument for the redescription of Islam as "Mahometan
Christianity"—and, consequently, for a policy of religious tolerance in
Christian Europe—is basically historical: insofar as the beliefs and practices of Islam are historically rooted in the beliefs and practices of early
Christianity, Islam is itself properly classified as Christianity. Toland's
novel taxonomy, however, cannot be fully explained as the product of his
critical historiography. When stating at the outset his thesis regarding
Islam, Toland draws an analogy between its historical origins and those
of Christianity:

> by perusing the following *Dissertation*, you'll be fully convinc'd there is
> a sense, wherin the Mahometans may not improperly be reckon'd and
> call'd a sort or sect of Christians, as Christianity was at first esteem'd a
> branch of Judaism (*N.*, 4–5).

If the analogy sums up Toland's historical argument for reclassifying
Islam as "Mahometan Christianity," it also exposes an element of tension
between that argument and his other novel category, "Jewish Christianity." If the issue is simply one of historical roots, how can we explain the
fact that he came ultimately to formulate the category "Jewish Christianity" rather than—as his own analogy would seem to suggest—"Christian
Judaism"? Why was the end result of Toland's historical argument a new
taxonomy of *Christianity* rather than a new taxonomy of *Judaism*, one that
accounted for Christian and "Mahometan" varieties?

The answer to this question lies less in Toland's historical analysis than in the cultural and rhetorical contexts in which it was produced; namely, a competition among Christian intellectuals to authorize rival mythological and ethical constructions as "true Christianity" in the midst of the English Enlightenment. There are two specific issues that must be reckoned with. The first concerns the authorizing power of the term *Christianity* itself, and particularly *original Christianity*, in the ecclesiastical discourse of Toland's Europe. The second concerns Toland's own mythological construction of that "Christianity," particularly in relation to Judaism.

It should be remembered at the outset how Toland came to the terms of his taxonomy in the first place. The category with which he began, "Mahometan Christianity," was formulated as an ironic and pointed appropriation of a term of ecclesiastical polemics. If Trinitarian intellectuals were characterizing Unitarians as "Mahometan Christians" in order to suggest that their views were something less than "actual" Christianity,[43] Toland would show that such "Mahometan Christians," on the contrary, had at least as much claim to the title *Christianity* as their Trinitarian critics. Indeed, Toland would press farther: not only Unitarianism, but Islam more generally should be understood to count as Christianity *and thus granted the same social and political rights in Christian Europe as any other form of the religion.* Laying claim to the term *Christianity*, in other words, was precisely the point. It was this term, not *Judaism*, that carried rhetorical power in Toland's Europe.

The same dynamic is at work in Toland's move from a term familiar to his contemporaries, "Jewish *Christians*," to one apparently never before previously used, "Jewish *Christianity*." If this category, along with its inevitable companion "Gentile Christianity," were somewhat less "apt to startle" than "Mahometan Christianity" (*N.*, 4), it was not, apparently, because they had ever been used before. There was, to be sure, a long-standing tradition of distinguishing Christians by ethnic derivation, that is, "*those from among the Jews, and those from among the Gentiles*" (*N.*, iv).[44] But Toland's work would not merely restate a distinction, he says, "*which no body denies*" (*N.*, iv). On the contrary, the move from Jewish and Gentile *Christians* as distinct types of *people* to Jewish and Gentile *Christianity*

---

43. Fouke (*Philosophy and Theology*, 218) notes that Charles Leslie, for example, "thought he had sufficiently discredited Socinianism, which denied the divinity of Christ, by showing its similarity to Islam" in this same era.

44. See further above, n. 7.

as discrete categories of *religion* gets to a point that, he says, "*every body denies*" and one that is in fact a central thesis of *Nazarenus*: not merely that such a distinction existed, but "*that* of right *it* ought *to have been so*"; "*that it was so design'd in THE ORIGINAL PLAN OF CHRISTIANITY*"[45] that there should for all times be different *and yet equally legitimate* forms of Christianity itself: one for Jews, and one for Gentiles.

Toland's quarrel with earlier accounts of the Nazarenes thus had less to do with historical description than with normative evaluation. "*Their History*," he says, "*I have here set in a truer light than other writers, who are generally full of confusion and misrepresentation concerning them; making them the first, if not the worst, of all* Heretics" (*N.*, iii). In fact his reconstruction of the Ebionites and Nazarenes largely echoes the reports of the church fathers, with one primary and very crucial difference: they were not, as the Fathers portrayed them, a heretical deviation from apostolic Christianity, but reflected apostolic Christianity itself, "the TRUE ORIGINAL PLAN OF CHRISTIANITY" as envisioned by both Jesus and the apostles (*N.*, 52). To redescribe the Nazarenes as "Jewish Christianity," then, was to dignify and authorize their form of Jesus veneration precisely *as* Christianity rather than as heresy. The Nazarenes, he concludes with a scathing irony, were disavowed as heretics "not only [on account] of their Judaism, but I may say of their Christianity too" (*N.*, 56).

It is important to note in this connection how seamlessly the discourse of *Nazarenus* moves between the descriptive and the normative, the historical and the apologetic. The hinge on which the discourse swings in this respect is the notion of "original Christianity"—a concept that recurs throughout *Nazarenus*, beginning with its subtitle[46] and ending with its closing thought:

> If in the history of this *Gospel* [of Barnabas] I have satisfy'd your curiosity, I shall think my time well spent; but infinitely better, if you agree, that, on this occasion, I have set THE ORIGINAL PLAN OF CHRISTIANITY in its due light, as farr as I propos'd to do. (*N.*, 85)

---

45. *N.*, iv, emphasis (nonitalicized font) added.

46. "The history of the antient GOSPEL OF BARNABAS, and the modern GOSPEL OF THE MAHOMETANS, attributed to the same APOSTLE: this last GOSPEL being now first made known among CHRISTIANS. ALSO, the ORIGINAL PLAN OF CHRISTIANITY occasionally explain'd in the history of the NAZARENS, whereby diverse CONTROVERSIES about this divine (but highly perverted) INSTITUTION may be happily terminated."

In ecclesiastical rhetoric, this concept is not merely or even primarily a term of history but one of myth and, inevitably, politics. To characterize something as "original Christianity" is less to draw a temporal distinction than to lay claim to the mythic authority of Christianity itself.[47] Indeed, Toland's argument for the normative legitimacy of "Jewish"—and, consequently, "Mahometan"—Christianity ultimately boils down to a single point: their religion was envisioned by, and indeed practiced by, Jesus and the apostles.

For all its significant innovation, then, Toland's *Nazarenus* is ultimately an expression of the same ecclesiastical rhetoric used by his adversaries.[48] The most basic common assumption is that there is in fact such a thing as "true Christianity" (or more generally "true religion") that can—and indeed must—be distinguished from the various iterations of Jesus veneration represented by different individuals and groups over human history. This assumption is apparent throughout the text of *Nazarenus*, but perhaps never more so than when Toland, taking a page from the book of his adversaries, denies *their* claims on the title "Christianity," accusing them indeed of "down-right ANTICHRISTIANISM."[49]

Two additional moves serve to transpose this normative assumption onto the stage of human history. Both Toland and his adversaries assume, first, that normative Christianity is to be identified with what was taught by Jesus and the apostles. "True Christianity" is in this way anchored in time and space so that the temporal category "original" becomes essen-

---

47. See further on this point Champion, *Pillars*, esp. 11–12: "The Christian past was a necessary determinant (for the Christian) of the morality or truth of the present. For the seventeenth-century Christian an essential part of religious experience was the continual re-evaluation of the present in terms of the past.... I wish to argue that that the developments in the writing of history were perceived as a means to securing a credible defence of ideological opinions rather than forging modern ways of writing history."

48. Cf. Fouke, *Philosophy and Theology*, 221–51. As noted above, Fouke argues that Toland's participation in this discourse was the result of a deliberate attempt to mock it. For a different view, see Champion, *Pillars*, and, more concisely, "Politics of Pantheism."

49. E.g., *N.*, 71; cf. vii; and with respect to Robert South in particular, the earliest draft of the introduction: "in which respect the Doctor is a very good Mahometan, how ill a Christian soever he may be" (BL 4465 f64r; cf. Champion, *Nazarenus*, 301). This move is the obverse of redescribing the Nazarenes as "Jewish Christianity."

tially synonymous with ecclesiastical category "authoritative."[50] Second, it is agreed that this "original" and "true" Christianity becomes subject to human corruption as it moves beyond the apostolic sphere—and that the nature of that corruption is such that heretical innovators are themselves wont to identify their own teaching as "apostolic."[51] Toland quite agreed with his adversaries, for example, that this was how "papism" was to be explained. The only real disagreement was whether the same was true of each of their own positions. Toland saw something analogous to "papism" at work in his adversaries, even as he anticipated that they would interpret his own reconstruction in just the same way. "I forsee that many of 'em ... will say, that I advance a new Christianity," he says, "tho I think it undoubt-edly to be the old one."[52]

This series of assumptions leads naturally to the sort of historical-critical study manifested in Toland's work and eventually, indeed, in the field of New Testament criticism: early Christian tradition must be criti-cally analyzed to distinguish the genuinely apostolic from the subsequent developments, the layers of later tradition peeled back in order to disclose

---

50. Note the repeated juxtaposition of the terms *original* and *true*, or *genuine*, in, e.g., *N.*, 5, 33, 52, 65. Note also that in the very passages where Toland denies the term *Christianity* to his adversaries, he simultaneously aligns his own position—using a phrase reminiscent of 1 Cor 2:16—with that of Jesus and the apostles—thus, "*I do here teach a very different doctrine, more consonant (I am persuaded) to the mind of* CHRIST *and his* Apostles, *as tis more agreeable to the Law of nature and the dictates of Humanity*" (*N.*, vii). Cf. further *N.*, 70–71 where, decrying the "Antichristianism" of his opponents, Toland identifies "the articles of their belief and the rubric of their practice" as "manifestly the very things which JESUS went about to destroy," and asks: "what can be less Christian, I say, or more contrary to the design of JESUS CHRIST, than all these things I have here enumerated?"

51. E.g., *N.*, 81–82: "In short, every side and sect pretended they were the onely true Christians, and each did peremtorlly (as many persons now do with as little ground yet equal confidence) appeal to APOSTOLICAL TRADITION AND SUCCESSION.... Just so it is at this day between some of the Protestants and all the Papists (not to speak of the Greecs) each of 'em boasting I know not what *uninterrupted Tradition and Succession*, which are the most chimerical pretences in nature."

52. *N.*, 68. Cf. his discussion in the preface of the rhetorical strategies "*corrupt Clergymen*" (xvii) employ against anyone (like Toland!) who offers alternative views: "*They never fail to accuse him of Innovation, which, if not his greatest merit (as new Reformations ought to be substituted to old disorders) yet his greatest crime is many times the reviveing of some obsolete unfashionable Truth, a novelty not to be endur'd by men who live upon error*" (xix).

the "original Christianity" assumed to lie beneath it all. If expressed in the genre of critical historiography, though, the assumptions themselves are simply the stuff of Christianity's own myth of origins and the rhetoric of ecclesiastical authority. To the extent that it is built on such assumptions, critical historiography itself is simply ecclesiastical politics in a new mode: a means to claim the power inherent in the term *original* or *apostolic Christianity* in order to authorize whatever it is that one values.[53]

The values that *Nazarenus* seeks to authorize in this way are those of an Enlightenment humanism.[54] More specifically, *Nazarenus* is built around the notion that *true* religion is neither the product of revelation nor something to be identified with the doctrines and practices of any one people. It is, rather, a "Moral Law of Nature" that, equated with rationality, is the "the fundamental bond of all society," and thus a human universal.[55] The various "civil and national rites" that are normally called religions are, to be sure, necessary means toward realizing the ends of the Law of Nature in human societies; but even as such they are nonetheless themselves less religion than politics.[56] Indeed, in the wrong hands—specifically, in the hands of priests—these social institutions can be twisted into something entirely opposed to religion. Ironically, then, such priests are themselves a principal cause of impiety:

> *for the little effect of Religion procedes in most places from the too great influence of the CLERGY, who make that to pass for Religion which is none, or quite the reverse, as they make Piety often inconsistent with Probity; and this they do to serve their own private ends, which in such places are ever opposite to the public good of the people....* In order to secure [wealth, and thus power] ... they train up their hearers in Ignorance, and consequently in Superstition and Bigotry. (*N.*, xv)

It is not actually religion that such so-called religious leaders preach, he says, but "*metaphysical riddles, or mythological tales, or mystical dreams*"—

---

53. Cf. above, n. 47.

54. Compare the synthetic treatments of Toland in Stephen H. Daniel, *John Toland: His Methods, Manners, and Mind* (Kingston: McGill-Queen's University Press, 1984); and, more briefly, Thomas Duddy, *A History of Irish Thought* (New York: Routledge, 2002), 82–98.

55. See esp. *Nazarenus*, ch. 17 (here pp. 66–67), where Toland cites Cicero's account of natural law at length.

56. E.g., *N.*, v–vi, speaking of Judaism in particular; cf. *N.*, 38.

in short, precisely that sort of "mystery" that Toland had exposed as the cynical invention of power-hungry priests in his earlier work *Christianity Not Mysterious*.[57]

What was promulgated by Jesus and the apostles, according to Toland, was no such "mystery." Nor was it even a new set of doctrines and civic practices, much less one intended to displace others. On the contrary, if there could be said to be any "mystery" in "original Christianity," it was precisely in the notion that humans could be unified even as cultural differences were perpetuated and affirmed. The "*Mystery that* PAUL *rightly says was hid from all other ages, till the manifestation of it by* JESUS," according to Toland, is just that "*Union without Uniformity*" that became manifest in the simultaneous existence of Jewish and Gentile Christianity (*N.*, v). This union is accomplished not by replacing the variety of existing civic institutions with a single new one but by disclosing the "true religion" that they all have in common: "and tis evident to all, but such as will not see," he writes, "that one main design of Christianity was to improve and perfect the knowledge of the Law of nature" (*N.*, 67). And if the second design was "to facilitate and inforce the observation of the same" (ibid.), it was less by creating a new civic institution than by breathing new life and new understanding into those, like Judaism, that already existed. Indeed, the primary error that would befall Gentile Christianity was "*confounding political with religious performances*" in the insistence that Jews no longer follow the "civil and national rites" of the Jewish law. Such Gentiles "absurdly [took] away the means" even as they came to at least partially understand the end.[58]

In this sense, Christianity for Toland represents something qualitatively different from all those systems of doctrine and practice that one might otherwise be inclined to call religion. Christianity alone, precisely as "*true religion*," is not culture at all, but rather the end for which culture, and particularly its so-called religions, should serve as means. The Gospel, he says,

---

57. *N.*, xv. For further on this notion of "mystery," see Champion, *Pillars*, 165–69; and H. F. Nicholl, "John Toland: Religion without Mystery," *Herm* 100 (1965): 54–65, esp. 60–65.

58. *N.*, v–vi. Toland explains this development in Gentile Christianity as the result of nothing but bigotry: an "inveterate ... hatred of the Jews" (vi).

consists not in words but in virtue; tis inward and spiritual, abstracted
from all formal and outward performances: for the most exact observation
of externals, may be without one grain of religion ... wheras true religion is
inward life and spirit. (N., v)

Christianity properly so called is not social and empirical but individual and spiritual. It is not a set of specific doctrines and practices but a spiritual disposition characterized only in generic terms like "Faith," "Piety," and "Virtue," that one brings *to* practice. As such, it can become manifest in any number of sociocultural institutions, thereby producing the "Union with Uniformity" envisioned in "the original plan of Christianity."

If "Christianity" thus stands for a spiritual disposition that transcends all cultural differences, "Judaism," for Toland, represents precisely the sort of civic and cultural difference that Christianity simultaneously affirms and overcomes. This emerges with particular clarity as Toland discusses the gospel of Jesus and the apostles in relation to the Judaism of their times. The passage merits quoting at length:

> Without this Faith and Regeneration (as a change from vice to virtue was properly call'd even by the Heathens) the ever so punctual performance of Ceremonies cou'd not justify a Jew, or render him a good man, agreeable and well-pleasing to God: but JESUS and his Apostles made it manifest that the Gentile, who believ'd one God and the necessity of Regeneration, might, contrary to the notions of the degenerate Jews (who then plac'd all religion in outward practices) be justify'd by such his Faith, without being oblig'd to exercise the ceremonies of the Law, being things no way regarding him, either as to national origin or civil government; while the Jew, on the other hand, must, to the outward observance of his country Law by eternal covenant, add this inward Regeneration and the Faith of the *Gospel*, or the Levitical Law wou'd avail him nothing tho ever so strictly observ'd. (*N.*, 64)

In short: Jews, as Jews, are bound by covenant to observe Jewish law forever and always. The fundamental Jewish mistake, however, was to confuse this "outward observance" with "religion," thereby confusing—much as would later Gentile Christians—the means with the end.[59] By clarify-

---

59. Cf. *N.*: "*But the Jews generally mistook the means for the end: as others, who better understood the end, wou'd not onely absurdly take away the means; but even those other civil and national rites which were to continue always in the Jewish Republick*

ing the distinction between Jewish law and religion, Jesus and the apostles showed that Gentiles could have true religion apart from Jewish law and be justified simply by faith. But this also meant that Jews, even with Jewish law, did not yet themselves have true religion. As Toland put it in the preface to *Nazarenus*, "*somthing else besides the Legal Ordinances, most of 'em political, was necessary to render a Jew religious: even that* FAITH, *which is an internal participation of the divine nature, irradiating the soul*" (*N.*, v). It was just that inward and spiritual "something else" that was made manifest by Jesus and the apostles.[60]

Toland's formulation of a new taxonomy of Christianity rather than Judaism, then, was inevitable quite apart from any detailed critical historiography he would generate. Judaism and Christianity represented fundamentally different kinds of things in his discourse. Judaism is the quintessential expression of the historical, the ethnic, the external, the political; Christianity, in contrast, is the timeless, the universally human, the internal/spiritual, the religious. Judaism symbolizes the very problem of cultural and civic difference that *Nazarenus* seeks to resolve, while Christianity, as a transcendent law of nature, is the solution. Indeed, Judaism cannot properly be called religion at all until it becomes "Jewish Christianity."[61]

... thus confounding political with religious performances" (v–vi). Cf. *Mangoneutes*: "a great many of the observances in the *Old Testament*, tho generally mistaken for Religion, were onely national and commemorative Ceremonies" (217).

60. In this sense, Henning Graf Reventlow's characterization of Toland as having gone "so far as to see the three monotheistic religions [of Judaism, Christianity, and Islam] on the same level" is misleading. See his "Judaism and Jewish Christianity in the Works of John Toland," *Proceedings of the Sixth World Congress of Jewish Studies* 3 (1977): 113 (and, more broadly, 111–16). To be sure, Toland elsewhere gives Mosaic law a very high appraisal, but precisely as a "political System": Moses was an "incomparable legislator," who instituted a theocracy that was "the most excellent and perfect" of all forms of commonwealth. *Hodegus*, 6; cf. *Tetradymus*, i (both cited from *The Theological and Philological Works*).

61. The model is encapsulated in Toland's interpretation of the Letter of James, which he takes to be an authentic writing of James and thus an articulation of original "Jewish Christianity." Interpreting the transition from *logos* to law in Jas 1:21–25, Toland writes that "*Christianity is by the same Apostle ... most properly stil'd* the engrafted word able to save their souls, *engrafted I say on the* Law of MOSES, *not sanctifying the inward man; yet for most wise reasons to be perpetually observ'd by the Jews, and wherof Christianity is the spirit:* for as the body without the breath is dead, so Faith without Works is dead also [Jas 2:26]" (*N.*, xiii). Here it is Jewish law itself that is understood to be lacking religion, not merely individual Jews.

On the other hand, Christianity, insofar as it represents an internal spiritual disposition, can manifest itself historically only within particular social-cultural institutions like Judaism, that is, as *Jewish*, or *Gentile*, or *Mahometan* Christianity.

Seen in this light, Toland's concept of "Jewish Christianity" represents little more than a humanistic retelling of Trinitarian Christianity's myth of origins. What had formerly been told as the story of a transcendent god manifesting itself historically in the form of a particular Jewish man has in Toland's hands become the story of a transcendent spirituality manifesting itself historically in Judaism itself, and indeed in humanity more generally. The spirit is less anthropomorphic, and the locus of the epiphany moved from one man to all humanity, but the incarnation remains. "Jewish Christianity" was not discovered by historical analysis. It was invented as a humanistic reclamation of Christian myth.

Bibliography

Carleton Paget, James. "The Definition of the Terms *Jewish Christian* and *Jewish Christianity* in the History of Research." Pages 22–52 in *Jewish Believers in Jesus: The Early Centuries*. Edited by Oskar Skarsaune and Reidar Hvalvik. Peabody, Mass.: Hendrickson, 2007.

Champion, Justin. *John Toland: Nazarenus*. British Deism and Free Thought 1. Oxford: Voltaire Foundation, 1999.

———. "John Toland: The Politics of Pantheism." *Revue de synthese* 2–3 (1995): 259–80.

———. *The Pillars of Priestcraft Shaken: The Church of England and Its Enemies, 1660–1730*. Cambridge Studies in Early Modern British History. Cambridge: Cambridge University Press, 1992.

———. *Republican Learning: John Toland and the Crisis of Christian Culture, 1696–1722*. New York: Manchester University Press, 2003.

Daniel, Stephen H. *John Toland: His Methods, Manners, and Mind*. Kingston: McGill-Queen's University Press, 1984.

Duddy, Thomas. *A History of Irish Thought*. New York: Routledge, 2002.

Fouke, Daniel C. *Philosophy and Theology in a Burlesque Mode: John Toland and "The Way of Paradox."* Amherst, N.Y.: Humanity Books, 2007.

Gager, John G. *Reinventing Paul*. New York: Oxford University Press, 2000.

Jackson-McCabe, Matt. "What's in a Name? The Problem of Jewish Christianity." Pages 7–38 in *Jewish Christianity Reconsidered: Rethinking Ancient Groups and Texts*. Edited by Matt Jackson-McCabe. Minneapolis: Fortress, 2007.

Jackson-McCabe, Matt, ed. *Jewish Christianity Reconsidered: Rethinking Ancient Groups and Texts*. Minneapolis: Fortress, 2007.

Klijn, A. F. J. "The Study of Jewish Christianity." *NTS* 20 (1973–1974): 419–31.

Luedemann, Gerd. *Opposition to Paul in Jewish Christianity.* Translated by M. Eugene Boring. Minneapolis: Fortress, 1980.

Nicholl, H. F. "John Toland: Religion without Mystery." *Herm* 100 (1965): 54–65.

Palmer, Gesine. *Ein Freispruch für Paulus: John Tolands Theorie des Judenchristentums mit einer Neuausgabe von Tolands 'Nazarenus' von Claus-Michael Palmer.* ANTZ 7. Berlin: Institut Kirche und Judentum, 1996.

Patrick, David. "Two English Forerunners of the Tübingen School: Thomas Morgan and John Toland." *Theological Review* 14 (1877): 562–603.

Reventlow, Henning Graf. "Judaism and Jewish Christianity in the Works of John Toland." *Proceedings of the Sixth World Congress of Jewish Studies* 3 (1977): 111–16.

Skarsaune, Oskar. "Jewish Believers in Jesus in Antiquity: Problems of Definition, Method, and Sources. Pages 3–21 in *Jewish Believers in Jesus: The Early Centuries.* Edited by Oskar Skarsaune and Reidar Hvalvik. Peabody, Mass.: Hendrickson, 2007.

Toland, John. *Nazarenus: Or, Jewish, Gentile, and Mahometan Christianity.* 2nd ed. London: J. Brotherton, J. Roberts, and A. Dodd, 1718.

———. *The Theological and Philological Works of the Late Mr. John Toland.* London: W. Mears, 1732.

Verheyden, Joseph. "Jewish Christianity, A State of Affairs: Affinities and Differences with Respect to Matthew, James, and the Didache." Pages 123–35 in *Matthew, James, and Didache: Three Related Documents in Their Jewish and Christian Settings.* Edited by Huub van de Sandt and Jürgen K. Zangenberg. SBLSymS 45. Atlanta: Society of Biblical Literature, 2008.

THE GENESIS, PURPOSE, AND SIGNIFICANCE
OF JOHN TOLAND'S *NAZARENUS*

F. Stanley Jones

Janus Junius Toland, soon to be called John to quell the other schoolboys' ridicule, became a student of divinity and found financial support for his talents first among the dissenting congregations in London.[1] This was the launching pad from which Toland industriously pursued a career in publishing and politics. Though he struggled financially to an end swamped in debt, Toland rubbed shoulders with many of the best and brightest of his time. His influence can still be felt today.

Toland's writings were mostly political—often in the service of his government benefactors and employers. But the divinity student in Toland never died, and during his lifetime politics and religion were closely intertwined; that they are less intertwined today is due in no little part to Toland's industry itself. But here it is possible to focus only on Toland as the father of modern critical study of Jewish Christianity—a small part of his work, even if it can also be judged as simultaneously the beginning of modern critical study of the New Testament and Christian origins.

The achievement of Toland's *Nazarenus*[2] has often been overlooked because of the style of the writing. It is not what one would consider a

---

1. Giancarlo Carabelli, *Tolandiana: Materiali bibliografici per lo studio dell'opera e della fortuna di John Toland (1670–1722)* (Florence: La Nuova Italia Editrice, 1975), 252, states that the most authoritative biography of Toland is by Pierre Desmaizeaux, "Some Memoirs of the Life and Writings of Mr. John Toland," in *A Collection of Several Pieces of Mr. John Toland* (2 vols.; London: J. Peele, 1726), 1:iii–xcii, which has been used here and in the following.

2. *Nazarenus: Or, Jewish, Gentile, and Mahometan Christianity* (2nd ed.; London: J. Brotherton, J. Roberts, and A. Dodd, 1718). The second edition is also currently online in the Gallica collection of the Bibliothèque Nationale de France (http://gallica

straightforward academic piece. While much in modern bookstores and book exhibits also does not qualify as strictly academic investigation, publisher-booksellers of Toland's time had just created a regular literary marketplace and were looking not only to survive on staple commodities but also possibly to hit a jackpot with a novelty. Toland sorely needed a jackpot, but he had to settle with minimal remuneration and another disappointment to be faced down.[3] Could he write enough to survive?

This essay will address, more specifically, the genesis, purpose, and significance of *Nazarenus*. The need for such an investigation is highlighted by a remark of the intellectual historian Justin Champion, who wrote in his reedition of *Nazarenus*: "The meaning and significance of *Nazarenus* can be teased out, but only with difficulty."[4] It is really high time for a student of the New Testament and ancient Christianity to evaluate the significance of this book.

To start with the genesis of the work, there are a number of issues that have yet to be resolved. Recent research has identified and published a French manuscript version dated to the year 1710.[5] The 1718 publication of *Nazarenus* notably has an unexplained subscription of July 16, 1709. These two pieces of the puzzle would seem at least to approach one another. More information is found in Toland's papers in the Brit-

---

.bnf.fr/ark:/12148/bpt6k67828g). Evidently the original typesetting of the second edition of *Nazarenus* (with the exception of the title page and the following page of contents of the appendix) was used in *The Theological and Philological Works of the Late Mr. John Toland* (London: W. Mears, 1732), which has now been reissued by Kessinger Publishing. Justin Champion, ed., *John Toland: Nazarenus* (British Deism and Free Thought 1; Oxford: Voltaire Foundation, 1999), 115–245, inexplicably reproduces the text of the first edition after having presented a replica of the title page of the second edition on p. 114.

3. On all this, see Robert E. Sullivan, *John Toland and the Deist Controversy: A Study in Adaptations* (HHS 101; Cambridge: Harvard University, 1982), 36.

4. Champion, *John Toland: Nazarenus*, 102.

5. Attention was drawn to this manuscript first by Guiseppe Ricuperati, "Libertinismo e deismo a Vienna: Spinoza, Toland e il 'Triregno,'" *RSIt* 79 (1967): 628–95, esp. 638. The French has been published by Champion, *John Toland: Nazarenus*, 255–86, and collated against the English in the appendix to Gesine Palmer, *Ein Freispruch für Paulus: John Tolands Theorie des Judenchristentums mit einer Neuausgabe von Tolands 'Nazarenus' von Claus-Michael Palmer* (ANTZ 7; Berlin: Institut Kirche und Judentum, 1996). Pierre Lurbe has kindly drawn my attention to another edition of the French by Lia Mannarino, ed., *John Toland: Dissertations diverses* (Libre pensée et littérature clandestine 24; Paris: Honoré Champion, 2005), 61–99.

ish Library. Justin Champion transcribed, somewhat inaccurately, BL add. 4465 folios 63v–64,[6] which date to 1698[7] and present the English that corresponds to the first chapter of the French manuscript along with a mock-up for a title page. The original title as found here was simply "Mahometan Christianity."[8]

With the help of the preface here and in the French manuscript, it can now be clearly seen that the genesis of *Nazarenus* lies in the aftermath of Toland's first and most notorious hit, *Christianity Not Mysterious*.[9] It was in reference to Toland's *Christianity Not Mysterious* that Robert South called Toland a "Mahometan Christian" in 1698.[10] Toland had indeed become infamous for this anonymously published work. In September 1697, Toland and the book were condemned by the Irish Parliament. Toland quickly fled Ireland. The one folded sheet of paper in the British Library (now bound into BL add. 4465 as folios 63–64) is thus the literary remains of the original kernel of *Nazarenus*. One can clearly see here the original impetus of attempting to turn a charge around into a positive.

That Toland did not proceed to write and publish this essay must likely be attributed to his occupation with some other works and the controversies they stirred up—particularly *Amyntor* (1699), which with its list of noncanonical writings under the names of the apostles began to be investigated alongside *Christianity Not Mysterious* by committees of the British Parliament in 1701—and then a period of active political work following

---

6. Champion, *John Toland: Nazarenus*, 301. The first sentence of the transcription of folio 64 should read: "A certain Doctor of Divinity, celebrated for satyr and punning (for of his deep learning or judgement you never heard) was pleas'd in the dedication of a volum of sermons to the Archbishop of Dublin, now primate of Ireland, to grace me with the title of a Mahometan Christian."

7. The date 1718, also found on the manuscript, is evidently later; the 1s in "1718" do not have a point to them, as Toland's generally do. "1718" may be from the hand of the cataloguer (or perhaps Pierre Desmaizeaux) who tried to place the papers in chronological order.

8. See Champion, *John Toland: Nazarenus*, 58, again with a few transcriptional mistakes. My transcription of folio 64 verso is: "Mahometan Christianity: An Account of the ancient Gospel of Barnabas, and the modern Gospel of the Turks; with some reflections on the Contest between Peter and Paul about the observation of the Law of Moses by Christian Believers."

9. See similarly Champion, *John Toland: Nazarenus*, 55–57.

10. Robert South, *Twelve Sermons upon Several Subjects and Occasions*, vol. 3 (London: Tho. Warren for Thomas Bennet, 1698), 7–8 of the unpaginated preface called "The Epistle Dedicatory."

the Act of Settlement (1701), particularly in the service of Robert Harley. It was during the hiatus of Harley's fall and return to power (February 1708 through August 1710) that Toland was in the Netherlands and wrote at least the French version of *Nazarenus*. From the construction of the argument (as well as from the 1698 fragment), it seems apparent that Toland wrote the account of the Muslim Gospel before he was exposed to the Gospel of Barnabas.

By 1710 Toland is back writing and publishing in England, most often anonymously.[11] There is evidence that in 1713 he was ready to publish something under the title "A New Gospel Discovered,"[12] which he equates with *Nazarenus* (xxv). But word got out, and publication was delayed apparently owing to Richard Bentley's criticism of the freethinkers. In 1718, Toland remarks that he made no secret of this tract (*Nazarenus*), because he had already sent it to Eugene of Savoy shortly after his discovery of the Gospel of Barnabas in 1709 (*Nazarenus*, ii). This controversy perhaps explains why Toland would backdate *Nazarenus* to 1709 in his subscription.

More political writings followed, reaching a high point in *State-Anatomy* (1717),[13] which was an argument for the admission of Dissenters to public office. A plea for the naturalization of Jews had already been published in 1714. Toleration is the theme. The year 1718 can thus now be viewed as a time for theological icing: a prophecy of the fall of the papacy (*The Destiny of Rome*) and *Nazarenus*. It is in this context that *Nazarenus* must be viewed as a plea for political toleration.

The Protestant underground that developed under Queen Mary historically lies at the root of the English push against established religion. The Enlightenment's pervasive argument against priestcraft is essentially an aggressive case against a state church. The other side of the coin is the argument for full liberty of conscience and, accordingly, toleration (explained in *State-Anatomy*, 27). For Toland, priestcraft was responsible for robbing humankind of liberty;[14] nurses, parents, schools, and the like pass on customs, which become prejudices and superstitions.[15] In a letter

---

11. See the documentation in Carabelli, *Tolandiana*, 145–69.

12. See Carabelli, *Tolandiana*, 169, 175.

13. [John Toland], *The State-Anatomy of Great Britain* (5th ed.; London: John Philips, [1717]).

14. Cf. Robert Rees Evans, *Pantheisticon: The Career of John Toland* (AmSt.H 98; New York: Lang, 1991), 97.

15. *Letters to Serena* (London: Bernard Lintot, 1704), 4–9.

of 1709,[16] Toland declares that the first letter to Serena, which is where these themes are enunciated, "can serve as the key to all his other works" and that the origin, force, and destruction of prejudices in all spheres of human activity is the central theme of his life. It is thus likely that the purpose of *Nazarenus* is to be understood along these lines.

Historical study can expose the origin of prejudice; here is where Toland's method of ecclesiastical history[17] and thus *Nazarenus* fits in. However one pronounces on its style, *Nazarenus* pursues a historical question about the nature of the earliest Christians. The answer Toland finds is that there were essentially two types of early Christians: Jewish Christians and Gentile Christians, and that the Jewish Christians were the first Christians. New here is not just the assertion that the Jewish Christians were the first Christians but also their equation with the Ebionites and Nazoraeans.[18] Toland had learned about the Ebionites and Nazoraeans doubtless from Spanheim[19] and LeClerc during his student years in Holland. LeClerc's reedition of the Pseudo-Clementines in 1698 delivered the Pseudo-Clementine citations that allowed Toland to bolster his new case that the Ebionites and Nazoraeans were equivalent to the first Christians, the Jewish Christians—in contrast to the ecclesiastical view from the church fathers to Spanheim that the Ebionites and Nazoraeans were a *later* perversion of the gospel.[20] This equation of the Ebionites and Nazoraeans with the first Christians, and thereby the isolation of "Jewish Christianity" as a subject

----

16. In F. H. Heinemann, "John Toland and the Age of Enlightenment," *RESt* 20 (1944): 125–46, esp. 129–30.

17. See Evans, *Pantheisticon*, 13; see Toland's use of the term *Church-history* as an area for study in *Nazarenus*, 60. In *An Apology for Mr.* Toland (London: n.p., 1697), 19, Toland comments on how "the Study of Ecclesiastical History perfected" his disposition.

18. *Nazarenus*, 25–26. Toland had already briefly stated this equation in *Amyntor: Or, A Defence of Milton's Life* (London: n.p., 1699), 64.

19. Toland writes in *Nazarenus*: "*I was long before directed to my materials by the celebrated* FREDERIC SPANHEMIUS, *when I study'd Ecclesiastical History under him at Leyden*" (iii).

20. For Spanheim, see Frederick Spanheim, *Ecclesiatical Annals* (trans. George Wright; Cambridge: T. Stevenson, 1829), 216–17 (the Bodleian copy may be found online). The page numbers that Toland lists for his citations from the Pseudo-Clementines (e.g., *Nazarenus*, 23 n. 33) correspond to LeClerc's 1698 reedition of Cotelier, ed., *Ss. patrum qui temporibus apostolicis floruerunt*, not to Cotelier's original edition of 1672.

for historical investigation, is Toland's historical-critical accomplishment[21] that would be reestablished one hundred fifty years later, and only very gradually, by F. C. Baur. For Baur, the determination that the Ebionites were the first Christians raised the question of the legitimacy of other forms of Christianity and led to deeper historical study of the evolution of the faith. For Toland, the equation of the first Christians with the Ebionites and their condemnation by the Gentile Christian wing indicated that none of the later forms of the faith could claim pristine heritage. This historical determination carried practical consequences for Toland: None of the churches in his day had a historical leg to stand on when they claimed such pristine heritage; therefore, they should tolerate one another.

The purpose of *Nazarenus* was thus to present a historical argument for toleration.[22] While this argument remains important in terms of broader religious and intellectual history, the significance of *Nazarenus* for the history of New Testament scholarship is different: here, the equation of Jewish Christianity with the first Christians and also with the Ebionites and the Nazoraeans served as the catalyst that kicked off the entire critical exploration of the genesis of the Christian faith.

Of particular interest, of course, is the question of how Toland lit upon the terms *Jewish Christian* and *Jewish Christianity*. From the history of the manuscripts, it now seems clear that Toland actually started the project that

---

21. This accomplishment has been correctly recognized by Emanuel Hirsch, *Geschichte der neuern evangelischen Theologie* (5th ed.; Gütersloh: Gütersloher Verlagshaus Gerd Mohn, 1975), 1:305. Adolph Schliemann, *Die Clementinen nebst den verwandten Schriften und der Ebionitismus: Ein Beitrag zur Kirchen- und Dogmengeschichte der ersten Jahrhunderte* (Hamburg: Friedrich Perthes, 1844), 364–65, however, lists a couple of supposed predecessors, yet Daniel Zwicker (*Irenicum irenicorum* [n.p., (1658)], 111, 115) does not really make the equation mentioned above. He just says that the Ebionites were among or out of the Nazoraeans and were tolerated by the apostles.

22. This element becomes express when he slaps at "Uniformity" on p. 56 and slyly argues for the toleration of Muslims "as any other Sectaries" on p. 61. See also pp. 70–71. Toleration as a Christian duty founded in the Gospel is asserted on p. 40 (see pp. 71, 75, 77 for contemporary anti-clerical application). Ancient disunity (invective) is presented as an analogy to the contemporary situation on pp. 81–82. Page 82 denies the uninterrupted apostolic tradition/succession of every contemporary succession. It is no accident that in "Mangoneutes," his defence of *Nazarenus*, Toland writes, "Civil Liberty and Religious Toleration ... have been the two main objects of all my writings" (*Tetradymus* [London: J. Brotherton, 1720], 223).

would become *Nazarenus* with the term *Mahometan Christian*[23] and then *Mahometan Christianity*. As Toland formed his ideas on how to respond to this objection to himself, there can be little doubt that Henry Stubbe's *An Account of the Rise and Progress of Mahometanism* was going to be the grist for Toland's mill.[24] Stubbe had argued that Ebionite or Nazarene Christianity formed the foundation for Islam.[25] Toland states that the term *Jewish Christianity* would be less strange to the ear.[26] As a matter of fact, English language exegetical literature of the mid-seventeenth-century witnesses to the term *Jewish Christian*,[27] to the term *Jew Christian*, and more often and earlier to the term *Hebrew Christian*. These terms are used largely in a neutral historical sense; the heretical term of the time, in contrast, is *Ebionite*,

---

23. Cf. Champion, *John Toland: Nazarenus*, 56.

24. Henry Stubbe, *An Account of the Rise and Progress of Mahometanism with the Life of Mahomet* (ed. Hafiz Mahmud Khan Shairani; London: Luzac, 1911). This treatise was written in the 1670s; see ibid., viii, xx. It is relevant that two manuscripts of Stubbe's work are found in the Harley collection (ibid., xi). Compare Champion, *John Toland: Nazarenus*, 86 (here, however, he states that the ultimate inspiration did not come from Stubbe and states that a close comparison of the manuscript version shows that Toland just used Stubbe to embellish his work—I am uneasy with this verdict) and Justin Champion, "Legislators, Impostors, and the Politic Origins of Religion: English Theories of 'Imposture' from Stubbe to Toland," in *Heterodoxy, Spinozism, and Free Thought in Early-Eighteenth-Century Europe: Studies on the 'Traité des Trois Imposteurs'* (ed. Silvia Berti, Françoise Charles-Daubert, and Richard H. Popkin; Dordrecht: Kluwer, 1996), 333–56, especially the following: "Thomas Mangey insisted that this work [sc. *Nazarenus*] was linked to Stubbe's, and I have shown elsewhere that Toland's work is heavily indebted to the 'Account'" (351). Mangey's reference to Stubbe is generally thought to be in Mangey's description: "A Physician of some note, a few Years ago wrote, as it is said, a thorough Defence of their Sentiments, a Manuscript Copy of which I have seen." See Thomas Mangey, *Remarks upon 'Nazarenus'* (London: William and John Innys, 1718), 43.

25. Stubbe writes, for example, "For my part I beleive [*sic*] that he [sc. Muhammed] was a convert to the Judaizing Christians and formed his Religion as far as possible in resemblance of theirs" (*An Account of the Rise and Progress of Mahometanism*, 145). Stubbe continues on p. 146: "This that I have said I hope is sufficient to evince that the Religion of Mahomet is cheifly [sic] founded on the Doctrines of the Nazarene Christians and the Arrians."

26. *Nazarenus*, 4.

27. E.g., Henry Hammond, *A Paraphrase and Annotations upon all the Books of the New Testament* (2nd ed.; London: J. Flesher, 1659), 725: "Jewes-Christian." Daniel Zwicker, writing in Latin in 1658, also uses the term *Judæo-Christianos* (*Irenicum irenicorum*, 116).

which was in wide use. Thus, as Toland intimates, *Jewish Christianity* is a term readily understandable on this exegetical background.

It is also possible that Toland knew the term *Jewish Christian* in connection with the Sabbatarians.[28] Indeed, this usage may well be the ultimate root of Toland's interest in Jewish Christianity. It is not an accident that, in an addition to the English edition of *Nazarenus* (54), Toland states that he was intimately acquainted with Joseph Stennett, the brother-in-law of Daniel Williams, from whom Toland had received support to study in the Netherlands in 1692. At this time, Stennett was the illustrious pastor and hymnwriter of the Baptist Sabbatarian congregation in London. This intimate connection makes it likely that Toland knew that the term *Jewish Christian* had been applied to the Sabbatarians, even if his reading of Stubbe, where he could read of Judaizing Christians and the Jewish Church,[29] also encouraged him to apply the term generally to the earliest Christians.

Despite such predecessors, it is not without justification to say that modern usage of the term *Jewish Christianity* owes a debt to Toland, particularly if he was the first to use this term.[30] What coalesces in Toland is the objectification of the Jewish Christians as "Jewish Christianity," an identifiable, independent, and distinctive type of Christians—as independent and identifiable as Islam, as the ancient Christian sects in common historical understanding of his time, and/or as such contemporary movements as the Sabbatarians. It is on the basis of this objectification that Jewish Christianity is identified as a religious entity (with its own rituals, beliefs, etc.) that is open to full investigation in and of itself.

That the first Christians were Jewish Christians also tacitly supported Toland's plea for the naturalization of the Jews.[31] More explicit, and

---

28. For usage of the term in reference to the Sabbatarians, see James Carleton Paget, "The Definition of the Terms *Jewish Christian* and *Jewish Christianity* in the History of Research," in *Jewish Believers in Jesus: The Early Centuries* (ed. Oskar Skarsaune and Reidar Hvalvik; Peabody, Mass.: Hendrickson, 2007), 22–52, esp. 25, and William Gouge, *The Progresse of Divine Providence* (London: G. M., 1645), 23. Toland discusses them on pp. 53–54 of *Nazarenus*.

29. See, e.g., Stubbe, *An Account of the Rise and Progress of Mahometanism*, 27.

30. This is the result of the historical investigation of terms by Matti Myllykoski in this volume.

31. According to *Nazarenus*, the law was given to the Jews for perpetual observation—a point acknowledged in the original plan of Christianity (see, e.g., pp. 43, 65).

radical, was Toland's case for Mahometan Christianity.[32] The Muslims demonstrably derive from old apostolic tradition and thus may even be viewed as a sort of Christians that deserves toleration.[33]

So Toland did achieve a significant accomplishment in historical research, even if it was the political significance that he assigned to this accomplishment that gave his achievement such prominence.[34] This insight that the first Christians were Jewish Christians and were also the first heretics may be said to be the catalyst behind modern critical study of the New Testament and Christian origins. Toland must also be credited with the insistence that the modern scholar of early Christianity use not only the New Testament but also *all* documents from the period including the noncanonical writings—on a par with the canonical.[35]

The notion that F. C. Baur is the father of the study of Jewish Christianity and of critical New Testament study is widely off the mark.[36] Toland seems to deserve the title.

BIBLIOGRAPHY

Carabelli, Giancarlo. *Tolandiana: Materiali bibliografici per lo studio dell'opera e della fortuna di John Toland (1670–1722)*. Florence: La Nuova Italia Editrice, 1975.

---

32. From Stubbe, *An Account of the Rise and Progress of Mahometanism*; see Champion, "Legislators, Impostors, and the Politic Origins of Religion," 353.

33. *Nazarenus*, 4–5, 61, 84–85.

34. Compare F. H. Heinemann, "John Toland and the Age of Reason," *APh* 4 (1950–1952): 35–66, esp. 55.

35. See Francis Schmidt, "John Toland: Critique déiste de la littérature apocryphe," *Apocrypha* 1 (1990): 118–45, esp. 142–45. For Toland as the instigator of the entire modern critical study of the New Testament canon, see Bruce M. Metzger, *The Canon of the New Testament: Its Origin, Development, and Significance* (Oxford: Clarendon, 1987), 11–14. For something of the background for Toland's work in this regard, see Justin Champion, "Apocrypha Canon and Criticism from Samuel Fisher to John Toland, 1650–1718," in *Judaeo-Christian Intellectual Culture in the Seventeenth Century: A Celebration of the Library of Narcissus Marsh (1638–1713)* (ed. Allison P. Coudert et al.; AIHI 163; Dordrecht: Kluwer, 1999), 91–117.

36. See the description of the fundamental nature of Baur's "accomplishment" in Werner Georg Kümmel, *The New Testament: The History of the Investigation of Its Problems* (Nashville: Abingdon, 1972), 127–33. See also Robert Morgan, "Ferdinand Christian Baur," in *Nineteenth Century Religious Thought in the West* (ed. Ninian Smart et al.; Cambridge: Cambridge University Press, 1985), 1:261–89, esp. 269–70. He speaks of Baur as "the pioneer" (p. 270) in this regard.

———. *Tolandiana: Materiali bibliografici per lo studio dell'opera e della fortuna di John Toland (1670–1722), Errata, addenda e indici*. Pubblicazioni della Facoltà di Magistero dell'Università di Ferrara 4. Ferrara: Università degli studi di Ferrara, 1978.

Carleton Paget, James. "The Definition of the Terms *Jewish Christian* and *Jewish Christianity* in the History of Research." Pages 22–52 in *Jewish Believers in Jesus: The Early Centuries*. Edited by Oskar Skarsaune and Reidar Hvalvik. Peabody, Mass.: Hendrickson, 2007.

Champion, Justin. "Apocrypha Canon and Criticism from Samuel Fisher to John Toland, 1650–1718." Pages 91–117 in *Judaeo-Christian Intellectual Culture in the Seventeenth Century: A Celebration of the Library of Narcissus Marsh (1638–1713)*. Edited by Allison P. Coudert, Sarah Hutton, Richard H. Popkin, and Gordon M. Weiner. AIHI 163. Dordrecht: Kluwer, 1999.

———, ed. *John Toland: Nazarenus*. British Deism and Free Thought 1. Oxford: Voltaire Foundation, 1999.

———. "Legislators, Impostors, and the Politic Origins of Religion: English Theories of 'Imposture' from Stubbe to Toland." Pages 333–56 in *Heterodoxy, Spinozism, and Free Thought in Early-Eighteenth-Century Europe: Studies on the 'Traité des Trois Imposteurs.'* Edited by Silvia Berti, Françoise Charles-Daubert, and Richard H. Popkin. Dordrecht: Kluwer, 1996.

Desmaizeaux, Pierre. "Some Memoirs of the Life and Writings of Mr. John Toland," Pages iii–xcii in vol. 1 of *A Collection of Several Pieces of Mr. John Toland*. 2 vols. London: J. Peele, 1726.

Evans, Robert Rees. *Pantheisticon: The Career of John Toland*. AmSt.H 98. New York: Peter Lang, 1991.

Gouge, William. *The Progresse of Divine Providence*. London: G. M., 1645.

Hammond, Henry. *A Paraphrase and Annotations upon all the Books of the New Testament*. 2d ed. London: J. Flesher, 1659.

Heinemann, F. H. "John Toland and the Age of Enlightenment." *RESt* 20 (1944): 125–46.

———. "John Toland and the Age of Reason." *APh* 4 (1950–1952): 35–66.

Hirsch, Emanuel. *Geschichte der neuern evangelischen Theologie*. Vol. 1. 5th ed. Gütersloh: Gütersloher Verlagshaus Gerd Mohn, 1975.

Kümmel, Werner Georg. *The New Testament: The History of the Investigation of Its Problems*. Nashville: Abingdon, 1972.

Mangey, Thomas. *Remarks upon 'Nazarenus.'* London: William and John Innys, 1718.

Mannarino, Lia, ed. *John Toland: Dissertations diverses*. Libre pensée et littérature clandestine 24. Paris: Honoré Champion, 2005.

Metzger, Bruce M. *The Canon of the New Testament: Its Origin, Development, and Significance*. Oxford: Clarendon, 1987.

Morgan, Robert. "Ferdinand Christian Baur." Pages 261–89 in vol. 1 of *Nineteenth Century Religious Thought in the West*. Edited by Ninian Smart, John Clayton, Patrick Sherry, and Stephen T. Katz. 3 vols. Cambridge: Cambridge University Press, 1985.

Palmer, Gesine. *Ein Freispruch für Paulus: John Tolands Theorie des Judenchristentums mit einer Neuausgabe von Tolands 'Nazarenus' von Claus-Michael Palmer*. ANTZ 7. Berlin: Institut Kirche und Judentum, 1996.

Ricuperati, Guiseppe. "Libertinismo e deismo a Vienna: Spinoza, Toland e il 'Triregno.'" *RSIt* 79 (1967): 628–95.

Schliemann, Adolph. *Die Clementinen nebst den verwandten Schriften und der Ebionitismus: Ein Beitrag zur Kirchen- und Dogmengeschichte der ersten Jahrhunderte*. Hamburg: Friedrich Perthes, 1844.

Schmidt, Francis. "John Toland: Critique déiste de la littérature apocryphe." *Apocrypha* 1 (1990): 118–45.

South, Robert. *Twelve Sermons upon Several Subjects and Occasions*. Vol. 3. London: Tho. Warren for Thomas Bennet, 1698.

Spanheim, Frederick. *Ecclesiatical Annals*. Translated by George Wright. Cambridge: T. Stevenson, 1829.

Stubbe, Henry. *An Account of the Rise and Progress of Mahometanism with the Life of Mahomet*. Edited by Hafiz Mahmud Khan Shairani. London: Luzac, 1911.

Sullivan, Robert E. *John Toland and the Deist Controversy: A Study in Adaptations*. HHS 101. Cambridge: Harvard University Press, 1982.

Toland, John. *Amyntor: Or, A Defence of Milton's Life*. London: n.p., 1699.

———. *An Apology for Mr. Toland*. London: n.p., 1697.

———. *Letters to Serena*. London: Bernard Lintot, 1704.

———. *Nazarenus: Or, Jewish, Gentile, and Mahometan Christianity*. 2nd ed. London: J. Brotherton, J. Roberts, and A. Dodd, 1718.

———. *The State-Anatomy of Great Britain*. 5th ed. London: John Philips, [1717].

———. *Tetradymus*. London: J. Brotherton, 1720.

———. *The Theological and Philological Works of the Late Mr. John Toland*. London: W. Mears, 1732.

[Zwicker, Daniel]. *Irenicum irenicorum*. N.p., [1658].

PART 3
FROM TOLAND TO BAUR

"Jewish Christianity" and "Christian Deism" in Thomas Morgan's *The Moral Philosopher*

Matt Jackson-McCabe

You know, *Theophanes,* that I am a profess'd Christian Deist. And, therefore, I must take Christianity, as to the Substance and doctrinal Parts of it, to be a Revival of the Religion of Nature....

—Philalethes, in Thomas Morgan's *The Moral Philosopher*[1]

Little is known about Thomas Morgan beyond his professional and intellectual interests.[2] Born sometime in the late seventeenth century, Morgan

---

1. Thomas Morgan, *The Moral Philosopher: In a Dialogue between Philalethes a Christian Deist, and Theophanes a Christian Jew* (2nd ed.; 1738; facsimile of the second edition with new introduction by John Valdimir Price; History of British Deism; London: Routledge/Thoemmes, 1995), 392. In what follows, all italics, small capitals, etc., in quotations from this work reflect the original text unless explicitly noted otherwise.

2. The literature on Morgan is unfortunately limited. In the introduction to his reprint edition of *The Moral Philosopher*, Price observes that "virtually the only substantial thing written on Morgan since his death" was Leslie Stephen's *History of English Thought in the Eighteenth Century*, which was first published in 1876 (3rd ed.; repr. in 2 vols.; New York: Harbinger, 1962 [see 1:140–42]) and suggests that Stephen's less than positive treatment may have itself "discouraged further study of Morgan" (introduction, xvi–xvii). For additional treatments, see John Leland, *A View of the Principal Deistical Writers that have Appeared in England in the last and present Century* (3rd ed., rev.; London: Benj. Dod, 1757; repr. ed., René Wellek; 3 vols.; British Philosophers and Theologians of the 17th & 18th Centuries; New York and London: Garland, 1978), 1:131–50 (Letter X); David Patrick, "Two English Forerunners of the Tübingen School: Thomas Morgan and John Toland," *Theological Review* 14 (1877): 562–603, esp. 564–87; and, more recently, Günter Gawlick's *Einleitung* to his own edition of Morgan's work (Thomas Morgan, *The Moral Philosopher*; facsimile repr. in one vol.; Stuttgart-Bad [Cannstatt: Frommann (Holzboog), 1969], 5–30); William Baird, *From Deism to Tübingen* (vol. 1 of *History of New Testament Research*; Minneapolis:

was ordained as a Presbyterian minister in 1717—the year before the publication of John Toland's *Nazarenus*—but by 1730 had become a physician.[3] He published a variety of works on both medicine and theology from 1725 until his death in 1743 but was remembered primarily alongside Toland, Matthew Tindal, Anthony Collins, and Thomas Chubb as a freethinker.[4]

It is not immediately clear whether Morgan was acquainted with Toland or his controversial *Nazarenus*. To be sure, given Toland's notoriety, their common freethinking leanings, and the fact that both published out of London, there is every reason to believe that Morgan had at least heard of his older contemporary.[5] Be that as it may, Morgan's own central work, initially published some fifteen years after Toland's death and under the guise of "the Moral Philosopher," provides no clear indications—explicit or implicit—of dependence on Toland. It is all the more interesting, then, that the work that came to be known as *The Moral Philosopher*, like *Nazarenus*, placed a concept of "Jewish Christianity" at the center of its own account of Christian origins.[6]

Fortress, 1992), 52–54; and James Carleton Paget, "The Definition of the Terms *Jewish Christian* and *Jewish Christianity* in the History of Research," in *Jewish Believers in Jesus: The Early Centuries* (ed. Oskar Skarsaune and Reidar Hvalvik; Peabody, Mass.: Hendrickson, 2007), 26–28.

3. Baird (*From Deism to Tübingen*, 52) seems to imply that Morgan spent his early life in Wales. Price (introduction, v), however, suggests that Morgan, while of Welsh extraction, was actually born in England's Somerset county, where he would later preach; Gawlick ("Einleitung," 5), noting that "Seine Anfänge liegen im Dunkel" speaks more generally of a "wallisischer Herkunft" and a youth spent "im Westen Englands."

Patrick ("Two English Forerunners," 564) reports that Morgan lost his ministerial position "in 1726 on account of his Arian views, and subsequently practiced as a physician in Bristol"; cf. Gawlick, "Einleitung," 6.

4. So already Edmund Burke, *Reflections on the Revolution in France* (7th ed.; London: Dodsley, 1790), 133; cited by Price, "Introduction," v.

5. Cf. Patrick, "Two English Forerunners": "In all the then extant theological literature, no one work is so likely to have given Morgan materials for his view of the apostolic Church as a once notorious dissertation by John Toland" (587).

6. Stephen notes that the "one peculiarity" that makes Morgan stand out from earlier deists is that "His book is more historical than his predecessor's writings"— with, interestingly, one exception: "some of the points raised by him are touched on in Toland's later writings." *History of English Thought*, 141. Stephen observes perceptively that this attempt by Morgan (and by implication, Toland) to "support … doctrine by a distinct historical theory" is "symptomatic of the coming change" in the intellectual discourse of the era.

More interesting still is the fact that, for all their similarities, the two works enlist this category to serve precisely opposite rhetorical purposes and, consequently, assign it precisely opposite historical roles. In both works, accounts of Christian history are structured around the same mythic paradigm of pristine origins and subsequent corruption.[7] What is more, good freethinkers both, Morgan and Toland also share common assumptions about the essentially rationalistic and humanistic essence of that pristine original and the too-external, too-priestly character of the subsequent corruption. But where Toland identifies "Jewish Christianity" as the authoritative original and foil to contemporary Christianity's bankrupt deviation,[8] Morgan casts it rather in the role of the mythic antagonist: not the pure original but the corrupt decline. In this way, Morgan is more precursor to Baur than successor of Toland.[9] In order to see how he gets there, it will be helpful to set his historical reconstruction in the context of his larger rhetorical project.

THE RHETORICAL STRATEGY OF *THE MORAL PHILOSOPHER*

The work Morgan published as *The Moral Philosopher* presents itself as the distillation of a running conversation that took place "many Years ago" among a "Club of Gentlemen" at a private home in some "pleasant retired Village."[10] The central topic of that conversation, which is said to have occurred at two-week intervals over a period of nearly two years, was "the Grounds and Principles of Religion in general, and particularly of Christianity as a Revelation distinct from the Religion of Nature."[11] Appar-

---

7. On this model, see further Jonathan Z. Smith, *Drudgery Divine: On the Comparison of Early Christianities and the Religions of Late Antiquity* (Chicago: University of Chicago Press, 1990), 1–35 passim.

8. See in the present volume Matt Jackson-McCabe, "The Invention of Jewish Christianity in John Toland's *Nazarenus*."

9. Patrick, "Two English Forerunners," esp. 581–83.

10. The circumstances, which are reminiscent of those portrayed in Cicero's dialogues (e.g., *Tusculan Disputations, On Ends*), are recounted in Morgan's own preface; see esp. vii–xi (here vii).

11. *Moral Philosopher*, viii; cf. the title page to the 1738 edition, which presents the work as a "DIALOGUE ... IN WHICH The Grounds and Reasons of RELIGION in general, and particularly of CHRISTIANITY, as distinguish'd from the Religion of Nature ... are fairly considered, and debated, and the Arguments on both Sides impartially represented."

ently for the purposes of publication, though, "the Moral Philosopher" recounts this conversation as a dialogue that occurred over a couple of days between two symbolically named men: "PHILALETHES a Christian DEIST AND THEOPHANES a Christian JEW."[12]

While the subtitle of *The Moral Philosopher* promises to present "the Arguments of both sides impartially," Morgan was himself scarcely a detached observer in this debate. In fact, Philalethes—that is, the Deist "Lover of Truth"—is quite plainly the protagonist here, with Theophanes— the defender of orthodox, revelation-based Christianity—cast in the role of interlocutor and foil.[13]

The work opens with a troubled Theophanes coming to visit Philalethes. The source of his anxiety is twofold. First and most generally, he is troubled about "the present growth of *Deism*," not only among "Men of little Sense and less Virtue," but most especially among those who would otherwise seem to be models of "Sobriety, Benevolence, and all the social Virtues." More to the point, he is concerned because a mutual friend has suggested that Philalethes himself "might be a little, or perhaps not a little tainted with *Deism*."[14]

Though Philalethes will explicitly and proudly confirm that suspicion over the course of the dialogue, he does not immediately address the question of his own religious leanings. What he seizes on, rather, is Theophanes's characterization of Deists, virtuous or not, as being "no great Friends if not real Enemies to Christianity."[15] This, Philalethes suggests, depends entirely on how one defines Christianity:

> this modern Controversy which has given you such Apprehensions may
> … be very much about Words of an indeterminate or no Signification;
> in my Opinion, we are not well agreed about the Meaning of the Words,
> *Deism, Christianity, Revelation, Inspiration,* &c.... I should be glad to

---

12. The book's title page as it appears after the preface (*Moral Philosopher*, 13); compare the book's title page.

13. This is apparent already from the very title of the work insofar as its ambivalence about the relationship of Christianity to "natural religion" and its characterization of Theophanes as a "Christian Jew" are both reflective of Philalethes's position in particular.

14. Morgan, *Moral Philosopher*, 14.

15. Ibid.

know what you mean by *Christianity*, or *reveal'd Religion*, as oppos'd to, or contradistinguish'd from the *Religion of Nature*.[16]

Thus begins the extended dialogue of *The Moral Philosopher*, the central task of which will be to clarify the true meaning of the term "Christianity," particularly in relation to Deism.[17]

It is important to note at the outset that Morgan, through Philalethes, does not pursue this question simply out of an academic interest in generating a usefully descriptive taxonomy of early British Enlightenment religion. Rather, the issue is engaged with a normative and indeed competitive edge. The core assumption around which the whole dialogue is built—as Theophanes will later put it when summarizing Philalethes's position—is that "the Christian religion, when rightly understood, is the *true* Religion."[18] *Christianity* is thus no neutral designation for a particular species of religion here, but an honorific for which the two men will compete by means of their debate. If then, as Theophanes will ultimately articulate it, "the great and main Question" is "wherein Christianity consists," the real question at issue in the dialogue is "how a Man may know whether he be *truly* and *really* a Christian or not."[19] To suggest, as Theophanes does, that Deists—regardless of what they might say about themselves—are not "really" Christians is itself, in effect, to discredit them. Conversely, to characterize Deism as Christianity is to authorize it as legitimate, true, and superior.

Accordingly, the rhetorical strategy of Morgan's *Moral Philosopher* is not limited to a demonstration of the philosophical and ethical superiority of Deism. To be sure, Philalethes argues throughout the work that it is neither intellectually defensible nor morally responsible to determine proper belief and practice by appealing to supernatural revelation or authorizing miracles, as orthodox Christianity does—and that the only "certain and infallible Mark or Criterion of divine Truth ... is the moral Truth,

---

16. Ibid., 15.

17. Note again the extended title of the work: "A DIALOGUE ... IN WHICH The Grounds and Reasons of RELIGION in general, and particularly of CHRISTIANITY, as distinguish'd from the Religion of Nature ... are fairly considered, and debated, and the Arguments on both Sides impartially represented"; see further Morgan's preface, viii.

18. Ibid., 358 (emphasis added). Theophanes clearly agrees, at any rate, with this much.

19. Ibid., 391 (emphasis added).

Reason or Fitness of the Thing itself" as determined by rational reflection.[20] But Philalethes is not satisfied to call himself simply a Deist. The identity he claims, rather, is *Christian* Deist. He cannot be content, therefore, to demonstrate the superiority of his "religion of nature" on philosophical grounds; he is also profoundly concerned to authorize it as being in fact *true Christianity*. As he quite candidly puts it:

> You know, *THEOPHANES*, that I am a profess'd Christian Deist. And, therefore, I must take Christianity, as to the Substance and doctrinal Parts of it, to be a Revival of the Religion of Nature.[21]

The larger thesis of the work, then, is that Christianity in the *true* sense of the word has nothing to do with revelation and mystery, with "speculative Opinions, doubtful Disputations, external Rituals, arbitrary Laws, and mere positive Institutions," nor with the hierarchy of clergymen who trade in such things.[22] It is, in short, in no way to be identified with what generally passes as orthodox Christianity.[23] Real Christianity, rather, is "purely an internal Thing, and consists ultimately in moral Truth and Righteousness, considered as an inward Character, Temper, Disposition, or Habit in the Mind."[24]

The question this raises, of course, is why Christianity as it exists in fact is generally identified, on the contrary, precisely with all the sorts of things that Deism rejects. In order to explain this, Morgan's Philalethes draws on the same rhetorical paradigm that has defined inter-Christian polemics for centuries, and never more since the Protestant Reformation: the identification of one's own position as the pure original, and that of

---

20. Ibid., 85–86; the words are repeated almost verbatim in the preface (viii–x); see further 99, 198, 256, 443–44.

21. Ibid., 392.

22. Ibid. These are running themes in the work as a whole.

23. Cf. *Moral Philosopher*, 165, where, regarding his understanding of "the true, genuine, and scriptural Ends and Reasons of Christ's Death," he notes: "if I should not happen, in this Case, to be an *orthodox Christian*, I shall content myself with the Honour of being a *Christian Deist*" (emphasis original).

24. Morgan, *Moral Philosopher*, 416. He here defines "true Religion," which is however synonymous with true Christianity in the context of the work; cf. 96–97: "I take Christianity to be that most complete and perfect Scheme of moral Truth and Righteousness.... This Definition, as I imagine, takes in all that is essential to Christianity, or that can be receiv'd and allow'd as a constituent Part of it."

one's opponent as a secondary corruption.[25] Ecclesiastical polemics, that is, must be fought in the arena of historiography.

Jesus, Paul, and Deism

The typically ecclesiastical correlation of the normative concept "true Christianity" with the temporal concept "original Christianity" is assumed throughout *The Moral Philosopher*, and by both parties in the debate. Within such a discourse, apologetic claims about how one *should* conceive of the world and act within it imply, simultaneously, historical claims about how certain ancient figures *did in fact* answer such questions. For Philalethes, in other words, Deism does not merely represent *true* Christianity; it represents Christianity *as taught in the first century*:

> I take ... Christianity to be that Scheme or System of Deism, natural Religion, or moral Truth and Righteousness, *which was at first preached and propagated in the World, by Jesus Christ and his Apostles*, and has since been convey'd down to us by probable, human Testimony, or historical Evidence, strengthened and confirm'd by the necessary, natural Truth, and intrinsick Goodness of the Doctrines themselves.[26]

---

25. See above, n. 7.

26. Morgan, *Moral Philosopher*, 412 (emphasis added). The historical claim is registered repeatedly in the *Dialogue*; e.g.: "I take Christianity to be that most complete and perfect Scheme of moral Truth and Righteousness, which was first preach'd to the World by Christ and his Apostles, and from them convey'd down to us under its own Evidence of immutable Rectitude, Wisdom and Reason" (96–97); "By Christianity, I mean that complete system of moral Truth and Righteousness, Justice and Charity, which, as the best Transcript of the Religion of Nature, was preach'd to the World by Christ and the Apostles, as the Rule of Equity and Rectitude, by which Men were to be rewarded or punished in the final Judgment by God himself, as the most powerful, wise, and righteous Creator, Governor, and Judge of the World" (439); "I am a profess'd Christian Deist. And, therefore, I must take Christianity, as to the Substance and doctrinal Parts of it, to be a Revival of the Religion of Nature; in which the several Duties and Obligations of moral Truth and Righteousness are more clearly stated and explained, enforced by stronger Motives, and encouraged with the Promises of more effectual Aids and Assistances by Jesus Christ, the great Christian Prophet, than ever had been done before by any other Prophet, Moralist, or Lawgiver in Religion" (392).

The Deist teaching of Jesus is a recurring, though largely undeveloped, theme of the work.[27] The issue of the apostles' teaching, on the other hand, is a bit more complicated than this passage might seem at first to suggest, as we shall see shortly. Despite the use of the plural here and in similar passages,[28] there is only one apostle who carries authoritative weight for the *Moral Philosopher*, and that is Paul. Indeed, Paul's status is such that Philalethes proposes at the outset that he be the ultimate arbiter in the debate:

> For what relates to St. *Paul*, I can assure you, Sir, that I have as good an Opinion of him as you can have, and shall willingly abide by the Judgment and Sense of that great Apostle in the present Debate between us.... [I]f I cannot make it appear that St. *Paul* (when he comes to be rightly understood) is plainly on my Side, I will give up the Argument.[29]

For all practical purposes, then, the Pauline corpus is itself effectively identified as "true" and "original Christianity" in the context of *The Moral Philosopher*. The period in which "St. *Paul* liv'd, and his *Gentile* Churches flourish'd," that is, represents not merely "the Apostolick Age," but "the first and purest Part" even of that mythic, paradigmatic time.[30] Much of the dialogue, then, will be spent negotiating that crucial parenthetical caveat: what exactly it means to render Paul's letters "rightly understood," particularly as this concerns revelation and the miraculous in general, and the apostle's understanding of Jewish scripture, law, and the death of Christ in particular. While a full accounting of Philalethes's reading of Paul lies beyond the scope of this essay, the basic gist of the matter is well captured by his striking characterization of him as "the great Free-thinker of his Age, the bold and brave Defender of Reason against Authority."[31]

---

27. In addition to the preceding note see, e.g., 393–94: "The Religion of Jesus consists in the inward, spiritual Worship of one true God, by a strict Regard to all the Duties and Obligations of moral Truth and Righteousness, in Opposition to all the animal Affections, and mere bodily Appetites." In this respect Morgan anticipates the full-blown rationalist lives of Jesus famously critiqued by Albert Schweitzer in *Quest of the Historical Jesus* (trans. W. Montgomery New York: Macmillan, 1966).

28. For examples, see above, n. 26.

29. Morgan, *Moral Philosopher,* 21 and 24.

30. Ibid., 395.

31. Ibid., 71.

If the Christian Deism of Philalethes thus represents the "original Christianity" of Jesus and Paul, what remains to be explained is what passes as "orthodox Christianity." Insofar as it contradicts Deism, of course, it can only be a subsequent, corrupting deviation from the pure original. But whence comes this deviation? The ultimate explanation, according to Philalethes, is psychological:

> But to avoid this [i.e., Deism's] strict Attention and Application of Mind to moral Truth and Reason, as too painful and laborious, Mankind have been generally befriended with several learned, mechanical Schemes and Systems of Faith and Religion, which they might easily learn and practise without understanding, and thereby be made very good and gracious, without being wise or reasonable.[32]

Historically speaking, however, Philalethes finds one central font from which all the particular "mechanical Schemes" that came to be misidentified as Christianity have been drawn. The central culprit, in a word, is Judaism. Despite its own claims to the contrary, then, so-called orthodoxy is *not* "original Christianity," but an overly Jewish deviation from the religion of Jesus and Paul. Less Christianity, that is, than *Jewish* Christianity.[33]

JEWISH RELIGION, JESUS' APOSTLES, AND "JEWISH CHRISTIANITY"

"[N]o two Religions in the World," according to Philalethes, "can be more inconsistent and irreconcileable, than *Judaism* and *Christianity*."[34] Indeed, if Jesus had been sent by a providential God "to restore, revive, and republish" the true religion of nature, "the inward, spiritual Worship of one true God,"[35]

---

32. Ibid., 417.

33. The polemical force of Morgan's taxonomic move is not lost on Leland: "he honoureth himself, and those of his sentiments, with the title of *Christian Deists* ... as if they only were the true Christians; and brandeth all others, *i.e.* those that acknowledge the divine authority of the Christian religion, as taught in the New Testament, with the character of *Christian Jews*" (*A View of the Principal Deistical Writers*, 138–39).

34. Morgan, *Moral Philosopher*, 441; cf. 394: "I am a Christian, and at the same Time a Deist, or, if you please, this is my Christian Deism; but as for *Moses* and the Prophets, though I admire them, as Politicians, Historians, Orators, and Poets, I have nothing to do with them in Religion, as I cannot possibly be of their Religion."

35. See Morgan, *Moral Philosopher*, 394 and 393.

[the Jewish] Nation was set up by Providence, as an Example to the World in all future Ages, of the natural Effects and Consequences of Ignorance, Superstition, Presumption, and Immorality.... [God] gave them up as an everlasting Name of Reproach, an eternal Scandal to the Profession of Religion, without moral Goodness, or any rational Dependence on God and Providence.[36]

Judaism, in short, is quite literally everything that Jesus and Paul opposed.

This applies above all to two particular "false Principles and fatal Errors," both of which are traced ultimately to superstitious habits of mind cultivated during two hundred years spent among magicians and sorcerers in the "Priest-ridden Country" of Egypt.[37] First, Israel began to set aside reason and nature as the only sure guides to the character of God and "his providential Government of the World" in favor of appeals to "Miracles, Prodigies, Dreams, Visions, Voices from Heaven, and such like Manifestations."[38] The result, among other things, was a total loss of moral discernment, as even "natural" evils "brought about by the Power and Malice of Tyrants and wicked Men," could now be authorized as the "positive Will of God." [39] Second, their delivery out of Egypt left them with "a strong and most invincible Prejudice" that "they were the peculiar People of God, and special Favourites of Heaven, by an absolute, irreversible Decree."[40] This "national Delusion" of an eternal, unconditional covenant, says Philalethes, itself had terrible moral consequences. For while the providential order of God gives all "Men sufficient, natural, and moral Means of Happiness" in the form of natural religion, the Jewish nation made "the most dangerous and fatal Presumption" that God would ulti-

---

36. Morgan, *Moral Philosopher*, 255; cf. 322: "this [Jewish] Nation, I believe, have been set up by God and Providence, as an Example and Warning to all other Nations." 1 Cor 10 (esp. 10:6) is likely in the background here.

37. Morgan, *Moral Philosopher*, 255 and 254. Morgan actually enumerates three such "errors" (256–65). I treat together under the heading of the covenant what he distinguishes as (a) the belief "that they were the peculiar People of God, and special Favourites of Heaven, by an absolute, irreversible Decree" (257) and (b) their interpretation of the "*Abrahamick* Covenant," particularly as it relates to the land of Canaan (258).

38. Morgan, *Moral Philosopher*, 256.

39. Ibid.

40. Ibid., 257. For Philalethes's own interpretation of the Abrahamic covenant, see esp. pp. 258–59 and 287.

mately "save and deliver them by Miracles ... without the necessary Condition and Qualification of their own Repentance and Reformation."[41]

In short, the immutable, internal, moral law established by God became indistinguishable from the variable, external rites established by a self-interested hierarchy of kings, priests, and corrupt prophets.[42] And the vision of a future in which all Nations might be unified in this natural, universal religion became an expectation that God, by miraculous means and according to a predetermined historical plan, would send a king from Israel's royal dynasty—a messiah—to establish their political sovereignty over all other peoples of the world.[43]

Jesus, according to Philalethes, was sent as "the last great Prophet" to Israel with a clear teaching about this religion of nature and, conversely, an explicit condemnation of Jewish religion.[44] Yet the orthodox Christianity that would succeed him would itself come to exhibit precisely those tendencies the deist Jesus opposed: it too relied on revelation over reason in matters of belief and ethics; it too rejected God's natural providence while expecting a savior from heaven, even accepting the validity of Jewish messianic prophecy in this respect. Philalethes states the problem most sharply in connection with the New Testament itself:

> it leans strongly towards *Judaism*, and seems, at first Sight, to connect two opposite and contradictory Religions one with another; ... if a man reads the *New Testament* as a plain, historical, and uncorrupted Account of Things ... he might be tempted to imagine, that *Judaism* and *Christianity* are both one and the same Religion, or at least have a necessary Dependence on, and Connexion with each other.[45]

---

41. Ibid., 264 and 263. The phrase *national Delusion* in the preceding sentence is found on p. 258.

42. See especially the extensive discussion of preexilic Israel in Morgan, *Moral Philosopher*, 266–322, particularly in light of the treatment Egyptian "Priestcraft" and hierarchy on 237–44 and 247–49.

43. Morgan, *Moral Philosopher*, 258–63; compare his treatment of the messianic interpretation of Jesus, esp. 325–29 and 349–54.

44. Ibid., 327; further on Jesus' role as "prophet," 167, 392, 394, 439.

45. Ibid., 441.

If Philalethes's understanding of "original Christianity" is right, how is this to be explained? His answer, in a word, is that the true Christianity of Jesus quickly became tainted by Judaism.[46]

Indeed, as Philalethes sees it, such corruption, despite the best efforts of Jesus and Paul, was happening from the very start. If Jesus taught the rational religion of nature, his Jewish audience could only hear him with ears conditioned by "Enthusiasm, Superstition, and predestinarian Presumption." Indeed, the "great Numbers" of Jews that followed Jesus during his lifetime did so precisely on the conviction that he was himself "their Messiah, or national Deliverer." It was precisely when they came to realize that this was in no way his own design that they finally turned on him and demanded his crucifixion.[47]

Nor did it end there. Those few Jews that continued to follow Jesus after his death did so with just this same messianic expectation, only now deferred to a "second Coming." Nor could it possibly have been otherwise: "for no *Jew*," he says, "would ever have embraced the Religion of Jesus, but upon the old Foundation of the Prophets, that the Messias should restore the Kingdom of *Israel* to the House of *David*" and wield imperial power over all the nations of the world.[48] This, indeed, was precisely "the *Jewish* Gospel, which Christ's own Disciples firmly adhered to, and preached."[49]

What is more, he argues, "[i]t is very plain ... that as many of the *Jews* in the Apostolick Age as embraced Christianity, continued as firm *Jews*, in Obedience to the whole Law afterwards, as they had been before."[50] In

---

46. A variety of images are used to convey the notion of an originally pristine Christianity subsequently tainted by Judaism, e.g.,: "the dead Weight of that most gross and carnal Institution [of Judaism]" was "hitherto ... laid upon" Christianity (142); Christianity "seems to be clogg'd with the *Jewish* Doctrine of Propitiation, or a penal Atonement by Blood, as a necessary Means of satisfying the Justice, and pacifying the Anger of an offended Deity" (145); "an Antichristian Tare came to be transplanted into the Church of Christ by *Peter's* successors" (264); "they ... who would transfer the *Egyptian* and *Jewish* Doctrine of Atonement and Propitiation to the Priesthood of Christ, have greatly mistaken the Christian Doctrines, and grossly imposed on the Christian world" (244).

47. All quotations in this paragraph are from Morgan, *Moral Philosopher*, 325; cf. 353–54 and above n. 43.

48. Morgan, *Moral Philosopher* 441, referring to Luke 1; cf. 328.

49. Morgan, *Moral Philosopher*, 328.

50. Ibid., 329.

effect, then, the only thing "new" about the religion of these "Christian Jews" was the identification of Jesus in particular as national messiah.[51]

> When they became Christians ... they did not alter their Temper, or their old Religion, in any one Particular.... And from hence Christianity ... as receiv'd and profess'd by them, was nothing but a political Faction among themselves, and a new State Division added to the three or four more which they had before.[52]

The religion of these "Judaizers," then, was in no way representative of the religion of Jesus. On the contrary, it was a religion "exactly agreeable to their old *Egyptian* Superstition, and the gross Notions they always had of Religion; which they placed chiefly in mere external, useless Rites and Ceremonies, [and] founded ... on Force." It was not *real* Christianity, then, but merely a *Jewish* Christianity that might just as well be called, as far as Philalethes is concerned, Christian *Judaism*.[53]

Insofar as "no Jew," according to Philalethes, could see things any other way, the Apostles themselves were scarcely immune. Jesus' initial limitation of their mission to Israel as reported in Matt 10, if apparently at odds with what Philalethes assumes to be Jesus' own deistic universalism, was nothing more than a prudent acknowledgment "that the Prejudices even of his own Apostles and Disciples, and of the whole Circumcision ... were invincible."[54] What is more, as Philalethes sees it, this "national Prejudice" on the part of the apostles would continue in force long past Jesus' death and resurrection. The point is developed with particular attention to Peter and John. With respect to the latter, Philalethes devotes a significant excursus to showing how the book of Revelation—which he understands (following Sir Isaac Newton) to have been composed by the apostle in the late 60s—is essentially consistent with "the Nature and Genius of the *Jewish* Religion."[55] More ongoing attention is devoted to Peter, who emerges as "the Head and Ring-Leader of the *Judaizers*, who would still keep up the Separation between *Jews* and *Gentiles* in the Christian Churches."[56] Even

---

51. Ibid.
52. Ibid., 374; cf. 328.
53. Ibid., 374.
54. Ibid., 375–76.
55. Ibid., 364–74 (here 373).
56. Ibid., 364.

once Peter finally did open up to Gentile involvement in the movement, says Philalethes, "neither he nor any of the rest of these circumcised Christians" ever could conceive of admitting non-Jews apart from "Proselytism or *Jewish* Naturalization"—which is to say, without at least some measure of compliance with Mosaic law.[57]

In Philalethes's reconstruction, the lone apostle who manages to transcend his Jewishness is Paul. And here even the avowed Deist Philalethes can appeal only to miraculous intervention to explain how this one-time "Rabbin" would himself become "the great Free-thinker of his Age, the bold and brave Defender of Reason against Authority."[58] That there was in any event an ongoing conflict between Paul and the other apostles around precisely these matters is, as Philalethes sees it, obvious to all but those who would "wilfully shut their Eyes" to the evidence of Acts and Paul's letters.[59] He gives particular attention in this connection to reports of the events surrounding the apostolic decree—an agreement, he says, that Paul himself considered to be an untenable "joining of two contrary and inconsistent Religions" that "could serve only to continue and propagate the old Superstition and Slavery."[60] The conflict thus pitted the "Apostolical Christian *Jews*" against "our truly Christian Apostle" Paul,[61] laying bare (as Theophanes will recapitulate the matter) that "the *Jewish* and *Gentile*

---

57. Ibid., 376; on Peter's understanding of the implications of the Gentile mission, see further 72–80.

58. Ibid., 120 and 71. Strikingly—and very significantly—the same exceptional invocation of the category of "miracle" in the case of Paul's conversion (albeit with a historicizing caveat) is also made by the otherwise insistently humanistic Baur: "We cannot call his conversion, his sudden transformation from the most vehement opponent of Christianity into its boldest preacher, anything but a miracle [*Können wir ... nur ein Wunder sehen*]; and the miracle appears all the greater when we remember that ... he broke through the barriers of Judaism and rose out of the particularism of Judaism into the universal idea of Christianity. Yet great as this miracle is, it can only be conceived as a spiritual process [*als ein geistiger Process*]; and this implies that some step of transition was not wanting from the one extreme to the other." See F. C. Baur, *Kirchengeschichte der drei ersten Jahrhunderte* (Tübingen: Fues, 1863), 45. The English translation is taken from *The Church History of the First Three Centuries* (trans. A. Menzies; 3rd ed.; 2 vols.; London: Williams & Norgate, 1878), 1:47.

59. Morgan, *Moral Philosopher*, 71.

60. Ibid., 57; further 55–80, 361–64.

61. Ibid., 71.

Christianity, or *Peter's* Religion and *Paul's*, were as opposite and inconsistent [with one another] as Light and Darkness, Truth and Falshood."[62]

If Paul and his Gentile Churches, as mentioned earlier, are thus styled as "the first [!] and purest Part" of "the Apostolick Age,"[63] his Christian Deism is said to have been all but swallowed up by "Jewish Christianity" soon after his death.[64] When Nero's persecution provided a common enemy for Jewish and Gentile Christians, the latter formed an unholy alliance with the former, "to the great Advantage of *Judaism* in the Christian Church."[65] Out of this unity was born the Catholic Church, which is merely a latter-day Jewish Christianity—albeit one consisting primarily of Gentiles—and in that sense indeed an "anti-Christian" institution.[66] This group established its own priestly hierarchy and devised a variety of strategies to protect their power, to settle the disputes that would inevitably arise about the details of their theological schemes, and to silence and exclude the remnants of their freethinking critics.[67] The pinnacle of this development was the establishment of the Pope as "*a living, infallible Judge*, with temporal Power enough in his Hands to controul and prevent all Difference of Opinion."[68]

These "Judaizers" eventually "collected, revis'd, and published" a "Canon of Scripture" that, not surprisingly, "leans strongly towards *Judaism*" and, as such, does indeed seem to "to connect two opposite and contradictory Religions one with another."[69] Insofar as Protestant Christians continue to rely naively on that same Bible, then, they are scarcely any closer to true Christianity than the Catholics they critique. Indeed, as Philalethes sees it, the Protestant Reformation as a whole amounted to little more than a changing of the guard: "they set up the Scriptures in

---

62. Ibid., 377.

63. Ibid., 395.

64. Ibid., 396.

65. Ibid., 378.

66. See Morgan, *Moral Philosopher*, 378–79, where a summary list of "judaizing" concessions includes the notion of priestly authority, and particular disdain for the "Catholick" exclusion of "all Hereticks, or Dissenters and Protestants, who would not submit to this Church Authority, or Antichristian Hierarchy" (379); cf. 381.

67. Regarding the latter, Philalethes thinks particularly of the gnostics, whom he identifies as "truly primitive Christians, who maintained Liberty of Conscience, and the Right of private Judgment" (Morgan, *Moral Philosopher*, 381; further 386–91).

68. Morgan, *Moral Philosopher*, 399.

69. Ibid., 441.

gross in its Prophecies, Histories, and Morals without Exception, as a *dead, infallible Rule*, in Opposition to a *living, infallible Judge*."[70] If one's object is actually the discovery of true Christianity, then what is required is rather an entirely different approach to the Bible:

> The Books of the *New Testament* ... ought to be read critically, with an Allowance for Persons, Circumstances, and the Situation of Things at that Time; and not taken in gross, as if every Thing contain'd in them had been at first infallibly inspired from God, and no Corruptions could have ever since happen'd to them.[71]

Philalethes, in other words, advocates a historical-critical approach to the New Testament as a means to separate the wheat of "original Christianity" from the Jewish chaff. Apart from such a critical orientation, Protestants like Theophanes, as much as any "Papist," will remain less "Christian" than "Christian Jew."

MORGAN, TOLAND, AND BAUR

Within two decades of one another—and roughly a century before the influential work of F. C. Baur—John Toland and Thomas Morgan, each advocating a humanistic, critical approach to the New Testament, produced provocative accounts of Christian origins that revolved around notions of an early "Jewish Christianity." If it is far from clear that Morgan got his concept of Jewish Christianity from Toland, neither is it satisfactory to explain their common appeal to this new interpretive construct merely as the independent discovery of the same "facts of history" by two pioneers of critical scholarship. While the notion of Jewish Christianity, to be sure, is intimately bound up with the rise of critical New Testament scholarship, the category itself is ultimately a construct of the theological apologetics of Enlightenment Christianity, and specifically its appeal to a mythic time of pure, authoritative origins.[72]

---

70. Ibid., 403.

71. Ibid., 442.

72. Indeed, as the immediately preceding section indicates, the rise of critical scholarship on the New Testament itself, insofar as it proceeded from the same mythic assumption, was just as intimately bound up in post-Enlightenment ecclesiastical apologetics. While Patrick ("Two English Forerunners," 586) well recognizes that Morgan's work was "at least as much a *Tendenz-schrift* as an impartial inquiry,"

Much like Toland, Morgan used the tools of critical historiography to authorize his humanistic, rationalistic religious views by identifying them as the pristine original Christianity of Jesus and the apostolic era while simultaneously delegitimating the traditional religion of his opponents as a corrupt deviation from that original. Strikingly, a central byproduct of this apologetic project, for both men, was the invention of an early "Jewish Christianity." More strikingly still, each employed the construct for opposite aspects of the same apologetic project. Toland, in order to denigrate contemporary Christianity as a Platonizing Gentile development, invoked *Jewish Christianity* as the term of contrast for the pure original.[73] Morgan was equally concerned to subvert dominant Christianity; his strategy, however, was to associate it not with Platonism but with Judaism. He thus invoked *Jewish Christianity* as a way to reframe the religion of his opponents, their own claims notwithstanding, as being something less than the pure original; not so much *real* Christianity as *Jewish* Christianity.

In addition to their respective appeals to different "others"—Platonism or Judaism—to symbolize the impurity of traditional Christianity while legitimating their own Enlightenment values as "the original," Morgan and Toland differ from one another in one other key respect. Where Toland's reconstruction renders Paul's relationship to the mythic original ambiguous, Morgan is clear and unwavering in his correlation of Paul, as much as Jesus, with authoritative "original Christianity." It is perhaps less than surprising, then, that as this apologetic paradigm came to be replicated again and again over subsequent centuries, it was Morgan's iteration, not Toland's, that would come to typify the critical scholarship of liberal Protestantism as its quest for "original Christianity" continued, not least in the work of F. C. Baur.

---

the contrast he wishes to draw between Morgan and Baur in this respect—citing "the immeasurable distance that separated the two in almost all the qualities most essential for historical research"—seems to me to be little more than a matter of degree insofar as Baur's work is itself driven by the same core assumption. It remains a solemn obligation of contemporary historians of religion to ask whether and to what extent the same continues to be the case in present-day "historical" analyses of early Christianity and its literature.

73. See in the present volume Matt Jackson-McCabe, "The Invention of Jewish Christianity in John Toland's *Nazarenus*."

BIBLIOGRAPHY

Baird, William. *From Deism to Tübingen.* Vol. 1 of *History of New Testament Research.* Minneapolis: Fortress, 1992.
Baur, F. C. *The Church History of the First Three Centuries.* Translated by A. Menzies. 3rd ed. 2 vols. London: Williams & Norgate, 1878. Translation of *Kirchengeschichte der drei ersten Jahrhunderte.* Tübingen: Fues, 1863.
Burke, Edmund. *Reflections on the Revolution in France.* 7th ed. London: Dodsley, 1790.
Carleton Paget, James. "The Definition of the Terms *Jewish Christian* and *Jewish Christianity* in the History of Research." Pages 22–52 in *Jewish Believers in Jesus: The Early Centuries.* Edited by Oskar Skarsaune and Reidar Hvalvik. Peabody, Mass.: Hendrickson, 2007.
Gawlick, Günter. *The Moral Philosopher.* Facsimile reprint in one volume. Stuttgart-Bad Cannstatt: Frommann (Holzboog), 1969.
Leland, John. *A View of the Principal Deistical Writers that have Appeared in England in the last and present Century.* 3rd ed., rev. London: Benj. Dod, 1757. Reprint edited by René Wellek. 3 vols. British Philosophers and Theologians of the 17th and 18th Centuries. New York: Garland, 1978.
Morgan, Thomas. *The Moral Philosopher: In a Dialogue between* Philalethes *a Christian* Deist, *and* Theophanes *a Christian* Jew. 2nd ed., rev. 1738. Facsimile of the second edition with a new introduction by John Valdimir Price. History of British Deism. London: Routledge/Thoemmes, 1995.
Patrick, David. "Two English Forerunners of the Tübingen School: Thomas Morgan and John Toland." *Theological Review* 14 (1877): 562–603.
Schweitzer, Albert. *The Quest of the Historical Jesus: A Critical Study of Its Progress from Reimarus to Wrede.* Translated by W. Montgomery. New York: Macmillan, 1966.
Smith, Jonathan Z. *Drudgery Divine: On the Comparison of Early Christianities and the Religions of Late Antiquity.* Chicago: University of Chicago Press, 1990.
Stephen, Leslie. *History of English Thought in the Eighteenth Century.* 3rd ed. Repr. in 2 vols. New York: Harbinger, 1962.

From Toland to Baur: Tracks of the History of Research into Jewish Christianity

F. Stanley Jones

John Toland's *Nazarenus* argued that the Jewish Christians were the first Christians. By equating these first Christians with the Ebionites and the Nazoraeans, Toland concluded that the first Christians were the first heretics.[1] Toland furthermore objectified these first Christians with the moniker *Jewish Christianity* and thereby opened them up for systematic historical investigation. The purpose of the following paper is to track how this seminal set of ideas made its way into F. C. Baur's later publications and thereby became a foundation stone for modern critical study of the New Testament and early Christianity. It is a distinctive set of ideas that can be traced like a red thread. This red thread is first found in prominence in the vicinity of Baur when his sharp-minded student Albert Schwegler wrote in 1846, "Primitive Christianity was Ebionitism."[2] The path that led from Toland to Baur was not a direct one, however, and, apart from the vague 1877 sketch by David Patrick,[3] it has never been traced.

Thus, even though Baur wrote voluminous histories of Christian doctrine as well as a treatise entitled "Epochs of Church Historiography," there is no evidence (to my knowledge) that Baur had read the English Deists. It may be a fair and interesting question as to why he did not, but this

---

1. *Nazarenus: Or, Jewish, Gentile, and Mahometan Christianity* (2nd ed.; London: J. Brotherton, J. Roberts, and A. Dodd, 1718), 76.

2. Albert Schwegler, *Das nachapostolische Zeitalter in den Hauptmomenten seiner Entwicklung* (2 vols.; Tübingen: Ludwig Friedrich Fues, 1846), 1:179. This "red thread" is quite distinct from the position of Thomas Morgan, who (like Marcion) thought that the apostles misunderstood Jesus and reintroduced Jewish ideas and practices.

3. David Patrick, "Two English Forerunners of the Tübingen School: Thomas Morgan and John Toland," *Theological Review* 14 (1877): 562–603.

question cannot be the focus of this essay. Instead, this study is going to track Toland's ideas as they made their circuitous route through German literature on their unacknowledged path to Baur.

One main figure in this history is going to be Johann Salomo Semler, though the story begins earlier, before Semler was a student and a resident in the home of his teacher Siegmund Jacob Baumgarten. Baumgarten was reading the English Deists and reviewing their works, among others, in his serial publication *Nachrichten von einer hallischen Bibliothek* (News from a Library in Halle), which was Baumgarten's own library in a city named Halle in Germany. Thanks to the Internet, some of this material is now generally available, including the review of Toland's *Nazarenus*, which, however, is little more than a summary of the book, though with reference to Johann Lorenz Mosheim's refutation of Toland.[4]

Nearly thirty years earlier, in 1720, Mosheim argued in an extensive review and point-for-point refutation of Toland's *Nazarenus* that the Ebionites and the Nazoraeans were later and different[5] sects and were not at all to be equated with the first Palestinian Christians.[6] According to Mosheim, the very fact of Ebion's existence, as well as the name *Ebionites*, points to a person and a sect that separated themselves from the other Christians.[7] The Nazoraeans are yet another group that arose no earlier than the fourth century;[8] the Nazoraeans came into existence in the time of Constantine as some Jews perceived the calamities and miseries that were growing against their people.[9]

Mosheim's study is thus not the red thread in its positive presentation, but the red thread is present and perceived as the position that must be refuted. As can be seen also in the British reactions to Toland, it is in the attempts to refute Toland's studies that the opponents are drawn into extensive historical argumentation; this discussion marks the beginning

---

4. [Siegmund Jacob Baumgarten], review of John Toland, *Nazarenus*, 2nd ed. *Nachrichten von einer hallischen Bibliothek* 3 (1749): 320–30. On 330 it is stated that Toland's *Nazarenus* was "widerleget" by Mosheim.

5. Johann Lorenz Mosheim, *Vindiciae antiqvae Christianorum disciplinae, adversus celeberrimi viri Jo. Tolandi, Hiberni, "Nazarenum"* (2nd ed.; Hamburg: Impensis Viduæ Benj. Schilleri & Jo. Christoph. Kesneri, 1722), 97–117.

6. Ibid., 182.

7. Ibid., 184, 201.

8. Ibid., 118.

9. Ibid., 145–46.

of the modern academic debate.[10] So the red thread has indeed made it across the channel to Germany.[11]

---

10. This was the case with the study of the New Testament canon, in which Toland's work (and the immediate attempts to refute him) sparked the extensive three-volume study by Jeremiah Jones, *A New and Full Method of Settling the Canonical Authority of the New Testament* (3 vols.; 1726–1727; Oxford: Clarendon, 1798). Historians of the Deist movement have properly pointed out that the opponents of the Deists get caught up in the same rationalistic thinking as the Deists themselves; for example, A. Tholuck, "Abriß einer Geschichte der Umwälzung, welche seit 1750 auf dem Gebiete der Theologie in Deutschland statt gefunden," in *Vermischte Schriften* (Hamburg: Friedrich Perthes, 1839), 2:1–147, esp. 28, accurately perceives such influence and complains about it. On p. 27, Tholuck mentions predecessors who had commented on this state of affairs. Cf. Gotthard Victor Lechler, *Geschichte des englischen Deismus* (Stuttgart: J. G. Cotta, 1841), 451.

11. Christoph Voigt, *Der englische Deismus in Deutschland: Eine Studie zur Rezeption englisch-deistischer Literatur in deutschen Zeitschriften und Kompendien des 18. Jahrhunderts* (BHT 121; Tübingen: Mohr Siebeck, 2003), fails to notice that Mosheim's work is indeed a point-for-point refutation and thus overlooks the significance of this work by Mosheim. Cf. Henning Graf Reventlow, "Johann Lorenz Mosheims Auseinandersetzung mit John Toland," in *Johann Lorenz Mosheim (1693–1755): Theologie im Spannungsfeld von Philosophie, Philologie und Geschichte* (ed. Martin Muslow et al.; Wolfenbütteler Forschungen 77; Wiesbaden: Harrassowitz, 1997), 93–110, esp. 100: "Beachtlich und für die Geschichte der Aufklärung bedeutsam ist jedoch, daß mit Mosheims Werk [sc. *Vindiciae antiqvae Christianorum disciplinae*] die Auseinandersetzung mit der deistischen Bewegung die Grenzen des Inselreichs überschreitet und nach Deutschland übergreift." Reventlow correctly sees, on p. 110, that the attempt to refute Toland's historical arguments forced Mosheim to methodological and critical historical reflection and initiated Mosheim's transformation from apologist to church historian ("Der Kirchengeschichtlicher wächst aus dem Polemiker und Apologeten heraus"). This point of contact and influence is precisely a good example of what Voigt downplays and disavows in his endeavor generally to deny the influence of the English Deists on German thought (e.g., *Der englische Deismus*, 211: "Die englisch-deistischen Büchern haben in der deutschen Diskussion also gerade keine neuen Fragen provoziert," or the summarizing statement on p. 213 that "man sich in Deutschland die Positionen der englischen Deisten auch nicht angeeignet [sc. hat]"). Voigt's radical thesis against the view of previous scholarship will not carry the day. Voigt's study does help explain, however, why Germans were not publicly citing the Deists. Hermann Samuel Reimarus, who is not even mentioned by Voigt, is a good case in point. Though Reimarus did not mention Toland in his published works, Reimarus says that Toland "alle andere Gegner der Offenbarung an Belesenheit und Scharfsinnigkeit weit übertrifft" in his *Apologie oder Schutzschrift für die vernüftigen Verehrer Gottes* (2 vols.; ed. Gerhard Alexander; Frankfurt am Main: Insel, 1972), 1:434, which he chose not to publish (see also 2:106, which seems to refer to Toland). Voigt's study does perhaps point to

Mosheim's "refutation" of Toland made him famous.[12] This type of fine work eventually led to his appointment as the first chancellor of the recently founded Universität Göttingen, in 1747. It is said that Mosheim was the most famous theologian of the time,[13] and his refutation of Toland is still praised in recent times.[14] In the particular case of the earliest Christians, Mosheim had saved them from the charge of heresy. The only problem is that Mosheim was wrong in this particular case, just as he was wrong in his initial insistence on the existence of a historical Ebion in his so-called refutation of Toland[15]—a position even he himself no longer defended later.[16]

---

the need to be more specific about precise instances and manners of influence, as the current study is attempting to do.

12. Karl Heussi, *Johann Lorenz Mosheim: Ein Beitrag zur Kirchengeschichte des achtzehnten Jahrhunderts* (Tübingen: J. C. B. Mohr [Paul Siebeck], 1906), 55: "Mosheims Widerlegung Tolands brachte ihm seinen ersten grösseren literarischen Erfolg und trug seinen Namen rasch in weitere Kreise." Cf. also Reventlow, "Johann Lorenz Mosheims Auseinandersetzung mit John Toland," 98: "Offenbar was es dieses Werk, das Mosheims wissenschaftlichen Ruhm begründete."

13. Bernd Moeller, "Johann Lorenz von Mosheim und die Gründung der Göttinger Universität," in *Theologie in Göttingen: Eine Vorlesungsreihe* (ed. Bernd Moeller; Göttinger Universitätsschriften, Serie A: Schriften 1; Göttingen: Vandenhoeck & Ruprecht, 1987), 9–40, esp. 12.

14. Moeller, "Johann Lorenz von Mosheim und die Gründung der Göttinger Universität," 15–16. Heussi, *Johann Lorenz Mosheim*, however, correctly saw that Toland was right with respect to Jewish Christianity and that Mosheim was wrong: "der Deist hat in diesem Punkte trotz aller Übertreibungen fraglos geschichtlich richtigere Anschauungen, als der lutherische Kirchenhistoriker" (54). Cf. also Reventlow, "Johann Lorenz Mosheims Auseinandersetzung mit John Toland," 100 ("Eine Apologie ist in Wirklichkeit das gesamte Werk, nicht etwa eine objektive historische Darstellung"). It should not be overlooked that Mosheim had to endure a "dark night of the soul" before his first appointment. There was resistance from the House of Hannover; it had been noted that Mosheim treated scholars of differing opinion with ridicule. See Heussi, *Johann Lorenz Mosheim*, 62–63. It needs to be investigated whether the personal problems for Mosheim in Hannover had some basis in Toland's earlier contact with this House. Toland was sent with Lord Macclesfield to present the Act of Settlement to Sophia of Hannover in 1701. See Robert E. Sullivan, *John Toland and the Deist Controversy: A Study in Adaptations* (HHS 101; Cambridge: Harvard University, 1982), 16. When Mosheim finally received the news of his appointment, he lay deathly sick in bed (see Heussi, *Johann Lorenz Mosheim*, 69).

15. *Vindiciae antiqvae Christianorum disciplinae*, 201–202.

16. John Lawrence Mosheim, *Ecclesiastical History, Ancient and Modern, from the Birth of Christ, to the Beginning of the Present Century*, vol. 1 (trans. Archibald MacLaine; Philadelphia: Stephen C. Ustick, 1797), 209.

I am referring now to Mosheim's mature *Ecclesiastical History*, which according to Karl Heussi was the occasion by which German research in the area of church history gained hegemony in relation to foreign countries.[17] Here, too, Mosheim abandoned his dating of the Nazoraeans to the fourth century.[18]

In Semler's autobiography, which is also now accessible via the Internet, Semler states that he had written some of the reviews in Baumgarten's *Nachrichten*, including review of some English books.[19] It has been suggested that Semler wrote the review of *Nazarenus*,[20] but this possibility cannot be verified. Semler expressly states that he had read the works of William Whiston and had written reviews of some of them.[21] Semler also reports that Baumgarten had evening discussions at the table with other academics: one evening Voltaire and Christian Wolff were there, and the discussion occurred in Latin. Semler saw Baumgarten take the side of an English Deist.[22] Semler states that Baumgarten never clearly indicated such views in his lectures and writings but that Semler himself took them to heart. It is true that in 1750 Semler wrote a master's thesis to refute William Whiston's text-critical analysis of 1 Tim 3:16 and 1 John 5:7. Semler, however, came to condemn his own thesis, and as justification he states that he had only gradually learned to differentiate theological metaphysics from actual history.[23] Semler expressly comments that he did not know a single German academic who had followed the path he found himself upon.[24] Without further entry into the psychological, intellectual, and historical

---

17. Heussi, *Johann Lorenz Mosheim*, 223.

18. It is no longer mentioned in *Ecclesiastical History*, 1:209.

19. Semler, *Lebensbeschreibung von ihm selbst abgefaßt* (Halle: n.p., 1781–1782), 1:117.

20. In "Two English Forerunners of the Tübingen School," Patrick states that it is "highly probable that the reviews of Nazarenus and of the Moral Philosopher are from his [sc. Semler's] own pen" (601). The review was published in 1749, which would be during Semler's initial time in Halle.

21. Semler, *Lebensbeschreibung*, 1:118.

22. Ibid., 1:108. See the commentary on this page in Semler in Martin Schloemann, *Siegmund Jacob Baumgarten: System und Geschichte in der Theologie des Überganges zum Neuprotestantismus* (FKDG 26; Göttingen: Vandenhoeck & Ruprecht, 1974), 55 n. 188

23. Semler, *Lebensbeschreibung*, 1:120.

24. Ibid., 2:121.

aspects of this transformation or development,[25] suffice it to say that the more mature Semler found himself promoting elements of the positions he first encountered with the wacko British Deists. Thus, Semler promoted the view that *Ebionites* and *Nazaraeans* were just two names for the same Jewish Christians.[26] While Semler apparently did not follow in the objectification of the Jewish Christians with the term *Jewish Christianity*, he did objectify the Jewish Christians with the term *Partey*.[27] It would seem fair to conclude that Semler essentially has his terminology and objectification from the Deists.[28] He stated that it was certain that these Jewish Christians did not accept the letters of Paul and other Greek writings of the apostles.[29] In his mature study of the canon (1771–1775), Semler expressed the view that the Jewish Christians accepted a body of writings that differed

---

25. For some of this, see Tholuck, "Abriß einer Geschichte der Umwälzung," 26–28.

26. Johann Salomo Semler, "Geschichte der christlichen Glaubenslehre," in Siegmund Jacob Baumgarten, *Untersuchung theologischer Streitigkeiten* (ed. Johann Salomo Semler; Halle: Johann Justinus Gebauer, 1762), 1:210.

27. Johann Salomo Semler, *Abhandlung von freier Untersuchung des Canon*, part 4 (Halle: Carl Hermann Hemmerde, 1775), Vorrede, b8(1).

28. The term "das jüdische … Christentum" appears in the translation of the title of Toland's *Nazarenus* in [Baumgarten], review of *Nazarenus*, 321, but noteworthily not prominently in the body of the review (cf. 322, which is essentially a repetition of the title; 324 speaks of "den jüdischen Christen"). Page 324 speaks of those "aus den Juden Bekerten"; p. 326 just says "die bekerten Juden." Hella Lemke, *Judenchristentum zwischen Ausgrenzung und Integration: Zur Geschichte eines exegetischen Begriffes* (Hamburger Theologische Studien 25; Münster: Lit, 2001), 200, finds usage of the term *Juden=Christ* by Mosheim as early as 1741 (the second edition reads "Judenchrist" [Johann Lorenz von Mosheim, *Erklärung des Ersten Briefes des heiligen Apostels Pauli an die Gemeinde zu Corinthus* (2nd ed.; ed. Christian Ernst von Windheim; Flensburg: Kortensche privilegirte Buchhandlung, 1762), 371]). Cf. the Latin *pars Iudaeorum Christianorum* in Io. Lavr. Mosheim, *Institutionum Historiae Ecclesiasticae Antiqvae et Recentioris* (rev. ed.; Helmstadt: Christianus Fridericus Weygang, 1764), 51. I find that Mosheim used the term *Iudaeos Christianos* as early as 1733 in *Dissertationum ad historiam ecclesiasticam pertinentivm volvmen* (Altonaviae: Sumptibus Ionae Korte, 1733), 572 (here he is presenting an opinion he rejects). It thus seems likely that Mosheim is largely responsible for the introduction of the German term and that he did this as a subconscious adoption from Toland. In Semler's "Geschichte der christlichen Glaubenslehre," 210, and *Abhandlung von freier Untersuchung des Canon*, part 4, Vorrede, b8(2), he uses the term *Judenchristen*. Cf. Lemke's interpretation of the evidence in Lemke, *Judenchristentum zwischen Ausgrenzung und Integration*, 250.

29. "Geschichte der christlichen Glaubenslehre," 210 n. 199.

from what the Gentile Christians accepted. Semler pointed to the Pseudo-Clementines as evidence of the negative attitude that the Jewish Christians held toward Pauline Christians.[30] These notions are highly likely to have come from Toland, who had emphasized that the first Christians (Jewish Christians, Nazoraeans, or Ebionites) had rejected Paul and all his letters.[31] Semler's reference to the Pseudo-Clementines as evidence certainly seems to be a clear, telltale sign that Toland is the source.[32] Toland had essentially spoken of different canons among a variety of early Christian groups in his *Amyntor*,[33] a work that had also been reviewed in Baumgarten's *Nachrichten von merkwürdigen Büchern* in 1756.[34]

In Baur's early days, around 1830, the scholar who caught Baur's attention with regard to the Ebionites was not Semler but rather Karl August Credner and his recent 1829 article.[35] Baur followed Credner in the view that the Ebionites shared a common root with the Essenes.[36] This perspective is indicated already in the title of the 1831 piece *De Ebionitarum origine et doctrina, ab Essenis repetenda*. Baur picked up the use of the Pseudo-Clementines in this context from both Credner and August Neander, who had not referred to any previous scholar when they did so. Baur furthermore adopted Neander's differentiation between the Nazoraeans and the Ebionites.[37] The Ebionites were later than the Nazoraeans[38] and arose after the war in the vicinity of Pella through admixture of Essene

---

30. Semler, *Abhandlung von freier Untersuchung des Canon*, part 4, Vorrede, b8(2).

31. Toland, *Nazarenus*, 25–29: "the Ebionites call'd Paul *an Apostate from the Law*; and rejected all his *Epistles*, as those of an Enemy and an Impostor" (25).

32. When Semler writes, "Ein Jude zugleich und ein Christ zugelich seyn ist mir und allen Juden und Christen unbegreiflich; ein Deist kan so etwas vorschlagen, aus Verachtung und zur Verspottung der Christen," he may well have had Toland in mind. See *Beantwortung der Fragmente eines Ungenanten insbesondere vom Zweck Jesu and seiner Jünger* (Halle: Verlag des Erziehungsinstituts, 1779), 129. Other references to Toland in Semler's works are listed in n. 21 of David Lincicum's contribution to this volume.

33. Toland, *Amyntor: Or, A Defence of Milton's Life* (London: n.p., 1699), 64.

34. Siegmund Jacob Baumgarten, review of John Toland, *Amyntor*, *Nachrichten von merkwürdigen Büchern* 9 (1756): 128–32.

35. K. A. Credner, "Über Essäer und Ebioniten und einen theilweisen Zusammenhang derselben," *ZWT* 1 (1829): 211–64, 277–328.

36. Ferdinand Christian Baur, *De Ebionitarum origine et doctrina, ab Essenis repentenda* (Tübingen: Typis Hopferi de L'Orme, 1831), 21.

37. Ibid., 8.

38. Ibid., 9.

doctrines and practices with the Christian faith.[39] Baur noted and rejected the position of Johann Karl Ludwig Gieseler that these two groups originally arose out of the earliest Christians.[40] It is precisely this point that gradually changes in Baur's publications.[41] By 1838, Baur could write "that all these Jewish Christians of the oldest time bore a more or less Ebionite character."[42] Baur will also eventually and explicitly reject the view that the Ebionites arose after the war.[43] The later Baur will even affirm that *Ebionites* was originally the name of the Jewish Christians generally.[44] In other words, "Ebioniten sind die ältesten Judenchristen überhaupt"[45] ("in general, Ebionites are the oldest Jewish Christians"). How did Baur advance to this position? Was he aware of a predecessor?

J. C. O'Neill stands in a long line of scholars (including H. J. Holtzmann) when he states that Baur was indebted to Semler in his view of two opposing parties in earliest Christianity.[46] While this opinion seems globally true, two observations speak against the particularity of this claim. First, Baur does not cite Semler in his various discussions of the issue. Second,

---

39. Ibid., 24, 30–31.

40. Ibid., 4–5.

41. For Baur's own description of his evolution, see his "Die Einleitung in das Neue Testament als theologische Wissenschaft: Ihr Begriff und ihre Aufgabe, ihr Entwicklungsgang und ihr innerer Organismus," *ThJb(T)* 10 (1851): 291–329, esp. 294–96.

42. *Über den Ursprung des Episcopats in der christlichen Kirche* (Tübingen: Ludwig Friedrich Fues, 1838), 123 ("daß alle diese Judenchristen der ältesten Zeit einen mehr oder minder ebionitischen Charakter an sich tragen"). On p. 124, he writes, "daß das ebionitische Element … ein den Judenchristen der ältesten Zeit überhaupt gemeinsames war."

43. *Das Christentum und die christliche Kirche der drei ersten Jahrhunderte* (2nd ed.; Tübingen: Ludwig Friedrich Fues, 1860), 174. Baur differentiates early Ebionitism from later Ebionitism in his *Von der apostolischen Zeit bis zur Synode in Nicäa* (part 1 of *Das Dogma der alten Kirche*, vol. 1 of *Vorlesungen über die christliche Dogmengeschichte* [ed. Ferd. Fr. Baur; Leipzig: Fues's Verlag (L. W. Reisland), 1865]), 144–45.

44. Baur, *Von der apostolischen Zeit bis zur Synode in Nicäa*, 146–47.

45. Ibid., 153.

46. J. C. O'Neill, *The Bible's Authority: A Portrait Gallery of Thinkers from Lessing to Bultmann* (Edinburgh: T&T Clark, 1991), 121; cf. also, e.g., Heinrich Holtzmann, "Baur und die neutestamentliche Kritik der Gegenwart," *PrM* 1 (1897): 177–88, esp. 187, and the references there, and Gerhard Uhlhorn, "Die älteste Kirchengeschichte in der Darstellung der Tübinger Schule: Eine Übersicht," *JDTh* 3 (1858): 280–349, esp. 347–48.

in his "Epochs of Church Historiography" (1852), Baur discusses Semler without reference to Semler's view of two early parties in Christianity; for Baur, Semler was lost in details and never developed a more general point of view.[47]

The scholar whom Baur cites in his discussion and who actually had held a similar position about the existence of two opinions among the earliest Christians was J. K. L. Gieseler. Ever since the decision of the apostolic council (according to Gieseler), there were (additionally) two opinions (or parties) among the Jewish Christians (though no separation).[48] Later, these two opinions or parties are found separate in the Nazoraeans and the Ebionites.[49]

What is interesting is that toward the beginning of his study Gieseler states that Semler was *the first* to express the opinion that Nazoraeans and Ebionites made up the same party ("Einer Partey").[50] While Gieseler differentiates his view from that of Semler, Semler's radical position is a motivating force behind Gieseler's effort. It is also clear that Gieseler is adopting Semler's term of objectification of the Jewish Christians ("Partey"). We know, of course, that, contrary to Gieseler's statement, Semler was *not* the first to equate the Nazoraeans and the Ebionites; Toland was.[51] So here we see the red thread, now under the name of Semler.

Besides the above, Gieseler furthermore promoted the view that the earliest Jewish Christians were all called Ebionites.[52] This opinion was picked up by Credner, who had stated that even the differentiation between Nazoraeans and Ebionites was inadequate.[53] We are close to the

---

47. Baur, *Die Epochen der kirchlichen Geschichtschreibung* (Tübingen: Ludwig Friedrich Fues, 1852), 144–45.

48. Johann Karl Ludwig Gieseler, "Über die Nazaräer und Ebioniten," *AANKG* 4 (1820): 279–330, esp. 313 (on p. 297 he calls them "parties").

49. Ibid., 314–15. On p. 322 he identifies Thebutis as the cause for the rise of the two parties.

50. Gieseler, "Über die Nazaräer und Ebioniten," 281.

51. Mosheim, *Vindiciae antiqvae Christianorum disciplinae*, 97, can indeed list some predecessors in this view, but Toland still remains the first to develop this perspective prominently and systematically.

52. "Über die Nazaräer und Ebioniten," 298. For Gieseler the name *Ebionites* came from the unbelieving Jews (301) as did also the name *Nazoraeans* (297). There were two parties among these Ebionites (298). Later the stricter party took the name *Ebionites* and left the milder party with the name *Nazoraeans* (323).

53. Credner, "Über Essäer und Ebioniten," 323–24.

red thread. What one is seeing here is a gradual convergence toward the idea that Nazoraeans, Ebionites, and Jewish Christians cannot be differentiated, particularly at the early time of the apostles—a good part of the red thread. Lobegott Lange, whom Baur knows and cites, perhaps contributed to this gradual convergence in his insistence that it was *not* a mistake or misunderstanding of the teaching of Christ when the apostles insisted on observance of the Mosaic law.[54] These two positions combined would be the red thread.

In his earliest piece on the Jewish Christians, Baur already referred to Gieseler and Lange as well as to Credner.[55] Besides being impressed (as indicated above) with the connection between the Ebionites and the Essenes that Credner spotlighted, Baur is in conversation mostly with Gieseler throughout the essay. He argues against Gieseler that the name *Ebionites* was not used generally of the earliest Christians[56] but that it arose when Jewish Christians in the vicinity of Pella mixed in Essene beliefs and practices with Christian doctrine.[57] Thus, the Ebionites arose after the war.[58] In the later context where Baur eventually asserts that *Ebionites* was originally the name of all Jewish Christians,[59] he is still discussing Gieseler's article from 1820.[60] Though in the course of his publications Baur makes both negative and positive comments about Gieseler's work,[61] it is difficult not to see the increasing influence of Gieseler in the position of the mature Baur on Jewish Christianity. Baur first rejects but then gradually adopts more and more of Gieseler's position, which we know to be indebted to Semler. Baur eventually goes beyond Gieseler essentially to agree with the opinion of Semler and Toland (Ebionites' Jewish Christian-

---

54. Lobegott Lange, *Die Ebioniten und Nicolaiten der apostolischen Zeit und das Verhältniß der neutestamentlichen Schriften zu ihnen* (Leipzig: Johannes Ambrosius Barth, 1828), 68. Baur cites Lange in *De Ebionitarum origine*, 5.

55. Baur, *De Ebionitarum origine*, 4–5.

56. Ibid., 28.

57. Ibid., 30–31.

58. Ibid., 24–25.

59. Baur, *Von der apostolischen Zeit*, 146–47.

60. Ibid., 144–47, 151.

61. See critical remarks in "Kritische Beiträge zur Kirchengeschichte der ersten Jahrhunderte, mit besonderer Rücksicht auf die Werke von Neander und Gieseler," *Theologische Jahrbücher* 4 (1845): 207–314, esp. 210–11, but praise of his work in *Die Epochen der kirchlichen Geschichtschreibung*, 232–33, as "das nützlichste Werk der neueren kirchenhistorischen Literatur."

ity was rooted in the Jerusalem congregation under the leadership of the original apostles).[62]

It will not be a surprise that Albert Schwegler was perhaps the first Tübinger clearly to deny the differentiations between Nazoraeans, Ebionites, and Jewish Christians and to state that "primitive Christianity was Ebionitism" and that "the Nazoraean point of view is just the earliest, most primitive developmental stage of Ebionitism."[63] Schwegler also uses the term *Judenchristentum* prominently and places it in contrast to Pauline Christianity.[64] Baur slowly followed suit.[65]

So this is the somewhat circuitous, though nevertheless traceable, path by which Toland's distinctive set of ideas reached Baur: Rejected and refuted in detail by Mosheim, Toland's ideas were known to Semler and appropriated under the concept of two "parties" with distinctive canons

---

62. This detailed response to Gieseler is found in his 1845 article "Kritische Beiträge," esp. 263–67. In effect, Baur is simultaneously arguing against his own earlier position. For Baur's later position that the Jerusalem congregation was led by the original apostles, see *Das Christenthum und die christliche Kirche der drei ersten Jahrhunderte* (2nd ed.; Tübingen: L. Fr. Fues, 1860), 42–43, 49–50; the connection between these "original" Jewish Christians and the Ebionites is mentioned on p. 85.

63. Schwegler, *Das nachapostolische Zeitalter*, 1:179–80 ("Das Urchristentum war Ebionitismus" [179]; "der nazaräische Standpunkt ist nur die früheste, primitivste Entwickelungsstufe des Ebionitismus" [180]). It is noteworthy that Schwegler is asserting his position explicitly against Gieseler (179).

64. E.g., Schwegler, *Das nachapostolische Zeitalter*, 1:25.

65. Baur sporadically uses the term *Judenchristenthum* in his earlier writings and then does so more frequently later. Fairly early examples are found in "Über Zweck und Veranlassung des Römerbriefs und die damit zusammenhängenden Verhältnisse der römischen Gemeinde: Eine historisch-kritische Untersuchung," *TZTh* 3 (1836): 59–178, esp. 138, and *Über den Ursprung des Episcopats in der christlichen Kirche*, 129. Later, more systematic usage is found in *Das Christenthum und die christliche Kirche der drei ersten Jahrhunderte*, e.g., 95 (in juxtaposition to "Paulinismus"). Cf. Lemke, *Judenchristentum zwischen Ausgrenzung und Integration*, 274. An earlier witness to this term of objectification in the realm of German scholarship is found already in the title of Heinrich Eberhard Gottlob Paulus's *Historia Cerinthi cuius partem priorem quae ad Iudaeochristianismum et canonicae apocalypseos fata illustranda pertingit* (Jena: Typis Goepferdtii, 1795). See also Wilhelm Martin Leberecht de Wette, *Biblische Dogmatik Alten und Neuen Testaments* (3rd ed.; Berlin: G. Reimer, 1831), 204, who distinguishes "das Judenchristenthum" as one of three main forms of apostolic Christianity (alongside "das alexandrinische" and "das paulinische Christentum"). Lemke, *Judenchristentum zwischen Ausgrenzung und Integration*, 240, draws attention to these instances.

in early Christianity. Gieseler refereed Semler's position to distinguish his own. Baur hammered out and modified his views with continual reference to Gieseler's overview until he finally arrived at the position ascribed to Semler but ultimately indebted to Toland. Toland's "Jewish Christianity" then became known as Baur's "Judenchristenthum."

BIBLIOGRAPHY

Baumgarten, Siegmund Jacob. Review of John Toland, *Amyntor. Nachrichten von merkwürdigen Büchern* 9 (1756): 128–32.

[Baumgarten, Siegmund Jacob]. Review of John Toland, *Nazarenus*, 2nd ed. *Nachrichten von einer hallischen Bibliothek* 3 (1749): 320–30.

Baur, Ferdinand Christian. *Das Christenthum und die christliche Kirche der drei ersten Jahrhunderte*. 2nd ed. Tübingen: L. Fr. Fues, 1860.

———. *De Ebionitarum origine et doctrina, ab Essenis repentenda*. Tübingen: Typis Hopferi de L'Orme, 1831.

———. "Die Einleitung in das Neue Testament als theologische Wissenschaft: Ihr Begriff und ihre Aufgabe, ihr Entwicklungsgang und ihr innerer Organismus." *ThJb(T)* 10 (1851): 291–329.

———. *Die Epochen der kirchlichen Geschichtschreibung*. Tübingen: Ludwig Friedrich Fues, 1852.

———. *Über den Ursprung des Episcopats in der christlichen Kirche*. Tübingen: Ludwig Friedrich Fues, 1838.

———. "Über Zweck und Veranlassung des Römerbriefs und die damit zusammenhängenden Verhältnisse der römischen Gemeinde: Eine historisch-kritische Untersuchung." *TZTh* 3 (1836): 59–178.

———. *Von der apostolischen Zeit bis zur Synode in Nicäa*. Part 1 of *Das Dogma der alten Kirche*. Vol. 1 of *Vorlesungen über die christliche Dogmengeschichte*. Edited by Ferd. Fr. Baur. Leipzig: Fues's Verlag (L. W. Reisland), 1865.

Credner, K. A. "Über Essäer und Ebioniten und einen theilweisen Zusammenhang derselben." *ZWT* 1 (1829): 211–64, 277–328.

Gieseler, Johann Karl Ludwig. "Über die Nazaräer und Ebioniten." *AANKG* 4 (1820): 279–330.

Heussi, Karl. *Johann Lorenz Mosheim: Ein Beitrag zur Kirchengeschichte des achtzehnten Jahrhunderts*. Tübingen: J. C. B. Mohr (Paul Siebeck), 1906.

Holtzmann, Heinrich. "Baur und die neutestamentliche Kritik der Gegenwart." *PrM* 1 (1897): 177–88.

Jones, Jeremiah. *A New and Full Method of Settling the Canonical Authority of the New Testament*. 3 vols. 1726–1727. Oxford: Clarendon, 1798.

Lange, Lobegott. *Die Ebioniten und Nicolaiten der apostolischen Zeit und das Verhältniß der neutestamentlichen Schriften zu ihnen*. Leipzig: Johannes Ambrosius Barth, 1828.

Lechler, Gotthard Victor. *Geschichte des englischen Deismus*. Stuttgart: J. G. Cotta, 1841.

Lemke, Hella. *Judenchristentum zwischen Ausgrenzung und Integration: Zur Geschichte eines exegetischen Begriffes*. Hamburger Theologische Studien 25. Münster: Lit, 2001.

Moeller, Bernd. "Johann Lorenz von Mosheim und die Gründung der Göttinger Universität." Pages 9–40 in *Theologie in Göttingen: Eine Vorlesungsreihe*. Edited by Bernd Moeller. Göttinger Universitätsschriften, Serie A: Schriften 1. Göttingen: Vandenhoeck & Ruprecht, 1987.

Mosheim, Johann Lorenz. *Dissertationum ad historiam ecclesiasticam pertinentivm volvmen*. Altonaviae: Sumptibus Ionae Korte, 1733.

———. *Ecclesiastical History, Ancient and Modern, from the Birth of Christ, to the Beginning of the Present Century*. Translated by Archibald MacLaine. Vol. 1. Philadelphia: Stephen C. Ustick, 1797.

———. *Erklärung des Ersten Briefes des heiligen Apostels Pauli an die Gemeinde zu Corinthus*. 2nd ed. Edited by Christian Ernst von Windheim. Flensburg: Kortensche privilegirte Buchhandlung, 1762.

———. *Vindiciae antiqvae Christianorum disciplinae, adversus celeberrimi viri Jo. Tolandi, Hiberni, "Nazarenum."* 2nd ed. Hamburg: Impensis Viduæ Benj. Schilleri & Jo. Christoph. Kesneri, 1722.

O'Neill, J. C. *The Bible's Authority: A Portrait Gallery of Thinkers from Lessing to Bultmann*. Edinburgh: T&T Clark, 1991.

Patrick, David. "Two English Forerunners of the Tübingen School: Thomas Morgan and John Toland." *Theological Review* 14 (1877): 562–603.

Paulus, Heinrich Eberhard Gottlob. *Historia Cerinthi cuius partem priorem quae ad Iudaeochristianismum et canonicae apocalypseos fata illustranda pertingit*. Jena: Typis Goepferdtii, 1795.

Reimarus, Hermann Samuel. *Apologie oder Schutzschrift für die vernüftigen Verehrer Gottes*. Edited by Gerhard Alexander. 2 vols. Frankfurt am Main: Insel, 1972.

Reventlow, Henning Graf. "Johann Lorenz Mosheims Auseinandersetzung mit John Toland." Pages 93–110 in *Johann Lorenz Mosheim (1693–1755): Theologie im Spannungsfeld von Philosophie, Philologie und Geschichte*. Edited by Martin Muslow, Ralph Häfner, Florian Neumann, and Helmut Zedelmaier. Wolfenbütteler Forschungen 77. Wiesbaden: Harrassowitz, 1997.

Schloemann, Martin. *Siegmund Jacob Baumgarten: System und Geschichte in der Theologie des Überganges zum Neuprotestantismus*. FKDG 26. Göttingen: Vandenhoeck & Ruprecht, 1974.

Schwegler, Albert. *Das nachapostolische Zeitalter in den Hauptmomenten seiner Entwicklung*. 2 vols. Tübingen: Ludwig Friedrich Fues, 1846.

Semler, Johann Salomo. *Abhandlung von freier Untersuchung des Canon*. Part 4. Halle: Carl Hermann Hemmerde, 1775.

———. *Beantwortung der Fragmente eines Ungenanten insbesondere vom Zweck Jesu and seiner Jünger*. Halle: Verlag des Erziehungsinstituts, 1779.

———. "Geschichte der christlichen Glaubenslehre." In Siegmund Jacob Baumgarten, *Untersuchung theologischer Streitigkeiten*. Vol. 1. Edited by Johann Salomo Semler. Halle: Johann Justinus Gebauer, 1762.

———. *Lebensbeschreibung von ihm selbst abgefaßt.* 2 vols. Halle: n.p., 1781–82.

Sullivan, Robert E. *John Toland and the Deist Controversy: A Study in Adaptations.* HHS 101. Cambridge: Harvard University Press, 1982.

Tholuck, A. "Abriß einer Geschichte der Umwälzung, welche seit 1750 auf dem Gebiete der Theologie in Deutschland statt gefunden." Pages 1–147 in *Vermischte Schriften.* Vol. 2. Hamburg: Friedrich Perthes, 1839.

Toland, John. *Amyntor: Or, A Defence of Milton's Life.* London: n.p., 1699.

———. *Nazarenus: Or, Jewish, Gentile, and Mahometan Christianity.* 2nd ed. London: J. Brotherton, J. Roberts, and A. Dodd, 1718.

Uhlhorn, Gerhard. "Die älteste Kirchengeschichte in der Darstellung der Tübinger Schule: Eine Übersicht." *JDTh* 3 (1858): 280–349.

Voigt, Christoph. *Der englische Deismus in Deutschland: Eine Studie zur Rezeption englisch-deistischer Literatur in deutschen Zeitschriften und Kompendien des 18. Jahhunderts.* BHT 121. Tübingen: Mohr (Siebeck), 2003.

Wette, Wilhelm Martin Leberecht de. *Biblische Dogmatik Alten und Neuen Testaments.* 3rd ed. Berlin: G. Reimer, 1831.

F. C. Baur's Place in the Study of Jewish Christianity

David Lincicum

1. Introduction

Ferdinand Christian Baur was born in 1792 and died in 1860, having lived in Württemberg in southwest Germany his whole life. After teaching briefly at the lower seminary in Blaubeuren, he was called to be professor of theology at the University of Tübingen in 1826, where he remained until his death thirty-four years later. Throughout his career, he produced an astonishingly wide range of work (Emanuel Hirsch reportedly counted 16,000 printed pages), on subjects ranging from the history and philosophy of religion to the critical study of the New Testament, from multi-volume works in the history of dogma to treatises on church history and polemical writings directed against his various detractors.[1] If one could claim that his work as a whole has an overriding theme, one could do worse than to suggest the relationship between history and theology—or perhaps better, the radical historicity of theology.

In this contribution I intend to examine one narrow but influential slice of that historical theological work: Baur's conception of Jewish Chris-

---

1. See the bibliography of Baur's works in Peter C. Hodgson, *The Formation of Historical Theology: A Study of Ferdinand Christian Baur* (Makers of Modern Theology; New York: Harper & Row, 1966), 285–91; Horton Harris, *The Tübingen School: A Historical and Theological Investigation of the School of F. C. Baur* (Oxford: Oxford University Press, 1975; repr., Grand Rapids: Baker, 1990), 263–74; note also Klaus Schuffels, "Der Nachlass Ferdinand Christian Baurs in der Universitätsbibliothek Tübingen und im Schiller-Nationalmuseum Marbach/Neckar," *ZKG* 79 (1968): 375–84. On Hodgson's work, see K. Penzel, "Will the Real Ferdinand Christian Baur Please Stand Up?" *JR* 48 (1968): 310–23.

tianity. Given the importance for the theme of two essays Baur published in 1831, it is necessary to focus attention on these works, especially seeking to locate his approach to Jewish Christianity among the work of his predecessors in search of Baur's distinctive contribution. I will then proceed to examine the phenomenon of Jewish Christianity in his later works and draw some general conclusions.

2. Baur in the Study of Jewish Christianity

When one examines the expansive and expanding literature on the phenomenon of Jewish Christianity, one quickly realizes that even the object of study itself is under debate: what precisely does the term *Jewish Christianity* refer to? Should the term be defined with reference to praxis (e.g., Torah observance), theology (e.g., belief in a human but not divine Messiah), ethnic background, geographical location in Palestine, chronology (before the destruction of the temple in 70 C.E.) or perhaps simply in terms of a Jewish or Semitic "conceptual frame of reference"?[2]

---

2. For histories of research on Jewish Christianity, see A. F. J. Klijn, "The Study of Jewish Christianity," *NTS* 20 (1974): 419–31; Gerd Lüdemann, *Opposition to Paul in Jewish Christianity* (trans. M. E. Boring; Minneapolis: Fortress, 1989), 1–32, 214–34; S. C. Mimouni, "Le judéo-christianisme ancien dans l'historiographie du XIXème et du XXème siècle," *REJ* 151 (1992): 419–28; H. Lemke, *Judenchristentum zwischen Ausgrenzung und Integration: Zur Geschichte eines exegetischen Begriffes* (Hamburger Theologische Studien 25; Münster: Lit, 2001); James Carleton Paget, "The Definition of the Term 'Jewish Christian'/'Jewish Christianity' in the History of Research," in *Jews, Christians and Jewish Christians in Antiquity* (WUNT 251; Tübingen: Mohr Siebeck, 2010), 289–324. For current approaches to Jewish Christianity, see, e.g., C. Colpe, "Das deutsche Wort 'Judenchristentum' und ihm entsprechende Sachverhalte," in *Das Siegel der Propheten: Historische Beziehungen zwischen Judentum, Judenchristentum, Heidentum und frühen Islam* (Arbeiten zur neutestamentlichen Theologie und Zeitgeschichte 3; Berlin: Institut Kirche und Judentum, 1990), 38–58; S. C. Mimouni, "Pour une définition nouvelle du judéo-christianisme ancien," *NTS* 38 (1992): 161–86; J. Carleton Paget, "Jewish Christianity," in *The Cambridge History of Judaism* (ed. W. Horbury, W. D. Davies, and J. Sturdy; Cambridge: Cambridge University Press, 1999), 3:731–75; G. Stemberger, "Judenchristen," *RAC* 19:228–45; M. Jackson-McCabe, "What's in a Name? The Problem of 'Jewish Christianity,'" in *Jewish Christianity Reconsidered* (ed. M. Jackson-McCabe; Minneapolis: Fortress, 2007), 7–38, 305–10; D. Boyarin, "Rethinking Jewish Christianity: An Argument for Dismantling a Dubious Category (To Which Is Appended a Correction of My Border Lines)," *JQR* 99 (2009): 7–36; J. Frey, "Zur Vielgestaltigkeit judenchristlicher Evangelienüberlieferungen," in *Jesus in*

Especially given the contested nature of the field, it is only natural to turn to the history of research for clarification: we may have lost our way, but might our forebears have known the path? Or, to change the metaphor, can a turn *ad fontes* purify the muddied waters of current scholarly contention? In the case of Jewish Christianity, this involves one in a double quest for origins: the origins of a certain story of origins, the beginning of a certain way of thinking about the beginning. In this *forschungsgeschichtliche* impulse, it is not uncommon to see Baur hailed as the originator of the concept. So, for example, A. F. J. Klijn, writing in 1974, says baldly: "Modern study of Jewish Christianity began with F. C. Baur in 1830."[3] Shortly after him, Stanley Riegel speaks of Baur as "the first to study Jewish Christianity as an entity."[4] Joan Taylor, in the course of an article questioning the utility of the term *Jewish Christianity*, is likewise explicit about her understanding of the roots of the concept: "The idea of a somehow 'Jewish' Christianity standing apart from a Gentile Church originated in the concepts of the Tübingen school, a hundred and sixty years ago."[5] Other examples could easily be adduced.[6]

It may come as a surprise, then, when we turn to Baur's 1831 essays, expecting to find there the *wissenschaftliche* equivalent of *creatio ex nihilo*, only to discover … his essays have footnotes! The fact that Baur's dependence upon predecessors was for so long overlooked may have more to do with a certain style of nineteenth-century footnote that appears to be designed to conceal as much as to reveal than anything else, but we have in fact seen a renewed interest in the predecessors of Baur in the study of

---

apokryphen *Evangelienüberlieferungen: Beiträge zu außerkanonischen Jesusüberlieferungen aus verschiedenen Sprach- und Kulturtraditionen* (ed. J. Frey and J. Schröter; WUNT 254; Tübingen: Mohr Siebeck, 2010), 93–137, esp. 94–98.

3. Klijn, "The Study of Jewish Christianity," 419; for "1830," one should probably understand "1831."

4. Stanley K. Riegel, "Jewish Christianity: Definitions and Terminology," *NTS* 24 (1977–78): 411.

5. Joan E. Taylor, "The Phenomenon of Early Jewish-Christianity: Reality or Scholarly Invention?" *VC* 44 (1990): 314.

6. E.g., Anette Rudolph, "Die Judenchristen in Justins Dialog mit Tryphon," in *Studia Patristica XXXVI* (ed. M. F. Wiles and E. J. Yarnold; Louvain: Peeters, 2001), 300–306, esp. 300–302; cf. also Lüdemann, *Opposition to Paul*, who is not unaware of Baur's predecessors but still thinks it justified to begin his survey of research of Jewish Christianity with Baur.

Jewish Christianity.[7] The recovery of an earlier phase of investigation into the phenomenon of Jewish Christianity leads, in fact, away from German shores, and to England.

Two English Deists in particular wrote works which examined the phenomenon of Jewish Christianity: John Toland's *Nazarenus: Or, Jewish, Gentile, and Mahometan Christianity*, first published in 1718, and Thomas Morgan's *The Moral Philosopher* (3 vols., 1737–1740).[8] It would be fair to describe each of these works as curious and lumbering, but this should not obscure the innovative way in which the apostolic era is conceived by both authors. Toland contended that the earliest Christianity was Jewish Christianity and that Paul came into conflict with this original Christianity by means of his preaching against the law. In fact, Toland identifies Paul as the target of the *Epistula Petri* prefixed to the Pseudo-Clementine *Homilies*, which speaks of an ἐχθρὸς ἄνθρωπος.[9] The earliest Christians were known interchangeably as Nazarenes or Ebionites, and the early church was therefore marked by a plurality of parties standing in tension with one another. Ultimately, however, a peaceful resolution was achieved, reflected in Acts 15, and both gospels—to the circumcised and to the uncircumcised—were allowed to coexist within the church. Morgan similarly sees

---

7. See esp. Lemke, *Judenchristentum*, and Carleton Paget, "Definition of the Term."

8. J. Toland, *Nazarenus: Or, Jewish, Gentile and Mahometan Christianity* (2nd ed.; London: J. Brotherton, J. Roberts, and A. Dodd, 1718), recently reedited twice, each with an extended introduction: Gesine Palmer, *Ein Freispruch für Paulus: John Tolands Theorie des Judenchristentums, mit einer Neuausgabe von Tolands Nazarenus von Claus-Michael Palmer* (Arbeiten zur neutestamentlichen Theologie und Zeitgeschichte 7; Berlin: Institut Kirche und Judentum, 1996); J. Champion, ed., *John Toland: Nazarenus* (British Deism and Free Thought 1; Oxford: Voltaire Foundation, 1999). Note also Henning Graf Reventlow, "Judaism and Jewish Christianity in the Works of John Toland," in *Proceedings of the Sixth World Congress of Jewish Studies III* (Jerusalem: World Union of Jewish Studies, 1977), 111–16; and M. Wiener, "John Toland and Judaism," *HUCA* 16 (1941): 215–42.

The second and third volumes of *The Moral Philosopher in a Dialogue between Philalethes a Christian Deist and Theophanes a Christian Jew* carry on controversy with Morgan's detractors. See Morgan, *The Moral Philosopher in a Dialogue* (3 vols.; London: n.p., 1737–1740). Cf. David Patrick, "Two English Forerunners of the Tübingen School: Thomas Morgan and John Toland," *Theological Review* 14 (1877): 562–603; Carleton Paget, "Definition of the Term," 293–97 (to whom I am indebted for drawing Patrick's article to my attention).

9. Toland, *Nazarenus*, letter 1, chap. 8: Champion, *John Toland: Nazarenus*, 148–50; Palmer, *Nazarenus*, 45–46.

the early church as marked by irreparable divisions between Paul and the Jewish apostles, though he argues that Paul is the one who stands in concert with Jesus, while the Jewish apostles have failed to perceive the universal impulse of Jesus' message (including, it should be added, the import of this for their continued reverence of the Old Testament).[10] It is also worth noting that, for Morgan, Paul becomes the great proponent of freethinking. As Morgan writes, "The Truth is, that St. Paul was the great Freethinker of his Age, and the brave defender of Reason against Authority."[11] His opposition to Peter at Antioch signifies a vote of protest: the individual conscience against Peter, the first pope, and the implicit ecclesiastical institutional authority of Jerusalem (or in the murky shadows, Rome or Canterbury) threatening from a distance. One notes a certain Pauline self-conception, or perhaps, if one may pardon the phrase, a self-like-Paul conception, in such statements—and this is a rhetoric which is not, as we shall see, foreign to Baur.

But Toland and Morgan are writing in English in the first half of the eighteenth century; this still leaves a gap of a hundred years and a foreign language between Baur and the English Deists. Whether Baur himself can read English is questionable, and he does not apparently find occasion to cite English texts—a favor that many English-speaking theologians have been only too happy to return. Certainly there is nowhere he evinces direct influence from either Toland or Morgan. Any influence from the English Deists must, it seems, be indirect.[12]

---

10. Patrick, "Two English Forerunners," 581–83, supplies nine points of convergence between Baur and Morgan: (1) Gal 2 is the central text; (2) the controversy at Antioch between Peter and Paul is the outcome of a standing controversy; (3) Paul has a different gospel from that of the twelve; (4) both Morgan and Baur have a similar view of the questions in dispute; (5) Paul's assertion of his apostleship is against the twelve; (6) the four requirements of the apostolic decree correspond to requirements for "proselytes of the gate"; (7) Morgan is closer, according to Patrick, to Schwegler than to Baur in viewing the Jewish side as developing into Catholicism; (8) the canon was a late formation of the Catholics, though Morgan does not know Baur's mediating books; (9) the apocalypse is by John and Jewish Christian—and so parochial rather than universal.

11. Morgan, *Moral Philosopher*, 1:71; I owe knowledge of the citation to Patrick, "Two English Forerunners," 572.

12. In the following, I am indebted to some of the general lines of influence traced in Lemke, *Judenchristentum*, and Carleton Paget, "Definition of the Term," though my analysis differs in the contours of its argument.

As it happens, during the eighteenth century one sees a rise in the reading, sales, and translation of English books in Germany. As the literary historian Bernhard Fabian has written,

> In the long history of intellectual exchanges between England and Germany the eighteenth century stands out as a period of special significance. It was a period in which Germany assimilated the contemporary literature of England to an extent and with an intensity that has few parallels in the relations between two national cultures. The flow of ideas began in the last decades of the seventeenth century and continued uninterrupted throughout the eighteenth into the early part of the nineteenth.[13]

Although the demand for French books continually exceeded the demand for English books throughout the eighteenth century,[14] the works of both Toland and Morgan were discussed and debated in German theological circles. While still a young man, the eminent historian Johann Lorenz Mosheim penned an early attack against Toland in 1722.[15] The fourth volume of U. G. Thorschmid's *Freydenker-Bibliothek*, published in 1767, contains nearly one hundred pages summarizing Toland's *Nazarenus* and the reaction to it.[16] The reaction to Thomas Morgan's *Moral Philosopher*

---

13. Bernhard Fabian, "English Books and Their Eighteenth-Century German Readers," in *Selecta Anglicana: Buchgeschichtliche Studien zur Aufnahme der englischen Literatur in Deutschland im Achtzehnten Jahrhundert* (Veröffentlichungen des Leipziger Arbeitskreises zur Geschichte des Buchwesens; Schriften und Zeugnisse zur Buchgeschichte 6; Wiesbaden: Harrassowitz, 1994), 11.

14. Ibid., 36.

15. Mosheim, *Vindiciae antiquae Christianorum disciplinae* (2nd ed.; Hamburg: B. Schiller and J. C. Kisner, 1722). Baur later discusses Mosheim as a historian without mentioning his polemic against the Deists in "The Epochs of Church Historiography," in *Ferdinand Christian Baur on the Writing of Church History* (ed. Peter C. Hodgson; New York: Oxford University Press, 1968), 142–52.

16. U. G. Thorschmid, *Versuch einer vollständigen Engelländischen Freydenker-Bibliothek* (Cassel: Johann Friedrich Hemmerde, 1766–1767), 4:188–277; cf. Christopher Voigt, *Der englische Deismus in Deutschland: Eine Studie zur Rezeption englisch-deistischer Literatur in deutschen Zeitschriften und Kompendien des 18. Jahrhunderts* (BHT 121; Tübingen: Mohr Siebeck, 2003), 226; cf. 174–200. In the fifth volume, Thorschmid intended to discuss Morgan (together with Bernard de Mandeville) but this never appeared; cf. Voigt, *Der englische Deismus*, 184. For other German reviews and reactions to Toland's *Nazarenus*, see Voigt, *Der englische Deismus*, 53–56.

was less explosive, but still significant.[17] Of course, Tübingen in the eighteenth century was not quite a hotbed of Enlightenment thinking, a sort of Göttingen of the south. In fact, an official document from 1757 in the Tübingen Stiftsbibliothek offers the guidance that Deist books should only be read for the purpose of refutation.[18] It is intriguing that a Württemberg contemporary of Baur's, Gotthard Victor Lechler, should publish the first history of English Deism just a decade after Baur's essay on the Christ-party at Corinth appeared.[19] What is more intriguing, however, is the fact that Lechler thanks Baur in the preface for his help in securing the Deist literature necessary for his study.[20] Though we have no way of knowing precisely which Deist works were lacking in Tübingen, this may offer some small confirmation of the suggestion that Deist influence on Baur was indirect.

---

17. Jan van den Berg, "English Deism and Germany: The Thomas Morgan Controversy," *JEH* 59 (2008): 48–61. He criticizes Voigt, *Der englische Deismus*, for ignoring Morgan (51 n. 20).

18. Martin Brecht, "Die Entwicklung der Alten Bibliothek des Tübinger Stifts in ihren theologie- und geistesgeschichtlichen Zusammenhang: Eine Untersuchung zur württembergischen Theologie," *Blätter für württembergische Kirchengeschichte* 63 (1963): 71.

19. Gotthard Victor Lechler, *Geschichte des englischen Deismus* (Stuttgart: J. G. Cotta, 1841). Lechler's work was reviewed by E. Zeller in the third fascicle of the first volume of the *Theologische Jahrbücher*, which appeared in 1842 (pp. 574–87), though Zeller does not discuss the views of Jewish Christianity of Toland and Morgan. *Pace* Carleton Paget ("Definition of the Term," 296 n. 30), Lechler does interact with Toland's *Nazarenus*, but relegates it to an appendix (469–72).

20. After thanking Baur, he goes on to write, "Es wurde nämlich der in den öffentlichen Bibliotheken von Tübingen und Stuttgart noch nicht vorhandene Theil der deistischen und antideistischen Literatur für die Universitätsbibliothek erworben, indem die Bücher unmittelbar aus London bezogen wurden. Was auch so noch zu vermissen war, holte ich in England im vorigen Jahre nach, wobei ich übrigens mich überzeugte, dass die grossen Bibliotheken, des *British Museum* zu London, die *Bodlean* [sic] zu Oxford, und die öffentliche Bibliothek zu Cambridge, wenn auch an antideistischer, doch nicht an deistischer Literatur Wesentliches enthalten, das mir zuvor entgangen wäre" (*Geschichte*, iv). Carleton Paget ("Definition of the Term," 296 n. 30) has also posed the question why Lechler refrained from calling attention to the similarities between Toland and Morgan's views and those of Baur; it may be that he initially refrains from doing so out of the personal debt he owes Baur, though this did not restrain him from publishing his *Apostolisches und Nachapostolisches Zeitalter* against Baur ten years later.

It is possible, however, to draw a connecting line between the English Deists and the Halle neologian Johann Salomo Semler (1725–1791). David Patrick, in a learned article from 1877, labors to demonstrate that Semler knew Toland and Morgan by means of his presence in Halle when a debate concerning their work took place, or by Semler's role as a reviewer for the *Nachrichten von einer Hallischen Bibliothek* when the works of Toland and Morgan were reviewed. This is entirely plausible, but it is now also possible to add to this several references to works by Toland and Morgan in works written or edited by Semler.[21] Of course, these are not always complimentary references, but they are sufficient to demonstrate that Semler knew their works. This becomes significant when one observes Semler's striking conception of early Christianity as marked by competing parties—or, as he sometimes calls them, different dioceses—the Judaizing and the Pauline.[22]

---

21. Semler mentions Morgan and/or Toland in his *Apparatus ad liberalem Novi Testamenti interpretationem* (Halle: J. Godofredi Trampii, 1767), 24–25; *Christliche freye Untersuchung über die so genannte Offenbarung Johannis aus der nachgelassenen Handschrift eines fränkischen Gelehrten herausgegeben* (Halle: Johann Christian Hendel, 1769), 314; *Institutio ad doctrinam christianam liberaliter discendam* (Halle: Carl Hermann Hemmerde, 1774), 78–82 (sec. 44); *Versuch einer freiern theologischen Lehrart* (Halle: Carl Hermann Hemmerde, 1777), 74–75. For Semler's oppositional understanding of early Christianity, Patrick ("Two English Forerunners," 596–97) further points to Semler's *Praefatio ad illustrandam catholicae ecclesiae originem*, which is prefixed to Semler's *Paraphrasis in Epistolam II. Petri, et Epistolam Iudae* (Halle: Hemmerde, 1784).

22. On Semler's view of two parties, see, e.g., his *Abhandlung von freier Untersuchung des Canon* (Halle: Carl Hermann Hemmerde, 1771–76), 4:b8(1–2): "Es ist aus den ältesten uns noch übrigen Schriften erweislich, daß es lange Zeit eine Partey von Christen gegeben, die zu der Diöces von Palästina gehöret, folglich Schriften dieser Apostel, welche unter die Beschneidung eigentlich ihre Dienste verwendeten, angenommen haben; und an diese Christen, die zu Jacobi, Petri, Diöces gehöreten, hat Paulus seine Briefe nicht gerichtet; sie hat also auch sie nicht unter ihren Lehrschriften gehabt. Dagegen hat die Partey Christen, welch zu Pauli Diöces gehöreten, auch gar wol gewust, daß Jacobus, Petrus, Judas, an sie keine Briefe geschickt hatten; sie haben folglich diese Schriften auch nicht unter ihren Gemeinden aufweisen und einfüren können. Beide Parteien sind Christen, und haben sich von den Juden abgesondert; aber die Denkungsart der palästinischen Judenchristen ist noch niedriger, und an mancherley locale Ideen und geringe Bilder gewönet, als daß andere Christen, welche nicht unter diesen Einwonern leben, eben diese Lehrart für sich." Also, in the same place, Semler recognizes the Pseudo-Clementine *Homilies* and *Recognitions* as reflecting the Petrine-Pauline conflict. Note also idem, *D. Joh. Salomo Semlers Lebenbeschreibung von ihm selbst abgefaßt* (2 vols.; Halle: 1781–1782), 2:27; cf. S. Alkier,

In his investigations on the canon, Semler anticipates Baur's tendency criticism by judging the nature of the books by whether they appeared more Judaizing or Pauline, or were involved in a process of uniting the two parties.[23] Semler's views do, in fact, seem to prefigure Baur's nicely. Might this suggest a direct influence of Semler on Baur?

Such influence is of course not unlikely but difficult to prove. Martin Brecht has demonstrated the influence of Semler and Neologie on the Tübinger Stift of the late eighteenth and early nineteenth centuries,[24] and it is possible that Baur has received Semler's conclusions secondhand through his teachers or those whom he read.[25] In the end, of course, whether Semler's conclusions reached Baur directly or by circuitous means is immaterial.

Finally, if we want to know the most proximate sources for Baur's conception of Jewish Christianity, we should attend to those works that he himself cites.[26] Restricting our attention to the year 1831, when Baur's first

---

Urchristentum: Zur Geschichte und Theologie einer exegetischen Disziplin (BHT 83; Tübingen: Mohr Siebeck, 1993), 34–40.

23. See Patrick, "English Forerunners," 597; cf. also R. W. MacKay, *The Tübingen School and Its Antecedents* (London: Williams & Norgate, 1863), 97; Adolf Hilgenfeld, "Ferdinand Christian Baur nach seiner wissenschaftlichen Entwickelung und Bedeutung," *ZWT* 36.1 (1893): 223, 232; note further those cited in Lemke, *Judenchristentum*, 260. Samuel Davidson, *The Canon of the Bible: Its Formation, History and Fluctuations* (3rd ed.; London: Kegan Paul, 1880), 247–51, already places Baur as a follower of Morgan, Toland, and Semler, though with more success than either Morgan or Toland. Likewise, in an off-handed manner, Robert Morgan notes that "Semler introduced Morgan's theory (1737–40) about the difference between Pauline and Petrine Christianity into Germany, and the door was opened for the modern historical study of the epistle [i.e., Romans], beginning with F. C. Baur's essay (untranslated) on its 'purpose and occasion' (1836)" (*Romans* [NTG; Sheffield: Sheffield Academic Press, 1995], 142–43). Perhaps here Morgan is dependent on O. Pfleiderer, whose 1885 Hibbert Lectures contain a section entitled, "Morgan, Semler, Baur"?

24. Martin Brecht, "Entwicklung der Alten Bibliothek," 76–84, citing H. E. G. Paulus, *Skizzen aus meiner Bildungs- und Lebensgeschichte zum Andenken an mein 50 jähriges Jubiläum* (Heidelberg: Karl Groos, 1839).

25. Though it is a mere argument from silence, it is perhaps worth noting that, when Baur discusses Semler in his 1852 work on the *Epochs of Church Historiography* (ET 153–62), a version of lectures delivered in the previous decade, he mentions neither English deists nor Semler's view of Pauline and Judaizing influences in early Christianity.

26. Between Semler and Baur, one might mention works on Jewish Christianity by H. E. G. Paulus, Christian Wilhelm Flügge, W. M. L. de Wette, Johann Ernst Chris-

real forays into the study of Jewish Christianity began, what do we gain by examining Baur's sources in his two essays that year, *De Ebionitarum origine et doctrina, ab Essenis repetenda* and his essay on the Christ-party in the Corinthian church? Four conclusions are worth emphasizing; together they pose the question of Baur's originality afresh.

First, we see that the language of "parties" to describe groups in early Christianity is widespread. Following on from Toland, Morgan, and Semler, we see Jewish Christians spoken of as a "party" (*partey*) by, for example, Lobegott Lange, who conceives of them as ethnically Jewish Christians who keep the law and had a view of Christ as merely human.[27] The extent, however, to which such parties are at odds with each other remains a matter of dispute. Lange himself claims that, while Paul can be seen as an opponent of Jewish Christianity, in raising the particularism of Judaism to a universal religion, he is only following the lead of the apostle Peter.[28]

Second, we encounter a discussion about different types of Jewish Christianity. Both Karl Ludwig Gieseler and August Neander propose a distinction between Nazarenes, tolerant Jewish Christians who think that Jews should keep the Torah but not Gentiles, on the one hand, and Ebionites, who think all Christians should observe the Law, on the other.[29] Paul's opponents are of the latter variety, though Gieseler appears to suggest that the Jewish apostles are of the former, tolerant variety.[30] The schism in early

tian Schmidt, and August Neander (see Lemke, *Judenchristentum*, 237–49); but it is especially the last two who are of importance to Baur. Lemke, however, fails to mention Gieseler and Credner, both important figures in the discussion of Jewish Christianity in the early nineteenth century. More surprising, she neglects to mention Baur's work *De Ebionitarum origine et doctrina, ab Essenis repetenda* (Tübingen: Hopferi de L'Orme, 1831).

27. Lobegott Lange, *Die Judenchristen, Ebioniten und Nikolaiten der apostolischen Zeit und das Verhältnis der neutestamentlichen Schriften zu ihnen historisch und exegetisch beleuchtet* (vol. 1 of *Beyträge zur ältesten Kirchengeschichte*; Leipzig: J. A. Barth, 1828); see esp. 13–32; 63–92; referenced in Baur, *De Ebionitarum*, 5 n. 3.

28. Cf. Lange, *Judenchristen*, 72–73.

29. Karl Ludwig Gieseler, "Über die Nazaräer und Ebioniten," *AANKG* 4.2 (1820): 279–330; August Neander, "Beylage: Über die Pseudoclementinischen Homilien, ein Beitrag zur Geschichte der Ebioniten," in his *Genetische Entwickelung der vornehmsten gnostischen Systeme* (Berlin: F. Dümmler, 1818), 361–421. Both are referenced in Baur, *De Ebionitarum*, 3–4.

30. Gieseler, "Über die Nazaräer," 317.

Christianity is not simply Paul versus the Jewish Christians but rather a schism, of which Paul is at least a partial cause, within Jewish Christianity itself: one line becoming Nazarenes, the other Ebionites. Lange mentions the view (with which he disagrees) that Peter changes his mind at Antioch once he hears from James and decides that all Christians, regardless of their ethnicity, must keep the Mosaic law: this could be described, using Gieseler's terms, as a conversion from Nazarene theology to Ebionite theology. One can observe, however, disagreements about whether both types of Jewish Christianity are present in the apostolic age, or only arise later.

Third, we find a general recognition of the relevance of the Pseudo-Clementine literature, together with the possibility, already noted by Toland and Semler, of its containing an anti-Pauline polemic. Neander countenances the possibility of an anti-Pauline polemic behind the portrayal of Simon Magus, but he is not ultimately convinced.[31] D. von Cölln, on the contrary, suggests that in *Hom.* 18.11 "the Clementine Peter contends against the Pauline principle" that one must love God rather than fear him. Likewise, Paul is certainly to be seen behind the figure of Simon Magus.[32] Von Cölln also suggests that the Pseudo-Clementine literature has its roots in Ebionite circles and may reflect the tensions of the late second century. Indeed, in his standard edition, Cotelier had ascribed the *Recognitions* to the second century: "secundo saeculo composite."[33]

---

31. Neander, "Über die Pseudoclementinischen Homilien," 364.

32. D. von Cölln, "Clementina," in *Allgemeine Encyclopädie der Wissenschaften und Künste* (ed. J. S. Ersch and J. G. Gruber; Leipzig: Johann Friedrich Gleditsch, 1828), 18:39. The article is referenced in Baur, "Die Christuspartei in der korinthischen Gemeinde, der Gegensatz des petrinischen und paulinischen Christentums in der ältesten Kirche, der Apostel Petrus in Rom," *Tübinger Zeitschrift für Theologie* 4 (1831): 133–35.

33. J.-B. Cotelier, *SS. Patrum qui temporibus apostolicis floruerunt, Barnabae, Clementis, Hermae, Ignatii, Polycarpi opera edita et non edita, vera et supposita, graece et latine, cum notis* (rev. ed.; ed. J. Leclerc; Antwerp: Huguetanorum sumtibus, 1698), 484. Note Baur, "Christuspartei," 116–36. Other elements of the Pseudo-Clementine *Homilies* were more contentious, not least Baur's later use of them as a witness to Christian Gnosticism, following Neander; for a full history of research, including Baur and Neander, see esp. F. Stanley Jones, "The Pseudo-Clementines: A History of Research," *SecCent* 2 (1982): 69–70. On the question of approaches to Jewish Christianity in the *Pseudo-Clementines*, see Jones, "Pseudo-Clementines," 84–96. Jones also notes that "subsequent research has antiquated most of the details in Baur's description of the place of the PsCl in the history of the early church" (86).

Fourth, and finally, even one of Baur's key interpretative moves in his essay on the Christ-party at Corinth, the reduction of four parties to two, had been anticipated over thirty years previously. Baur cites a short essay by Johann Ernst Christian Schmidt in which he contends that the Pauline and the Apollo parties are one, and the Petrine and Christ parties are one,[34] the latter being Jewish Christians. It would also be possible to point to the analogy of Semler's reduction of the two parties, Nazarenes and Ebionites, to one party, to which Gieseler refers.[35]

Turning now, with this context in mind, to Baur's essay on the Christ-party at Corinth, we find that Baur's contribution, while not to be downplayed, is perhaps less innovative than one might have been led to believe by the claims of *creatio ex nihilo* with which this contribution began. When Baur suggests, "Let us investigate first of all the question in what the chief opposition between the Pauline and Petrine parties consisted," he answers, perhaps tellingly, that "Usually [*gewöhnlich*] the Petrine party has been taken as a strictly judaising party."[36] This seems to imply Baur's awareness of his siding with an extant interpretation. Indeed, Baur is also, in this early essay, careful to ascribe the conflict between the Judaizing and Pauline parties not to the Jewish apostles themselves, but to their followers.[37] Likewise, perhaps one of the most contestable of Baur's interpretative moves, the two-sided assumption that there are agitators being

---

34. Johann Ernst Christian Schmidt, "Über die Stelle I Kor. I, 12. und die ursprüngliche Bedeutung des Namens χριστιανοι," in *Bibliothek für Kritik und Exegese des neuen Testaments und älteste Christengeschichte* (N.p.: In der neuen Gelehrtenbuchhandlung, 1797), 1:86–100: "wenn Paullus in unserer Stelle gleich von vier Partheyen zu redden scheint, so redet er doch nur von zwey; die Paulliner und Apollonier sind Eine, die Petriner und Christianer ebenfalls Eine Parthey" (91). The article is referenced in Baur, "Christuspartei," 76–77, 82–83; and, later, in *Paul*, 1:274–76.

35. Semler, "Geschichte der christlichen Glaubenslehre," preface to vol. 1 of S. J. Baumgarten, *Untersuchung theologischer Streitigkeiten* (ed. J. S. Semler; Halle: Johann Justinus Gebauer, 1762), 210, as cited in Gieseler, "Über die Nazaräer," 281 (which, it will be recalled, Baur cites in his *De Ebionitarum*).

36. Baur, "Christuspartei," 77; cf. 114.

37. "Petrus selbst hatte an dieser seinen Namen in Korinth führenden Partei keinen Antheil, wie schon daraus zu schließen ist, daß Petrus nicht selbst nach Korinth gekommen war, wohl aber müssen, wie aus allem hervorgeht, umherreisende Pseudoapostel, die sich auf den Namen des Petrus beriefen, auch nach Korinth gekommen seyn" (83).

addressed in 1 Corinthians and that these are Judaizing agitators, recalls Schmidt's similar contentions.

At this stage, Baur thinks of the Ebionites as a sect of Jewish Christianity, though later he will come to identify Ebionism with Jewish Christianity.[38] He follows D. von Cölln in ascribing the Pseudo-Clementine *Homilies* to these Ebionites, and in seeing them as containing anti-Pauline polemic.[39] But Baur does not achieve interpretive mileage from the Pseudo-Clementine literature by dating it early (which, by the standard of his day, he does not) but by making the suggestion, again paralleled in von Cölln, that the *Homilies* mark a late development of a process that must have been ongoing. As Baur writes, "The Pauline letters to the Corinthians and the Galatians on the one hand, and the Clementina on the other, mark the outlying points by which it is possible to determine the polemic which arose in the ancient church against the apostle Paul."[40] Between these two points, of course, Baur locates the development of what he takes to be legends concerning Peter's presence in Rome, as evidence of an ongoing anti-Pauline polemic in the early church. An option which Baur does not consider is to follow Neander and Gieseler in distinguishing between Nazarene and Ebionite Jewish Christianity, the former insisting on law keeping only for ethnically Jewish Christians, the latter insisting on Torah observance for all Christians regardless of their ethnicity. Baur does not, however, believe the Nazarenes are attested early.[41] Might Baur have made sense of Peter in Nazarene rather than Ebionite terms? However problematic those terms may now appear, they demonstrate that within Baur's day he had the option of constructing a less oppositional account of Jewish Christianity.[42] The reason he did not may be related to one of the motifs that consistently recurs throughout his later writing on Jewish Christian-

---

38. So he writes that the Pseudo-Clementine *Homilies* are "unläugbar nicht blos ein judenchristliches, sondern ein namentlich mit der Secte der Ebioniten in irgend einem nähern Zusammenhange stehendes Product" (Baur, "Christuspartei," 116). It is Schliemann who points out that originally Ebionites are a sect for Baur, but then they come to be synonymous with Jewish Christianity; see Adolph Schliemann, *Die Clementinen nebst den verwandten Schriften und der Ebionitismus* (Hamburg: Friedrich Perthes, 1844), 368.

39. E.g., Baur, "Christuspartei," 127–28.

40. "Christuspartei," 136.

41. Baur, *De Ebionitarum*, 7–8.

42. Baur does not explicitly define Jewish Christianity, but it seems to involve (1) ethnically Jewish Christians who (2) insist on keeping the Torah and (3) have a

ity: the struggle for universalism. The issue between Paul and his opponents was "whether Judaism should be a material and integrated part of Christianity or not."[43] To Paul is ascribed a "decisive bursting through the constraints of Judaism."[44]

Almost two decades later, Baur, in the course of writing the recent history of the Theology Faculty in Tübingen, had occasion to reflect on his Christ-party essay (which he now tells us had arisen from lectures on the Corinthian epistles). With what now appears as inflated rhetoric, he speaks of how he departed from the previous harmonious conceptions of the apostolic age, how he emphasized the various parties and their tendencies, and how he looked on the Catholic Church as something that could only emerge at the end of a long historical process.[45] It is not without irony that one can point out the tendencies reflected in Baur's writing of a victor's history. The Christ-party essay was important as a synthesis of previous work, an integration of various independent theses in the service of the whole. But mostly it is important in retrospect as, in Zeller's words, "die ersten schüchternen Flügelschläge"—the first timid beating of the wings.[46]

---

particularistic rather than universal vision for Christianity. On Baur's view of Jewish Christianity, see esp. Lemke, *Judenchristentum*, 257–91.

43. Baur, "Christuspartei," 108.

44. Ibid., 109.

45. See Baur, "Die evangelisch-theologische Fakultät vom Jahr 1812 bis 1848," in *Geschichte und Beschreibung der Universität Tübingen* (ed. K. Klüpfel; Tübingen: L. F. Fues, 1849), 407–408: "sehr abweichend von der hergebrachten Ansicht, welche in der apostolischen Zeit und der unmittelbar auf sie folgenden alles nur in der schönsten Harmonie und Einigkeit, in der gleichmäßigsten Entfaltung vor sich gehen läßt, vielmehr die heterogenen Elemente, in deren Gegensatz sich jene Zeit bewegte, ihre Parteien und Tendenzen, ihre Kämpfe und Vermittlungen nachzuweisen, und überhaupt die Entstehung einer katholischen Kirche nur als das Resultat eines vorangehenden tief eingreifenden geschichtlichen Processes zu begreifen suchte." Cf. Heinz Liebing, "Historical-Critical Theology: In Commemoration of the One Hundredth Anniversary of the Death of Ferdinand Christian Baur, December 2, 1960," *JTC* 3 (1967): 55–69: "In later years Baur repeatedly designated the 1831 essay as the foundation of his total conception of the development of primitive Christianity" (62).

46. E. Zeller, "Ferdinand Christian Baur," in his *Vorträge und Abhandlungen geschitlichen Inhalts* (Leipzig: Fues's Verlag [L. W. Reisland], 1865), 1:414; cf. also Dilthey's comments on the fact that Baur had still not come to all his critical conclusions in the 1831 essay, cited in Lüdemann, *Opposition to Paul*, 218 n. 38.

3. Baur's View of History and Philosophy

Before continuing on to examine the function of Jewish Christianity in Baur's later writings, it is worth pausing briefly to make the point that Baur was not a crass Hegelian who simply imposed a rigid scheme of dialectical oppositions upon history.[47] Baur had undertaken two years of philosophical training in the Tübinger Stift before he came to study theology, and he was especially attracted to the idealist philosophy of Plato, Fichte, and Schelling during those years.[48] In idealist thought, Baur found a way to overcome the dualism with which he had been faced in his theological training: rationalism versus supernaturalism.[49] In Schelling especially, Baur encountered a dialectical thinking that proceeded by way of opposition and mediation.[50] So, for example, in Schelling's *System of Transcendental Idealism*, which Baur had read and recommended to a student by 1822, he found the following type of statement: "This advance from thesis to antithesis, and from thence to synthesis, is therefore originally founded in the mechanism of the mind [which Schelling has been attempting to demonstrate], and so far as it is purely formal (as in scientific method, for

---

47. Against the charge that Baur is simply a crass Hegelian, see Hodgson, *Formation* (note also Penzel, "Real Ferdinand Christian Baur"); Robert Morgan, "F. C. Baur's Lectures on New Testament Theology," *ExpTim* 88 (1977): 202–206; idem, "Baur's *Paul*," *ExpTim* 90 (1978): 4–10; idem, "Non Angli sed Angeli: Some Anglican Reactions to German Gospel Criticism," in *New Studies in Theology*, (ed. S. Sykes and D. Holmes; London: Duckworth, 1980), 1:1–30, esp. 9–10, 28; idem, "Ferdinand Christian Baur," in *Nineteenth Century Religious Thought in the West* (ed. N. Smart et al.; Cambridge: Cambridge University Press, 1985), 1:261–89.

48. Zeller, "Ferdinand Christian Baur," 358–59.

49. This is at least a strong way of reading Baur's emerging idealism; cf. Liebing, "Historical-Critical Theology"; Hodgson, *Formation*; Harris, *Tübingen School*.

50. For the importance of Schelling for Baur, see Zeller, "Ferdinand Christian Baur," 364; Gotthold Müller, "Ferdinand Christian Baur und David Friedrich Strauss in Blaubeuren (1821–1825)," in *Glaube, Geist, Geschichte: Festschrift für Ernst Benz zum 60. Geburtstage am 17. November 1967* (ed. G. Müller and W. Zeller; Leiden: Brill, 1967), 217–30; Carl E. Hester, "Gedanken zu Ferdinand Christian Baurs Entwicklung als Historiker anhand zweier unbekannter Briefe," *ZKG* 84 (1973): 249–69; K. Scholder, "Baur, Ferdinand Christian (1792–1860)," *TRE* 5:353; Carl E. Hester, "Baurs Anfänge in Blaubeuren," in *Historisch-kritische Geschichtsbetrachtung. Ferdinand Christian Baur und seine Schüler* (ed. U. Köpf; Contubernium 40; Sigmaringen: Jan Thorbecke, 1994), 67–82. For Schelling in Baur's later works, note, e.g., *Epochs*, 240–41 n. 1.

example), is abstracted from this original, material sequence established in transcendental philosophy."[51] As a corollary of this, Schelling states that "philosophy can enumerate only those actions which constitute epochs, as it were, in the history of self-consciousness, and establish them in their interrelations with one another."[52] In his early days of teaching—and certainly well before he read Hegel—Baur already operates with an understanding of the opposition of principles as what moves history.[53] In his early work is where Baur utters his famous—perhaps infamous—phrase, "Ohne Philosophie bleibt mir die Geschichte ewig todt und stumm."[54] And in the preface to the first edition (1847) of Baur's *Lehrbuch der christlichen Dogmengeschichte*, written over twenty years later, Baur says: "Only the coarsest empiricism can think that one should simply surrender oneself to the materials, that the objects of historical reflection could be taken just as they lie before us."[55] His philosophical and theological commitments change over time (and such changes are of course a matter of some debate), but whether he is in his Schleiermachian phase, his Hegelian phase, or his late return to Kant, his historical thinking is still marked by the oppositional dialectics that he learned early under the tutelage of Schelling.

4. Jewish Christianity in Baur's Thought after the Christ-Party Essay

The development of Baur's thought through time has been traced often enough, and an attempt to repeat the experiment will not be ventured here. Rather, the rest of this chapter sketches some of the major elements of what Baur calls in the preface to his book on the Gospels, the *Totalanschauung*, especially in so far as these impinge on Baur's view of Jewish

---

51. F. W. J. Schelling, *System of Transcendental Idealism (1800)* (trans. Peter Heath; Charlottesville: University Press of Virginia, 1978), 47; cf. 42–50; originally published as *System des transcendentalen Idealismus* (Tübingen: J. G. Cotta, 1800).

52. Ibid., 50.

53. See esp. Hester, "Baurs Anfänge," with reference to a lecture Baur gave in 1819 entitled "Vergleichung der griechischen und deutschen Nation" just before Christmas (a handwritten manuscript in Baur's Nachlaß in the Universitätsbibliothek Tübingen [Mh 970, 8b]).

54. *Symbolik und Mythologie oder die Naturreligion des Alterthums* (Stuttgart: J. B. Metzler, 1824–25), 1:xi.

55. Cited in Hodgson, *Baur on the Writing of Church History*, 364 n. 45.

Christianity.[56] For this, in the end, is why the Christ-party essay is distinctive, and what marks Baur's work on Jewish Christianity out from his predecessors.

4.1. PRINCIPLE, UNIVERSALISM, AND THE END OF JUDAISM

In his programmatic analysis of the writing of church history, Baur makes clear how he thinks church history should be written. One must grapple with a period or a movement until one has grasped its principle or idea:

> everything proceeds from a starting point in which the Idea that is to be realized through its entire temporal manifestation is clearly and definitely expressed; and once initiated, the development proceeds from one point to another in a continuity in which it should not be difficult to relate everything individual to the Idea that is the basis of the whole, or to determine the relation in which one thing stands to another.[57]

In the *Church History of the First Three Centuries*, which Klaus Scholder calls "perhaps the work which most fully brings together his life's work,"[58] Baur suggests that the Christian principle "looks beyond the outward, the accidental, the particular, and rises to the universal, the unconditioned,

---

56. *Kritische Untersuchungen über die kanonischen Evangelien, ihr Verhältnis zu einander, ihren Charakter und Ursprung* (Tübingen: L. F. Fues, 1847), iv, vi; cf. also "Die evangelisch-theologische Fakultät," 408.

57. *Epochs*, 47–48; cf. 44: "no one can deny it to be in the nature of the case that, whereas on the one hand historical research must immerse itself in the mass of details (not without the danger of losing itself in the particular), on the other hand it must also rise again to the universal, to those Ideas that must be the guiding points of view and illuminating stars on the long journey through the centuries." "Symbolics, rather, seeks to reconstruct the two opposed doctrinal concepts as systems by grasping each in the unity of its principle, for at the root of each system lies a primary determination of the religious consciousness that bears in itself its own well grounded claim to truth." *Der Gegensatz des Katholicismus und Protestantismus nach den Principien und Hauptdogmen der beiden Lehrbegriffe* (2nd ed.; Tübingen: L. F. Fues, 1836), 3, as translated and cited in Joseph Fitzer, *Moehler and Baur in Controversy, 1832–38: Romantic-Idealist Assessment of the Reformation and Counter-Reformation* (AAR Studies in Religion 7; Tallahassee, Fla.: American Academy of Religion, 1974), 45.

58. Scholder, "Baur," 357; Baur, *The Church History of the First Three Centuries* (trans. Allan Menzies; 2 vols.; Theological Translation Fund Library; London: Williams and Norgate, 1878).

the essential."[59] One sees this most clearly in the proclamation of Jesus: the call to love one's neighbor is a privileging of the universal over the particular, the objective over the subjective. In this sense, Baur's summary of Jesus' teaching sounds very Kantian: "This universal is that form of action in accordance with which we do to others what we wish that others should do to us. The morally good is thus that which is equally right and good for all, or which can be the object of action for all alike." And this ethical idealism is a hallmark of Baur's late thought. But his emphasis on universalism as belonging to the essence of Christianity belongs to all stages of Baur's thought. In this light, both paganism and Judaism were sorts of *praeparatio evangelica*. Precisely because Christianity has such a clearly universal mandate, coupled with Baur's understanding of history as teleologically progressing toward a dialectical resolution, he is almost bound to regard Judaism as a dead religion once Christianity is on the scene: "Thus Judaism is nothing more than the religion of the law in contradistinction to Christianity, which is the religion of the spirit. Both its position in the world and its inner constitution declare that the function of Judaism is that of effecting a transition, of filling up an interval."[60] Paul "places Judaism and Christianity together under the light of a great religio-historical contemplation, and of a view of the course of the world before the universal idea of which the particularism of Judaism must disappear."[61] "The particularism of Judaism must disappear"—the political potential of those words is haunting in the shadow of the Holocaust, though it would be unfair to Baur to attribute to him their full import.

But against paganism and Judaism, Christianity is the "absolute religion." To Judaism belong the mere "hollow forms" of religion, because the spirit has outgrown them.[62] The self-revelation of the spirit in history "eliminates more and more completely all that bears the stamp of particularism and subjectivity, we see that it can have no other issue than at the point where the origin of Christianity is found."[63] Paul subsequently becomes "the first to lay down expressly and distinctly the principle of Christian universalism as a thing essentially opposed to Jewish particularism" and sets this principle before him "as the sole standard and rule of

---

59. Baur, *Church History*, 1:33.
60. Ibid., 1:58.
61. Ibid., 1:59.
62. Ibid., 1:10.
63. Ibid., 1:22; cf. 18.

his apostolic activity."[64] This is precisely why Jewish Christianity is such a bother to the apostle: by insisting on the particular, Jewish Christians impede the progress of the divine in history. They are fundamentally hybrid since they partake of that universal principle of Christianity but refuse to allow that principle to flourish and burst the bonds of a constrictive religion that belongs to a past era.

Where does Jewish Christianity therefore have its origin? Is it only based in a misunderstanding? In a remarkable passage in his *Church History*, Baur claims that in fact both the Pauline universalism and the Jewish Christian particularism can trace their roots back to Jesus. In a statement that almost sounds Chalcedonian, in structure if not in content, Baur writes:

> there was the moral universal in him, the unconfined humanity, the divine exaltation, which gave his person its absolute significance. On the other side there was the cramping and narrowing influence of the Jewish national Messianic idea.[65]

Jesus, one might say, clothes himself in Jewish particularism in order to burst it from the inside out. That particularism is basically a concession to the needs of the historical consciousness of the day, but something to be surrendered as soon as possible—like a rocket's fuel tank that can be discarded once the vessel has been propelled along its true course. It is precisely this duality in Jesus that accounts for the duality among his followers.[66] In this sense, then, Jesus does intend to found a new religion.[67]

4.2. JEWISH CHRISTIANITY AND THE DEVELOPMENT OF EARLY CHRISTIANITY

If one wants to press Baur for historical detail about his conception of Jewish Christianity, this is only possible to some extent. He uses the term

---

64. Ibid., 1:47.
65. Ibid., 1:49.
66. Ibid., 1:49–50.
67. In his *Vorlesungen über Neutestamentliche Theologie* (ed. Ferdinand Friedrich Baur; Leipzig: Fues's Verlag, 1864), Baur claims that "Jesus ist Stifter einer neuen Religion; was aber das Wesen einer Religion an sich ausmacht, ist nicht ein dogmatisch ausgebildetes Religionssystem, ein bestimmter Lehrbegriff, es sind nur Grundanschauungen und Principien, Grundsätze und Vorschriften, als unmittelbare Aussagen des religösen Bewusstseins" (45–46, cited in Lemke, *Judenchristentum*, 265).

Judenchristentum assuming that its meaning is self-evident (which, of course, it is not), but clearly it stands in contrast to *Heidenchristentum.*[68] At one point, Baur states that "Jewish Christians were Jews by birth,"[69] and clearly his emphasis falls on the Torah observance upon which they insist for themselves and for new members of the Christian movement. He elsewhere suggests that "[t]he Ebionites ... are just what the Jewish Christians were originally, as distinguished from the Pauline Christians. ... it cannot be deemed an unjustifiable use of the name to say that Jewish Christianity in general was a kind of Ebionitism,"[70] and in context Baur is arguing against Epiphanius's view that the Ebionites did not arise until after the destruction of the temple. In this sense, we observe the completion of the move from seeing the Ebionites as a sect of Jewish Christianity to seeing the Ebionites as, for all intents and purposes, coextensive with Jewish Christianity. Baur does mention "the more tolerantly disposed Nazarenes," but perhaps their tolerant natures do not attract Baur, with his love of conflict, since he does not devote much attention to them.[71] In a footnote, Baur at least mentions Hilgenfeld's view that "the Nazarenes and Ebionites are not so much two separate sects of Jewish Christianity as rather different modifications of the old hostility against Paulinism as it softened down to a more tolerant attitude toward Gentile Christianity."[72]

In broad strokes, Baur's picture of the development of early Christian history is well known. According to Baur's book on *Paul,* which Zeller calls Baur's "Lieblingswerk,"[73] the "bounds of the national Judaism" were a hindrance to the conscious idea of Christianity actualizing itself.[74] After the persecution of Stephen, the Hellenistic part of the church leaves Jerusalem and allows Jewish Christianity to become firmly entrenched there,[75] with

---

68. "Baur verwendet sowohl die Form 'Judenchristen' als auch 'Judenchristentum' wie selbstverständlich und ohne jede ausdrückliche Erklärung oder Einführung" (Lemke, *Judenchristentum*, 274).

69. Baur, *Church History*, 1:107–8

70. Ibid., 1:181, 182; cf. 181–83.

71. Ibid., 1:182.

72. Ibid., 1:182 n. 3; further on the Ebionites, see *Church History*, 1.89–92, including discussion of the Pseudo-Clementine *Homilies* and *Recognitions* and the famous identification of Simon Magus with Paul which we observed in Baur's earlier essay on the Christ-party at Corinth.

73. Zeller, "Ferdinand Christian Baur," 366.

74. Baur, *Paul*, 1:3.

75. Ibid., 1:39–42.

Peter in due course becoming "the head of the Judaizers."[76] The subsequent conflict unfolds in three stages: an initial period of intense conflict between the Pauline and Judaizing parties; the authentic Pauline letters (the four so-called *Hauptbriefe*) belong to this earliest phase,[77] as does John's Revelation on the Jewish Christian side, which contains, on Baur's view, anti-Pauline polemic.[78]

In the time after Nero's persecutions, there was a second period in which the prevailing tendency was to "bring the two opposing parties nearer to each other, by a process of smoothing down their differences, and finding the mean between their opposing principles."[79] The process of reconciliation, in which each side slowly yielded on its hardened convictions, took some time. So, for example, the requirement of circumcision was abandoned over time as a concession to the historical success of the Gentile mission, though circumcision was now simply exchanged for baptism.[80] As the period of reconciliation presses onward, we meet with a mixed group of Pauline and Jewish compositions: we are told that Hebrews is a product of Jewish Christianity, "but a Jewish Christianity more free and spiritual, which is broad enough to have Paulinism itself as a presupposition."[81] Likewise, the Pastoral Epistles have in view pastoral instructions "in the interest of Paulinism as well as of Jewish Christianity."[82] Over time, Christian universalism became an accepted fact (the idea had been successful in realizing itself, we might say), but there were residual ill feelings toward Paul which caused the impulse toward universalism to be ascribed by, for instance, the book of Acts, to none other than Peter—contrary to Baur's historical knowledge otherwise.[83] Eventually the conflict subsides entirely and the Catholic Church can be regarded as fully estab-

---

76. Ibid., 1:7.

77. In a later period, Baur contends that the Gospel of Luke is, aside from the Pauline epistles, "the purest and most important source we possess for the knowledge of Paulinism." *Church History*, 1:77. If this is reminiscent of Marcion, it is not accidental; cf. 82–84: "In the early history of Paulinism he [i.e., Marcion] is, next to the author of the Gospel of Luke, the most characteristic representative and champion of the pure Pauline principle" (82).

78. Baur, *Church History*, 1:84–87.

79. Ibid., 1:77.

80. Ibid., 1:106–8.

81. Ibid., 1:115.

82. Ibid., 1:128.

83. Ibid., 1:109.

lished; and here Johannine Christianity represents a form of Christian consciousness beyond the Judaizing–Pauline divide.

Nevertheless, it would be a mistake to read this process of development as suggesting merely that the error of Jewish Christianity opposes the truth of Paulinism until the latter eventually wins out. In disagreement with Ritschl, Baur contends that "Jewish Christianity is necessary for Paulinism."[84] Baur is certainly clear that Paulinism is the "higher principle," and he does not attempt to hide his loyalties, but he does suggest that "neither of the two tendencies is absolutely true; each has its justification as against the other."[85] Thus, the productivity of this tension should be kept in view, and one should not allow the naturally more one-sided exposition of Baur's *Paulus* to obscure it.[86]

Finally, it is worth noting that in Baur's reconstructions of pre-Christian Judaism, the most immediate parent of Paul's Jewish nationalistic opponents, Baur is content to see everything through Paul's eyes, making precious little use of the literature of early Judaism itself.[87] "The relation of Christianity to heathenism and Judaism is," according to Baur's Paul, "defined as that between the absolute religion and the preparatory and subordinate forms of religion. We have here the progress from servitude to freedom, from nonage to majority, from the age of childhood to the age of maturity, from the flesh to the spirit."[88] For Baur, Judaism after the advent

---

84. Ibid., 1:102–3.

85. Ibid., 1:103.

86. Among some of the more interesting contentions of Baur's concerning Jewish Christianity in his book on *Paul*: In the Corinthian epistles, "indisputably the same Judaizing opponents [as in Galatians] are in question" (1:267, 269). Of Romans, Baur suggests that "Now in the Epistle to the Romans [Paul] proceeds to do away with the last remaining portion of the Jewish exclusiveness, by taking up and representing it as the mere introduction to the Christian Universalism which extended to all nations" (1.322). Baur goes on to call Rom 9–11 the "centre and pith of the whole, to which everything else is only an addition" (1:327), anticipating in some ways some of the social and ethnic concerns of the New Perspective on Paul. On the relationship of Baur's essays on Corinth and Rome to his book on Paul, see Hodgson, *Formation*, 204–5 n. 15. On Baur's Paul more broadly, see Hodgson, *Formation*, 202–12.

87. On Paul's view of Judaism's relationship to Christianity, see Baur, *Paul* 2:188–204. According to Paul, the "ante-Christian period was the period of the reign of sin; and in this description Judaism is included: in Judaism also sin reigned" (2:188).

88. Baur, *Paul*, 2:212.

of Christianity is simply encased in silence, consigned to the perpetual immaturity of belonging to a bygone age.

4.3. ANTI-CATHOLICISM, ANTI-JUDAISM?

This leads immediately on to the final observation I would like to make: one finds a striking confluence between anti-Catholic rhetoric and anti-Jewish rhetoric in Baur's reconstruction of early Christianity. In fact, Judaism provides a direct inheritance to Catholicism in the form of its hierarchy and external institutions:

> For whence were all those theocratic institutions and aristocratic forms derived, in which the Catholic Church found ready to her hand the elements of her future organisation, and which contained in themselves all the conditions of a power that should conquer the world, whence but from Judaism? ... It was Paulinism that conquered the soil for Catholic Christianity: it was the Pauline mission to the Gentiles which added to the original congregation of the sealed the great multitude of those who came from all nations, and kindreds, and people, and tongues. But it was Jewish Christianity which supplied the forms of organisation and erected the hierarchical edifice upon this basis.[89]

One could be forgiven for confessing to being underwhelmed by this praise of Jewish Christianity, coming, as it does, from a Protestant idealist. But what Baur goes on to say next is telling:

> when Paulinism rebutted the aristocratic claims of Jewish particularism, and destroyed the very root from which these claims sprang, it made the principle of Christian universalism an integral element of the general Christian consciousness. It thus secured for itself, for the whole future of the Church, the power to step forward again and again with all its original keenness and decision, whenever hierarchical Catholicism should again overgrow evangelical Christianity, and offend the original Christian consciousness in its most vital element.[90]

Paulinism's contention with Jewish Christianity elides seamlessly into Protestantism's conflict with Catholicism.

---

89. Baur, *Church History*, 1:112–13.
90. Ibid., 1:113; cf. 113–14.

If we apply Baur's own *Tendenzkritik* to his writings, if we turn back upon him with what Baur once refers to as "the keen-sightedness of Protestant mistrust,"[91] do we see a confluence of anti-Catholicism with anti-Judaism? We should recall that Baur's polemical exchanges with the Catholic theologian Möhler take place during the period that produced Baur's greatest Pauline works.[92] Indeed, often one could simply substitute Protestantism for Paulinism and Catholicism for Jewish Christianity and the essence of his argument would remain the same. For example, one needs merely to place side by side two citations to observe the similarities. In his *Epochs of Church Historiography*, he writes, "Protestantism is the principle of subjective freedom, of the freedom of faith and conscience, of the autonomy of the subject in opposition to the heteronomy of the Catholic conception of the church."[93] And in his *Church History*, commenting on 2 Cor 3:17, he writes,

> The Lord is the spirit: and the spirit is liberty. That is to say, the principle and essence of Paulinism is the emancipation of the consciousness from every authority that is external or exercised through human means, the removal of all confining barriers, the elevation of the spirit to a standpoint where everything lies revealed and open in luminous clearness to its eye, the independence and immediateness of the self-consciousness.[94]

When Baur finally calls "free thinking" the principle of Protestantism,[95] alongside the "emancipation of the consciousness of authority" that Paulinism brings, one cannot help but recall Thomas Morgan and see Baur, like his later disciple Ernst Käsemann, as reading Paul in his own image and seeing himself in the *imago Pauli*.

---

91. Baur, *Epochs*, 87.

92. For a study of the conflict and an analysis of the writings on both sides, see Fitzer, *Moehler and Baur in Controversy*.

93. Baur, *Epochs*, 249. Cf. 250: "From a higher level one can understand for the first time the true significance of a subordinate level, because it now appears for the first time for what it really is—not the whole and complete truth, but only a momentary aspect of the same, through which the Idea in the course of its development must first pass, or a form of consciousness that must first be fully lived in order to be able to move on with the awareness of having the maturity for a higher level."

94. Baur, *Church History*, 1:65.

95. Baur, *Introduction to the History of Christian Dogma*, 362 (in Hodgson, *Baur on Church History*).

5. Conclusions

In conclusion, it is clear that Baur is not the first to study Jewish Christianity or to treat it as an entity. Many of the key interpretative moves in his early essays had been anticipated by exegetes working in the thirty or forty years or so before he wrote. In addition, he stood in a line that stretched back through Semler to Thomas Morgan and John Toland, though we cannot ascertain with any certainty whether he was conscious of following in their footsteps. Nonetheless, if Baur did have his predecessors, he transposes the conversation about Jewish Christianity into a new key by making the study of parties in early Christianity subservient to the *Totalanschauung*, the holistic grasp of the process of the absolute religion establishing itself within history. It is precisely this conviction that enables his historical work to function as theology, and conversely motivates the precise historical work that he attempts.

It is also, we would have to say from our current perspective, what tempts Baur to distort the evidence—though of course one person's distortion is another's interpretation. But can earliest Christianity be seen as determined by the struggle between Pauline and Judaizing tendencies? Baur's reading arguably rests on a tendentious reading of Paul, though it would stray beyond the bounds of this contribution to substantiate this claim. Nonetheless, it is a possible reading of Paul, seen not least in the fact that he has been followed by scholars such as Daniel Boyarin, Gerd Lüdemann, Michael Goulder, and C. K. Barrett—though for Boyarin the universalizing Paul is to be lamented rather than celebrated. One might suggest that Baur's conception of early Christianity is a play with very few characters: the same Jewish Christian opponents lurk behind all of Paul's certainly authentic letters; the plurality of parties at Corinth is really reducible to two; James and Peter are in agreement rather than, as Gal 2 might suggest, in some tension with one another. That tensions existed in early Christianity is undeniable, but today one is prone to see rather more and varied tensions than Baur in his day saw.

Bibliography

Alkier, S. *Urchristentum: Zur Geschichte und Theologie einer exegetischen Disziplin.* BHT 83. Tübingen: Mohr Siebeck, 1993.
Baur, Ferdinand Christian. *The Church History of the First Three Centuries.* Translated by Allan Menzies. 2 vols. Theological Translation Fund Library. London: Williams & Norgate, 1878.

———. *De Ebionitarum origine et doctrina, ab Essenis repetenda.* Tübingen: Hopferi de L'Orme, 1831.

———. *Der Gegensatz des Katholicismus und Protestantismus nach den Principien und Hauptdogmen der beiden Lehrbegriffe.* 2nd ed. Tübingen: L. F. Fues, 1836.

———. "Die Christuspartei in der korinthischen Gemeinde, der Gegensatz des petrinischen und paulinischen Christentums in der ältesten Kirche, der Apostel Petrus in Rom." *TZTh* 4 (1831): 61–206.

———. "Die evangelisch-theologische Fakultät vom Jahr 1812 bis 1848." Pages 389–426 in *Geschichte und Beschreibung der Universität Tübingen.* Edited by K. Klüpfel. Tübingen: L. F. Fues, 1849.

———. *Kirchengeschichte der drei ersten Jahrhunderte.* 3rd ed. Tübingen: L. F. Fues, 1863.

———. *Kritische Untersuchungen über die kanonischen Evangelien, ihr Verhältnis zu einander, ihren Charakter und Ursprung.* Tübingen: L. F. Fues, 1847.

———. *Paul the Apostle of Jesus Christ, His Life and Work, His Epistles and His Doctrine: A Contribution to a Critical History of Primitive Christianity.* 2 vols. Translated by Allan Menzies. London and Edinburgh: Williams & Norgate, 1875.

———. *Paulus, der Apostel Jesu Christi: Sein Leben und Wirken, seine Briefe und seine Lehre, Ein Beitrag zu einer kritischen Geschichte des Urchristenthums.* 1st ed. Stuttgart: Becher und Müller, 1845. 2nd ed. Edited by E. Zeller. 2 vols. Leipzig: Fues's Verlag, 1866–1867.

———. *Symbolik und Mythologie oder die Naturreligion des Alterthums.* 2 vols. Stuttgart: J. B. Metzler, 1824–1825.

———. *Vorlesungen über Neutestamentliche Theologie.* Edited by Ferdinand Friedrich Baur. Leipzig: Fues's Verlag, 1864.

Berg, Jan van den. "English Deism and Germany: The Thomas Morgan Controversy." *JEH* 59 (2008): 48–61.

Boyarin, D. "Rethinking Jewish Christianity: An Argument For Dismantling a Dubious Category (to Which Is Appended a Correction of My Border Lines)." *JQR* 99 (2009): 7–36.

Brecht, Martin. "Die Entwicklung der Alten Bibliothek des Tübinger Stifts in ihren theologie- und geistesgeschichtlichen Zusammenhang: Eine Untersuchung zur württembergischen Theologie." *Blätter für württembergische Kirchengeschichte* 63 (1963): 3–103.

Carleton Paget, James. "The Definition of the Terms 'Jewish Christian'/'Jewish Christianity' in the History of Research." Pages 289–324 in idem, *Jews, Christians and Jewish Christians in Antiquity.* WUNT 251. Tübingen: Mohr Siebeck, 2010. Originally published as "The Definition of the Terms *Jewish Christian* and *Jewish Christianity* in the History of Research." Pages 22–54 in *Jewish Believers in Jesus: The Early Centuries.* Edited by Oskar Skarsaune and Reidar Hvalvik. Peabody, Mass.: Hendrickson, 2007.

———. "Jewish Christianity." Pages 731–75 in *The Early Roman Period.* Vol. 3 of *The Cambridge History of Judaism.* Edited by W. Horbury, W. D. Davies, and J. Sturdy. Cambridge: Cambridge University Press, 1999.

Champion, J., ed. *John Toland: Nazarenus*. British Deism and Free Thought 1. Oxford: Voltaire Foundation, 1999.

Cölln, D. von. "Clementina." Columns 36–44 in vol. 18 of *Allgemeine Encyclopädie der Wissenschaften und Künste*. Edited by J. S. Ersch and J. G. Gruber. Leipzig: Johann Friedrich Gleditsch, 1828.

Colpe, C. "Das deutsche Wort, 'Judenchristentum' und ihm entsprechende Sachverhalte." Pages 38–58 in *Das Siegel der Propheten: Historische Beziehungen zwischen Judentum, Judenchristentum, Heidentum und frühen Islam*. Arbeiten zur neutestamentlichen Theologie und Zeitgeschichte 3. Berlin: Institut Kirche und Judentum, 1990.

Cotelier, J.-B. *SS. Patrum qui temporibus apostolicis floruerunt, Barnabae, Clementis, Hermae, Ignatii, Polycarpi opera edita et non edita, vera et supposita, graece et latine, cum notis*. Rev. ed. Edited by J. Leclerc. Antwerp: Huguetanorum sumtibus, 1698.

Davidson, Samuel. *The Canon of the Bible: Its Formation, History and Fluctuations*. 3rd ed. London: Kegan Paul, 1880.

Fabian, Bernhard. "English Books and Their Eighteenth-Century German Readers." Pages 11–94 in *Selecta Anglicana: Buchgeschichtliche Studien zur Aufnahme der englischen Literatur in Deutschland im Achtzehnten Jahrhundert*. Veröffentlichungen des Leipziger Arbeitskreises zur Geschichte des Buchwesens; Schriften und Zeugnisse zur Buchgeschichte 6. Wiesbaden: Harrassowitz, 1994.

Fitzer, Joseph. *Moehler and Baur in Controversy, 1832–38: Romantic-Idealist Assessment of the Reformation and Counter-Reformation*. AAR Studies in Religion 7. Tallahasse, Fla.: American Academy of Religion, 1974.

Frey, J. "Zur Vielgestaltigkeit judenchristlicher Evangelienüberlieferungen." Pages 93–137 in *Jesus in apokryphen Evangelienüberlieferungen: Beiträge zu außerkanonischen Jesusüberlieferungen aus verschiedenen Sprach- und Kulturtraditionen*. Edited by J. Frey and J. Schröter. WUNT 254. Tübingen: Mohr (Siebeck), 2010.

Gieseler, Karl Ludwig. "Über die Nazaräer und Ebioniten."*AANKG* 4.2 (1820): 279–330.

Harris, Horton. *The Tübingen School: A Historical and Theological Investigation of the School of F. C. Baur*. 2nd ed. Grand Rapids: Baker, 1990. Originally published at Oxford: Oxford University Press, 1975.

Hester, Carl E. "Baurs Anfänge in Blaubeuren." Pages 67–82 in *Historisch-kritische Geschichtsbetrachtung: Ferdinand Christian Baur und seine Schüler*. Contubernium 40. Edited by Ulrich Köpf. Sigmaringen: Jan Thorbecke, 1994.

———. "Gedanken zu Ferdinand Christian Baurs Entwicklung als Historiker anhand zweier unbekannter Briefe." *ZKG* 84 (1973): 249–69.

Hilgenfeld, Adolf. "Ferdinand Christian Baur nach seiner wissenschaftlichen Entwickelung und Bedeutung." *ZWT* 36.1 (1893): 222–44.

Hodgson, Peter C., ed. *Ferdinand Christian Baur on the Writing of Church History*. New York: Oxford University Press, 1968.

Hodgson, Peter C. *The Formation of Historical Theology: A Study of Ferdinand Christian Baur*. Makers of Modern Theology. New York: Harper & Row, 1966.

Jackson-McCabe, M. "What's in a Name? The Problem of 'Jewish Christianity.'" Pages 7–38, 305–10 in *Jewish Christianity Reconsidered.* Edited by M. Jackson-McCabe. Minneapolis: Fortress, 2007.

Jones, F. Stanley. "The Pseudo-Clementines: A History of Research." *SecCent* 2 (1982): 1–33, 63–96.

Klijn, A. F. J. "The Study of Jewish Christianity." *NTS* 20 (1974): 419–31.

Lange, Lobegott. *Die Judenchristen, Ebioniten und Nikolaiten der apostolischen Zeit und das Verhältnis der neutestamentlichen Schriften zu ihnen historisch und exegetisch beleuchtet.* Vol. 1 of *Beyträge zur ältesten Kirchengeschichte.* Leipzig: J. A. Barth, 1828.

Lechler, Gotthard Victor. *Geschichte des englischen Deismus.* Stuttgart: J. G. Cotta, 1841.

Lemke, H. *Judenchristentum zwischen Ausgrenzung und Integration: Zur Geschichte eines exegetischen Begriffes.* Hamburger Theologische Studien 25. Münster: Lit, 2001.

Liebing, Heinz. "Historical-Critical Theology: In Commemoration of the One Hundredth Anniversary of the Death of Ferdinand Christian Baur, December 2, 1960." *JTC* 3 (1967): 55–69.

Lüdemann, Gerd. *Opposition to Paul in Jewish Christianity.* Translated by M. E. Boring. Minneapolis: Fortress, 1989.

MacKay, R. W. *The Tübingen School and Its Antecedents.* London: Williams & Norgate, 1863.

Mimouni, S. C. "Le judéo-christianisme ancien dans l'historiographie du XIXème et du XXème siècle." *REJ* 151 (1992): 419–28.

———. "Pour une définition nouvelle du judéo-christianisme ancien." *NTS* 38 (1992): 161–86.

Morgan, Robert. "Baur's *Paul.*" *ExpTim* 90 (1978): 4–10.

———. "F. C. Baur's Lectures on New Testament Theology." *ExpTim* 88 (1977): 202–6.

———. "Ferdinand Christian Baur." Pages 261–89 in vol. 1 of *Nineteenth Century Religious Thought in the West.* Edited by Ninian Smart, John Clayton, Patrick Sherry, and Steven T. Katz. Cambridge: Cambridge University Press, 1985.

———. "Non Angli sed Angeli: Some Anglican Reactions to German Gospel Criticism." Pages 1–30 in vol. 1 of *New Studies in Theology.* Edited by S. Sykes and D. Holmes. London: Duckworth, 1980.

———. *Romans.* NTG. Sheffield: Sheffield Academic Press, 1995.

Morgan, Thomas. *The Moral Philospoher in a Dialogue between Philalethes a Christian Deist and Theophanes a Christian Jew.* 3 vols. London: n.p., 1737–1740.

Mosheim, Johann Lorenz von. *Vindiciae antiquae Christianorum disciplinae.* 2nd ed. Hamburg: B. Schiller and J. C. Kisner, 1722.

Müller, Gotthold. "Ferdinand Christian Baur und David Friedrich Strauss in Blaubeuren (1821–1825)." Pages 217–30 in *Glaube, Geist, Geschichte: Festschrift für Ernst Benz zum 60. Geburtstage am 17. November 1967.* Edited by G. Müller and W. Zeller. Leiden: Brill, 1967.

Neander, August. "Beylage: Über die Pseudoclementinischen Homilien, ein Beitrag zur Geschichte der Ebioniten." Pages 361–421 in *Genetische Entwickelung der vornehmsten gnostischen Systeme*. Berlin: F. Dümmler, 1818.

Palmer, Gesine. *Ein Freispruch für Paulus: John Tolands Theorie des Judenchristentums, mit einer Neuausgabe von Tolands Nazarenus von Claus-Michael Palmer*. Arbeiten zur neutestamentlichen Theologie und Zeitgeschichte 7. Berlin: Institut Kirche und Judentum, 1996.

Patrick, David. "Two English Forerunners of the Tübingen School: Thomas Morgan and John Toland." *Theological Review* 14 (1877): 562–603.

Paulus, H. E. G. *Skizzen aus meiner Bildungs- und Lebensgeschichte zum Andenken an mein 50 jähriges Jubiläum*. Heidelberg: Karl Groos, 1839.

Penzel, K. "Will the Real Ferdinand Christian Baur Please Stand Up?" *JR* 48 (1968): 310–23.

Reventlow, H. Graf. "Judaism and Jewish Christianity in the Works of John Toland." Pages 111–16 in *Proceedings of the Sixth World Congress of Jewish Studies III*. Jerusalem: World Union of Jewish Studies, 1977.

Riegel, Stanley K. "Jewish Christianity: Definitions and Terminology." *NTS* 24 (1977–1978): 410–15.

Rudolph, Anette. "Die Judenchristen in Justins Dialog mit Tryphon." Pages 300–306 in *Studia Patristica XXXVI*. Edited by M. F. Wiles and E. J. Yarnold. Leuven: Peeters, 2001.

Schelling, F. W. J. *System of Transcendental Idealism (1800)*. Translated by Peter Heath. Charlottesville: University Press of Virginia, 1978. Originally published as *System des transcendentalen Idealismus*. Tübingen: J. G. Cotta, 1800.

Schliemann, Adolph. *Die Clementinen nebst den verwandten Schriften und der Ebionitismus*. Hamburg: Friedrich Perthes, 1844.

Schmidt, Johann Ernst Christian. "Über die Stelle I Kor. I, 12. und die ursprüngliche Bedeutung des Namens χριστιανοι." Pages 86–100 in vol. 1 of *Bibliothek für Kritik und Exegese des neuen Testaments und älteste Christengeschichte*. N.p.: In der neuen Gelehrtenbuchhandlung, 1797.

Scholder, K. "Baur, Ferdinand Christian (1792–1860)." *TRE* 5:352–59.

Schuffels, Klaus. "Der Nachlass Ferdinand Christian Baurs in der Universitätsbibliothek Tübingen und im Schiller-Nationalmuseum Marbach/Neckar." *ZKG* 79 (1968): 375–84.

Semler, J. S. *Abhandlung von freier Untersuchung des Canon*. 4 vols. Halle: Carl Hermann Hemmerde, 1771–1776.

———. *Apparatus ad liberalem Novi Testamenti interpretationem*. Halle: J. Godofredi Trampii, 1767.

———. *Christliche freye Untersuchung über die so genannte Offenbarung Johannis, aus der nachgelassenen Handschrift eines fränkischen Gelehrten herausgegeben*. Halle: Johann Christian Hendel, 1769.

———. *D. Joh. Salomo Semlers Lebensbeschreibung von ihm selbst abgefaßt*. 2 vols. Halle: 1781–1782.

———. "Geschichte der christlichen Glaubenslehre." Preface to vol. 1 of *Untersuchung theologischer Streitigkeiten*, by S. J. Baumgarten. Edited by J. S. Semler. Halle: Johann Justinus Gebauer, 1762.

———. *Institutio ad doctrinam christianam liberaliter discendam.* Halle: Carl Hermann Hemmerde, 1774.

———. *Paraphrasis in Epistolam II. Petri, et Epistolam Iudae.* Halle: Hemmerde, 1784.

———. *Versuch einer freiern theologischen Lehrart.* Halle: Carl Hermann Hemmerde, 1777.

Stemberger, G. "Judenchristen." *RAC* 19:228–45.

Taylor, Joan E. "The Phenomenon of Early Jewish-Christianity: Reality or Scholarly Invention?" *VC* 44 (1990): 313–34.

Thorschmid, U. G. *Versuch einer vollständigen Engelländischen Freydenker-Bibliothek.* 4 vols. Vols. 1–2: Halle: Carl Hermann Hemmerde, 1765–1766. Vols. 3–4: Cassel: Johann Friedrich Hemmerde, 1766–1767.

Toland, John. *Nazarenus: Or, Jewish, Gentile and Mahometan Christianity.* 2nd ed. London: J. Brotherton, J. Roberts, and A. Dodd, 1718.

Voigt, Christopher. *Der englische Deismus in Deutschland: Eine Studie zur Rezeption englisch-deistischer Literatur in deutschen Zeitschriften und Kompendien des 18. Jahrhunderts.* BHT 121. Tübingen: Mohr Siebeck, 2003.

Wiener, M. "John Toland and Judaism." *HUCA* 16 (1941): 215–42.

Zeller, E. "Ferdinand Christian Baur." Pages 354–434 in *Vorträge und Abhandlungen geschichtlichen Inhalts.* Leipzig: Fues's Verlag (L. W. Reisland), 1865.

NAZARENUS:

OR,

Jewish, Gentile, and *Mahometan*

CHRISTIANITY.

CONTAINING

The history of the antient GOSPEL OF BARNABAS, and the modern GOSPEL OF THE MAHOMETANS, attributed to the same APOSTLE: this last GOSPEL being now first made known among CHRISTIANS.

ALSO,

The ORIGINAL PLAN OF CHRISTIANITY occasionally explain'd in the history of the NAZARENS, wherby diverse CONTROVERSIES about this divine (but highly perverted) INSTITUTION may be happily terminated.

WITH

The relation of an IRISH MANUSCRIPT of the FOUR GOSPELS, as likewise a Summary of the antient IRISH CHRISTIANITY, and the reality of the KELDEES (an order of Lay-religious) against the two last Bishops of Worcester.

By Mr. *TOLAND.*

Intacta & Nova? graves Offensae, levis Gratia.   Plin. lib. 5. Epist. 8.
Ast Ego Coelicolis gratum reor ire per omnes
Hoc opus, & Sacras populis notescere Leges.   Lucan. lib. 10. ver. 197

The SECOND EDITION Revised.

LONDON, Printed: And Sold by J. BROTHERTON at the Black Bull in Cornhill, J. ROBERTS in Warwick-Lane, and A. DODD at the Peacock without Temple-Bar. 1718.

[Price Two Shillings Stich'd.]

PREFACE

TO

Mr. *D. S.*

SIR,

SINCE you are determin'd to continue in town this whole Winter, and that I know none of my friends to be a nicer judge of exact Printing, I just beg the favor of you, to convey (during my necessary absence, for some time, in the country) the inclos'd DISSERTATION to the Press, and to see it every way correctly finish'd: tho I hope to be with you again, before you have half done. But tis good to provide against all chances. I design to publish it next spring, for the same reason that all books are or ought to be publish'd: namely, that I may inform others of what I know, which in many things I apprehend to be my duty; or that, if misinform'd, I may be set right by those, who show themselves rather lovers of Truth than of Contention. [ii] They are, for the most part, easily distinguish'd: tho, thro some men's management, even Truth does often wear the badges of Falshood. I have in the first chapter so farr declar'd the Contents of the first Letter, as to render any other Preface (I once thought) entirely unnecessary, at least a very long one. But the better nevertheless to prepare you for the reading of it, as also of the second Letter, especially since they are both swell'd beyond their original bulk; and that you may not possibly ly under any mistake by that too short Introduction, I shall reduce the sum of what you are to expect to the following heads: not thinking it needful to indicate every particular, no nor every general subject, in a work of so moderate a size.

I. *IN the first place you'll find the succinct history of a* NEW GOSPEL, *which I discover'd at Amsterdam, in the year* 1709. *It is a* Mahometan *Gospel, never before publicly made known among Christians, tho they have much talkt about the Mahometans acknowledging the* Gospel. *I strait sent an account of this discovery to his most serene Highness, the ever victorious* PRINCE EUGENE OF SAVOY, *to whom I had the honour of writing sometimes, by the way of his Adjutant General the Baron de* HOHENDORF, *who comes behind very few in the knowledge of all curious and useful books: and tis really surprizeing how much the Prince himself has read, how minutely, how critically, in how many languages; considering his perpetual series of action as well in the Court as in the Camp. He's now master of this book, as may be seen in the* Appendix. *But our Turkish Gospel being father'd upon* BARNABAS, *and all Christians agreeing that* MAHOMET *acknowledg'd the* Gospel; *I have shown by unexceptionable authorities, that Ecclesiastical writers did antiently attribute a* Gospel *to* BAR[iii]NABAS, *whether there be any remains of it in this new-found* Gospel, *or not: and therfore upon this occasion I have given a clearer account, than is commonly to be met, of the Mahometan sentiments with relation to* JESUS *and the* Gospel; *insomuch that it is not (I believe) without sufficient ground, that I have represented them as a sort of Christians, and not the worst sort neither, tho farr from being the best.*

II. *BUT happening to spend that summer in the delicious gardens of Honslaerdyk (a palace formerly belonging to King* WILLIAM *of immortal memory) from which I cou'd easily make an excursion to Leyden, upon any occasion of consulting the public Library, I was naturally led by the* Gospel *of* BARNABAS *to resume some former considerations I had about the* NAZA-RENS; *as being the Primitive Christians most properly so call'd, and the onely Christians for some time. Their History I have here set in a truer light than other writers, who are generally full of confusion and misrepresentation concerning them; making them the first, if not the worst, of all* Heretics: *nor did they want their mistakes, to be sure, any more than the* Apostles *themselves, who were often reprehended by their master and by one another. One of the mistakes, in common with the* Apostles *for some time, was a gross and worldly notion of the person and spiritual kingdom of* CHRIST; *which, with some opinions falsly imputed to them, and others as falsly held by them, are not the immediate subject of their* History *(these requiring too nice a discussion for this place) but tis the very groundwork of the Christian Economy, of which I shall presently give you the detail. I was long before directed to my materials by the celebrated* FREDERIC SPANHEMIUS, *when I* study'd Ecclesiastical History under him at Leyden, tho I differ [iv] widely from my master in this point. But the Bible and the Fathers, the Hebrew and the Greec Originals, being what he ever exhorted his disciples to consult as their fountains, without giving up their judgements to any thing short of truth; I have follow'd his excellent advice to the best of my power, and tis for the able and equitable readers to decide, how I have profited by it. They who have read the same history and languages in the same Class with me, have not (that I can see) receiv'd any such change of organs or understanding from any of the Professions they have since espous'd, as to capacitate them for comprehending these things better than one without any Profession: and therfore the more likely to be freer from prejudices, as he has more leisure maturely to consider; neither being ty'd down by Articles upon Oath, too frequently productive of perjury, nor crampt by any other partial or politic restraint. But such reflections not being always so justly made as they ought to be, men of candor will accurately judge of the things themselves, without regarding whether he be a Clergyman or a Layman that delivers them.

   III. FROM the history of the NAZARENS, and more particularly from the evident words of Scripture, I inferr in this discourse a distinction of two sorts of Christians, viz. those from among the Jews, and those from among the Gentiles: not onely that in fact there was such a distinction (which no body denies) but likewise that of right it ought to have been so (which every body denies) and that it was so design'd in THE ORIGINAL PLAN OF CHRISTIANITY. I mean that the Jews, tho associating with the converted Gentiles, and acknowledging them for brethren, were still to observe their own Law thro-out all generations; and that the Gentiles, who became so farr Jews [v] as to acknowledge ONE GOD, were not however to observe the Jewish Law: but that both of them were to be for ever after united into one body or fellowship, and in that part of Christianity particularly, which, better than all the preparative purgations of the Philosophers, requires the sanctification of the spirit, or the renovation of the inward man; and wherin alone the Jew and the Gentile, the Civiliz'd and the Barbarian, the Freeman and the Bondslave, are all one in CHRIST, however otherwise differing in their circumstances. In comparison of the New Creature, Circumcision and Uncircumcision are as nothing: which yet no more takes away the distinction of Jewish and Gentile Christians, than the distinction of sexes; since it is likewise said in the same sense, and in the same place, that in CHRIST there is neither Male nor Female. This fellowship in Piety and Virtue is the Mystery that PAUL rightly says was hid from all other ages, till the manifestation

Rom. x.12.
Gal. iii.28.
Col. iii.11.

Gal. iii. 28.

Rom. xvi. 25. Ephes. i. 9, 10. & iii.3,5,6,9. Col. i. 26, 27.

of it by JESUS; *and this Union without Uniformity, between Jew and Gentile, is the admirable Economy of the* Gospel. *Now, this* Gospel *consists not in words but in virtue; tis inward and spiritual, abstracted from all formal and outward performances: for the most exact observation of externals, may be without one grain of religion. All this is mechanically done by the help of a little book-craft, wheras true religion is inward life and spirit. So that somthing else besides the Legal Ordinances, most of 'em political, was necessary to render a Jew religious: even that* FAITH, *which is an internal participation of the divine nature, irradiating the soul; and externally appearing in beneficence, justice, sanctity, and those other virtues by which we resemble God, who is himself all Goodness. But the Jews generally mistook the means for the end: as others, who better understood the end, wou'd not onely absurdly take away the means; but even* [vi] *those other civil and national rites which were to continue always in the Jewish Republick (as I particularly prove) thus confounding political with religious performances. From this doctrine it follows (its true) that* JESUS *did not take away or cancel the* JEWISH LAW *in any sense whatsoever, Sacrifices only excepted; but neither does this affect any of the Gentile Christians now in the world, who have nothing at all to do with that Law. It follows indeed that the* JEWS, *whether becoming* CHRISTIANS *or not, are for ever bound to the* LAW OF MOSES, *as now limited: and he that thinks they were absolv'd from the observation of it by* JESUS, *or that tis a fault in them still to adhere to it, does err not knowing the* Scriptures; *as did most of the converts from the Gentiles, who gave their bare names to* CHRIST, *but reserv'd their Idolatrous hearts for their native superstitions. These did almost wholly subvert the TRUE CHRISTIANITY, which in the following Treatise I vindicate; drawing it out from under the rubbish of their endless divisions, and clearing it from the almost impenetrable mists of their sophistry. So inveterate was their hatred of the Jews (tho indebted to them for the* Gospel) *that their observing of any thing, however reasonable or necessary, was a sufficient motive for these Gentile converts to reject it. They wou'd neither fast nor pray at the same time with them, where they could possibly avoid it. They had no other reason for changing the time of* Easter, *to the dividing and distracting of all Christian Churches; but that they might have nothing in common with the Jews, as being so expresly commanded by* CONSTANTINE *the great, which we are told by* EUSEBIUS *in the 17th chapter of the 4th book of that Emperor's Life. And all Christians are enjoin'd by the 11th Canon of the 6th General Council (in Trullo) to have no familiarity or commerce with the Jews, not to call for their assistance when sick, nei*[vii]*ther to receive any physic from them, nor to wash in the*

same bath with them. I do here teach a very different doctrine, more conso-
nant (I am persuaded) to the mind of CHRIST *and his Apostles, as tis more*
agreeable to the Law of nature and the dictates of Humanity. As for what
I think of Christianity in general, contrary to the malicious suggestions of
wicked men (whose Godliness is Gain) I referr you to the perpetual tenor of
this present book. Yet they are in the right of it, if they mean that I disbelieve
their sort of Christianity; which no good man can approve in practice, no
more than any wise man can understand in theory. Tis Paganism or Policy,
but not Christianity or Humanity. This will be evident from the account I
give of CHRISTIANITY *in general in the first Letter, and after a more particu-*
lar manner in the second Letter.

IV. *VARIOUS difficulties, and such as have hitherto exercis'd many Pens*
to no purpose, or to the bad purpose of needlesly divideing mankind, are
readily solv'd by this healing and uniteing SCHEME; not that I have arbi-
trarily contriv'd it, tho for so good an end, as several Systems have upon other
occasions been merely coin'd for accomodation: but I maintain it, because
I judge it to be most right and true, the genuin primary Christianity; and
therfore produceing the promis'd effects of the Gospel, GLORY TO GOD ON   Luc. ii.14.
HIGH, PEACE ON EARTH, GOOD-WILL TOWARDS MEN. *Among those seem-*
ingly insoluble difficulties clear'd by it, is that of eating blood, *and* things
strangl'd, *and* things dead of themselves; *which I have brought (I fancy) to*
be no longer a subject of doubt or scruple to any one. I have moreover prov'd,
that the distinction of Jewish and Gentile Christians, *and this distinction*
onely, reconciles PETER *and* PAUL *about Circumcision and the other Legal*
Ceremonies, as it does PAUL *and* JAMES *about Justification by Faith* [viii] *or*
by Works; it makes the Gospels *to agree with the* Acts *and the* Epistles, *and*
the Epistles *with the* Acts *and one another: but, what is more than all, it*
shows a perfect accord between the Old Testament *and the* New; *and proves*
that God did not give two Laws, wherof the one was to cancel the other,
which is no small stumbling block to the opposers of Christianity, as the
resolving of this difficulty is no sign, I hope, of my want of Religion. Many are
the salutary fruits I foresee from the obtaining of this SCHEME in the world,
and but one sad consequence; I mean the turning to waste paper an infinite
number of volums, particularly on Justification in the modern sense, on the
several meanings of the Law (a thing, by the way, inconsistent with all Law)
on the calling of the Jews to quit the Religion they receiv'd from MOSES, *and*
the utter exploding of those forc'd or unintelligible Allegories, which have no
manner of foundation in the Scriptures; *but are the precarious inventions of*

fanciful or worse men, fit only to puzzle the curious, to amuze the indifferent, and to distract the ignorant. One main objection against Cartesianism *in its infancy, was, that a great many booksellers wou'd be undone, and cart-loads of books become useless in Libraries, shou'd this pernicious sect prevail. But they need not be alarm'd.*

V. *I SHALL mention here no other difficulty remov'd by the SCHEME I espouse, but onely two more, which I have barely toucht as I go along: for the master-key being once found, tis easy opening all the doors. The first of these regards the controversy about* the Seventh day, *or* Saturday-Sabbath; *and the second, that of* anointing sick persons: *points which some of late have labor'd to introduce, and which I have no less clearly than briefly terminated. I might have instanc'd several others, cou'd the circumstances of my writing this* [ix] *DISSERTATION have admitted it: nor am I willing to inlarge it at present so very much beyond its primitive size, tho several things I have occasionally added, amounting at least to a third part of the whole. Whatever may be the reception of this piece at the beginning, I doubt not but after a while the most judicious and moderate will approve of those Explications, which appear to be the most singular in it: for this is not the first time I have known them, who were the forwardest to write against me, afterwards to fall in themselves with the same sentiments; which has not past unobserv'd by the public, especially with regard to certain late compounders for* MYSTERY. *Yet I might hazard to prophesy, that some of these same gentlemen may now be among the foremost to contest my explications; merely because they are mine, or rather because they are not originally theirs: as others will oppose them, because contrary to some of the receiv'd opinions, or not precisely suteing with their interest. I onely desire that in doing this they wou'd deal cautiously, and not commit such mistakes, as Dr.* BLACKHALL *did formerly, expos'd in* Amyntor. *I made no objections then, nor do I make any now, to invalidate or destroy, but in order to illustrate and confirm the* Canon of the New Testament; *wherof I have written the* History *in two parts, to be publish'd in convenient time. And as for my being so particular in relating, what the Nazarens or Ebionites objected against* PAUL, *besides that my subject manifestly requir'd it; tis likewise as manifest that it was to show their mistakes, which I have done, and that they had unjustly charg'd him with abolishing the Law. Let others make his Apology better if they can.*

VI. *THIS much I had to say to you, Sir, in relation to the first* Letter *of the book you are to see printed. But, as to the second* Letter, *be pleas'd* [x] *to understand, that in the beginning of the same year 1709, I discover'd at the Hague a manuscript of the four Gospels (then lately brought from France) all written in Irish characters, which were mistaken for Anglosaxon, but yet the whole text in the Latin tongue. Some little thing in Irish it self is here and there mixt among the NOTES, which are very numerous, and other passages in the Irish language occurr also elsewhere. Of what age or importance this book may be, and what Father* SIMON *has said about it, with my censure of him; you'll find so particularly discuss'd in their due place, that I need say no more of these things here. However, besides doing justice on this occasion to the Learning and florishing Schools of the* ANTIENT IRISH, *while the rest of Europe continu'd distracted by warrs and overshadow'd with ignorance; I have set in its true light, beyond what most others had an opportunity of doing, the Christianity originally profest in that nation (wherof I have given a distinct SUMMARY in 17 paragraphs) and which appears to be extremely different from the religion of the present Irish. I mean the posterity of the aboriginal Proprietors, to whom, as my countrymen and fellow-subjects, I do most earnestly recommend the impartial consideration of this matter. If they are fond of antiquity, this Religion is much ancienter than the Popery which most of'em now profess: it haveing been the peculiar honor of Ireland, as they'll find in perusing this* Letter, *to have asserted their Independency more strenuously against the usurpations of Rome, and to have preserv'd their Faith unpolluted against the corruptions of it longer, than any other nation. But truth being what people ought to value more than either country or kindred, as I have not been wanting to commend whatever I thought deserving; so I have never palliated what I judge blame-worthy in Ireland, no more than in any other country: nor* [xi] *have I any where exceeded the reverend Dr.* PRIDEAUX's *expressions, who (in the 241st page of the first part of the 2d volume of his excellent performance,* The Old and New Testament connected) *says, that, in the ages I mention, Ireland was the prime seat of Learning in all Christendom. What he has said I have prov'd, and this from Authors unexceptionable, many of 'em contemporaries, and none of 'em Irish. I shall dispatch with the APPENDIX, which consists of three small pieces. The two PROBLEMS (wherof the first piece consists) are preparatory to a Treatise concerning the* REPUBLIC OF MOSES, *about which few men have hitherto written common sense: not excepting* SIGONIUS, *or* CUNEUS, *or even* HARRINGTON *the author of* Oceana; *who, tho the best of 'em, is yet very defective, and in many things erroneous. Next follows an account of the TURKISH GOSPEL by Monsieur* DE LA MONNOYE *(to whom the Baron* DE HOHENDORF *show'd it, after the owner had parted with it to* PRINCE EUGENE) *and which I have*

The 189th page of the folio edition.

added, as a further illustration of the book; and withall as a confirmation of my own description of it, which I am persuaded the Baron did not show to that ingenious Academician. Lastly, come certain QUERIES *I drew up for my private satisfaction, and that of some others; haveing already sent diverse copies of them to Asia and Africa, as well as to Greece.*

VII. *IN the marginal* NOTES *I have commonly exprest my self in Latin, the obviousest language on such occasions: besides that it is intelligible to all who are conversant with such passages, and about which others must rely on the skill of those they can trust. But my text is plain and perspicuous enough, even to the meanest capacity; haveing, after* [xii] *the great example of the antients, interwoven those passages into my own discourse in a continu'd thread: and not onely being of opinion that the simplest Stile (not incompatible with the politest) is in teaching the best; but that every man, who clearly conceives any subject, may as clearly express it. Witty conceits and harmonious florishes are for another-guess sort of writing: but obscurity is to be avoided in all sorts, and nothing to be affected but not to be misunderstood; if too great a care of being intelligible, can be reckon'd affectation. In the Greec* NOTES *at the foot of the page, I shou'd have avoided ligatures and contractions, which are no more useful in this Tongue than in the Latin; or rather they are still as troblesom and deform'd in the one, as they were once in the other. I admire therfore that* WETSTEIN's *example is not more follow'd by other printers. For the same reason the Greec is printed without Accents, which are a useless, perplexing, and no very ancient invention, on the foot they now stand. But let it be specially remember'd, with regard to all citations of Authors, that I give them onely for what they are; haveing always had recourse to the* Originals, *whether quoted by others or not, except where I hint the contrary for want of such* Originals, *and neither wilfully curtailing, garbling, or misrepresenting any of them: produceing* Fathers *as* Fathers, Heretics *as* Heretics, Antients *and* Moderns *for just such; and therfore not answerable for any thing they say, unless where I expresly approve it, as I may probably disapprove them on other accounts. I answer in others for no more than what I say with them, which is nothing the worse for what they may elswhere say against it. Their judgement of things cannot alter the nature of them. I allow all of 'em to be judges of the opinions of their own times as to fact (if they be any thing fair or accurate) but not always to reason for me, much less implicitly to lead* [xiii] *me. The* PASSAGES OF SCRIPTURE *I hope will be read at length, in the few places where I have not quoted them so, particularly those in the beginning of the*

twelfth chapter: and I have taken care in general not to overburthen the
reader with citations of any sort, contenting my self to prove or illustrate my
allegations by no more authorities than are necessary; tho I often abound
with others, which I judge needless, or reserve against Answerers.

VIII. *THESE Answerers naturally put me in mind of Cavillers, whom I*
wou'd not have to run away with a notion, as if I thought FAITH *did every*
where signify the Christian Institutions; because, in the 16th chapter of the
first Dissertation, *I say it does so whenever oppos'd to the Works of the Law:*
or as if I maintain'd WORKS *did every where signify the Levitical Rites,*
because I say they do so, whenever oppos'd to Faith. The various meanings
of these words are obvious to every reader, as Faith *(for example) in the 6th*
verse of the 1st chapter of JAMES, *signifies a full persuasion: but in the 1st and*
5th verses of the second chapter, it signifies the whole Christian belief. So does
it in the 14th verse of the same chapter, as Works *there betoken the Leviti-*
cal Rites: and the instance of Charity in the 15th and 16th verses is plainly
a simile, of what is inforc'd in the 17th verse. The examples of ABRAHAM
and RAHAB *in the 21st, 22d, 23d, 24th, and 25th verses, show that works*
here betoken the positive, not the moral Law. For Christianity is by the same
Apostle, in the 21st verse of the 1st chapter, most properly stil'd the engrafted
word able to save their souls, *engrafted I say on the* Law of MOSES, *not sanc-*
tifying the inward man; yet for most wise reasons to be perpetually observ'd
by the Jews, and wherof Christianity is the spirit: for as the body without   Jam. ii.26.
breath is dead, so Faith without Works is dead also; *yea and* by [xiv] Works
a man is justify'd, and not by Faith onely. *This is literally true of the Jews,*   Ibid. v. 24.
and had LUTHER *understood this distinction, he wou'd never have rejected*
(which he once did) the Epistle of JAMES *as stramineous and contrary to the*
doctrine of PAUL: *which stands upon the same foot with that of* JAMES, *as in*
our first Dissertation *one running may read. The* LAW *was given by* MOSES,   John i. 17.
but GRACE *and* TRUTH *came by* JESUS, *who has confirm'd that Law. I hope*
no small advantage will accrue to Christianity from the system advanc'd in
the said 16th and 17th chapters of this Dissertation; *in which, as well as*
by the SUMMARY OF CHRISTIANITY *contain'd in the second* Dissertation,
tho not onely the reality, but (as I am reasonably to hope) the soundness of
my Religion sufficiently appears: yet seeing learned disquisitions are not for
every body's taste or capacity, however grateful to the curious, and neces-
sary for the proof of things; I shall hereafter (God willing) give a more dis-
tinct account of my Religion, stript of all literature, and laid down in naked
theorems, without notes of any kind. I promise you (Sir) before-hand, that it

will not be a mechanical and artificial Religion, consisting more in a stupid respect for receiv'd forms, and a lifeless round of performances by rote, than in a reasonable worship or unaffected piety. There will be more objects of practice than of belief in it; and nothing practis'd but what makes a man the better, nor any thing believ'd but what necessarily leads to practice and knowledge: yet nothing that does not concern people to know, or that they cannot possibly know at all. It will contain nothing fabulous or mysterious, nothing hypocritical or austere; nothing to divert people from their imploy-ments, or tending to beget idleness and licentiousness: nothing, in short, that contributes to enslave their minds or bodies, nothing to serve the purposes of Princes or Priests against the interest of mankind. This you'll say, after what I have alread[xv]dy perform'd in the following book, seems to be superflu-ous: but, by that time the year comes round, you'll find reason for your self to change your mind, and for me to publish that System of Religion.

FREQUENT complaints are deservedly made about the want of PIETY, wherof the cause nevertheless is known but to very few: for the little effect of Religion procedes in most places from the too great influence of the CLERGY, who make that to pass for Religion which is none, or quite the reverse, as they make Piety often inconsistent with Probity; and this they do to serve their own private ends, which in such places are ever opposite to the public good of the people. But let it be always understood, that I mean corrupt and inter-ested PRIESTS, the bitterest enemies to good MINISTERS, for whom I both have, and shall ever retain the highest veneration. The functions and views of the latter I shall specify on another occasion. The practices and pretences of the former are too flagrant to be deny'd. Every day yields fresh instances of the ambitious and traiterous designs of degenerate Clergymen,

Whose lives make Atheists, and whose doctrine Slaves.

The ultimte designs of such men are to procure to themselves Riches, and consequently Power and Authority; as, in order to secure both, they train up their hearers in Ignorance, and consequently in Superstition and Bigotry. *Their constant Preaching will be made an objection to this asser-tion: but constant Preaching is not always effectual Teaching. If the things preach'd be metaphysical riddles, or mythological tales, or mystical dreams; if they are Politics instead of Faith and Repentance, the People are as farr from being taught, as if they heard nothing: but with this difference, that they* [xvi] *imagine they know somthing, while they onely make good the charac-*

ter of ever learning, but never being able to come to the knowledge of the 2 Tim. iii.
Truth. *The most libertine Priests, the most illiterate Mendicants, can easily* 7.
make what impressions they please upon a People thus previously dispos'd;
who believe, when those Empirics are maliciously blackening the lovers of
Truth, that they are strenuously asserting the cause of God against the ser-
vants of the Devil: and thus they are commonly workt up to become the
mortal enemies of such as are pleading their own cause; and who wou'd
generously set 'em free, from the bondage of their spiritual Task-masters.
They are accustom'd to look upon them no longer with eyes of Humanity,
no nor to believe their own senses concerning them; for once they know 'em
to differ from their Leaders (whose human Inventions they are taught to be
the Oracles of God) they abhorr 'em as the most licentious and abandon'd
Libertines, be their lives and conversations ever so irreproachable: not being
able to conceive how one, who is not right in his notions, that is, in their
notions of things, can be just in his actions; even tho such notions shou'd not
relate to practice at all, but end in pure speculation. The GENTRY in some
countries know little more than the VULGAR, being industriously molded to
their own purposes by the CLERGY, to whose care their Earliest Education
is preposterously committed: or if in some other countries they happen to be
more discerning, yet out of a sordid principle of Interest, to which they basely
sacrifice Truth and Virtue, they affect to be more credulous than the very
VULGAR; and this with a view of being recommended to the PRINCE by
the CLERGY, who preach up his absolute Power over the People, that their
own Authority may become arbitrary both over these and him too. But have-
ing nothing to apprehend in this last respect (our British Throne [xvii] being
happily fill'd with a Prince no less discerning and judicious, than just and
magnanimous, and abhorring Tyranny as much as he despises Superstition)
I shall, in spite of all discouragements, openly profess the Religion I believe
to be most for the instruction and benefit of mankind; for what is not so, can
never be true, much less divine. This Religion, I say, I shall fairly deliver: and
to the present reward, which the consciousness of doing my duty necessarily
brings along with it, I shall add the certain prospect I have, that the few in all
ages who are wise and good (which qualities ought to be inseparable) will do
justice to a man who dar'd to own his affection to Truth, the beauty wherof
had set him above all fears and expectations.

    I AM farr from being ignorant of the ARTS, which those corrupt Clergy-
men wherof I have spoken, and such onely of the Clergy, daily use, to decry
their Antagonists; experience as well as observation haveing abundantly

discover'd to me those Mysteries of iniquity, and convinc'd me of this maxim: that all curious Enquiries and useful Discoveries wou'd be for ever stopt, shou'd men put a stop to their Pens for fear of Obloquy, or any other Opposition. *The most learned and universally celebrated Mr.* LE CLERC *has written an entire* Dissertation (Argumentum Theologicum ab Invidia ductum) *to expose the Calumnies of Divines, when other Arguments fail them. Every little Chaplain's transforming himself into the Catholick Church, and making Christianity (forsooth) to suffer by the exploding of his whimsies, ought no more to terrify us from appearing for Truth; than we shou'd be scolded or buffoon'd out of it by others, who write, as if they had the high office of being the Church's Jesters and Merry-Andrews. To speak against any one of these, if you take their own word for it, is to be an enemy to all Clergymen, to disbelieve the Christian Religion,* [xviii] *and not to own the being of a God. Numberless are the wiles and artifices of such mercenary Priests, to puzzle the cause, or to discredit the person of an Adversary; wherof I think it con-*
1. *venient here, to specify the most principal. They are sure, in the first place, to misrepresent the state of the Question, and to make it more or less important than it is, as may best sute their ends; their implicite followers being ever ready to acquiesce in their report of the matter, without once dareing to think*
2. *for themselves. They commonly deliver the Sense of the man, whose book they oppose, in their own words instead of his; under pretence of setting it in a clearer light, when indeed they design to involve and perplex it: or if they produce the words of the Original, they are always disjointed and imperfect; and their observations upon them, for fear their sophistry might be detected,*
3. *are equivocal, industriously confuse, and obscure. They conceal his chief Reasons and strongest Arguments, loudly insisting at the same time upon Incidents either not essential or foren to the subject; and nibbling at unguarded expressions or inaccuracies of Stile, into which, thro more attention to the matter than to the words, the correctest writers are sometimes apt to fall,*
4. *especially in a work of any length. Unfairly dropping the main Question, they attribute Designs to their opponent the most remote from his views, and from the evident scope of his whole writing: judgeing of others by themselves, as if there were a trick at the bottom of every thing men did; and that, upon a proper occasion, they wou'd make no scruple of saying one thing and meaning*
5. *ing another. This puts me in mind of another of their main artifices, for so impotent is their malice, that almost in the same breath they make the same man equally stupid and cunning; telling you in this page, that his whole Performance is so insuperably dull and incoherent, as scarce to deserve animadversion: which in* [xix] *the next page they contradict themselves, not onely in*

the oil and sweat they expend to confute him; but in laying his plot so deep
for him, and reporting his skill so formidable, as to call for abler hands, nay
sometimes for the Magistrate, to take him to task. They draw invidious Con- 6.
sequences from his positions, which either follow not by any Logical deduc-
tion, or are disown'd by him as wrested and unforeseen; yet by them popu-
larly imputed to him, as if he had actually intended and maintain'd them. 7.
They never fail to accuse him of Innovation, which, if not his greatest merit
(as new Reformations ought to be substituted to old disorders) yet his great-
est crime is many times the reviveing of some obsolete unfashionable Truth,
a novelty not to be endur'd by men who live upon error. But what do I talk of 8.
Truth? to which they are so little us'd, that they ever charge their Antagonist
with not believing what he affirms, and as writing onely out of Singularity,
or vainly to get a Name; not considering with what greater probability it may
be retorted upon them, that the sincerity of their own belief is much more
justly to be call'd in question, since it is rewarded with Riches, Fame, and
Authority: which is the reason, that the real Infidels are (in appearance) the
most zealous Professors and Persecutors in all national Churches, ever over-
acting their parts; it being visibly absurd, that an Atheist shou'd be a Noncon-
formist, or that any man who does not care for Truth wou'd suffer for what
he does not believe. No, no: such people can bawl Orthodoxy, and never fail
going to Church. If the Stile of the man they love not, be chaste and unaf- 9.
fected, stript of the enthusiastic cant of the Fathers, *the barbarous jargon of*
the Schools, *and the motly dialect of later* Systems, *then his Principles are*
vehemently suspected; and by how much more they are intelligible, judg'd to
be by so much the more dangerous. If the dispute be about matters of Fact, 10.
[xx] and that a man produces Authorities no less apt than numerous, this
they call a show of Reading, or borrow'd Learning: endeavoring to depreci-
ate what they cannot disprove, and sanctifying their illiberal Scurrility with
the name of Zeal: for of all men they are the most bitter and foul-mouth'd
against an Adversary; which the Popish Jesuits commend as meritorious,
and which the Protestant Jesuits practise as if it were so; meaning by these
last, such as act like the first. He must, among other epithets, be branded 11.
with the odious denomination of some ancient or modern HERESY, which
often happens to be onely a nickname for Truth: and, whether he will or
no, he's made to agree with those in every thing, with whom he happens
to agree in any one thing; as if every Sect did not hold some truth, were it
but to countenance their falshoods. If neither any nor all these methods can 12.
run down his Doctrine, they will next attack his Person, running away with
every idle story they can catch, and poorly rakeing into the frailties of his

life, tho he shou'd be less obnoxious to censure than the best of his neighbors;
and chargeing him even with the actual guilt, of what they pretend to follow
from his Notions: never hesitating at the vilest insinuations, to the end some
calumny may stick; for, of all men, they have the quickest knack of circula-
teing Scandal. Yet they wou'd do well to assign the time, when a Layman
is not to be twitted with the follies of his childhood, or reproach'd with the
excesses of his youth (shou'd he be guilty of any) since they will not admit it
fair to accuse a Clergyman, of anything he did before Ordination, or rather
before he's Doctor'd or Dignify'd.

    THESE are some of the ordinary ARTS of Corrupt Clergymen (of which
alone I speak, to say it once for all) and by these marks you shall know them:
but by none more than the charge of ATHEISM, [xxi] *which, in their pas-*
sion or malice, they bully out against any person that presumes to contradict
them: and, what extremely contributes to the scandal of Religion, and to
make Atheists in good earnest, they commonly lay this aspersion on men
of the clearest sense and the soberest lives; while they bestow the appella-
tion of GOOD CHURCHMEN on the most ignorant sots and rakes, if they
but appear devoted to their persons or their interest. The PRIEST-RIDDEN
LAITY imitate more or less these practices of their Clerical Guides, till at last
a man becomes an INFIDEL for differing from another about the meanest
trifle in nature. It becomes a Spirit that haunts them, and they meet it every
where. Of this a notable example is furnisht us by the author of the Builder's
Dictionary, *who inveighing (in the 5th page of his Proem) against the despis-*
ers of Architecture, I must and will tell such men (*says he*) the plain truth,
that they must certainly be INFIDELS, and do not deserve the title of a Jew,
and much less of a Christian: *for which his weighty reason is, that if they*
were Jews, they must have been acquainted with the buildings appointed in
the Old Testament; *and that if they were Christians, they must have read*
the books of the Jews. But it happens unluckily for him, that Heathens and
Infidels have been much better Architects, than either Jews or Christians. He
concludes the page by telling us, that CHRIST *was pleas'd to exercise this art*
of Architecture, and to be a Mechanic, even a Carpenter; which I must
needs tell you (*adds he*) is no small honor to the Mechanics and to Architecture: *and I must needs tell him, that he might as well conclude a man an*
Infidel for being merry with his neighbors, or having a house of his own; since
we read that JESUS *had not a hole wherin to lay his head, and that he wept*
but never laught that we know. Tis seldom that Divines fix their accusa[xxii]
tion of Atheism more conclusively, which makes it as contemtible as the

Pope's Bulls at Constantinople. Nay Hell-fire it self, in their mouths, has lost much of its antient terror; since they assign no less a punishment than eternal damnation, to the rejecting of certain chimerical notions about Priesthood and Schism, alembick'd out of the Fathers: *and to the disbelief of certain Doctrines of their own coining, which they neither practice nor believe; and therefore ought to pass for counterfeit with all others, such, for example, as* Passive Obedience, Indefeasible Hereditary Right, *and the like, whether impiously father'd upon* GOD, *or* MOSES, *or* JESUS. *These however are the stratagems against which I am to guard, against which my Readers, being forewarn'd, ought to be forearm'd; but which piece of justice, owing to themselves as well as to me, I am not to hope they will be all judicious and equitable enough to observe.*

WHEREFORE, after all these necessary precautions, I yet expect to be unmercifully pelted by those; who are the least able to confute me, shou'd I happen to be any where in the wrong, as no person on earth is infallible. This answering for answering sake, whether the thing be answerable or not; and the allowing of nothing where any thing is thought fit to be deny'd, is so vulgar and customary a practice, that all wise men do as much despise as they detest it: and, for my own part, I have, without pretending to be one of their number, resolv'd before-hand to receive all that sort of fire unmov'd; and to repel at the same time the attacks of my enemies, tho not with the like stink-pots to those they may throw at me. Of this I gave a specimen in Amyntor. *The only favor I desire is, that as I wrote my book alone, I may answer alone for it; and that* MEGALETOR *be not made to adopt the contents of all the Letters he receives, no more than of all the Books in his* Li[xxiii]*brary. But being a forener, he's happily out of the reach of their spite. I say as much however on the behalf of my other Friends at home; for it is an artifice peculiar to certain folks, to hook in every one they dislike, to what they first proclaim a crime. Besides, that in other respects, the thing is very unfair: for if the Book be good, the true Author ought not to be rob'd of the praise he deserves; and if it be bad, no others ought to suffer for a fault, they did not commit. Thus (for example) have I my self been, by more than one, no less confidently than falsely reported, to have had a hand in the* Discourse of Freethinking; *of which charge, nevertheless, I am quite as clear as themselves. I never club brains, I do assure them. But my Adversaires thought it enough, that I am well acquainted with the writer of that book, who is a very worthy Gentleman and a stanch Englishman. With such I shall ever think it a happiness to be acquainted, let their speculative Sentiments be what they will; for which I*

*am no more bound to be accountable, than they for mine. Otherwise I shou'd
have a fine task indeed on my hands, being intimate with Turks and Jews,
with Christians of most denominations, with Deists and Sceptics, with men
of wit or worth in every nation of Europe, and with some out of it. I wish I
were with more so every where. This was the laudable manner of the Antients, this I take to be the way to solid Knowledge, this I am certain is true
Humanity: and as I set no value on the judgment of peevish narrow-soul'd
Bigots of any kind, by whom no Improvement is to be made, cramping on the
contrary all generous Researches; so I am persuaded, that whatever is afraid
to trust it self alone abroad, is not able to stand alone at home. A good Cause
dares hear the worst that can be said against it, having no disirust of its own
Worth. I dare venture my Belief with any man. If tis right he may come into
it, if wrong he may con[xxiv]vince me, and if he'll do neither he's at his liberty: it breaks no squares at all, provided he's master of any Art, or Science,
or other good Quality, by which I may reap any benefit or entertainment.*

*ALL the arts of defamation I have enumerated, are now jointly put
in practise in this nation against one man; for being nobly ingag'd in the
cause of Mankind, in the cause of Christianity, in that of the Reformation,
and in that of the Laity. By this account every one must conclude, I mean
the right reverend the Bishop of* BANGOR: *who, tis to be hop'd, will not be
deserted by the Laity; whose privileges as men and Christians, as Reasonable creatures and Protestants, he does with no less honesty than courage
assert, against the encroachments of the Popishly affected part of the Clergy.
The malice of Devils is set at work, and the tongues of wicked men are set
on edge against him, for the stand he makes against Popery; which is the
heaviest curse that can light on any nation, the greatest unhappiness that
can befall men, with respect to their civil or religious Liberties. They who
are for setting up themselves instead of God (no matter under what name)
and erecting a Political empire over the understandings and consciences of
others; cannot bear with a man, who preaches that as* CHRIST *is King in
his own Kingdom, so his Kingdom is not of this World, nor Religion consequently to be propagated or promoted by secular Rewards and Punishments. Or if for mere shame, because the words are in* Scripture, *some of
his Antagonists own, that* CHRIST's *Kingdom is not of this World; yet it is
in such a manner, as to be content with nothing less than the whole World
for their possession: and favoring or distinguishing the household of Faith,
is in their sense to rob others of their Rights, to make religion a Monopoly,
and to confine* [xxv] *the* Gospel *to their Peculium, instead of giving it a free*

passage over all the earth. This Antichristian spirit is the source of infinite evils, that will certainly attend this Church and Nation; unless, in behalf of Christian Liberty, other able persons do seasonably interpose, after the example of this magnanimous Bishop, who, tho unknown to him, I profoundly reverence for his main Principle: however he may differ from me in any thing of less importance, or that I may possibly differ from his Lordship in many of the things I advance in this very book.

BUT to conclude this Letter, the first of these DISSERTATIONS (which I made a secret to no body, since in the Year aforesaid I sent it to MEGALETOR*) did, upon a mistaken notion of the Subject, probably occasion the alarm that was founded four or five years ago, by the ingenious author of* the Clergyman's thanks to PHILELEUTHERUS LIPSIENSIS; *as if a* new Gospel *were to be foisted, I know not how, into the room of the four old ones. But now I hope his fears will abate, and that, for all this same* BARNABAS *of Turkey,* MATTHEW, MARK, LUKE, *and* JOHN, *may still make good their posts. And so, my Friend, the* Letters *I wrote in that time of warr, and sent by the post under the feign'd name of* PANTHEUS, *I communicate to you this day without any disguize, in order to publish them to all the world. I am, with perfect respect,*

Dear Sir,

Jan. 20. 1718.   *Your most obedient servant,*

J. T.

NAZARENUS:

OR,

Jewish, Gentile, and Mahometan

CHRISTIANITY.

LETTER I.

CHAP. I.

IN my last Letter I promis'd to send you a *Dissertation* upon a subject altogether new (most illustrious MEGALETOR) and now I design to be as good as my word. But first I must make one or two reflections, which however will not lead us much out of our way. You know what vast sums have been publicly promis'd, and I have known much ampler rewards privately propos'd to be given that man, who shou'd recover the remaining parts of the incomparable historians, [2] LIVY and TACITUS. Yet I am persuaded, from the present practice of mankind, as well as from several instances that have formerly happen'd of this very nature: that if any person were so happy, as to discover those or the like valuable manuscripts; he wou'd, contrary to his own and the world's expectations, be left to the mercy of the bookselllers, or the generosity of subscribers. Do we not find all the books of the learned fill'd with complaints, that the ancient Egyptian language and letters, with the means to decypher their Hieroglyphicks, are irreparably lost? What labor, what expence do they not profess they wou'd lay out, to obtain those hidden, and therefore by them reckon'd inestimable, treasures? cou'd they perceive the least probability, or even possibility of succeeding. But for all this, THOMAS HYDE, the late Bodleian library-keeper at Oxford, Doctor of Divinity, Canon of Christ-Church, and Professor of the Oriental languages, after publishing to the world that he was become a perfect master of the ancient Persian literature, that he understood their language and letters, which are suppos'd long ago extinct; nay, and that he cou'd prove the genuin works of ZOROASTER, with several other books of the Mages (containing their history, religion, government, agriculture, and the like) were still extant: after asserting all these particulars, I say, and giving various specimens of their characters, in whole passages of his *Latin* [1] *history of the Religion of the ancient Persians*, tho reserving the Alphabet a secret to himself; yet he cou'd neither engage the public of any sort (applying to Whig and Tory ministers by turns) nor a sufficient number of pri[3]vate benefactors, to enable him to print the books of that kind he had already procur'd, nor to purchase those others which he knew were now in being. He was at the charge of casting a sett of those ancient Persian letters, and he once show'd me one of the books, by means wherof he attain'd the interpretation of the rest, written in alternate lines; the one red and the other black (if I remember right) the one in the old, the other in the modern character: which sorts of writing had not the least affinity or similitude together, no more than the two languages. Tho I confess I never had any extraordinary opinion of Dr. HYDE's judgement, when he took upon him to reason in matters of philosophy or theology; yet I generally found him a competent judge of facts in his most peculiar profession, and cou'd not therefore forbear wishing he had receiv'd due encouragement: that, after his translating of those books, we might likewise judge for our selves, and see how farr what the present [2] fire-worshippers in Persia, with their exil'd brethren the Persées in the East-Indies, believe with so much zeal, and conceal with so much industry, might agree with what the Greec and Roman authors have recorded concerning ZOROASTER and his Mages, the Persians themselves, their customs, language, and religion. Nor is it less to be wish'd, that some body, out of the Malabar language, wou'd publish the *Shaster*, now lying useless in the [3] Bodleian library at Oxford;

---

1. Historia Religionis veterum Persarum, eorumque Magorum, &c. Oxoniae, 1700.

2. *So they are commonly, tho erroneously nick-nam'd (as the Mahometans likewise call 'em Gaurs, Heretics or Unbelievers) from their respecting the fire as a symbol of the Divinity.*

3. MSS. Bodl. supra P. 3. Art. num. 2861.

and which contains the Religion of the present Indian Bramans, transmitted to them from the ancient Brachmans, who affirm'd they receiv'd it from heaven. It [4] signifies nothing how fabulous, contradictory, or mysterious such books may prove; since they serve not only to discover what the modern Indians believe, but to illustrate what old authors have deliver'd concerning the Indian Religion and Philosophy. But that I may not wander too farr, I cou'd never admire at our ignorance about things contain'd in dead languages, or the concerns of nations quite abolish'd, when we are so shamefully at a loss in the affairs of a people, that have flourish'd farr and wide for above a thousand years, that are contemporary with our selves, that are diversify'd into numerous sects and dialects, and with whom we not only daily converse and traffic; but who are also in some places polite and extreamly subtil, abounding with men of letters in their way, and a great variety of books. Nevertheless, tis but very lately that we begun to be undeceiv'd about MAHOMET's pigeon, his pretending to work miracles, and his tomb's being suspended in the air: pious frauds and fables, to which the Musulmans are utter strangers. The truly learned and candid Mr. RELAND, the celebrated professor of the Oriental languages at Utrecht, has exploded not a few vulgar errors relating to the Alcoranists; as others in other articles have, with that moderate Divine and finish'd Scholar, Dr. PRIDEAUX Dean of *Norwich*, done 'em the like justice. But the subject of this *Letter*, Sir, is a point not yet clear'd, if indeed touch'd by any: and tho the very title of *Mahometan Christianity* may be apt to startle you (for *Jewish* or *Gentile Christianity* shou'd not sound quite so strange) yet I flatter my self, that, by perusing the following *Dissertation*, you'll be fully convinc'd there is a sense, wherin the Mahometans may not improperly be reckon'd and call'd a sort or sect of Christians, as Christianity was at [5] first esteem'd a branch of Judaism; and that consequently, shou'd the GRAND SEIGNIOR insist upon it, they might with as much reason and safety be tolerated at London and Amsterdam, as the Christians of every kind are so at Constantinople and thro-out all Turkey. You'll further see reasons here to persuade you of a great paradox, namely; JESUS did not, as tis universally believ'd, abolish the Law of MOSES (Sacrifices excepted) neither in whole nor in part, not in the letter no more than in the spirit: with other uncommon particulars, concerning THE TRUE AND ORIGINAL CHRISTIANITY. Finally, you'll discover some of the fundamental doctrines of Mahometanism to have their rise, not from SERGIUS the Nestorian monk (a person who has hitherto serv'd for a world of fine purposes) but from the earliest monuments of the Christian religion. And tho for the most part I am only a historian, resolv'd to make no Reflections but what my facts will naturally suggest, which facts are generally collected from the *Bible* and the *Fathers*; yet I am not wanting, when there's occasion for it, to chalk out the methods, whereby the errors of simple or designing men may be seasonably confuted: as particularly, by showing the most material difficulties they object; and by exhorting our Divines, with all others that are equal to the task, to prove the authenticness, divinity, and perfection of the *Canon of Scripture*, the best means to silence all gainsayers. Concerning the *new Gospel* I discover, you'll receive due satisfaction in the next chapter, and in those immediately following it. In the mean while, we may (I hope) be as reasonably allow'd to lay out some portion of our time and diligence about the Mahometan doctrine (wherin we are not wholly unconcern'd) as in explaining the old Heathen Mythology, which [6] makes so great a part of our studies, both at school and in the university. So much by way of Introduction: now our subject.

CHAP. II.

AMONG the numerous *Gospels*, *Acts*, *Epistles*, and *Revelations*, which were handed about in the primitive Church, which since that time have been pronounc'd apocryphal by the majority of Christians, and wherof some remain entire to this day, as the *Gospel of* JAMES for example (tho we have only a few fragments of several others) among these, I say, there was a *Gospel* attributed to BARNABAS, as appears from the famous *Decree of* GELASIUS [4] Bishop [7] of *Rome*, who inserts it by name in his roll of apoc-

---

4. *Hujus Decreti verba huc spectantia, cum variantibus quorundam codicum lectionibus, sic se habent.* Itinerarium nomine Petri apostoli, quod appellatur sancti Clementis, libri octo [*potius decem*] apocryphum: Actus, nomine Andreae apostoli, apocryphi: Actus nomine Philippi apostoli, apocryphi: Actus nomine Petri apostoli, apocryphi: Actus nomine Thomae apostoli, apocryphi: Evangelium, nomine Thaddaei [*ut & Matthiae*] apocryphum: Evangelium, nomine Thomae apostoli, quo utuntur Manichaei, apocryphum: Evangelium, nomine BARNABAE, apocryphum: Evangelium nomine Bartholomaei apostoli [*etiam nomine Jacobi minoris*] apocryphum: Evangelium, nomine Andreae apostoli [*ut & Petri*] apocryphum: Evangelia, quae falsavit Lucianus, apocrypha: Evangelia, quae falsavit Hesychius, apocrypha: liber de Infantia Salvatoris, apocryphus: liber de nativitate Salvatoris, & de Sancta Maria, & de Obstetrice Salvatoris, apocryphus: liber qui appellatur Pastoris, apocryphus: libri omnes, quos fecit Lenticius [*potiùs Leucius, Charinus scilicet*] discipulus Diaboli,

ryphal books. Yet GELASIUS, who only augmented and confirm'd it, is not generally allow'd to be the first author of his *Decree*; but DAMASUS before him, as it was augmented again by HORMISDAS after him. The *Gospel of* BARNABAS is likewise quoted in the *Index of the Scriptures*, which COTELE-RIUS has [5] publish'd from the 1789th manuscript of the *French* King's library. Tis further mention'd in the 206th manuscript of the BAROCCIAN collection in the Bodleian [6] library, and is follow'd by the *Gospel according to Matth:* which, to be sure, signifies MATTHIAS and not MATTHEW; since not only in some copies of the *Gelasian Decree* there is a *Gospel* attributed to MATTHIAS, but also by ORIGEN, EUSEBIUS, JEROM, and AMBROSE, as may be seen by the Catalogues [8] of such as have written concerning the Apocryphal books of the *New Testament*. However we must not conceal that in the foresaid *Index of* COTELERIUS, which is the very same with that of the Bodleian library, MATTHEW is printed at length; whether it be erroneously exprest so in the manuscript, or that the transcriber has from MATTH, unaware of this distinction, made MATTHEW. But notwithstanding ancient testimonies, there appears not one single word or fragment of

---

apocryphi: liber, qui appellatur Actus Theclae & Pauli apostoli, apocryphus: Revelatio, quae appellatur Thomae apostoli, apocrypha: Revelatio, quae appellatur Pauli apostoli, apocrypha: Revelatio, quae appellatur Stephani, apocrypha: liber, qui appellatur Transitus Sanctae Mariae, apocryphus: liber, qui appellatur Sortes Apostolorum, apocryphus: liber, qui appellatur Laus Apostolorum, apocryphus: liber Canonum Apostolorum, apocryphus: Epistola Jesu ad Abgarum regem, apocrypha—*Apud Gratian. distinct.* 15. *can.* 3. *& in tomo* 4. *Concilior. ac alibi passim.*

5. Indiculus Scripturarum, *in Judicio de Constitut. Apostolic.*

6. *Catalogus hicce Barroccianus, cui nostras observationes uncinulis inclusas interspergemus, sic se habet in praedicto codice post* Damascenum de mensibus Macedonum. Αδαμ (libri nimirum Adamo olim a Judaeis afficti, speciatim *parva Genesis)* Ενωχ (scilicet *prophetia)* Λαμεχ (*itidem prophetia)* Πατριαρχαι (*Testamentum duodecim Patriarcharum)* Ιωσεφ προσευχη, Ελδαμ και Μοδαμ (Eldad & Medad*)* Διαθηκη Μωσεως (legitur & alius liber dictus Αναληψις Μοϋσεως) Ψαλμοι Σαλμοντος (vel Ωδαι Σολομωντος*)* Ηλιου Αποκαλυψις (vel prophetia*)* Ησαιου όρασις (alias Αναβατικον*)* Σοφονιου Αποκαλυψις (habetur & Ζαχαριου Αποκαλυψις, patris nempe Joannis Baptistae) Εσδρου Αποκαλυψις, Ιακωβου Ίστορια, Πετρου Αποκαλυψις, Περιοδοι και Διδαχαι Αποστολων (Petri nempe, Pauli, Joannis, Thomae, & ceterorum) βαρναβου Επιστολη, Παυλου πραξις, Παυλου Αποκαλυψις, Διδασκαλια Κλημεντος, Ιγνατιου Διδασκαλια [Πολυκαρπου Διδασκαλια] ΕΥΑΓΓΕΛΙΟΝ ΚΑΤΑ ΒΑΡΝΑΒΑΝ, Ευαγγελιον κατα Ματθ. *Habentur & inter apocrypha in Nicephori Chronographia (vel potius in Stichometria eidem addita)* Thomae Evangelium, Clementis prima & secunda Epistola, Ignatii Epistolae omnes, cum Hermae pastore.

the *Gospel of* BARNABAS, printed by any author under this title: yet in the 39th *Baroccian* [7] manuscript there is one fragment of it in the following words. *The Apostle* BARNABAS *says, he gets the worst of it, who overcomes in evil contentions; because he thus comes to have the more* [8] *sin.* BARNABAS is here call'd an Apostle, as he's more than once so term'd by [9] CLEMENS ALEXANDRINUS, and indeed by LUKE himself, or whoever was the writer of the *Acts of the Apostles.* But no particular work of BARNABAS being quoted in the *Baroccian* manuscript, I know (Sir) that a person of your exactness will presently ask me, how I come to affirm that this Saying did belong to his *Gospel?* since it can be no sufficient proof hereof, that it is not to be found in the *Epistle* extant under his name. The objection must be granted to be pertinent, because he might have written other books to us unknown; and therfore I promise a satisfactory answer in a few words, [9] which will appear in a better light further on in this *Letter,* the longest I ever sent you. As for the *Epistle* ascrib'd to BARNABAS, which is still extant, it has been prov'd long since to be spurious by several able hands: but let it be of what authority you will, the modern *Gospel,* of which we shall speak presently, cou'd not be written by the same person; seeing the *Epistle* is purposely directed against the Judaizing Christians.

Acts xiv. 14.

CHAP. III.

AFTER giving this account of the ancient *Gospel* of BARNABAS, or rather a bare proof that formerly there was such a *Gospel,* I come now to the *Gospel of the Mahometans,* which very probably is in great part the same book with that of BARNABAS; and so not yet extinct, as all Christian writers have hitherto imagin'd. But here I know you'll be surpriz'd, that I shou'd talk of any *Gospel of the Mahometans* at all. You'll cease your wonder nevertheless, when you consider how the Mahometans believe, as a fundamental article, that there have been six most eminent persons, who were the authors of new Institutions; every one of these gradually exceding each other in perfection, tho in substance it be still one and the same religion. These six are ADAM, NOAH, ABRAHAM, MOSES, JESUS, and

---

7. *Vide* Grabii Spicilegium Patrum, tom. 1. p. 302.

8. Βαρναβας ὁ αποστολος εφη, εν ἁμιλλαις πονηραις αθλιωτερος ὁ νικησας; διοτι επερχεται, πλεον εχων της ἁμαρτιας.

9. Stromat. lib. 2. *Sic etiam audit apud plerosque Patres, & parum abest quin Epistola ipsi tributa, a quibusdam hodieque habeatur Canonica.*

MAHOMET; wherin all Christians (excepting only as to this latter) agree with them, reckoning up in their several Systems so many [10] periods or dispensations, and calling the [10] whole GOD's ECONOMY. Nor are there wanting who continue subdividing such periods to the end of the world; and, according to some, there's but one period and a piece of one yet remaining: so exactly they know the beginning, the end, the measure of time and things! Now, altho the Mahometans do hold by tradition that ADAM, NOAH, ENOCH, ABRAHAM, and other patriarchs and prophets, had several books divinely sent 'em (even to the number of 104) containing the reveal'd will of God; yet the only obligatory ones are, according to them, these four, *viz.* the *Pentateuch* of MOSES, the *Psalms* of DAVID, the *Gospel of* JESUS, and the *Alcoran* of MAHOMET. Of all and every of these books they pronounce in this manner, nay and in these terms: *whoever denies these volumes, or doubts of the whole or part, or any chapter, verse, or word of the same, is certainly an infidel.* I cou'd allege for this formulary many undeniable authorities; but shall content my self at present to refer you to the third chapter of *The* [11] *compendious Mahometan Theology*, translated, illustrated with *Notes*, and publish'd five or six years ago by the eminent Professor ADRIAN RELAND, before mention'd. In the mean time you may perceive, that the Mahometans are not only more careful in preserving the integrity of their sacred books, than the Christians have generally been; but that they are likewise, as many of 'em assert, more consistent with themselves: since if any book be divinely inpir'd, say they, every line and word of it must necessarily be so; and therfore no room left, one wou'd imagine, [11] for *various Readings*, or such other Criticisms. The minute the learned may alter, add, or substitute, what to them shall seem most becoming the divine spirit, there's an end at once of *Inspiration*, (according to these gentlemen) and the book becomes thenceforth their own: meaning, that it is then the production of different times and diverse authors, till nothing of the original be left, tho the book continues as bulky as ever. But it must be carefully observ'd, that the Mahometan *system* of *Inspiration*, and that of the Christians, are most widely different: since we do not so much stand

---

10. *Tritum est illud Theologorum, genus scilicet humanum ab Adamo ad Noachum fuisse sub lege Naturae, a Noacho ad Abrahamum sub praeceptis Noachicis, ad Abrahamo ad Mosen sub Circumcisione, a Mose ad Christum sub ritibus Leviticis, & sic inde sub Evangelio usque ad Millennium, vel secundùm alios ad supremum Judicium.*

11. Adriani Relandi de Religione Mahommedica libri duo, pag. 25.

upon words, phrases, method, pointing, or such other niceties; as upon the matter it self, and the design of the whole, tho circumstances shou'd not be always so exact. 'Tis here we cast our sheet-anchor, and tis here we are confirm'd by matter of fact; notwithstanding the 30000 variations, which some of our Divines have discover'd in a few copies of the *New Testament:* nor have the copies of the *Alcoran* escap'd such variations (which is impossible in nature for any book to do) whatever the Mahometans pretend to the contrary, and even some of themselves have produc'd such different readings.

CHAP. IV.

TIS for the abovesaid reason, no doubt, of joining the *Pentateuch*, the *Psalms*, and the *Gospel* to the *Alcoran*, that I have heard some *Arabians* call Mahometanism the Religion of the four books, as the Christian Religion that of the two books. Nor is there any thing more evident to those who have taken pains in this matter, than that the Mahometans openly profess to believe the *Gospel:* tho they charge our copies with so [12] much corruption and alteration, that our *Gospel* is not only no longer certain or genuine; but, according to them, the farthest of all books in the world from being divine. About this charge, and the four books which they acknowledge divine, may be particularly consulted *The historical Compend of* [12] LEVINUS WARNER. But why shou'd I mention WARNER, or any other? Since the *Alcoran* it self does so often referr to the *Pentateuch*, the *Psalms*, and the *Gospel*, the inspiration on and authority wherof it always allows. This cannot be disputed. That the four books constitute the foundation of their Religion, is so much their general and constant belief, that one might as well be at the troble of quoting authors to prove the Christians receiv'd the *Old* and *New Testament*. But since in a late conversation certain persons, who ought to know better, appear'd surpriz'd at this; I desire that, over and above the now-mention'd *historical Compend of* WARNER, and the *Mahometan Theology of* RELAND, they wou'd please to read the formulary or profession of JACOB BEN SIDI ALI, produc'd by the Maronite [13] GABRIEL SIO-

---

12. Compendium historicum eorum quæ Mahommedani de Christo, & praecipuis aliquot Religionis Christianae capitibus tradiderunt.

13. De nonnullis Orientalium urbibus nec non indigenarum religione ac moribus. Tractatus brevis; auctoribus Gabriele Sionita & Joanne Hesronita, Maronitis e Libano. cap. 14.

NITA. Beyond exception is the testimony of the celebrated Divine ALGAZEL, in his *Exposition of the faith of the Sonnites,* or the Turkish Mahometans, in contradistinction to the *Schafites,* or the sect of the Persians; where, in the article *of the word of God,* he thus speaks: *we are bound to believe that the* Alcoran, *the* Pentateuch, *the* Gospel, *and the* Psalms *of* DAVID, *are books* [13] *given by God, and reveal'd to his Ambassadors.* Whoever has a mind to see the original Arabic passage, may read it in the 89th page of the third part of MARACCI's *Prodromus to the Alcoran.* In another Mahometan formulary, quoted in the 94th page of the same third part by MARACCI, you have the names of those Ambassadors in these words: *the* Pentateuch *was sent to* MOSES *the son of* AMRAM, *and the Gospel to* JESUS *the son of* MARY, *and the* Psalms *to* DAVID, *and the* Alcoran *to* MAHOMET. It were superfluous to add the concurrent testimonies of others. But still that *Gospel* is not ours, which, as I said, they decretorily brand with falsification. Every travellor almost will tell you, that where JESUS promises to send the *Paraclete* to complete or perfect all things, the Mahometans maintain the original reading was [14] *Periclyte,* or the famous and illustrious, which in Arabic is *Mohammed:* so that their prophet was as much, in their account, foretold by name in the *Gospel;* as CYRUS is believ'd by the Jews and Christians, to have been foretold by name in the *Old Testament.* Here's one instance of Mahometan Criticism; not less subtil or more slightly grounded, than abundance of such discoveries hammer'd out of sounds or letters by Jews and Christians: and I own that I have always admir'd so few other examples of *various Readings* or Interpolations were produc'd by learned travellors (tho some they do) since the Mahometans have so different an account of the person of JESUS CHRIST, of his ministry on earth, and the circumstances of his ascent into heaven. I was somtimes temted to fancy, that the excessive veneration of the Mahometans for the *Alcoran,* made them suffer their *Gospel* to perish by neglect: but [14] corrected that thought again, when I found such multitudes of citations out of it in their writings, over and above those contain'd in the *Alcoran;* the passages somtimes agreeing with those in our *Gospels,* often with those we count apocryphal, and oftner with neither. Hence I concluded, that since they counted the *Gospel* a divine book, and had more knowledge of it than their *Alcoran* furnish'd, they must needs have a *Gospel* of their own; tho I was always astonish'd (as I said) at the negligence of travellors, or whatever other reason it might

John xiv. 16, 26. & xv. 26. & xvi. 7. *compar'd* with Luke xxiv. 49. Isaiah xliv. 28. & xlv. 1.

---

14. Περικλυτος, & non Παρακλητος.

be, that hinder'd 'em from producing that *Gospel*, and yet so positively talk of its variety from ours. Nay, some of 'em have directly deny'd the Mahometans had any such *Gospel* now remaining; and Mr. RELAND, in his foremention'd Treatise, adopts their [15] opinion: not to speak of MARACCI, and divers other Writers of most Christian communions.

Pag. 23.

CHAP. V.

BUT at length (Sir) after wholly despairing of ever having a better account, it was my good fortune, instead of other information, to light on the *Gospel* it self; and translated into Italian, by or for the use of some renegades: for it is most certainly the performance of a Mahometan scribe. Yet knowing a more particular account will not be ungrateful, be pleas'd to receive it as follows. The learned gentleman, who has been so kind as to communicate it to me (*viz.* Mr. CRAMER, [15] Counsellor to the King of *Prussia*, but residing at [16] *Amsterdam*) had it out of the Library of a person of great name and authority in the said city; who, during his life, was often heard to put a high value on this piece. Whether as a rarity, or as the model of his religion, I know not. It is in the very first page attributed to BARNABAS, and the title of it runs in these [17] words: *The true* Gospel *of* JESUS *called* CHRIST, *a new prophet sent by God to the world, according to the relation of* BARNABAS *his apostle.* Here you have not only a new *Gospel*, but also a true one, if you believe the Mahometans. But how honest soever they may be represented, this is a topic where none are to be credited without the utmost caution; since, tho every *Gospel* forbids lying, yet never are more lies told than about the *Gospel*. The first chapter of it begins [18] thus. BARNABAS *an apostle of* JESUS *of Nazareth, called* CHRIST, *to all those who dwell upon the earth, wisheth peace and consolation.* Whatever may become of the truth, this is the Scripture-stile to a

---

15. *But having better information since that time, he does in an edition he has made of his book this very year, affirm, that the Mahometans have a* Gospel *of their own* (page 23) *and I suppose he means those of Barbary, because he says this* Gospel *is in Spanish and Arabic.*

16. *He's dead since the writing of this* LETTER.

17. Vero Evangelio di Jessu chiamato Christo, novo profeta mandato da Dio al mondo, secundo la descritione di Barnaba Apostolo suo.

18. Barnaba Apostolo di Jessu Nazareno, chiamato Christo, ha tutti quelli che habitano sopra la terra, pace he consolatione desidera. Charissimi.

hair. The book is written on Turkish paper delicately gumm'd and polish'd, and also bound after the Turkish manner. The ink is incomparably fine; and the orthography, as well as the character, plainly show it to be at least three hundred years old. I ever chuse to speak rather under than over in such cases. Any proper name of God, and the appellative word DIO it self, are constantly writ in red letters out [16] of respect, and so are the Arabic *Notes* in transverse lines on the margin. The contents of the chapters are likewise written in red letters, and reach about the twentieth; a void space being left for the rest before each chapter, but no where fill'd up. The author of these summaries was a zealous Musulman, who charges the Christians all along with falsification, from this his only authentic *Gospel.* But they'll be nothing behind hand with him, whenever his *Gospel* comes to be better known. Much care and ornament was bestow'd upon the whole, and the Arabic word ALLAH is in red letters superstitiously interline'd over DIO, for the first three times it occurs. The Story of JESUS is very differently told in many things from the receiv'd *Gospels,* but much more fully and particularly; this *Gospel,* if my eye has not deceiv'd me, being near as long again as any of ours. Some wou'd make this circum- stance a prejudice in favor of it, because as all things are best known just after they happen; so every thing diminishes, the further it proceeds from its original. But in this case the rule will be found not rightly apply'd, till the Book is prov'd to be the genuine issue of BARNABAS. MAHOMET is therein expresly nam'd for the *Paraclete,* as we have been told that he's so esteem'd, by all the historians of the Mahometan Religion: the Musulmans accusing our *Gospels* of corruption (as I noted before) in the 16th and 26th verses of the 14th Chapter of JOHN; and pretending further that MAHOM- ET's name was struck out of the *Pentateuch* and the *Psalms.* MAHOMET is nam'd again or foretold in some other places of this book of BARNABAS, as the design'd accomplisher of God's economy towards man. Tis, in short, the ancient Ebionite or Nazaren System, as to the making of JESUS a mere man (tho not with them the Son of JOSEPH, but [17] divinely conceiv'd by the Virgin MARY) and agrees in every thing almost with the scheme of our modern Unitarians; excepting the history of his death and resurrec- tion, about which a very different account is given from that in our *Gos- pels:* but perfectly conformable to the tradition of the Mahometans, who maintain that another was crucify'd in his stead; and that JESUS, slipping thro' the hands of the Jews, preach'd afterwards to his disciples, and then was taken up into heaven.

See also John xv. 26. & xvi. 7. *compar'd with* Luke xxiv. 49.

CHAP. VI.

HOW great (by the way) is the ignorance of those, who make this an original invention of the Mahometans! for the Basilidians, in the very beginning of Christianity, deny'd [19] that CHRIST himself suffered, but that SIMON of *Cyrene* was crucify'd in his place. The Cerinthians before them, and the Carpocratians next (to name no more of those, who affirm'd JESUS to have been a mere Man) did believe the same thing; that it was not himself, but one of his followers very like him, that was crucify'd: so that *the Gospel of* BARNABAS, for all this account, may be as old as the time of the Apostles, bateing several interpolations (from which, 'tis known, that no *Gospel* is exemt) since CERINTHUS was contemporary with PETER, PAUL, and JOHN, if there be any truth in [20] *Ecclesiastical history.* Thus PHOTIUS tells us, that he read a book, entitul'd, *The Journeys of the Apostles*, relating the [18] acts of PETER, JOHN, ANDREW, THOMAS, and PAUL: and among other things contain'd in the same, this was [21] one, *that* CHRIST *was not crucify'd, but another in his stead, and that therfore he laught at the crucifiers*, or those who thought they crucify'd him. Some said it was JUDAS that was executed. This laughing of JESUS at the Jews was also affirm'd by the Basilidians, as you may see in the place I quoted about them just now out of EPIPHANIUS. Tis a strange thing, one wou'd think, they shou'd differ about a fact of this nature so early; and that CERINTHUS, who was contemporary, a countryman, and a Christian, shou'd with all those of his Sect, deny the [22] resurrection of CHRIST from the dead: tho we cou'd easily solve the difficulty, were this a proper occasion for it; and I may, in convenient time, send you my observations on this subject. But they who deny'd his crucifixion, deny'd also his Genealogy, as it stands according to MATTHEW. In an Irish manuscript of the four *Gospels* (of which I shall give you an account in my next Letter) the Genealogy of JESUS is inserted apart, among certain preliminary pieces; and the first chapter of *Matthew*

Ver. 18. begins at these words, *Now the birth of* JESUS CHRIST *was on this wise.* The

---

19. Iren. lib. 1. cap. 23, &c. Item Epiphan. Haeres. 24. num. 3.

20. Iren. l. 3. c. 3: Euseb. Hist. Eccles. l. 3. c. 28: item l. 4. c. 14: Epiphan. Haeres. 28. n. 2, 3, 4. Idem asserunt Augustinus, Theodoretus, cum reliquis.

21. Και τον Χριστον μη σταυρωθηναι, αλλ᾽ ἑτερον αντ᾽ αυτου, και καταγελαν δια τουτο των σταυρουωτων. In Bibliotheca, cod. 14.

22. Haeres. 28. n. 6.

Ebionites, according to EPIPHANIUS, had not the [23] Genealogy in their *Gospel*; which makes it needless for him to say [24] elsewhere that the Cerinthians rejected it, whose *Gospel* was the same. But yet EPIPHANIUS, who confounds every thing [19] (as particularly this *Gospel of the Hebrews* with that of MATTHEW) tells us that CERINTHUS and CARPOCRAS wou'd needs prove by this very GENEALOGY, that JESUS was the [25] Son of JOSEPH and MARY. Nay, he farther acquaints us, how in the fourth Century, while CONSTANTINE the great reign'd, this Genealogy, with other curious pieces in Hebrew, was found by a certain JOSEPH in a cell of the treasury at Tiberias, which he honestly broke open to [26] steal some mony; and that this odd accident was the chief reason of his becoming a Christian. But whether the word [27] there signifies the Genealogy by it self according to PETAVIUS, or the whole *Gospel of* MATTHEW, according to FABRICIUS, tis certain that TATIAN left the Genealogy out of his *Gospel*; which so impos'd on the Orthodox themselves, that THEODORET affirms he had [28] remov'd above 200 of those *Gospels* out of public Churches, and plac'd others in their stead. So that the want of this Genealogy in the Irish copy of MATTHEW is not so strange a thing, as it may seem at first sight; which is all the consequence I shall now draw from it, referring the further discussion of it to another time, as it particularly relates to our Irish Manuscript.

[20] CHAP. VII.

BUT that I may not forget, what I promis'd above concerning the fragment of BARNABAS in the *Baroccian* Manuscript, I found it almost in terms in this *Gospel*, and the sense is evidently there in more than one place; which naturally induces me to think, it may be the *Gospel* anciently attributed to BARNABAS, however since (as I said) interpolated. I had not time to see if it contain'd the four sayings, or rather discourses of CHRIST, inserted by LEVINUS WARNER out of Mahometan books, into his *Notes* on the [29] *Century of Persian Proverbs*, which he publish'd at the end of his

---

23. Haeres. 28. n. 5. & 30. n. 3.
24. Haeres. 28. n. 5.
25. Haeres. 30. n. 14.
26. Ibid. n. 6.
27. Το κατα Ματθαιον Εβραικον φυτον.
28. Haeret. Fabul. l. 1. c. 20.
29. *Ad proverb.* 61. in Appendice Compendii historici, *pag.* 30

Historical Compend, cited before. I found many sayings ascrib'd to JESUS by [30] KESSEUS (as I read his *Lives of the Patriarchs and Prophets* cited) and by other Mahometan writers, exprest in this *Gospel of* BARNABAS: tho I have not yet examin'd all of that kind I have observ'd, no more than any of those in the *Alcoran*, the grossest of all impostures. But from what I have already had opportunity to do, two discoveries naturally result; which

I. cannot, Sir, but be agreeable to you. The first is, that we now probably know, whence the Mahometans quote most passages of this kind, they have concerning CHRIST: some having for this very reason rashly charg'd 'em with forgery, and others gravely asserting, that they took them all out of the known Apocryphal pieces; as if they had kept these with more care than the Christians, and without ever naming or producing any of the Apocryphal books they cou'd so easily suppose. [21] *The Gospel of the Infancy of* CHRIST, publish'd some years ago out of the Arabic, appears not only from the invocation of the Trinity to be no Mahometan imposture; but from *Ecclesiastical history*, and the extant original Greec Manuscripts, unknown to Mr. SIKE, the editor of it, to be long anterior to MAHOMET. This is as true of *the Gospel of* JAMES, which boasts of being the first of all the *Gospels*, or the PROTOEVANGELION: nor is it less true of *the Gospel of* NICODEMUS, which last is only extant in Latin; and seems by diverse of its expressions and doctrines, to be one of the latest of all those spiritual cheats. I deny not, that the Mahometans have borrow'd some of their fables from these and the like *apocryphal Scriptures:* I only deny it of all such; as believing most of 'em to be cull'd out of their own *Gospel of* BARNABAS. They are not ignorant however, either of the existence or imposture of the just mention'd *Gospel of the Infancy*, which AHMED EBN EDRIS cites by name, calling it also *the fifth Gospel* (as you may see in the 2d Chapter of the first part of MARACCI's *Prodromus*) *but redundant*, says he, *in*

II. *many things, and in many things defective.* Our next discovery is, that the Mahometans not only believe, as is well known, many things recorded of JESUS in our *Gospels*; but that they have likewise a peculiar *Gospel* of their own, tho probably in a few hands among the learned, from which perhaps some passages in ours may be farther illustrated: for very ancient books, tho never so spurious, always speak the language, often express the traditions, and commonly allude to the customs of their own times. I would

III. here add, as a third discovery, that we have at length found out the *Gospel*

---

30. Abu-Mohammed Abd-Alla.

father'd of old upon BARNABAS, tho not in its original purity. But I had not the perusal of the [22] book long enough, to form any peremtory decision in this case; notwithstanding the force of those presumtions, I have already alleg'd. I know how difficult a thing it is, to come at any *Alcoran* it self; and how few have it in their hands, even in Turky: Yet I have taken the most proper measures to gain all the further light about *the Gospel of* BARNABAS that can possibly be procur'd; as you'll perceive by some QUERIES I have drawn up, and which I shall do my self the honour to [31] communicate to you in a few days.

CHAP. VIII.

NOW, as I have before given the first words of this *Gospel*, I shall add the last words of it in this place. JESUS *being* [32] *gone* (that is into heaven) *the Disciples scatter'd themselves into many parts of Israel, and of the rest of the world: and the truth, being hated of* SATAN, *was persecuted by falshood, as it ever happens. For certain wicked men, under pretence of being Disciples, preach'd that Jesus was dead, and not risen again: others preach'd that* JESUS *was truely dead, and risen again: others preach'd, and still continue to preach, that* JESUS [23] *is the Son of God, among which persons* PAUL *has been deceiv'd. We therfore, according to the measure of our knowledge, do preach to those who fear God, to the end they may be sav'd at the last day of his divine judgment; Amen. The end of the Gospel.* Tis plain that the writer of this book has known of the dissention between BARNABAS and PAUL, recorded in *the Acts of the Apostles:* and it will be said, perhaps, that this quarrel set BARNABAS a writing. PAUL had likewise no little contest with PETER, about his manner of preaching the *Gospel* to the Gentiles. Neither do I doubt but tis the Apostle to the Gentiles, that is aim'd at in *an Epistle of* PETER *to* JAMES, prefixt by COTELERIUS to the *Clementines.* The words

Acts xv. 36, 37, 38, 39, 40. *Compare* Acts x. *with* Gal. ii. 11, 12.

---

31. *See the* Appendix, num. III.

32. Partito Jessu, si divisse per diversse parte de Isdrahelle he del mondo li dissepoli; he la verita, hodiata da Sattana, su persheguitata dalla Bugia, chome tutavia si trova: perche alchuni malli homeni, sotto pretesto di dissepoli, predichavano Jessu essere morto he non rissuscitato; altri predichavano Jessu essere veramente morto, he rissuscitato; altri predichavano, he hora predichano, Jessu essere fiolo di DIO, fra li qualli he Paullo ingannato. Noi pero, quanto habia sciuto, predichiamo ha cholloro che temono DIO, aziocche siano salvi nello ultimo giorno dello juditio di DIO; Amen. Fine dello Evangelio.

of PETER (after entreating JAMES not to communicate his *Preachings* to any Gentile, nor even to any Jew without previous examination) are [33] these. *For if this be not done, says he, our speech of truth* [24] *will be divided into many opinions. Nor do I know this thing as being a prophet, but as seeing even now the beginning of this very evil: for some from among the Gentiles have rejected my Legal preaching; embracing the trifling and Lawless doctrine of a man, who is an enemy. And these things some have endeavor'd to do now in my own life-time, transforming my words by various interpretations to the destruction of the Law; as if I had been of the same mind, but durst not openly profess it, which be farr from me. For this were to act against the Law of God spoken by Moses, and which has the testimony of our Lord for its perpetual duration, since he thus has said:* heaven and earth shall pass away, yet one jot or one tittle shall not pass from the Law. *And this he said, that all might be fulfill'd. But these, I know not how, promising to deliver my opinion, take upon them to explain the words they heard from me, better than I that spoke them; telling their disciples my sense was that, of which I have not so much as thought. Now, if in my own life-time they dare feign such things; how much more will those, that come after me, do the same?* This most remarkable and incontestably ancient piece, with others at least as ancient, which I cou'd cite were it needful, do manifestly show; that this notion of PAUL's having wholly metamorphos'd and perverted the true Christianity (as some of these Heretics have exprest it) and his being blam'd for so doing by the other Apostles, especially by JAMES and PETER, is nei-

See Gal. ii. 11, 12, 13, 14.

Mat. v. 18.
Luke xvi. 17.
See Gal. as above.

---

33. Επει εαν μη ουτως γενηται, εις πολλας γνωμας ο της αληθειας ημων διαιρεθησεται λογος. Τουτο δε ουχ᾽ ως ο προφητης ων επισταμαι, αλλ᾽ ηδη αυτου του κακου την αρχην ορων. Τινες γαρ των απο εθνων, το δὶ εμου νομιμον απεδοκιμασαν κερυγμα, του εχθρου ανθρωπου ανομον τινα και φλυαρωδη προσηκαμενοι διδασκαλιαν. Και ταυτα επι μου περιοντος επεχειρησαν τινες ποικιλαις τισιν ἑρμενειαις τους εμους λογους μετασχηματιζειν εις την του Νομου καταλυσιν; ως και εμου αυτου ουτω μεν φρονουντος, μη εκ παρρησιας δε κερυσσοντος: οπερ απειη. Το γαρ τοιουτο αντιπρασσειν εστι τω του θεου νομω, τω δια Μοϋσεως ρηθεντι, και υπο του κυριου ἡμων μαρτυρηθεντι περι της αϊδιου αυτου διαμονης, επει ουτως ειπεν: ο ουρανος και ἡ γη παρελευσονται, ιωτα ἑν η μια κεραια ου μη παρελθη απο του νομου. Τουτο δε ειρηκεν, ίνα τα παντα γινηται. Όι δε, ουκ οιδα πως, τον εμον νουν επαγγελλομενοι, οὑς ηκουσαν εξ εμου λογους, εμου του ειποντος αυτους φρονιμωτερον επεχειρουσιν ερμενευειν: λεγοντες τοις υπ᾽ αυτων κατηχουμενοις, τουτο ειναι το εμου φρονημα, ὃ εγω ουδ᾽ ενεθυμηθεν. Ει δε εμου ετι περιοντος τοιαυτα τολμωσιν καταψευδεσθαι, τοσω γε μαλλον μετ᾽ εμε ποιειν ὁι μετ᾽ εμε ποιησουσιν. Tom. 1. Patr. Apostolic. pag. 602.

ther an original invention of the Mahometans, nor any sign of the novelty of their *Gospel*: but rather a strong presumtion of its antiquity, at least as to some parts of it; since this was the constant language and profession of the most ancient Sects, as I shall convince you beyond any room for doubt.

[25] CHAP. IX.

TO set this matter therfore in the clearest light, it is to be noted, that the Ebionites call'd PAUL *an Apostate from the Law*; and rejected all his *Epistles*, as those of an Enemy and an Impostor. This is recorded by [34] ORIGEN [35] and EUSEBIUS, which shows that EPIPHANIUS (whose testimony we shall produce hereafter) is neither the only, nor the first, nor without an author, that said this is of the Ebionites, as the acute Mr. NYE has too positively affirm'd in his *Judgement of the Fathers*; denying this of ORIGEN by name, whom I have this moment quoted for it. The like charge against PAUL is acknowledg'd of the Nazarens, who were the same people under another name, or rather this of NAZARENS is the only name they own'd: and both of 'em, if they must needs be made two, were the first converts among the Jews to Christianity; that is to say, the first Christians, and consequently the only Christians for some time. Mr. SELDEN, never to be mention'd without honor, shows, that at least for the space of seven years after the death of CHRIST, none of the Gentiles embrac'd his doctrine; all his followers, till the conversion of CORNELIUS the Centurion, who was a proselyte of the gate, having been of the Jewish [36] nation and religion. [26] Now, these Jewish converts were term'd Nazarens from JESUS *of Nazareth*, as it appears that all the first Christians were so; since PAUL himself is, in *the Acts of the Apostles*, call'd *a ringleader of the Heresy of the Nazarens*. EPIPHANIUS not only affirms, *that all Christians were at* [37] *first by the Jews term'd Nazarens, and even by the Apostles themselves*, PETER *saying*, JESUS *of Nazareth, a man approv'd of God*, &c: but also *that the NAZARENS took*

Pag. 35.

Acts x. 47, 48.
Ibid. x. 38.
& iii. 6. &
iv. 10.
Ibid. xxiv. 5.
Ibid. ii. 22.
& x. 38.

---

34. Contra Cels. l. 5.

35. Hist. Eccles. l. 3. c. 27. Ὁυτοι δε του μεν Αποστολου πασας τας Επιστολας αρνητειας ἡγουντο ειναι δειν, Αποσταταν αποκαλουντες αυτον του νομου. *Item* Nicephor. Hist. Eccles. l. 4. c. 4. *Videatur & ejusdem* l. 5. c. 12.

36. De Synedriis, l. 1. n. 8.

37. Ναζωραιων, ὁ εστι χριστιανων, ὁ κληθεις εν ολιγῳ χρονῳ ὑπο Ιουδαιων χριστιανισμος, και ὑπο αυτων των Αποστολων, λεγοντος Πετρου, Ιησουν τον Ναζωραιον, ανδρα αποδεδειγμενον εκ του θεου, &c. Haeres. 19. n. 4.

this name to [38] *themselves, but not that of* JESSEANS *after* JESUS, *nor of*
CHRISTIANS *after* CHRIST; *and that all Christians whatsoever were then*
stil'd Nazarens, before they were call'd Christians at Antioch. TERTUL-
LIAN speaks to the same [39] purpose. They were likewise call'd by way of
contemt EBIONITES or beggars (just as the first Protestants in Flanders
Gueux) which is very evident, not only from the silence of IRENEUS concerning any such person as EBION, but also from the express testimonies
of [40] ORIGEN and EUSEBIUS, that they were thus nick-nam'd because of
their mean condition: and even from the Hebrew word *Ebion* it self, which
signifies *poor,* and was a most proper epithet of the first Christians; as [27]
JAMES asks the question concerning them, *has not God chosen the POOR*
of this world, rich in faith; and as CHRIST order'd JOHN to be told, *that the*
Gospel was preach'd to the POOR; or, to say it in Hebrew, to the *Ebionites.*
Yet afterwards some persons, that were equally ignorant of the Jewish language and of the Christian history, ridiculously invented a certain EBION
(of whom they tell very formal stories) to be the author of the Ebionites; as
they saw several other Sects had peculiar founders, of whom they deriv'd
their appellation. But we ought much sooner to believe the Ebionites themselves about their own name of Nazarens, and nick-name of Ebionites,
than JEROM, or EPIPHANIUS, or any other of their enemies; who either did
not know them enough, or wilfully and maliciously misrepresented them.
Others again, who cou'd no more digest this very gross account, than content themselves with the lovely simplicity of truth, insinuated that those
first Christians were call'd Ebionites from their [41] poor and low notions of
CHRIST's person: a derivation as farr fetcht as any other, and which diverse
learned men have deservedly exploded. Nevertheless, whatever confusion and diversity may be observ'd concerning them in IRENEUS, JUSTIN
MARTYR, EUSEBIUS, EPIPHANIUS, AUGUSTIN, THEODORET, and others of
those they call the old *Fathers,* tis constantly agreed among them, '*that the*
Nazarens and Ebionites affirm'd JESUS *to have been a mere man, as well by*

Ibid. xi.
26.

אביון

Jam. ii. 5.

Mat. xi. 5.
לאביונים

---

38. Ὅυτοι γαρ [ὁι Ναζωραιοι] ἑαυτοις ονομα επεθεντο, ουχι Χριστου, ουτε αυτο
το ονομα του Ιησου, αλλα Ναζωραιων; και παντες δε Χριστιανοι Ναζωραιοι τοτε
ὁσαυτως εκαλουντο. Id Haeres. 29. n. 1. & ibid. n. 6, 7.

39. Nazaraeus vocari habebat, secundùm prophetiam, Christus creatoris: unde &
ipso nomine nos Judaei Nazaraeos appellant per eam. *Contra Marcion. l. 4. c. 8.*

40. Origen. contra Cels. l. 2: & Philocal. c. 1: Euseb. Hist. Eccles. l. 3. c. 27.

41. Εβιωναιους τουτους οικειως επεφημιζον ὁι πρωτοι, πτωχως και ταπεινως τα
περι του Χριστου δοξαζοντας. Euseb. Hist. Eccles. l. 3. c. 27.

the father as the mother's side, namely the Son of Joseph [28] *and* Mary; *but that he was* [42] *just, and wise, and excellent, above all other persons, meriting to be peculiarly call'd* The Son of God, *by reason of his most virtuous life and extraordinary endowments: and that they join'd with their Christain profession, the necessity of circumcision, of the observation of the Sabbath, and of the other Jewish ceremonies'*; which necessity must be understood only of the Jewish Christians, for the reasons I shall produce by and by. Eusebius says, that some few of 'em in his time (that is, in the fourth century) believ'd, like the Gentile Christians, the mother of Christ to have been a [43] Virgin; and that he was conceiv'd by virtue of the Spirit of God, tho still but a mere man (which is just the Socinianism of our times) but that they enjoin'd the observation of the Legal ceremonies, as strictly as the others. There were diversities of opinion among 'em, no doubt, no less than among other societies, as this same distinction is as old as Origen's time: yet tho these latter were a quite different sort from the former, as the best Critics fairly acknowledge; they rejected Paul's *Epistles* equally with the others, and were as highly irritated [44] against him. But the *Fathers* acted with inexcusable confusion and injustice, to call men professing two such contrary sentiments by the same name of Ebionites, if such a Heretic as Ebion had ever existed; which some of 'em, as I said, did most ignorantly averr, especially Jerom and Epiphanius: tho the Ebionites [29] themselves (as even Epiphanius [45] confesses, who yet will not believe them) deny'd any such Ebion; and glory'd in their name, alledging their poverty was occasion'd by the laying of all their substance at the Apostles feet, for the first and most powerful support of Christianity, by a community of goods. These Nazarens therfore or Ebionites were mortal enemies to Paul, whom they stil'd *an Apostate* (as we saw just now) and [46] *a transgressor of the Law:* representing him as an intruder on the genuin Christianity, and, tho a stranger to the person of Christ, yet substituting his own pretended Revelations to the doctrines of those with whom Christ had convers'd, and to whom he actually communicated his will. This is the sum of what

Acts ii. 44, 45. & iv. 34, 35, &c.

42. Iren l. 1. c. 26: Euseb. Hist. Eccles. l. 3. c. 27: Epiphan. Haeres. 7. n. 2. 28. n. 1. & 30. n. 2. 18: Theodoret. Haeret. fab. l. 2. c. 1, 2. cum reliquis.
43. Hist. Eccles. l. 3. c. 27. *Idem dicunt* Origen. contra Cels. l. 2: Hieronym. in Epist. ad Augustin: & Thodoret. in loco jam notato.
44. Origen. contra Cels. l. 5.
45. Haeres. 30. n. 17.
46. Hieronym. in cap. 12. Matth.

we certainly know concerning them; for in other things, one or two points excepted, the *Fathers* are not of accord. Moreover, the Christians are to this day by the Arabians and Persians call'd NAZARI, and NOZERIM by the Jews, who call'd them at the beginning (as I suppose upon occasion they do still) MINEANS or Heretics: since all sectaries, of all sorts, are so nam'd by them; and that Christianity was then reckon'd but a Jewish Heresy, tho it was rather truely and properly their Reformation. The Nazarens or Mineans, whose Churches florish'd over all the [47] east, us'd to be curs'd by the Jews in their synagogues, at morning, noon, and evening pray[30]ers, under this very name of [48] Nazarens; as being excommunicate persons, and apostates from their body. In effect, they were commonly confounded together by the Heathens, even a good while after the Gentile converts made another Church: nor is SELDEN the only person, that, in later times, has asserted CHRISTIANITY to be no more than [49] REFORMED JUDAISM; the true religion being one and the same in substance from the beginning, tho in circumstances the Institutions of it at different times be different, and consequently more or less perfect. But we must not forget how his adversaries us'd the Apostle of the Gentiles.

מינים

CHAP. X.

Rom. ii. 16. & xvi. 25. Gal. i. 11. & ii. 2. 2 Tim. ii. 8. Gal. i. 11, 12. Ver. 17, 18, 19.

NOR does PAUL deny the charge of the Ebionites, that he did not learn *his Gospel* (a phraze familiar to him) from those who were immediately taught by CHRIST himself. For he tells the Galatians plainly, that *the Gospel which he preach'd was not after man; for I neither receiv'd it of man* (says he) *neither was I taught it but by the revelation of* JESUS CHRIST: *neither went I up to Jerusalem to them which were Apostles before me, but I went into Arabia and Damascus. Then after three years I went up to Jerusalem to see* PETER, *and abode with him fifteen days; but other of the Apostles saw I none, save* JAMES *the* [31] *Lord's brother.* And so he went on preaching this

---

47. Usque hodie per totas Orientis Synagogas inter Judaeos haeresis est, quae dicitur MINAEORUM, & a Pharisaeis nunc usque damnatur, quos vulgò Nazaraeos nuncupant. *Hieronym. in Epist. ad Augustin.*

48. Usque hodie perseverant in blasphemiis, & ter per singulos dies in omnibus Synagogis, sub nomine Nazaraeorum, anathematizant vocabulum Christianum. *Id. in Isaiam, cap.* 5. *ver.* 18.

49. Nec disciplina illa apud eos alia, quam Judaismus verè Reformatus, seu cum fide in Messiam, seu Christum, ritè conjunctus. *De Synedr. l.* 1. *c.* 8.

Gospel to the Gentiles, as he informs us in the same *Epistle* and elsewhere; expresly absolving them (and, as tis now generally believ'd, the Jews themselves) from Circumcision, and all the Levitical ceremonies, against which he strenuously argues every where. Then he declares, how that *fourteen* **Ibid. ii.** *years after he went again to Jerusalem, and communicated unto them that* **1, 2.** Gospel, *which he had preach'd among the Gentiles; yet but privately to them who were of reputation,* for fear of those who did not approve of the liberty **Ver. 2.** he preach'd from the Jewish ceremonies. Next he tells of what past between him and the other Apostles, *who, tho they seem'd to be somewhat, in con-* **Ver. 6, 7,** *ference added nothing to him: but contrarywise,* says he, *when they* (that **8, 9.** is, JAMES, and CEPHAS, and JOHN, who seem'd to be pillars) *saw that* THE GOSPEL OF THE UNCIRCUMCISION *was committed unto me, as* THE GOSPEL OF THE CIRCUMCISION *was unto* PETER, *and perceiv'd the grace that was given unto me; they gave to me and* BARNABAS *the right hands of fellowship, that we shou'd go unto the* HEATHEN, *and they unto the* CIRCUMCISION. This consent of JAMES, PETER, and the rest, the Ebionites flatly deny'd; maintaining, that if these had approv'd of PAUL's practice, they wou'd as well have gone in that manner to the Gentiles themselves, which cou'd be no less than the duty of some of them: and that his rivalling of PETER and JAMES for superiority, being ambitious to be the head of a party, is undeniable from these his own declarations. They further objected that he gave onely his own word for his revelations: and that some few miracles recorded in *the Acts of the Apostles* were no demonstration of [32] his mission, for a reason we shall alledge presently, which reason consists in the opinion they had of this book. But to go on with PAUL's account, *when* PETER (says he) *was come to Antioch, I withstood him to the face, because he* **Ver. 11.** *was to be blam'd;* since he had already, it seems, departed from the foresaid consent, recorded also in the fifteenth chapter of *the Acts of the Apostles: for before that certain came from* JAMES (adds PAUL here to the Galatians) *he did eat with the Gentiles; but when they were come, he withdrew and* **Ver. 12.** *separated himself, fearing them which were of the* CIRCUMCISION. This account the Ebionites again rejected as contradictory, since JAMES was one of those, that according to PAUL himself, had approv'd of his preaching to the Gentiles: and yet now they were those, who came from JAMES, that made PETER withdraw from the Gentiles. There's but one way in the world of reconciling these things, which we shall see a little further, and firmly hope it will satisfy the most incredulous. The Nazarens or Ebionites (for I use these words promiscuously) wou'd likewise probably say, it was this very misrepresentation of his sense, that PETER meant in his fore-cited

Letter to JAMES. And tis indeed more than probable, when PETER says

As above, page 24. there, *that certain took upon them to explain his words better than himself,* *giving out that he was of their mind, but durst not openly profess so much*; tis pritty plain, I say, that the author of this *Letter* had that passage in his view, where PAUL, as we saw just now, charges PETER with not daring to own his opinion, for fear of them which were of the Circumcision: adding,

Ver. 13. *that the other Jews dissembled likewise with them, insomuch that* BARNABAS *was carry'd away with their dissimulation.* But we ought not slightly to [33] run over this passage, since from the history of the Nazarens we shall take occasion (and a very natural occasion it is) to set THE ORIGINAL PLAN OF CHRISTIANITY in its proper light; the want of which made it a Mystery to both Jew and Gentile, before the declaration of it by JESUS: but since that declaration it ceases to be longer a MYSTERY to any, but to such as love darkness better than the light; or that take upon them to teach others, what they profess not to understand themselves. Wheras, after the manifestation of it by the *Gospel*, nothing is more intelligible or conceivable, as nothing is more amiable or interesting, than the true and genuin Christianity: so plain and perspicuous indeed, that it was preach'd at the very beginning to men of the most ordinary capacities; who were not puzzl'd but enlightn'd, not banter'd but thoroly instructed.

CHAP. XI.

Gal. i. 13. TO be *carry'd away* therfore here (MEGALETOR) must signify purely by opinion, or difference of sentiments, and not by any separation of company: or else it wou'd be a contradiction to the reason of the contest between PAUL and BARNABAS, that is given in *the Acts of the Apostles*; the time and the place, at Antioch, being unquestionably the same. For

Acts ix. 26, 27. in the *Acts*, BARNABAS (who first entertain'd and introduc'd PAUL to the Apostles, wheras before none wou'd receive him, nor believe him to be a disciple) is represented all along as his fellow-Apostle to the Gentiles without showing the least scruple in this affair of the Levitical rites. He was deputed with him from the Church of Antioch, to represent the [34] state of this same controversy to the Apostles at Jerusalem; and came back again in his company with the determination they made in this case, wherin he's ever mention'd as of PAUL's side. Then follows this different

Ibid. xv. 36, 37, &c. account of the quarrel in these words. PAUL *said unto* BARNABAS, *let us go again, and visit our brethren in every City, where we have preach'd the word of the Lord, and see how they do. And* BARNABAS *determin'd to take with them* JOHN *whose Surname was* MARK: *and* PAUL *thought not good to take him with them, who departed from them from Pamphylia, and went not with them to the work. And the contention was so sharp between them, that they departed asunder one from the other: and so* BARNABAS *took* [50] MARK, *and sail'd unto Cyprus; and* PAUL *chose* SILAS, *and departed.* This is quite another story, and we learn from it that BARNABAS now preach'd apart; which probably gave a handle to Impostors, of framing a *Gospel* in his name. But the Ebionites did not troble themselves with this difference seeming or real, nor with any thing else in *the Acts of the Apostles*, which they rejected as a [51] spurious piece; not deserving the title, were the contents of it true: since nothing was said therin of many of the Apostles, and comparatively very little of PETER or JAMES, being almost wholly taken up about PAUL. Neither did the [52] Cerinthians (a branch of the Ebionites) any more than the [53] Marcionites, acknowledge it: and the Ebionites had very different *Acts of the Apostles*, wherin it was recorded, among other [35] things, *that* [54] PAUL *was of Tarsus, which he owns and denies not,* says EPIPHANIUS. It was added, *that he was originally a Heathen, from that passage where it is truely said by him, I am a man of Tarsus, a citizen of no mean city; whence they conclude him to have been a Heathen both by the father and mother's side.* It was further affirm'd in those *Acts* that *he came to Jerusalem, stay'd there for some time, and had a mind to marry the High Priest's daughter; on the account of which he became a proseltye, and was circumcis'd* (contrary to what he relates of himself in his *Epistle to the Philippians*, as well as often elsewhere) *but that afterwards not obtaining the young woman, he was angry, and wrote against Circumcision, against the Sabbath, and against the keeping of the Law.* The Ebionites likewise retorted the charge of dissimulation on PAUL himself, not only in cir-

Acts xxi. 39.

Phil. iii. 5. Acts xxiii. 6. Rom. xi. 1. 2 Cor. xi. 22, &c.

Acts xvi. 1, 2, 3.

---

50. *His Sister's Son*, Col. 4. 10.

51. Epiphan. Haeres. 30. n. 36.

52. Philastr. Haeres. 36.

53. Tertullian. contra Marcion. l. 5. c. 2.

54. Ταρσεα μεν αυτον, ὡς αυτος ὁμολογει και ουκ αρνειται, λεγοντες: ἐξ Ἑλλήνων δε αυτον ὑποτιθενται, λαβοντες την προφασιν εκ του τοπου δια το φιλαληθες ὑπ' αυτου ρηθεν, ὁτι Ταρσευς ειμι, ουκ ασημου πολεως πολιτης. Ειτα φασκουσιν αυτον ειναι Ἑλληνα, και Ἑλληνιδος μητρος και Ἑλληνος πατρος παιδα: αναβεβηκεναι δε εις Ἱεροσολυμα, και χρονον εκει μεμενηκεναι, επιτεθυμηκεναι δε θυγατερα του Ιερεως προς γαμον αγαγεσθαι, και τουτου ἑνεκα προσηλυτον γενεσθαι, και περιτμηθηναι: ειτα μη λαβοντα την κορην ωργισθαι, και κατα περιτομης γεγραφεναι, και κατα σαββατου, και νομοθεσιας. Epiphan. Haeres. 30. n. 16, 25.

cumcising TIMOTHY, tho the son of a Heathen, because of the Jews that
dwelt at Lystra and Iconium; but particularly as to his conduct on another
occasion, which was thus. After he had gone up to Jerusalem, and delar'd
to JAMES and all the Elders, what had past in his ministry among the
Gentiles, *they said unto him: thou seest, brother, how many thousands of
the Jews there are which believe, and they are* ALL *zealous of the Law* (as
we show'd be[36]fore of the Nazarens) *and they are inform'd of thee, that
thou teachest all the Jews, which are among the Gentiles, to forsake* MOSES;
*saying, that they ought not to circumcise their children, neither to walk after
the custom.* So he's now understood, I am sure. *What is it therfore? the
multitude must needs come together: for they will hear that thou art come.
Do therfore this that we say to thee. We have four men, which have a vow
on them; take them, and purify thy self with them, and be at charges with
them, that they may shave their heads: and all may know that those things,
wherof they are inform'd concerning thee,* ARE NOTHING; *but that thou
thy self also walkest orderly, and keepest the Law. As touching the Gentiles
which believe, we have written and concluded, that they observe no such
thing; save only that they keep themselves from things offer'd to Idols, and
from blood, and from things strangl'd, and from fornication.* By the way,
here is no restriction made as to time or place, either in the abstinence
of the Gentile Christians from these four heads, or in the keeping of the
Law by the Jewish Christians. But of this presently. *Then* PAUL *took the
men, and the next day purifying himself with them, enter'd into the Temple;
to signify the accomplishment of the days of purification, that an offring
shou'd be offer'd for every one of them.* It follows therfore irrefragably, that
PAUL contended onely for the liberty of the Gentiles from Circumcision
and the rest of the Law, but not by any means of the Jewish Christians:
for if the matter was not so, how cou'd it be truly said, *that those things
were nothing,* with which he was charg'd? namely, that he taught the Jews
to forsake MOSES, and that they ought not to circumcise their children,
neither to walk after the customs. And, upon any other foot, wou'd not the
other Apostles be as great dissem[37]blers as he? this being, as I hinted
before, the onely way in the world to reconcile things; and reconcile them
it absolutely does, without any doubt or difficulty. Abstruse and multi-
form are the windings of error; but the clew of truth is uniform and easy.
Yet to what unaccountable shifts are most Commentators driven, to save
their own precarious System, and withal the integrity of the Apostles!
what loose maxims, incompatible even with ordinary morals, do they not
authorize! when nothing can ever do, but the real distinction of Jewish

Ibid. xxi.
20–26.

Ver. 26.

Ver. 24.

and Gentile Christians; who are ever to subsist in the Church, as in the sequel will be made evident. Neither am I altogether singular in this point: for this very passage of PAUL's justifying himself to his countrymen in this manner, appear'd so decisive to JAMES RHENFERD, Professor of the Oriental tongues in [55] Franeker, that he doubted not in one of his excellent [56] *Dissertations* to maintain, that PAUL taught onely the Gentile Christians (and never the Jewish, as is universally suppos'd) to abstain from Circumcision, and the observation of the rest of the Law. He confirms his opinion by these words of PAUL himself to the Corinthians: *but as God has distrib-* *uted to every man, as the Lord has call'd every one, so let him walk; and* *so ordain I in all the Churches. Is any man call'd being* CIRCUMCIS'D? *let him not become* UNCIRCUMCIS'D: *is any call'd in* UNCIRCUMCI-SION? *let him not become* CIRCUMCIS'D. CIRCUMCISION *is nothing,* *and* UNCIRCUMCISION *is nothing, but the keeping of the commandments* *of God. Let every man* [38] *abide in the same calling, wherin he was called.* I repeat it again, that PAUL can never be otherwise defended against the Ebionites; tho I know at the same time, that this will be call'd contradicting all the Churches in the world: and I despair not of setting the argument here in its due light, as I said before, without making my *Dissertation* too bulky. Yet let Criticism and Reason be ever so clear in the case, let *Scripture* and History be ever so positive, or an Accommodation with the Jews be ever so much facilitated; some of the reigning Divines will be as fond of their errors as of their benefices, and sooner keep up an eternal warr between the Jews and the Gentiles, than own themselves to have been ever in the wrong. *No Innovation* is the word, when the question is all the while about reducing things to the *Old Foundation*.

1 Cor. vii. 17, 18, 19, 20.

CHAP. XII.

BUT waving what the Ebionites further urg'd, and, as you see, very unjustly concerning PAUL's dissimulation, let's now procede with incontestable matter of fact; and observe from the foregoing discourse of JAMES and the Elders to him, that all the Jews which became Christians were still Zealous for the Levitical Law. This Law they look'd upon to be no less national and political, than religious and sacred: that is to say, expressive

Acts xxi. 20.

---

55. *He's dead since the writing of this Letter.*
56. De fictis Judaeorum & Judaizantium Haeresibus.

Exod.
xii. 26,
27. & xiii.
8, 9. *and*
in many
other
places, as
Deut. iv.
5–10. &
vi. 2, 7,
8. & xi.
18–21. &
xx. 25.

Gen xvii.
7, 10, 13.
Exod
xxxi. 16,
17. & xxix.
9. & xl.
15. Levit.
vii. 36,
&c, Deut
iv. 40. &
vi. 2.

of the history of their peculiar nation, essential to the being of their Theocracy or Republic, and aptly commemorating whatever befell their
ancestors or their state; which, not regarding other people, they did not
think them bound by the same, however indispensably subject to the Law
of Nature. *Our teacher* Moses, [39] says [57] Maimonides, *did not deliver
the inheritance of the Law and the Ordinances, but to the Israelites only;
according to that of* Deuteronomy, Moses *commanded us a Law, even the
inheritance of the congregation of* Jacob: *and also to all those, who become
Proselytes out of other nations; according to that of* Numbers, *as you are, so
shall the stranger be. But no body, against his will, must be forc'd to embrace
the Law and the Ordinances.* Besides this, the Jews were persuaded of the
Law's eternal duration, of Circumcision's being an everlasting covenant,
and of the Sabbath's being no less plainly deem'd than call'd such a covenant, not to speak of the passover, *&c,* from the manifold express declarations and promises of the *Old Testament:* and all this without any other
limitation, but that of *the days of heaven upon earth,* and the final period
of *their generations,* or the utmost date of time. They were further rooted
in this persuasion from the repeated words and constant practice of Jesus,
who they believ'd came not as a diminisher or an abolisher, but (as he
himself openly profest) an accomplisher or perfecter of the Law, the
restorer of the same, and a reformer of the abuses which had gradually
crept in upon it: for the Pharisees had almost wholly perverted,
transform'd, and made it of no effect, by their Traditions, Explications,
and even Dispensations; as all Institutions (tho ever so sacred) come to be
corrupted and disguiz'd in time, by men of weak or worldly minds. Thus
therefore the Nazarens, following the precept and example of their master
Jesus, concluded they might be very good Christians, yet still observe
their own country rites (Sacrifices excepted) [40] there not being one
word in any *Gospel* concerning the abolition of them, but directly the
contrary in all others, as well as in their own *Gospel of the Hebrews,* or *of
the twelve Apostles,* as it was indifferently call'd. This is so manifest, that in
the late disputes about *Occasional Conformity,* the example of Jesus and
the Apostles has been alledg'd a thousand times, as continuing in the
practice of the Jewish rites and worship, frequenting the Temple and the
Synagogues, observing the solemn feasts and particularly the Passover,
like the rest of their Countrymen. And this indeed is undeniable fact: the

Deut.
xxxiii.
Num. :
15.

Deut. x
21. Lev
xl. 15, *e*
Mat. v.
18, 19, 2
& xv. 3,
6, 9. M:
vii. 7, 8,
Luc. xv
17, *&c.*

57. Tractat. de Reg. cap. 8.

Apostles were so farr from condemning the Nazarens, that they confirm'd their doctrine by their own practice. But then I challenge any in the world to show me as plainly, that it was onely by way of prudential condescention for a certain season, as it is now taken for granted on all sides. I am as much as any man for *Occasional Conformity*, among Churches not differing in essentials; which was evidently the practice of the primitive Church most properly so call'd, and founded upon unanswerable grounds. *Toleration* also (in *Scripture*, among other names, call'd *Long-suffering* and *Forbearance*) is no less plainly a duty of the *Gospel*, than it is self-evident according to the Law of Nature: so that they who persecute others in their reputations, rights, properties, or persons, for merely speculative opinion, or for things in their own nature indifferent, are so far equally devested both of Humanity and Christianity. But the present case is nothing at all to the matter, nor can there be any solution given of it (otherwise than on the foot of our scheme) that will not appear perfectly precarious, if not subject to several great inconveniences: as no other scheme can reconcile Christianity, and the promises of everlasting duration [41] made in favor of the Jewish Law: which are poorly, I will not say sophistically, evaded, by making the words *eternal, everlasting, for ever, perpetual,* and *throout all generations,* to mean onely *a great while*; that the way of Christ's *accomplishing the Law,* was to *abolish it*; and that *till heaven and earth shall pass,* signify'd *till the reign of* TIBERIUS CESAR. Consonant to both the example and the doctrine of JESUS and his Apostles is the judgment of JUSTIN MARTYR, who is very express, and repeats it over and over; that the Jews believing on CHRIST may safely observe their own Law, provided they neither persuade nor force the Gentile Christians to do the same. Nay and he highly disapproves such of these last, *as* [58] *made a scruple of having any commerce and conversation with the first, or even to live in the same house with them.* Tis true, he's of opinion the Nazarens were no longer under the obligation of their country Law: but he's so farr from damning or excommunicating them for their observation of it, as did most of the other *Fathers*; that, notwithstanding this mistake, he acknowledges them for brethren, and teaches communion with them in all things else. *If they will needs,* [59] says he, *out of a weak opinion, observe*

---

58. Και μηδε κοινωνειν ὁμιλιας η ἑστιας τοις τοιουτοις τολμωντες, ὁις εγω ου συναινος ειμι. In dialogo cum Tryphone Judaeo.

59. Αλλ' εαν αυτοι, δια το ασθενες της γνωμης, και τα ὁσα δυνανται νυν εκ των Μωσεως (ἁ δια το σκληροκαρδειον του λαου νοουμεν διατεταχθαι) μετα του επι

[42] *whatever they can of the Laws of* MOSES (*which we think were ordain'd out of regard to the hardness of the people's hearts*) *and add to these their hope in* JESUS, *with the practice of the eternal and natural virtues of Justice and Piety; being further desireous to make one society with Christians and Believers* (*as I said before*) *yet so as not to persuade them to be circumcis'd like themselves, not to keep the sabbath, nor to observe any such other of their rites: I think they ought not only to be receiv'd, but likewise to be admitted to a communion of all things, as those of the same bowels and brethren.* Tho I cannot approve his notion of their being in a mistake, yet I applaud his charity for bearing with them. AUGUSTIN, as we shall see hereafter, went further than JUSTIN; and maintain'd for some time the very notion that I now do, without any material difference: that the Christian Jews shou'd ever observe their own Laws, without imposing the Levitical ceremonies on the Gentiles. But the Jewish Believers did not in the least pretend, to oblige the Christians from among the Gentiles to the like things with themselves; as many wou'd inferr from one passage in *the*

Acts xv. 1. *Acts of the Apostles,* rashly ascribing the opinion of a few private persons to the whole Church. For after it is there related that *certain men, which came from Judea, taught the brethren at Antioch, that except they were circumciz'd after the manner of* MOSES, *they cou'd not be sav'd;* and that

Ver. 5. some of the believing Pharisees said, *it was necessary to circumcise them, and to command them to keep the Law of* MOSES: it was the sentence of the

Ver. 19, 20. Apostles, given by the mouth of JAMES, *that those shou'd not be trobl'd, which from among the Gentiles were* TURN'D TO GOD; *but that we write unto them* (says he) *that they abstain from pollutions of Idols, and from fornication, and from things* [43] *strangl'd, and from blood.* Here is no setting of the believing Jews free from the Law, but onely of the Christian Gentiles: and the last were enjoin'd the observation of these, not indiffer-

Ver 28. ent, but *necessary things*; without which there cou'd be no tolerable communication or commerce between them and the first. The greatest endearment shou'd ever reign among brethren. And what is it, I pray, but the non-observance of these precepts, that makes society so difficult a thing even at this time between the Christians and the Jews, tho the latter are in

---

τουτον τον χριστον ελπιζειν, και τας αιωνιους και φυσει δικαιοπραξιας και ευσεβειας φυλασσειν βουλωνται, και άιρωνται συζην τοις χριστιανοις και πιστοις, ὡς προειπον, μη πειθοντες αυτους μητε περιτεμνεσθαι ὁμοιως αυτοις, μητε σαββατιζειν, μητε αλλα, ὁσα τοιαυτα εστι, τηρειν; και προσλαμβανεσθαι, και κοινωνειν ἁπαντων, ὁμως ὁμοσπλαγχνοις και αδελφοις, δειν αποφαινεσθαι. Id. Ibid.

a sort of slavery to the former? It is a known observation, that there can never be any hearty fellowship, where people don't eat and drink together. This was evidently design'd in the ancient Sacrifices, national, urbical, and familiar; as it was practis'd likewise in their solemn Treaties of peace or friendship, and was instituted in CHRIST's last Supper. I need not mention the primitive Love-feasts. But in the Apostolical decree no accommodation is hinted in the least, no time is limitted either unto the one for quitting the old Law, or unto the other for neglecting the four Precepts; as is positively taught in all our Systems or Catechisms. When PETER preach'd the *Gospel* to CORNELIUS, a Gentile proselyte of the gate; and publickly declar'd, contrary to the inveterate prejudices of many of the Jews, *that in* Acts x. 35. *every nation he that fears God, and works righteousness is accepted of him:* Ver. 45. they were astonish'd at it, and expostulated with him for as much as eating Ibid. xi. 1, with the Gentiles. But afterwards he gave full satisfaction to the Apostles 2, 3. and others at Jerusalem, as to his proceeding in this respect; and they were joyfully convinc'd, *that God had also to the Gentiles granted repen-* Ver. 18. *tance unto life:* this being the great MYSTERY, which [44] as PAUL says Rom. xvi. more than once or twice, had been hid from ages and generations, till it 25. Ephes. was now manifested by the *Gospel.* But in all this account, there is not one i. 9, 10. & word of PETER's subjecting those converted Gentiles to the Mosaic Law, iii. 3, 5, 6, nor of exemting the Jewish Christians from the observation of it: and tho 9. Col. i. he did eat with CORNELIUS, it does not appear that he ate any thing pro- 26, 27. hibited by the Law; any more than those Jews do, with whom we eat, and who eat with us, every day. Thus therefore THE REPUBLIC OF MOSES might still have subsisted entire, such as it was, or rather ought to have been, in Judea, and yet the inhabitants be very good Christians too: requiring no more from their brethren of the Gentiles that liv'd among them (and agreed with them in the main article of the unity of the Deity, as well as in other important tho not so essential points) than a strict abstinence from the four things now mention'd, which were likewise originally prohibited by the Jewish Law to the *Proselytes of Justice.*

CHAP. XIII.

THIS Abstinence from blood and things strangl'd, was the undoubted sense of all the primitive Christians: and did not only continue in all places (as it does still in the Eastern Churches) till AUGUSTIN's time; but, even till the eleventh century, in most parts of the Western Church. Cardinal HUMBERT, who wrote about the middle of that century, amply justifies the Latin against the Greec Church, as [45] to this point; *for retaining* (says [60] he) *the ancient usage or tradition of our ancestors, we in like manner do abominate these things: insomuch that a severe penance is impos'd on those, who, without extreme peril of life, do at any time feed on blood, or any animal dead of itself, either choak'd in the waters, or strangl'd by what accident soever.* I admire how those persons can herein be satisfy'd in their consciences, or by virtue of what nice distinction they can coin to themselves a dispensation from this abstinence; who make the practice of the primitive Church to be the best commentary on *Scripture*, when the doctrine of it too is so express and uniform in this respect. But I have ever observ'd, that they, who make the loudest pretences this way, are either the farthest of all others from primitive practice, or the least acquainted with primitive history. What is it, I pray, that has the *Fathers*, that has Tradition and Succession more or as much of its side, as this very Abstinence? It was commanded in an assembly of the *Apostles*, without limitation of time. Tis injoin'd in the [61] *Canons* antiently attributed to them. Tis alleg'd as a proof of their innocence by the first *Apologists* of Christianity, to all whom, that mention it, I appeal without exception; which makes particular citations unnecessary, as they wou'd make my *Letter* too prolix. Tis confirm'd by the Decrees of several *Councils*; and has been defended by some of the [46] most learned men in the last century. The citations, I say, wou'd be endless. Not to speak of HUGO GROTIUS, CLAUDIUS SALMASIUS, or GERARD JOHN VOSSIUS (what mighty names!) the great STEPHEN CURCELLEUS has written an elaborate discourse on this [62] subject, wherin he shows abstinence from blood to have continu'd in many places to almost his own time; and CHRISTIAN BECMANNUS made a Theological Exercitation to the same [63] purpose before CURCELLEUS. They all maintain'd it was no part of the ceremonial Law of the Jews, but [64] a

---

60. Antiquam etenim consuetudinem, seu traditiônem majorum nostrorum, diligenter retinentes, nos quoque haec abominamur: adeo ut sanguine, vel quocunque morticino, aut aquis seu quacunque negligentiâ praefocato, apud nos aliquando vescentibus, absque extremo periculo vitae hujus, poenitentia gravis imponatur. *In bibliotheca Patrum, tom.* 4. *pag* 202.

61. Can. 63, aliis vero 52.

62. Diatriba de esu sanguinis.

63. Exercitat. 26.

64. *The Jews maintain that* NOAH *and his children, did, before the flood, govern themselves by the six following precepts, as an abstract of the Law of Nature, viz.* I. *Not to worship Idols, or any other creature.* II. *Not to blaspheme God, or his holy name.* III.

Noachic precept, equally binding all the world upon a moral account. The words spoken to NOAH and his sons (and consequently, say they, to all mankind) in the ninth chapter of *Genesis*, are these: *every moving thing that lives shall be meat for you, even as the green herb have I given you all things; but flesh with the life therof, which is the blood therof, shall you not eat.* This indeed is confirm'd in the Levitical Law, tho properly no part of the same according to those Gentlemen, a great many other moral duties being occasionally mention'd there; and they think it observable, that thro-out the whole *Pentateuch*, the Stranger as well as the Jew are forbidden to eat the blood of any manner of flesh (as being the [47] life or soul therof) under the penalty of being *cut off from his people*, or, in plainer language, of being sent into banishment: for the deservedly famous Mr. LE CLERC has, in all the texts where it occurrs, prov'd this [65] phrase of being *cut off from his people*, to signify disfranchising and banishing quite out of the countrey; but not to dy an untimely death, and much less to be eternally damn'd, in one or both which senses most people have absurdly learnt to understand it. This prohibition of eating blood, is repeated in several places of the *Pentateuch*; chiefly, as is suppos'd by those who allow not the moral reason, to create a horror against the shedding of human blood, as well as for the avoiding of unwholsom or infectious diet: and being in the *Apostolical decree* neither restrain'd to any time, nor counted an indifferent, but plainly *a necessary thing*; there are still many Christians here in the West who think themselves as much bound to refrain from things strangl'd and from blood, as from meats offer'd to idols and from fornication, which are join'd together as of equal obligation. I said, that I wonder'd by what distinction certain moderns cou'd justify themselves, in their eating of birds caught in gins, black puddings, and such other things; and yet a distinction there is, but on which neither they, nor the *primitive Apologists* cou'd ever hit, or at least wou'd never stick to it, by reason of their being utter strangers to the true constitution of the THE MOSAIC REPUBLIC: for the case out of Judea, or any place where the Jews and Gentiles don't cohabit in one society, is quite another [48] thing. They are not

Marginal notes:
Gen. ix. 3, 4.

Gen xvii. 14. & alibi passim.

Levit. iii. 17. & vii. 26. xvii. 10–14. & xix. 26. Deut. xii. 16, 23. & xv. 23. Acts xv. 28.

Not to shed Blood, or not to kill. IV. Not to commit incest, or adultery. V. Not to rob or steal. VI. To appoint Judges, who shou'd see these precepts duly executed: to which the Rabbins add a VIIth, as commanded after the flood, namely, Not to eat the member of any living creature.

65. *In* Genesi *suo ad versum* 14 *capitis* 17, *&* in Commentariis *ad reliquos* Pentateuchi *libros.*

Levit.
xvii.
10–14.

Deut. xiv.
21.

Exod. xii.
48, 49.
Num ix.
14.
Ibid. xv.
16.

Pag. 39.

Pag. 47.

1 Cor. viii.
8, 9.

all strangers indefinitely, but expresly *the strangers who shou'd sojourn among the Israelites*, that are forbid to eat blood: and so farr were these points concerning blood, or things strangl'd, from being parts of the moral Law; that the Jews were freely permitted to give or sell things that dy'd of themselves, to travelling strangers and aliens, *that they might eat them:* which wou'd be highly immoral, were their own abstinence from eating such things grounded on the Law of nature. And just as they granted this liberty to aliens, and to *Proselytes of the gate*; or those strangers, who, tho believing in one God, yet were not circumcis'd, but worship in the outer court of the Temple, not conforming to the *Jewish* Law: so the Egyptians, who, no less than the Jews, had the distinction of meats clean and unclean, us'd to sell the [66] head of the sacrific'd beast to strangers, it being to themselves an abomination and an accursed thing. But as for the *Proselytes of justice*, or those strangers, who not onely were settl'd among the Jews, and inhabitants of their cities, but also receiv'd Circumcision as well as the belief of one God, and did in every thing conform to the Jewish Law; they were bound in all parts of social life (as in the feast of the pass-over, and in meat and drink-offerings particularly) to comply in the strictest sense with the establish'd Laws and Customs. *One Law*, says MOSES speaking of these very things, *and one Manner shall be for you, and for the stranger that sojourneth with you*: which is there directly call'd *a perpetual ordinance*. To this purpose also MAIMONIDES, as above-[49] cited. of the same nature and necessity therfore was the case of the Jewish and Gentile Christians, who, in the infancy of Christianity, made up one Church or society at Antioch; as it wou'd be again so, shou'd all the Jews become Christians, and be resettl'd in Judea: and upon a due examination the general prohibition in *Genesis* will be found to be no barr to this doctrine; as many other seeming generals there, were written nevertheless with special regard to the people of Israel, and to them onely. Of such general prohibitions, yet only meaning the particular usages of the Jews, LE CLERC will afford you many instances in his most learned *Commentary* before quoted. And therfore PAUL writing to the Corinthian Gentiles, with whom the Jews were not so much intermixt, tells them that *meat commended us not to God; for neither if we eat are we the better, neither if we eat not are we the worse: but take heed, lest by any means this liberty of*

---

66. Κεφαλη δ'εκεινου πολλα καταρησαμενοι, φερουσι τοισι μεν αν η αγορη, και Έλληνες σφι εωσι επιδημοι εμποροι; όι δε φεροντες ες την αγορην, απ' ών εδοντο. Herodot. l. 2. c. 39.

yours become a stumbling-block to them that are weak. This scandalizing
of others (whether about eating of blood, or about meat offer'd to idols)
was all that wise men had to avoid, as PAUL further acquaints the same
Christians, saying, *whatsoever is sold in the shambles that eat, asking no*
question for conscience sake: for the earth is the Lord's, and the fullness
therof. If any of them that believe not, bid you to a feast, and you be dispos'd
to go; whatsoever is set before you eat, asking no question for conscience
sake: but if any man say unto you, this is offer'd in sacrifice to Idols, eat not
for his sake that show'd it and for conscience sake (for the earth is the Lord's
and the fullness therof) Conscience, I say not thine own, but of the others;
for why is my liberty judg'd of another man's conscience? — Give none
offence, neither to the Jews, nor to the Gentiles, nor to the Church of God.
This regard to the Jews and to [50] their observations is so evident every
where, that I wonder it cou'd ever become a subject of controversy: but
the true reason is, the belief which so early obtain'd, that the Levitical Law
was quite abolisht, and that the Jews were no more oblig'd to keep it than
the Gentiles. This is the source of numberless errors, to the great deprava-
tion of Christianity; and this, with relation to the eating of blood in particular (after recommending the whole fourteenth chapter *to the Romans*
to your perusal) may be easily made out against the *primitive Apologists*
and *Fathers*, as well as against CURCELLEUS, Mr. WHISTON, and such
others: who for want of observing the said distinction of Jewish and Gentile Christians, have run into one extreme; as they, who limit the prohibition to a certain time, absolving all men and in all places alike, have run
into one another. But the first extreme is the more tolerable of the two,
not onely for being the least mischievous in its consequences, and that the
Jewish Christians are still oblig'd to this abstinence; but as being withall
both innocent and wholsom, as well as easy enough in its practice. But to
return, the fifteenth chapter of *the Acts* cou'd not but be a strong prejudice
in behalf of the Ebionites, and the stronger, as being the testimony of a
book they believ'd compil'd in favor of PAUL: besides that PETER in his *first*
Epistle (indisputably addrest to the believing Jews) calls them *a chosen*
generation, a royal priesthood, a holy nation, a peculiar people. He does not
say they were formerly such, but shou'd be accounted so no longer; he
desires 'em, on the contrary, *to have their conversation honest among the*
Gentiles, from whom they were therfore to be distinct: so that they might
still enjoy all the prerogatives and distinctions of their nation, no less than
in Judea (the Temple [51] and Sacrifices excepted) as a separate people
even among the Gentiles, and yet be very true Christians also.

Ibid. x. 25,
26, 27, 28,
29, 32.

1 Pet. i. 1.
Ibid. ii. 9.

Ver. 12.

CHAP. XIV.

THIS, I am persuaded, was in this particular point (for I approve of no men's errors) the genuin Theology of the Nazarens; however mistaken or misrepresented by the Christians from among the Gentiles, as if they wou'd have them likewise to observe the whole Law of MOSES. They indeed in their turn may have mistaken PAUL's meaning, *in whose Epistles are some things hard to be understood*, as is well remark'd in *the second Epistle* attributed to PETER. But if the Nazarens did so mistake PAUL, the Gentiles have sufficiently reveng'd their Apostle's quarrel. The *Fathers* are shamefully inconsistent, both with one another and each with himself, concerning the Ebionites: splitting them where they ought to be united (as they unite them where they ought to be split) turning their blessings sometimes into curses, and making their godly prayers to pass for diabolical conjurations. The Gentile Christians (as I have said more than once) show'd on all occasions an inexpressible hatred against those from among the Jews, even to the speaking many times irreverently if not profanely of the Law; tho they were acknowledg'd debtors to the Nazarens for the *Gospel*, the Jewish Church having been form'd, before any Gentiles had embrac'd Christianity. But none of any sort has treated them with more undisguiz'd rancor than EPIPHANIUS, the most ignorant and partial of all Historians; as has been made out in multitudes of instances by the best writers of the two last and the present cen[52]tury, not to mention any more ancient. Passing over his palpable ignorance in Grammar, History, Chronology, and the Hebrew tongue (tho a converted Jew) this may be truly said in general of him; that as none was more ready to make every man heretical, so none was more backward to find any man orthodox: and those, who displeas'd him in one thing, he was sure to misrepresent in every thing. Nevertheless, this same bungling and confus'd EPIPHANIUS owns, that the Nazarens [67] *differ'd in this* ONE THING, *as well from the Jews as the Christians: not agreeing with the former, because they believe in* CHRIST; *nor being of one mind with the latter, because they continue still addicted to the Jewish Law, to Circumcision, to the Sabbath, and to the other ceremonies.* You may take notice that he does not say, they urg'd these things on others, but only observ'd them

2 Pet. iii. 16.

---

67. Εν τουτω δε μονον προς Ιουδαιους διαφερονται και χριστιανους: Ιουδαιοις μεν μη συμφωνουντες, δια το εις χριστον πεπιστευκεναι; χριστιανοις δε μη ομογνωμονουντες, δια το ετι νομω πεπεδησθαι, περιτομη τε, και σαββατω, και τοις αλλοις. Haeres. 29. n. 7.

among themselves; which is what I precisely insist upon, not merely as
their real sentiment: but likewise as a very innocent and harmless thing,
nay and will maintain it to be so far the TRUE ORIGINAL PLAN OF
CHRISTIANITY. For all this he'll have them a little lower to be [68] down-
right Jews, tho he says in the very same place they are declar'd enemies to
the Jews; and that the Jews on the other hand do mortally hate them, cursing them three times a day in their Synagogues, as we learnt from JEROM
before. Any man else, but EPIPHANIUS, wou'd have remember'd the distinction he had [53] just made himself: and not reckon 'em Christians the
less in religion, that they had [69] Synagogs and Elders as Jews by nation;
nor, because they were partly Jews in the outward man, deny 'em to be in
the inward man entirely Christians. Here I wou'd desire those among us,
who press the necessity of observing the Jewish Sabbath (for which reason
they are call'd *Sabbatarians,* or *Seventh-day-sabbath-men*) to consider,
that they were not the Christians from among the Gentiles, but the Nazarens from among the Jews, that anciently observ'd, or rather were onely
bound to observe, the Jewish Sabbath: for we of the Gentile stock are not
oblig'd *to observe days, or months, or times, or years*; we are to be *judg'd by*   Gal. iv. 10.
no man in meat or in drink, or in respect of a holy day, or of the new moon,   Col. ii. 16.
or of the sabbaths. And indeed had the original distinction of two sorts of
Christians been heeded, this dispute had never risen: neither had the vol-
untary complaisance of the Gentile Christians in somtimes celebrating the
Sabbath of the Jews, nor of the Jewish Christians in observing the first day
of the week with the Gentiles, been ignorantly drawn by any into the
nature of a precept, or as an example of indispensable imitation; which yet
was done by many *Fathers* and *Councils* (not necessary at present to name)
by the [70] *Apostolical Constitutions,* and by the *Edicts* of [71] CONSTANTINE
the Great. Our Sabbatarians therfore (so call'd) a[54]mong whom I was
intimatly acquainted with the late excellent Mr. STENNET, being right in
their position, tho wrong in the application of it, into which they were

---

68. Ibid. n. 9.

69. Haeres. 30. n. 18.

70. Το σαββατον μεν τοι και την κυριακην ἑορταζετε; ὁτι το μεν δημιουργιας
εστιν ὑπομνημα, ἡ δε αναστασεως. l. 7. c. 23.

71. Ὑπο την Ρωμαιων αρχην πολιτευομενοις ἁπασι σχολην αγειν ταις επονυμοις
του Σωτηρος ἡμεραις ενουθετει: ὁμοιως δε και τας του σαββατου τιμαν; μνημης ἑνεκα
μοι δοκειν των εν ταυταις τῳ κοινῳ σωτηρι πεπραχθαι μνημονευομενων. Euseb. de
vita Constantini, l. 4. c. 18.

misled by so great authorities and examples, have this advantage however; that they may alter their practice, without recanting their opinion, namely, *that the Jewish Sabbath is to be observ'd in all ages.* After the same manner may be readily terminated abundance of other difficulties, solely arising from the misapplication to all, of what peculiarly belongs to one sort of Christians. Thus, to name no others, came into the Church *Extreme Unction*, which in time has been erected into a Sacrament. Yet this Unction originally was neither sacred nor extreme. Every one knows in what high estimation Oil was among the eastern nations, and he has not read the *Old Testament,* who is not acquainted with the most frequent use of Anointing among the Jews. It was especially practis'd on a medicinal account, and administr'd publicly in the synagogues by the Elders on the Sabbath; where the applying of this remedy to poor sick people, was accompany'd by the prayers of the faithful for their recovery, and the pardon of their sins: or if the persons were in a very weak condition, the Elders came home to them. LIGHTFOOT [72] observes out of the *Jerusalem* [73] *Talmud,* that *Rabbi* SIMEON, *the Son of* ELEAZAR, *permitted Rabbi* MEIR *to mingle wine with the oil, when he anointed the sick on the Sabbath:* and quotes as a Tradition from [74] thence, *that anointing on the Sabbath was permitted. If his head akes, or a scald comes upon it,* [55] *he anoints with oil.* So, in the *Babylonian* [75] *Talmud,* tis said almost in the same words; *if he be sick, or a scald be upon his head, he anoints according to his manner.* The Apostle JAMES therfore writing to the Jewish Christians, whose synagogues and rites were precisely the same with those of the other Jews, *is any sick among you* (says he) *let him send for the Elders of the Church, and let them pray over him, anointing him with oil in the name of the Lord; and the prayer of the faithful shall save the sick, and the Lord shall raise him up; and if he have committed sins, they shall be forgiven him.* This, you see, was nothing like the extreme unction of the Roman Church, but peculiar to the Jewish nation: as tis recorded of the other Apostles, who were not onely Jews, but likewise Elders of the Jewish Churches, that *they anointed with oil many that were sick, and healed them.* Several of our Protestant Divines, ignorant of the Jewish customs, yet perceiving the absurdity of the Roman practice, wou'd have this Apostolic Unction to be miraculous and temporary; tho others were for extending it

Jam. v. 14, 15.

Mar. vi. 13.

---

72. *Harmony of the N. Testament,* Works, vol. 1. pag. 333.

73. In Beracoth. fol. 3. col. 1.

74. Id. in Maazar Sheni, fol. 53. col. 3.

75. In Joma. fol. 77. 2.

to all men and times, as some did the observation of the Sabbath. But they were onely the Nazarens that were to keep their national Sabbath, and yet this is one of the heinous crimes the Gentiles cou'd never forgive them; and for which they must not, forsooth, so much as deserve the appellation of Christians: *since while they wou'd be both Jews and Christians*, says [76] JEROM, *they are neither Jews nor Christians*; and speaking of these Nazarens in another place, *they* [56] *so receive* CHRIST, says [77] he, *as not to quit the ceremonies of the old Law*. Well: where's the harm of all that? and why shou'd it trouble him, or me, or any other, that were to observe no such thing? Yet this, it seems, is the chief thing, even more than their opinion concerning the person of CHRIST, for which the new inmates unjustly expell'd the old inhabitants: for the same JEROM roundly tells [78] us, *that the Cerinthians and Ebionites, who were the Jews that believ'd in* CHRIST, *were anathematiz'd by the* Fathers *for this* ONELY THING, *that they intermixt the Ceremonies of the Law with the* Gospel *of* CHRIST; *and so profest the new matters, as not to part with the old*. Very nice and deliberate! Here you see the antiquity of pressing *Uniformity*, and the effects of it too: and I am entirely satisfy'd, that, were it not for this execrable treatment of them (so contrary to the practice of JESUS, and the doctrine of the *Gospel*) not a Jew, but, many ages since, had been likewise a Christian; as it must be on this foot alone, that their conversion to Christianity can ever be reasonably expected. Thus then the poor Jews were expell'd at once, and none of 'em to be ever receiv'd again, according to the mind of those *Fathers*, without a particular abjuration not only of their Judaism, but I may say of their Christianity too.

[57] CHAP. XV.

AUGUSTIN indeed made some small effort in favor of the Nazarens, as may be seen in the Letters that past between him and JEROM on this Subject; where, as it happens in most disputes, they quickly lost the main

---

76. Dum volunt & Judaei esse & Christiani, nec Judaei sunt nec Christiani. *In Epist. ad Augustin.*

77. Nazaraei ita Christum recipiunt, ut observationes Legis veteris non amittant. *Id. ad Jes.* 8.

78. Qui [Ebionei & Cerinthiani] credentes in Christo, propter hoc solum a Patribus anathematizati sunt, quòd Legis cerimonias Christi Evangelio miscuerunt; & sic nova confessi sunt, ut vetera non amitterent. *In Epist. ad Augustin.*

point, and ran after foren matters, trivial incidents, or personal reflections, till they came at last to fight perfectly in the dark, and to make the reader admire about what it is they contend. JEROM, endeavoring upon a wrong supposition to reconcile those seeming contradictions, which I have easily accorded above upon the bottom of truth, had recourse to *the lawfulness of an officious Ly for the sake of a good end*; and so asserted that PAUL, in accusing PETER, had prevaricated in effect himself, but all well done, it seems, for the important end of gaining the Jews, and excusing his own conduct. This doctrine however cou'd not but scandalize AUGUSTIN, who wrote smartly to him about it, and justify'd PAUL by saying as I do, and as the things say themselves, that when he speaks against the Law as danger-ous or useless, he means this of the Gentiles: and that all passages spoken by him or others in favor of the Law, or enjoining the observation of it, relate purely to the Jewish Christians: besides that PETER had onely misled some Gentiles by his example, which they mistook, but not by his doc-trine, which ought to have been better explain'd. To this purpose AUGUS-TIN. *But of all your discourse* (says [79] JEROM) *which you* [58] *have spun out into so prolix a disputation, this in short is the sense; that* PETER *did not err, in thinking the Law shou'd be observ'd by those, who believ'd among the Jews: but that he declin'd from the right way, in forceing the Gentiles to Juda-ize; which you say he did, not by the precept of his doctrine, but by the exam-ple of his conversation. You maintain therfore that* PAUL *did not say any thing, contrary to what he had done himself: but had truly accus'd* PETER, *of having compell'd the Christians from among the Gentiles to observe the Law. The sum therfore of your question, or rather of your judgment, is this; that, even after the* Gospel, *the Jews who believe, do well to observe the ordinances of the Law: that is to say, if they offer sacrifices as* PAUL *did, if they circumcise their children, if they keep the sabbath, &c.* This he's so far from approv-ing, that he utterly detests it: tis turning Christianity into Judaism. *If we*

---

79. Totius sermonis tui, quem disputatione longissimâ protraxisti, hic sensus est; ut Petrus non erraverit in eo, quòd his qui ex Judaeis crediderant, putaverit Legem esse servandam: sed in eo a recti linea deviarit, quòd gentes coegerit Judaizare; coegerit autem non docentis imperio, sed conversationis exemplo. Et Paulus non contraria sit locutus his, quae ipse gesserat; sed quare Petrus eos, qui ex gentibus erant, Judaizare compelleret. Haec ergo summa est quaestionis, immo sententiae tuae; ut, post Evan-gelium Christi, bene faciant Judaei credentes, si Legis mandata custodiant: hoc est, si sacrificia offerant, quae obtulit Paulus, si filios circumcidant, si Sabbatum servent, &c. *Id. ibid.*

must ly, says [80] he, *under the necessity of receiving the Jews together with their observations of the Law; and that they may perform in the Churches of* CHRIST, *what they exercis'd in the Synagogues of* SATAN: *I'll tell you my opinion freely, they will not become Christians, but make us* [59] *Jews;* as if the Jews and Gentiles were not to have their Churches apart, and as if the former wou'd not perform their peculiar ceremonies in their own Churches, which he blasphemously calls the synagogues of SATAN. But this is nothing to JEROM's perpetual sophistry, which yet is infinitely exceeded by his warmth and virulence. He sweats thro-out this whole Letter, he turmoils and turns himself every way. Now he disputes and argues, then he scolds and expostulates: and after producing a passage out of AUGUSTIN's Letter, justifying PETER for persevering in the Law, as being by nation a Jew: *I must speak to the contrary,* says [81] he, *and, the whole world shou'd be of another mind, pronounce with a loud voice, that the ceremonies of the Jews are pernicious and damnable to Christians; and that whoever will observe them, be he of the Jewish or Gentile race, is plung'd into the gulf of the Devil.* Thus this hotheaded raving monk, who to such a degree frighted AUGUSTIN (for convinc'd he cou'd never be) with his vehemence and bawling, that he slunk to the poorest subterfuges imaginable for getting well off; first giving another sense to an opinion, which he had before exprest in the plainest terms, and then quite giving it up to the overbearing weight of the majority. He was a Bishop, and wou'd continue so. The Jews therfore were cut off for ever, as I said, from the body of that Church which they had founded, wherin their Law is continually read to this day, where the Gentiles are proud to bear their proper names, and where they must in some man[60]ner become Jews before they can be reckon'd good Christians. Nor ought this proceding to appear any way surprizing, or the intrigue be reckon'd so very flagitious, when we consider what a damning crew the *Fathers* were; and how prone on the slightest occasions, somtimes for mere punctilios of Criticism or Chronology (wherin they were generally wrong) to send not onely private persons, but even whole societies, churches, and

---

80. Sin autem haec nobis incumbit necessitas, ut Judaeos cum legitimis suis suscipiamus, & licebit eis observare in Ecclesiis Christi quod exercuerunt in synagogis Satanae; dicam quod sentio, non illi Christiani fient, sed nos Judaeos facient. *Id. ibid.*

81. Ego e contrario loquar, &, reclamante mundo, liberâ voce pronuntio, ceremonias Judaeorum & perniciosas esse & mortiferas Christianis: & quicumque eas observaverit, sive ex Judaeis, sive ex Gentibus, eum in barathrum Diaboli devolutum. *Id. ibid.*

nations, a packing to the Devil. This is well known to all that have lookt into *Church-history*. But I am weary of transcribing so many citations out of books, that are very unpleasant to read, as are almost all the works of the *Fathers:* and wou'd think my self bound to make an apology for it, were it not that the thing is unavoidable in this kind of writing; where altho the best proofs imaginable, and the most clear are requisite, the worst in the world are generally us'd, the most precarious, perplext, and obscure. And, if the truth may be freely spoken, there remains very little on record, very little that's any way certain or authentic, concerning *the originals of Christianity*, from the beginning of NERO to the end of TRAJAN or ADRIAN, that I may take the narrowest compass I can: for others will bring this period of uncertainty much lower, which shou'd the more engage us to keep close to the *Scriptures*, where alone we can find rest for the soles of our feet. Yet in this labyrinth of the *Fathers* we have been at no loss (you see, MEGALETOR) tho sometimes a little at a stand, to find out the unsophisticated sentiments of the Nazarens or Ebionites, so farr as here insisted on, for of their other opinions we shall discourse another time: and this for the most part by the light of such testimonies, as if justly doubted or oppos'd, there will [61] be no evidence left for any sort of Christianity whatever. Now, from all these things, and particularly from *the Letter of* PETER *to* JAMES above cited, as well as from *the Acts of the Apostles*, and from other places of *the New Testament*, together with what some ancient Sectaries believ'd concerning the death and resurrection of JESUS, it manifestly appears from what source the Mahometans (who always most religiously abstain from things strangl'd and from blood) had their peculiar Christianity, if I be allow'd so to call it; and that their *Gospel*, for ought I yet know, may in the main be the ancient *Gospel of* BARNABAS. For the Mahometan Interpolations are too palpable, not to be easily distinguish'd: I wish we cou'd as easily come by the omissions, if there be any. PETER MARTYR (by the way) does, in the first chapter of the 4th part of his *Common places*, maintain, with other eminent Divines, that Mahometanism is nothing else but a Christian Heresy; from which I still inferr, that, whether upon a prospect of advantaging Traffic, or of putting them in the way of conversion to a better Christianity, the Mahometans may be as well allow'd Moschs in these parts of Europe, if they desire it, as any other Sectaries: and certainly it would not onely be highly unreasonable, but withall be the highest ingratitude, in the King of Sweden to oppose it at Stockholm; considering the generous and human treatment, I will not say the charitable and pious reception, he found so many years at Bender with his Christian followers. No future

Pag. 23.

misunderstanding may cancel the obligation: for if we are bound to forgive the injuries of our enemies, we ought certainly much rather to forget the miscarriages of our friends.

[62] CHAP. XVI.

I SHALL conclude these reflections concerning the perpetual observation of the Mosaic Law by the Jewish, and of the Noachic Precepts by the Gentile Christians living among them, with remarking, that the Apostle JAMES does not in his *Epistle* mean by WORKS the moral Law, nor by FAITH a merit in believing, as is suppos'd by the current of Expositors, the one half at least of Scholastic Divinity being built on this very interpretation: but that WORKS there signify the *Levitical Law*, as FAITH is put for *Christianity*. This likewise is apparently PAUL's meaning, whenever he uses the same expressions: and thus onely may these two Apostles be reconcil'd, without recurring to evasions, suppositions, and sophisms, that will satisfy no reasonable man, however he may think fit perhaps to hold his tongue. JAMES writes expresly to the scatter'd tribes of the Jews, Cap. i. v. 1. and therfore tells them that FAITH (i. e. Christianity) *can neither profit or save them without* WORKS (i. e. the Levitical rites) as being oblig'd by Cap. ii. v. an eternal and national covenant to the Law of MOSES: but PAUL, writing 14. by the Jewish converts to the Romans, tells them, that *a Man is justify'd* Cap. iii. v. *by* FAITH *without the works of the* LAW, the Gentiles not being at all 28. concern'd in the Mosaic rites or ceremonies. JAMES says, that *the* FAITH of Cap. ii. v. a Jew (for to such onely he writes) *without the* WORKS *of the Law is dead:* 26. and PAUL says, that the Gentiles (for such he himself calls the Romans) Cap. vii. *are dead to the* LAW *by the body of* CHRIST. In the same manner is to be v. 4. understood the *Epistle to the Galatians*, Gen[63]tiles whom certain more zealous than knowing Jews wou'd needs compel to be circumcis'd: and in the same manner also ought we carefully to distinguish what is said to the *Colossians, Philippians*, or any other Christians from among the Gentiles (as such) from what is said by way of parenthesis in PAUL's *Epistles*, or more directly elsewhere, to the Jewish Christians, and proper to them onely. Thus that *the* LAW *was our Schoolmaster to bring us unto* CHRIST, Gal. iii. and that its *ordinances were blotted out and nail'd to* CHRIST's *cross*, are 24, 25. phrases to be understood onely of us Gentiles. I might with equal facility Col. ii. 14. run over all the *Epistles*, and not onely show this distinction perpetually reigning thro them; but remark at the same time those infinite mistakes that the want of observing such a distinction has occasion'd: especially

those grosser errors, which have been too commonly advanc'd into fundamental Doctrines, administring fuel for endless contentions; but neither
reforming men's manners, nor informing their understandings. They are
the prime handles, on the contrary, for the opposition made to all Christianity; which such writers are in the mean time combating a Phantom,
and wou'd some of them be the zealousest advocates for the Christian
Institution, cou'd they but see its original beauty, stript of all such paint
and disguize. A person (Sir) of your great penetration and solid judgement, cannot fail making such observations to himself; tho, in regard of
the *Epistle to the Hebrews*, the case is peculiar: for which reason I reserve
what I have to say about it, till I come to treat of the nature and end of Sacrifices, without which the scope of the author *to the Hebrews* is obscure if
not unintelligible. For in this respect I grant there is a change of the Law,
as the Lawgiver himself has expresly foretold there shou'd be; wherin he's
[64] follow'd by JEREMIAH, EZEKIEL, JOEL, and such others, as must be
acknowledg'd to have well understood the reason and design of the Jewish
Sacrifices. Wherfore desiring you to suspend your judgement till you see
the [82] RESPUBLICA MOSAICA, I return to my general position. Besides

Pag. 37. the passage alledg'd before out of *the first Epistle to the Corinthians*, the
following passage also out of that to the Romans, may serve for a perpetual key to this System of reconciling JAMES and PAUL, *viz.* that WORKS,
as oppos'd to FAITH in their writings, signify the *opus operatum* of the
Levitical Law, or the outward practice of it; and that FAITH signifies the
belief of one God, a persuasion of the truth of CHRIST's doctrine, and the
inward sanctification of the mind. Without this Faith and Regeneration
(as a change from vice to virtue was properly call'd even by the Heathens)
the ever so punctual performance of Ceremonies cou'd not justify a Jew,
or render him a good man, agreeable and well-pleasing to God: but JESUS
and his Apostles made it manifest that the Gentile, who believ'd one God
and the necessity of Regeneration, might, contrary to the notions of the
degenerate Jews (who then plac'd all religion in outward practices) be
justify'd by such his Faith, without being oblig'd to exercise the ceremonies of the Law, being things no way regarding him, either as to national
origin or civil government; while the Jew, on the other hand, must, to
the outward observance of his country Law by eternal covenant, add this
inward Regeneration and the Faith of the *Gospel*, or the Levitical Law

---

82. *See the* Appendix, *number I.*

wou'd avail him nothing tho ever so strictly observ'd. Here PAUL himself speak. [65] *Where is boasting then? It is excluded: by what Law? of* WORKS? *Nay; but by the Law of* FAITH. *Therfore we conclude, that a man is justify'd by* FAITH *without the Works of the* LAW. *Is he the God of the* JEWS *onely? is he not also of the* GENTILES? *Yes of the* GENTILES *also; seeing it is one God which shall justify the* CIRCUMCISION *by* FAITH, *and the* UNCIRCUMCISION thro FAITH. *Do we then make void the* LAW *thro* FAITH? *God forbid: yea we establish the* LAW. What can be more plain or pertinent? and is not this the onely way to reconcile the *Gospels* with the *Acts* and *Epistles,* as well as these with the *Old Testament?* Is not this the onely method of according the Jews and the Gentiles? yea and of justifying God himself against those, who object the mutability or imperfection of giving one Law at one time, and another Law at another time? wheras there is no such abrogating or obrogating according to the ORIGINAL PLAN OF CHRISTIANITY. The Religion that was true yesterday is not false to day; neither can it ever be false, if ever it was once true.

Rom. iii. 27–31.

CHAP. XVII.

THUS therfore the Jewish Christians were ever bound to observe the Law of MOSES, and the Gentile Christians, who liv'd among them, only the Noachic precepts of abstinence from blood and things offer'd to Idols: for the Moral Law was both then, and before, and ever will be, of indispensable obligation to all men, it being the grossest absurdity and impiety to assert the contrary; since sound Reason, or the light of common sense, is a catholic and eternal rule, [66] without which mankind cou'd not subsist in peace or happiness one hour. It is the fundamental bond of all society, where there is or there is not a reveal'd religion: and 'tis the onely thing that's approv'd by the most opposite Revelations, or by any sort of parties and divisions in each other. Nothing can be more apposite in this place, than what CICERO divinely writes to the same purpose. RIGHT REASON, says [83] he, *is a true Law; suteable to nature, diffus'd among all*

---

83. Est quidem vera Lex recta Ratio, naturae congruens, diffusa in omnes, constans, sempiterna: quae vocet ad officium jubendo, vetando a fraude deterreat; quae tamen neque probos frustra jubet aut vetat, nec improbos jubendo aut vetando movet. Huic Legi neque obrogari fas est, neque derogari ex hac aliquid licet, neque tota abrogari potest; nec verò aut per Populum, aut per Senatum, solvi hac Lege possumus. Neque est quaerendus explanator, aut interpres ejus alius; nec erit alia lex

people, constantly the same, everlasting: which obliges men to their duty by commands, and deterrs them from wickedness by prohibitions; but which never commands or prohibits the virtuous in vain, tho the vitious are not mov'd by menaces or injunctions. Of this Law nothing must be chang'd, nor may any part of it be repeal'd, nor can the whole be ever abolish'd; neither can we be absolv'd from observing it, by the authority of the Senate or the People. No other expounder or interpreter therof, but it self, is to be sought; nor is it one Law at Rome, another at Athens, one at this time, another hereafter: but the same Law, both eternal and immortal, is to govern all nations and at all times. And there will be, as [67] *we may say, one common master and ruler over all, even GOD, the proposer, debater, and enacter of this Law: to whom he that will not yield obedience must fly from himself, and shake off the nature of a man; in doing which very thing he suffers the highest punishments, tho he shou'd escape those other torments which are commonly believ'd.* It was a saying of Dr. WHITCHCOT, that natural Religion was eleven parts in twelve of all Religion: and PAUL was so farr from exhorting his disciples of the Gentiles against this Moral Law of Nature (as he justly did against the Levitical Law of MOSES) that the FAITH which he recommends to them instead of this last Law (even that FAITH *which works by love,* and whose end is to beget *a new creature*) is made by him radically productive of the Moral Law. *The fruit of the Spirit* (says he) *is love, joy, peace, patience, gentleness, goodness, fidelity, meekness, termperance: against such there is no Law.* No certainly, neither against any other virtue; nor wou'd any Religion be receiv'd in the world, that shou'd go about to contradict or annul them: and tis evident to all, but such as will not see, that one main design of Christianity was to improve and perfect the knowledge of the Law of nature, as well as to facilitate and inforce the observation of the same; tho tis very true, that when we have done all, we have done but our duty, and that but ever imperfectly. JAMES was also in the right, by pressing upon the Jews the WORKS of the Levitical no less than those of the Moral Law, for the reasons given before (particularly in the 12th chapter) and therfore needless to be repeated here, since he

Gal. v. 6.
Ibid. vi. 15.
Ibid. v. 22, 23.

Romae, alia Athenis, alia nunc, alia posthac: sed & omnes gentes, & omni tempore, una Lex, & sempiterna & immortalis, continebit. Unusque erit communis quasi magister & imperator omnium, Deus ille, Legis hujus inventor, disceptator, lator: cui qui non parebit, ipse se fugiet, ac naturam hominis aspernabitur; atque hoc ipso luet maximas poenas, etiamsi cetera supplicia (quae putantur) effugerit. *Cic. de Repub. l. 3. ex Lactant. l. 6. c. 8.*

recommends FAITH as earnestly as PAUL himself. Now, all this is very
intelligible, easy, and consistent, according to the Nazaren System: wheras
nothing in the world is more intricate, difficult, [68] or incoherent, than
the controversies between the Protestants and the Papists, about *Merit
of Works* and *Justification by Faith*, occasion'd by the seeming contradiction of JAMES to PAUL. But these are nice speculations, of which those
plain men never dreamt; being founded on Scholastic distinctions and
Roman Law-terms, to which most of the Apostles were utter strangers.
Good works, as moral duties are commonly call'd, were no part of the
question at all: not the WORKS mention'd by PAUL and JAMES, in contradistinction to FAITH. The Papists are no better agreed among themselves in all their divisions and subdivisions, than the Protestants, who
are no less split about these points of Merit and Justification; which as we
all know, have occasion'd as much looseness and libertinism on the one
hand, as they have produc'd superstition and bigottry on the other. Anti-
nomianism and Supererogation are the two monstrous extremes of their
disputes. They keep still a woful pother: and I foresee that many of 'em
(not onely on account of this explication, but also for what I have deliver'd
concerning the perpetual observation of the Levitical Law) will say, that I
advance a new Christianity, tho I think it undoubtedly to be the old one.
But minding the calumny of some as little as they do the truth, I leave all
impartial persons to examine; if what has been written by either side on
these heads, be for the most part any thing else but elaborate nonsense,
mere jingle, and logomachy? and consequently, whether all the barbarous
stuff that's deliver'd in the Scholastic Systems concerning *Faith* and *Justification*, be not an after-device of Priests to puzzle the cause; and so to raise
scruples in mens consciences (to the bringing of them often into despair)
that they may have recourse to them for the solution of their doubts, to
the no small [69] increase both of their pay and their power? However
the matter may appear to others, I am persuaded that my explication was
the real sense of JAMES; and I am every whit as certain, that he can never
be made to agree with PAUL, as well as that PAUL can never be fairly made
to agree with him, on any other foot. As to the substance of what our
modern Divines wou'd seem to contend about, for my own part I readily
acknowledge that no man can merit any thing of God by his good works,
be they ever so many or great; and that whatever he receives is by mere
grace and mercy, even the best of us being, strictly speaking, unprofitable
servants: but I deny that any thing of all this matter is meant in the phraze
of *Justification by Works* or *by Faith* in the whole *New Testament*.

CHAP. XVIII.

HITHERTO then we have partly seen what the true original Christianity in many things was not, and partly what it was; especially as to the Jews perpetual keeping of their own rites, and the cohabiting Gentiles no less perpetual observation of the Noachic precept about blood: while both of 'em agreed to the necessity of Regeneration, and subjecting themselves to JESUS as their spiritual Lawgiver. To these things I cou'd add much greater lustre, had I time to digest and methodize my observations touching the rise and growth of Christianity. There it wou'd appear, how strangely the most part of the Jews of his time mistook the true design of JESUS, having been deluded and prepossest by the artifice of a prevailing faction, that had not the sincere interest of their country, nor the purity of their Constitution, at heart. But they [70] were chiefly irritated against him by the influence of a rampant Priesthood, who, for their own profit and power, had openly and shamelessly perverted the Law of MOSES; rather than to see which restor'd to its primitive institution, and themselves oblig'd to change their formal into a spiritual life, they wou'd not have even the kingdom restor'd at that time to Israel. Yet for rejecting the salutiferous doctrine and admonitions of the holy JESUS, they brought upon themselves swift destruction. And indeed the divine wisdom of the Christian Institution (the original, uncorrupted, easy, intelligible Institution; but not the fabulous systems, lucrative inventions, burthensom superstitions, and unintelligible jargon early substituted to it) is so apparent in enlightning the minds and regulating the conduct of men, in procuring their highest happiness in all respects, particularly in the admirable Economy of uniting the Jews and the Gentiles into one Family, and thus leading all the world to the knowledge of one God: that nothing, I am persuaded, but a perfect ignorance of what it really is, or private interest, a worse enemy to truth than ignorance, cou'd keep any from cheerfully imbracing it. I do not onely mean those who declare against both name and thing, and this somtimes very justly as they are represented to them: but likewise too many of those who make loud professions of their Christianity, nay, and who restrain the benefits of it solely to those of their own cant and livery; tho the articles of their belief and the rubric of their practice, be manifestly the very things which JESUS went about to destroy. A change in names makes no change in things: and tho' I cannot say, that I wish there was but one communion of Christians, since this in nature is impossible, nei[71]ther is it in it self desireable, nor the thing intended by the communion of Saints: yet

I wish with all my heart that there were none in any communion, whose CHRISTIANITY, notwithstanding all their boasts and pretences, cou'd be shown to be down-right ANTICHRISTIANISM; for we must govern our selves by things, as I said just now, and not by names, which frequently continue after things are chang'd quite contrary to what those words at first imported. And for God's sake, Sir, what can be more Antichristian than heathenish Polytheism and Idolatry, pious Frauds and superstitious Fopperies, sophistical Subtilties and unintelligible Mysteries, damning Uncharitableness and inhuman Persecutions, vain Pomp and ridiculous Pageantry, absolute Authority over conscience, and making temporal Rewards or Punishments the means of supporting Religion? what can be less Christian, I say, or more contrary to the design of JESUS CHRIST, than all these things I have here enumerated; with a factious engrossing of Gain, and an artful propagation of Ignorance to support the Trade, or whatever else our Deliverer oppos'd in the degenerate Jew and in the bewilder'd Gentile? These and the like corruptions wherever they are found, be it in any one society, or among several societies calling themselves Christians, are yet the very reverse of genuin CHRISTIANITY, and consequently ANTICHRISTIANISM. But tis no wonder Christianity shou'd in process of time be misunderstood or misrepresented, when the author of it was very early disbeliev'd by his own nearest relations, and charg'd with madness, John vii. nay and dealing with the Devil, by others: this charge of madness having 4, 5–8. x. been often since laid by men of craft and interest against those, that wou'd 20–34. generously risk life or reputa[72]tion, an employment or a benefice, for the sake of truth and the public good, or whatever they take to be such. Is not Mr. WHISTON (for example) reckon'd mad, tho no man in England writes more coherently? This truth bids me willingly acknowledge: and yet I am much farther than his detractors from allowing all his premisses, or admitting every one of his consequences to be just. Sit still, says the sly Pharisee, if you are a private man, and sooth the knavery of the great, that you may enjoy their protection: or if you chance to be a man in power, keep what you have got by what title soever, and be sure to make the most of the people's folly; for he that does otherwise is a madman. This language I have heard a thousand times, and as many times rejected such advice. Tho I declar'd long since that I love not to call names in Religion, and that I am neither of PAUL, nor of CEPHAS, nor of APOLLOS; yet since men are sure to be distinguish'd by their friends as well as by their foes, and that the designations they bestow are often inexpressive, but generally false or improper: so I own that, for more than one reason, I have less exception to

Pag. 26.

the name of NAZAREN than to any other. My first reason is, because this name, as I have already prov'd, was that which the followers of JESUS took to themselves at the beginning, even preferably to that of CHRISTIAN, which was given them next: and my second reason is, because this name was afterwards peculiarly apply'd to those, who understood the design of Christianity as I do; namely, that the Jewish nation shou'd always continue to observe their own Law under the Christian dispensation, tho nevertheless the disciples from among the Gentiles do stand under no obligation to keep that Law, either as it is ceremonial or judicial. This is the sense wherin [73] I understand NAZARENISM, as now betokening a distinct society of Christians: for with regard to any other opinions justly or unjustly attributed to the old NAZARENS, as I have neither expresly adopted nor defended such; so they do not enter into the idea I give of the word, and therfore am not hereafter to be charg'd, with what I before-hand disclaim.

CHAP. XIX.

AS most of the Jews mistook the design of JESUS, so the Gentiles did as much mistake the few Jews who adher'd to him. You know already to what a prodigious degree Imposture and Credulity went hand in hand in the primitive times of the Christian Church; the last being as ready to receive, as the first was to forge books, under the names of the Apostles, their companions, and immediate successors. IRENEUS, speaking of those primitive false coiners, says, that *in order to* [84] *amaze the simple, and such as are ignorant of the Scriptures of truth, they obtrude upon them an inexpressible multitude of apocryphal and spurious Scriptures of their own devizing.* This evil grew afterwards not onely greater, when the Monks were the sole transcribers, and (I might say in a manner) the sole keepers of all books good or bad; but in process of time it became almost absolutely impossible to distinguish history from [85] fable, or [74] truth from error, as to

---

84. Αμυθητον πληθος αποκρυφων και νοθων γραφων, ἁς αυτοι επλασαν, παρεισφερουσιν εις καταπληξιν των ανοητων, και τα της αληθειας μη επισταμενων γραμματα. Adversus Haeres. l. 1. c. 17.

85. Veteribus illis bono animo multa & scribentibus & legentibus, quae aliquo saltem modo instruere possent plebem; quorum crassis ingeniis, & temerariis Monachis patientiam sequentibus, alta nox etiam clarissimis Christianismi principiis tandem invecta est: fabulis & sophismatis veritatis regnum dolo & vi occupantibus. *Gaspar Barth. in Notis ad Claudiani Mamerti lib. 1. de Statu Animae.*

the beginnings and original monuments of Christianity. The truth of this
you may particularly see in all the treatises written about *the Canon of the
New Testament*, where there occurr a pritty ample list of difficulties, not
to be slightly answer'd, or past over indifferently, by any who are sincere
lovers of truth; these being in themselves matters of the highest importance, as well as subjects of the greatest curiosity, and therefore deserving
all the pains of the most able Critics to solve them satisfactorily. Those
Apocryphal books occasion'd me to start a difficulty formerly in *Amyntor*, which, for ought I yet perceive, must be solv'd at last by my self. It was
this. *How the immediate successors of the Apostles cou'd so grossly confound
the genuin writings of their masters, with such as were falsely attributed to
them? or, since they were in the dark about these matters so early, how came
such as follow'd 'em by a better light?* And observing, that such Apocryphal
books were often put upon the same foot with the Canonical books by the
Fathers; and the first cited as *divine Scriptures* no less than the last, or somtimes when such as we reckon divine were disallow'd by them, I propos'd
these two other questions: *why all those books, which are cited as genuin
by* CLEMENS ALEXANDRIRUS, ORIGEN, TERTULLIAN, *and the rest of such
writers, shou'd not be accounted equally authentic? and what stress ought
to be laid on the testimony of those* Fathers, *who not onely contradict one
another, but* [75] *are often inconsistent with themselves in their relations of
the very same facts?* Nor do I think it a mean service to true Religion, to set
objections of this nature in their clearest light, no less to acquaint the persons concern'd with those scruples of many, which had otherwise perhaps
never come to their knowledge; than to put 'em hereby in the right way
of removing such, by answering them as fairly as they are propos'd. I am
farr from being ignorant that the woodden Priests and Divinelings of all
communions (easily distinguish'd from the true Pastors) instead of labor-
ing for satisfaction in such cases to themselves or others, are accustom'd
immediately to rail and raise a cry against those that do, as profest Heretics
or conceal'd Atheists: wheras if they had been such indeed, they shou'd
the more earnestly study to inform and convince them, which Billingsgate
and defamation can never effect. This conduct, on the contrary, will make
them suspect all to be a cheat and imposture, because men naturally cry
out when they are touch'd in a tender part. Those Smatterers and Hypo-
crites, its true, wou'd ordinarily cover their malice with the pretence of
zeal: but the real cause of all their passion, is either their ignorance which
they wou'd not have expos'd, or their laziness which they wou'd not have
distrub'd, with the business of their profession. Tis not possible, however,

for any Church or Community to be rid of such; since there's a mob of Priests, a mob of Lawyers, a mob of Gentlemen, a mob of Physicians, and a mob (to be short) in all numerous societies. But the able, the exemplary, and conscientious Divine, who merits all the honor and respect that is sure to be paid him, acts quite another part: for misrepresentation of his very enemies is as little to be fear'd from him, as much [76] as it is to be despis'd from those of another character; and information will be much more agreeably receiv'd from his hands, as it is more likely to be sound and sincere. Being therfore sure, that no man will be angry at a question who's able to answer it, I shall here add one more to the difficulties relating to our present *Canon of the New Testament*. Tis this. *Since the Nazarens or Ebionites are by all Church-historians unanimously acknowledg'd to have been the first Christians, or those who believ'd in* CHRIST *among the Jews, with which his own people he liv'd and dy'd, they having been the witnesses of his actions, and of whom were all the Apostles: considering this, I say, how it was possible for them to be the first of all others (for they are made to be the first Heretics) who shou'd form wrong conceptions of the doctrine and designs of* JESUS? *and how came the Gentiles, who believ'd on him after his death, by the preaching of persons that never knew him, to have truer notions of these things; or whence they cou'd have their information, but from the believing Jews?* To the customs of the Jews I grant the Gentiles were most averse, and their language they so little understood, as to commit on diverse occasions endless and monstrous mistakes, many instances of which may be seen

Pag. 37. in RHENFERD's *Dissertations* before-cited; which (by the way) I approve not in all things, particularly in his confounding the Nazarens of the first with some of those of the third and fourth centuries: yet still the Gentiles must have their water from the Jewish stream, or their cisterns will be very muddy and unwholsom. But not to digress, tho I am my self most firmly rooted in what I am thoroly persuaded to be the right belief concerning CHRIST and CHRISTIANITY, which I shall particularly deduce in the account of my [77] Religion, which I have often promis'd you; yet, for the sake of others, I wou'd passionately recommend (in the mean time) the clear solution of this difficulty about the Ebionites to the most capable Critics, be they Divines or Laymen: since not onely of old it occasion'd two eminent parties, but even now in a manner in our own days; and that one of them does affirm, the true Christianity of the Jews was overborn and destroy'd by the more numerous Gentiles, who, not enduring the reasonableness and simplicity of the same, brought into it by degrees the peculiar expressions and mysteries of Heathenism, the abstruse doctrines and distinctions of their Philosophers, an insupportable pontifical Hierarchy, and even the altars, offrings, the sacred rites and ceremonies of their Priests, tho they wou'd not so much as tolerate those of the Jews, and yet owning them to be divinely instituted. The Socinians and other Unitarians no less confidently assert, that the Gentiles did likewise introduce into Christianity their former polytheism and deifying of dead men: thus retaining (add they) the name of Christianity, but quite altering the thing; and suteing it, as their interest or the necessity of their affaris requir'd, to all the opinions and customs any where in vogue from that time to this. The time-serving and fickleness of many Christians are too manifest to be deny'd. This is the nature of man. Yet for all the pretences of the Socinians to reason, they are in many things relating to this very subject, and in several other respects, not proper here to be mention'd, guilty of as palpable absurdities and contradictions, as any sect whatsoever: so little consistent is man in his opinions, any more than in his actions.

[78] CHAP. XX.

TO solve the said difficulty then about the Ebionites, it will not be enough barely to quote our *Gospels, Epistles,* and the *Acts of the Apostles;* but their genuinness and integrity must be likewise establish'd by those arguments, of which every good Christian may and ought to be appriz'd: since the Nazarens and Ebionites (whose Synagogues or Churches were numerous, as I said above, over all the orient, as well as particularly in Judea) had a *Gospel* of their own, somtimes call'd by Ecclesiastical writers [86] THE GOSPEL OF THE HEBREWS, and somtimes THE GOSPEL OF THE TWELVE APOSTLES; but ignorantly mistaken by IRENEUS, EPIPHANIUS, and their followers for THE GOSPEL OF MATTHEW interpolated. This *Gospel* was publickly read in their Churches as authentic, for above [87] 300 years; which

---

86. Papias apud Euseb. Hist. Eccles. l. 3. c. 39: Ignat. in Epist. ad Smyrn. n. 3: Iren. adversus Haeres. l. 3. c. 11: Clem. Alex. stromat. l. 1: Origen. homil. 1. in Luc: tract. 8 in Mat: homil. 15 in Jerem: & in tom. 2. comment. in Joan: Just. Martyr (*ut videtur*) in dialogo cum Tryphone: Ambros. in prooem. commentarior. in Luc: Euseb. Hist. Eccles. l. 3. c. 25 & 27: item l. 4. c. 22: Epiphan. Haeres. 29 & 30, passim: Hieronym. in Catalogo, n. 4: Contra Pelagian. l. 3. c. 1: Comment in cap. 12. Mat; & alibi saepissimè: Theophylact. comment. in Luc: Tit. Bostr. comment. in eundem.

87. Vid. Augustin. contra Faust. l 19. c. 18: & contra Cresconium, c. 31: *ut de* HIERONYMO, EPIPHANIO, *reliquisque sileam.*

might very well be for the most part, and yet the other *Gospels* never be the less authentic also. Doctor GRABE (who has [79] Doctor [88] MILLS and other very able men on his side) is of opinion it was written before the *Gospels* now receiv'd for [89] Canoncial, as being collected by the eye and ear-witnesses of CHRIST, or by such as were familiarly acquainted with

Luc. i. 1.

the Apostles, and that it was one of the many mention'd by LUKE. As several celebrated Divines have shown, that true Christianity might have subsisted, tho any particular book of our present *Canon* had perish'd, or if but any one of our *Gospels* had remain'd: so none of 'em, that ever I cou'd learn, has approv'd the extravagant fancy of IRENEUS, who wou'd needs inferr, that of necessity there cou'd neither be more nor fewer than four *Gospels*; because (says he) there are four regions of the world, and four principal winds. The *Gospel of the Hebrews* therfore might be one of those many mention'd by LUKE, as written before his own; and which he does not reject as false, or erroneous, or for any other reason. But, for ought appears hitherto, tis long ago destroy'd, a few fragments excepted; as are a world of other ancient monuments, that were sacrific'd to blind zeal or too clearsighted interest: and were it still remaining, it wou'd have finish'd or prevented abundance of Controversies, otherwise not easy to be determin'd; for which reason diverse pious and learned men do now highly regret the loss of the same. Nor were there wanting who would persuade the world, that it lies yet cover'd with dust in the French King's library, as others said it was in other places. It was translated into Greec and Latin by [90] JEROM, who very often makes use [80] of it, as likewise did ORIGEN and EUSEBIUS; not rejecting it as *Apocryphal*, nor receiving it as *Canonical*, but placing it among what they call'd the *Ecclesiastical books:* that is, books whose antiquity they were not able to deny, but whose authority they were not willing to acknowledge. Long before these *the Gospel of the Hebrews* was by PAPIAS, IGNATIUS, CLEMENS ALEXANDRINUS, and others alleg'd as a true *Gospel*. So it seems to have been by JUSTIN MARTYR, in his Dialogue with TRYPHON the Jew, as before cited: so was it by HEGESIPPUS, who was himself a Jew, and the father of Ecclesiastical, as HERODOTUS of Civil history. In his list of the first *Heresies*, preserv'd in his own words by EUSEBIUS, he is farr from reckoning the Nazarens or Ebionites among 'em: as good a

---

88. In Prolegomenis ad Novum Testamentum. pag. v. col. 2. & pag. vi. col. 2.
89. In Spicilegio Patrum, tom. 1. pag. 17, 18.
90. In Catalogo, n. 4 *& alibi.*

proof that he was one himself, as that he [91] delighted to quote their *Gospel*. The same EUSEBIUS says that SYMMACHUS was [92] an Ebionite, which is the reason that the Nazarens were by their antagonists call'd [93] Symmachians, as from CERINTHUS Cerinthians, but still by themselves NAZARENS. The Ebionites likewise (or if you had rather, the Nazarens) the Encratites, and the Severians their offspring, rejected the [94] *Acts of the Apostles*, with all [81] PAUL's *Epistles*; and the first had other *Acts*, as I took notice before, very different: so that the authority of this book must withall be clearly made out by the historians of the *Canon*, as very easily it may be; espe- cially since CHRYSOSTOM, in a *Homily* he made on the title of the *Acts*, says [95] that *in his time* (which was the end of the fourth century) *not onely the author and collector, but even the book it self, was unknown to many*. In short, every side and sect pretended they were the onely true Christians, and each did peremtorily (as many persons now do with as little ground yet equal confidence) appeal to APOSTOLICAL TRADITION AND SUCCES- SION, which are the very words of the Heretic [96] PTOLOMY to his female correspondent FLORA; and that they onely being the Church, no others were to be heard or credited. One wou'd imagine it was SCHELSTRATE or DODWEL that spoke. But what do I talk of PTOLOMY? the numerous and entire sects of the Valentinians, Marcionites, and others, accus'd our *Scrip- tures* of error and imperfection, of contradiction and insufficiency, with- out Tradition (forsooth) as we are inform'd by [97] IRENEUS: and that such

Pag. 34.

91. Euseb. Hist. Eccles. l. 4. c. 22: Item. 3. 25.

92. Hist Eccles. l. 6. c. 17: *Item Ambros. in Galat.* Omnis (inquit) credens in Chris- tum, & observans leges factorum, male intelligit Christum: sicut & Symmachiani (qui ex Pharisaeis originem trahunt) qui, servatâ omni Lege, Christianos se dicunt.

93. Et nunc sunt quidam Haeretici, qui se Nazarenos vocant; a nonnullis tamen Symmachiani appellantur, & Circumcisionem habent Judaeorum, & Baptismum Christianorum. *Augustin. contra Crescon. l. 1. c.* 31.

94. Tertullian, contra Marcion. l. 5. c. 2: Euseb. Hist. Eccles. l. 4. c. 29: & ubi supra in cap. 13: Origen. ubi supra: Epiphan. Haeres. 28. n. 5: & 30. n. 16: Nicephor. Hist. Eccles. l. 4. c. 4: Philastr. Haeres. 36: *Item Manichaei* apud Augustin. contra Adimant; & alibi: Hieronym. Tom. 6. in Mat.

95. Πολλοις τουτι το βιβλιον ουδ' ὁτι γνωριμον εστι, ουτε αυτο, ουτε ὁ γραψας αυτο και συνθεις. Homil. in Act.

96. Μαθηση γαρ (θεου διδοντος) ἑξης και την τουτο αρχην τε και γεννησιν, αξιουμενη της ΑΠΟΣΤΟΛΙΚΗΣ ΠΑΡΑΔΟΣΕΩΣ, ἑν εκ ΔΙΑΔΟΧΗΣ και ἡμεις παρειληφαμεν, μετα και του κανονισαι παντας τους λογους τη του Σωτηρος Διδασκαλιᾳ. Epiphan. Haeres. 33. n. 7.

97. Adversus Haeres. l. 1. c. 2.

Traditions there were, even some of the reputed Orthodox inferr'd from
1 Cor. ii. 6. this and such other texts alledg'd by the Heretics, *we speak wisdom among
them that are perfect.* This their adversaries also freely acknowledg'd, but
asserted the Traditions [82] were solely of their side, loudly glorying that
they themselves were the Church and the Orthodox, while those whom
others call'd Orthodox were Heretics and Intruders. Every one of them
likewise had APOSTOLICAL SUCCESSION ever in his mouth. But

> *Non nostrum inter vos tantas componere lites:*
> *Et vitulâ tu dignus, & hic* ——— Virgil.

Just so it is at this day between some of the Protestants and all the Papists
(not to speak of the Greecs) each of 'em boasting I know not what *uninterrupted Tradition and Succession*, which are the most chimerical pretences
in nature; and which not only shows how little any oral tradition whatever
is to be valu'd; but that no truth of universal concern can possibly depend
on so slight a foundation, as the way of bandying about an old story for
numerous generations. *To the Law* therfore *and to the Testimony.* To the
New Testament, I say; and to that alone both for doctrine and discipline.
So farr is the Succession of Bishops in any ancient See from being uninterrupted, that it is not so much as certain fact, no not for the first half-dozen
of pretended Bishops in the See of Rome, from which our English High-
church Pharisees are proud to derive their Succession; which I deliberately and positively defy 'em to make out to me, either in Rome, or here in
Great Britain with respect to the first British Bishops. Besides that several
even of the Bishops who are not contested, were Schismatics, Heretics,
Apostates, Atheists, and monsters of men for wickedness, by the consent
of all historians. These were cleanly conveyances for the pure doctrine
of CHRIST, farr better preserv'd in the *Scriptures*, and in the successive
profession of the faithful. [83] Shou'd the validity of Ordination and Ordinances depend on the succession of Sees, it wou'd then be downright Con-
juring, and not a reasonable, much less a divine Institution. If Tradition
therfore, and this Episcopal succession be not *weak and beggarly elements*;
I know not what can be so call'd with any propriety. This Succession, in
a word, and Apostolical, that is to say, Oral Tradition, are literally in the
1 Tim. i. 4. Apostle PAUL's words, *Fables and endless Genealogies, ministring questions
rather than godly edifying*: intricate questions that can never be solv'd, and
division instead of edification. This business puts me in mind of a learned
Gentleman, who told me some time since, that he was about to collect the

Traditions of his Church since the *Reformation*: and if he goes on with this design, he'll be strangely surpriz'd to find such prodigious variety, alteration, and uncertainty, within so small a compass as from LUTHER's time to ours. The first dispute will be (and no logomachy I assure him) whether his Church was well reform'd or not? The next, whether the Clergy or the Laity made this alteration, whether the motives to it were temporal or spiritual? and the third, to name no more, who were precisely the persons, or those that were the chief instruments of the same? Every one of these points will be eagerly contested. Yet they are trifles to the confusion and intricacy he'll meet at every step about the discipline and doctrine, the ceremonies and usages of this Church: when even stories void of all rivalship or interest, where neither point of honor nor preferment is concern'd, are scarce ever told twice the same way. APOSTOLICAL TRADITION, to say it in few words, was the engine us'd formerly, as it is at present, to introduce or countenance whatever men had a mind to advance without the authori[84]ty of *Scripture*, or contrary to it: and thus (to give an example in the very point we have been hitherto chiefly clearing) AUGUSTIN, speaking of the Nazarens by name, says, that *tho they* [98] *acknowledge the son of God to be the Messias, yet they observe all the precepts of the old Law; which the Christians*, continues he, *have learnt by* APOSTOLICAL TRADITION *not to observe carnally, but to understand spiritually.* JESUS no where, the *Gospel* no where, forbids the practice of the Jewish Law to the Jews; but the Tradition of the Apostles is here made to supply the defect of their writeing. And so this very Tradition is alledg'd by others to warrant the invocation of Saints, prayers for the Dead, the worship of Images, with the whole train of Greec and Romish superstitions, wherof the least footstep appears not in the *Bible*. Again therfore I say, *to the Law and to the Testimony*: since it will not avail any thing to say here (for there's nothing some men will not say) that by *Apostolical Tradition* AUGUSTIN means the written doctrine of the Apostles, till it appears that they have written any such matter. You perceive by this time (MEGALETOR) that what the Mahometans believe concerning CHRIST and his doctrine, were neither the inventions of MAHOMET, nor yet of those Monks who are said to have

---

98. Nazaraei, cùm Dei filium confiteantur esse Christum, omnia tamen veteris Legis observant; quae Christiani per APOSTOLICAM TRADITIONEM non observare carnaliter, sed spiritualiter intelligere didicerunt. Ebionei Christum etiam tantummodo hominem dicunt: mandata carnalia legis observant, circumcisionem scilicet carnis, & cetera, quorum oneribus per novum Testamentum liberati sumus. *De Haeres. c. 9.*

assisted him in the framing of his *Alcoran*; but that they are as old as the time of the Apo[85]stles, having been the sentiments of whole Sects or Churches: and that tho the *Gospel of the Hebrews* be in all probability lost, yet some of those things are founded on another *Gospel* anciently known, and still in some manner existing, attributed to BARNABAS. If in the history of this *Gospel* I have satisfy'd your curiousity, I shall think my time well spent; but infinitely better, if you agree, that, on this occasion, I have set THE ORIGINAL PLAN OF CHRISTIANITY in its due light, as farr as I propos'd to do. I am with inexpressible admiration and respect,

Your most faithful, obedient,

Honslaerdyke,   *and devoted Servant,*

$17\frac{16}{7}09$

J. T.

CONTRIBUTORS

F. Stanley Jones is Director of the Institute for the Study of Judaeo-Christian Origins and Professor of Religious Studies at California State University, Long Beach. He co-edited *Le judéo-christianisme dans tous ses états* and has recently released *Pseudoclementina Elchasaiticaque inter Judaeo-christiana: Collected Studies.*

David Lincicum is University Lecturer in New Testament at the University of Oxford. He is the author of *Paul and the Early Jewish Encounter with Deuteronomy* and, together with Martin Bauspieß, is currently producing a translation of F. C. Baur's essay on the Christ party in Corinth.

Pierre Lurbe is professor in the Département d'Études Anglophones at the Université PaulValéry Montpellier 3. He specializes in the history of ideas in the seventeenth and eighteenth centuries, with particular emphasis on the interconnection between political thought and religious ideas. He has co-edited *Le joug normand: La conquête normande dans la pensée politique anglaise des XVIIe et XVIIIe siècles* and *La question de l'athéisme au XVIIème siècle*, translated Toland's *Reasons for Naturalizing the Jews* (*Raisons de naturaliser les Juifs*), and published numerous articles on John Toland and his age.

Matt Jackson-McCabe is Associate Professor and Chair of the Department of Religious Studies at Cleveland State University. He edited *Jewish Christianity Reconsidered* and has authored, among related studies, *Logos and Law in the Letter of James.*

Matti Myllykoski is Chief Information Specialist at Helsinki University Library and docent in the New Testament. Recent relevant publications include "James the Just in History and Tradition: Perspectives of Past and Present Scholarship" in *Currents in Biblical Research* (2006–2007) and "Ohne Dekret: Das Götzenopferfleisch und die Frühgeschichte der Didache," in *Aposteldekret und antikes Vereinswesen: Gemeinschaft und ihre Ordnung.*

Index of Modern Authors

Abbot, Robert 15, 15 n. 40, 36
Alkier, S. 144–45 n. 22, 161
Allix, Pierre 28 n. 88, 36
Aucher, John 13 n. 31, 36
Baird, William 105–6 n. 2, 106 n. 3, 122
Barrett, C. K. 161
Baumgarten, Siegmund Jacob 124, 124 n. 4, 127, 128 nn. 26 and 28, 129, 129 n. 34, 134, 148 n. 35, 165
Baur, Ferdinand Christian 3, 68, 96, 99, 99 n. 36, 107, 118 n. 58, 120–21, 121 n. 72, 122, 123–24, **129–34**, **137–39**, 141, 141 n. 10, 142 n. 15, 143, 143 n. 20, **145–62**
Becmann, Christian 216
Berg, Jan van den 143 n. 17, 162
Biddle, John 27, 27 n. 84, 37
Blackall, Offspring 47, 48 n. 5, 174
Boyarin, Daniel 138 n. 2, 161, 162
Brecht, Martin 143 n. 18, 145, 145 n. 24, 162
Bridges, John 11, 11 n. 24, 37
Brown, Edward 8, 8 n. 13, 37
Burgess, Anthony 27 n. 83, 37
Burke, Edmund 106 n. 4, 122
Carabelli, Giancarlo 45 n. 1, 65, 91 n. 1, 94 nn. 11–12, 99–100
Carleton Paget, James 68 n. 3, 89, 98 n. 28, 100, 106 n. 2, 122, 138 n. 2, 140 nn. 78, 141 n. 12, 143 nn. 19–20, 162
Champion, Justin 45 n. 1, 49 n. 9, 54 n. 20, 55 n. 23, 65, 67 n. 1, 69 n. 10, 70–71 n. 12, 71–72 n. 16, 72 nn. 17–18, 73 nn. 19–21, 74 n. 24, 75 nn.

26–27, 83 n. 47–49, 86 n. 57, 89, 92, 92 nn. 2 and 4–5, 93, 93 nn. 6 and 8–9, 97 nn. 23–24, 99 nn. 32 and 35, 100, 140 nn. 8–9, 163
Chibald, William 18 n. 48, 37
Cirillo, Luigi 53, 53 n. 19, 55, 55 nn. 24–25, 65
Clarke, Samuel 48 nn. 4–5, 65
Cölln, D. von 147, 147 n. 32, 149, 163
Cohn-Sherbock, Dan 8 n. 14, 37
Colpe, Carsten 138 n. 2, 163
Copley, Anthony 7, 7 n. 11, 37
Cotelier, Jean-Baptiste 53, 95 n. 20, 147, 147 n. 33, 163, 191, 201
Cramer, Johann Jacob 52, 196
Credner, Karl August 129, 129 n. 35, 131, 131 n. 53, 132, 134, 146 n. 26
Cressy, Serenus 21 n. 56, 37
Cun, Pieter van der 175
Curcellus, Stephen 216, 219
Curione, Celio Secondo 18–19, 18–19 n. 49, 37
Daniel, Samuel 11 n. 23, 37
Daniel, Stephen H. 85 n. 54, 89
Davidson, Samuel 145 n. 23, 163
Dekker, Thomas 7, 7 n. 12, 37
Desmaizeaux, Pierre 49, 49 n. 8, 65, 91 n. 1, 93 n. 7, 100
Dodwell, Henry 239
Doran, Susan 20 n. 52, 37
Duddy, Thomas 85 n. 54, 89
Du Moulin, Pierre 22–23, 22–23 nn. 60–61, 37
Dunston, Christopher 20 n. 52, 37
Ehrman, Bart D. 50 n. 14, 65

Evans, Robert Rees   94 n. 14, 95 n. 17, 100

Fabian, Bernhard   142, 142 nn. 13–14, 163

Fabricius, Johann Albert   199

Falconer, John   16, 16 n. 44, 37

Finch, Henry   14, 14 n. 35, 23, 23 nn. 62–63, 37

Fitzer, Joseph   153 n. 57, 160 n. 92, 163

Flügge, Christian Wilhelm   145 n. 26

Fouke, Daniel C.   69–70 n. 10, 75 n. 26, 81 n. 43, 83 n. 48, 89

Fox, George   17, 17 n. 46, 37

Foxe, John   5, 6, 6 n. 6, 37

Frémaux, Michel   53, 53 n. 19, 55, 55 nn. 24–25, 65

Frey, Jörg   138 n. 2, 163

Gager, John G.   78, 78 n. 38, 89

Gaston, Lloyd   78

Gauden, John   17, 17 n. 45, 38, 48

Gawlick, Günter   105 n. 2, 106 n. 3, 122

Gieseler, Johann Karl Ludwig   130, 131, 131 nn. 48–50 and 52, 132, 132 n. 61, 133 nn. 62–63, 134, 146–47, 146 nn. 26 and 29–30, 148, 148 n. 35, 149, 163

Gouge, William   20–21, 20 n. 53, 21 nn. 54–55, 38, 98 n. 28, 100

Goulder, Michael   161

Grantham, Thomas   17, 17–18 n. 47, 38

Grascome, Samuel   10 n. 18, 38

Groot, Huig de   32, 216

Hammond, Henry   5, 23–26, 23–25 nn. 65–73, 26, 26 n. 81, 38, 100

Harrington, James   175

Harris, Horton   137 n. 1, 151 n. 49, 163

Haugaard, William P.   4 n. 4, 38

Hegel, Georg Wilhelm Friedrich   151–52, 151 n. 47

Heinemann, F. H.   95 n. 16, 99 n. 34, 100

Hesronita, Joannes   194 n. 13

Hester, Carl E.   151 n. 50, 152 n. 53, 163

Heussi, Karl   126 n. 12, 14, 127, 127 n. 17, 134

Heylyn, Peter   14 n. 38, 38

Hill, Craig   68 n. 4

Hilgenfeld, Adolf   145 n. 23, 156, 163

Hirsch, Emanuel   96 n. 21, 100, 137

Hoadly, Benjamin   184

Hodgson, Peter C.   137 n. 1, 151 nn. 47 and 49, 152 n. 55, 158 n. 86, 160 n. 95, 163

Holtzmann, Heinrich   130, 130 n. 46, 134

Hooker, Richard   12–13, 12 nn. 28–29, 13 n. 30, 38

Hyde, Thomas   188

Jackson-McCabe, Matt   67–68 n. 2, 89, 107 n. 8, 121 n. 73, 138 n. 2, 164

Jewel, John   22, 22 n. 59, 38

Jones, F. Stanley   45 n. 1, 67 n. 1, 68 nn. 4–5, 147 n. 33, 164

Jones, Jeremiah   49, 49–50 nn. 10–13, 55, 65, 125 n. 10, 134

Katz, David S.   5, 5 n. 5, 38

Klijn, A. F. J.   68 n. 3, 89, 138 n. 2, 139, 139 n. 3, 164

Kümmel, Werner Georg   99 n. 36, 100

Lake, Arthur   14–15, 15 n. 39

Lange, Lobegott   132, 132 n. 54, 134, 146–47, 146 nn. 27–28, 164

Lechler, Gotthard Victor   125 n. 10, 135, 143, 143 nn. 19–20, 164

LeClerc, Jean   95, 95 n. 20, 147 n. 33, 163, 180, 217, 218

Leigh, Edward   6, 6 n. 9, 38

Leland, John   105 n. 2, 113 n. 33, 122

Lemke, Hella   3 n. 1, 36 n. 121, 38, 128 n. 28, 133 n. 65, 135, 138 n. 2, 140 n. 7, 141 n. 12, 146 n. 23, 147 n. 26, 150 n. 42, 155 n. 67, 156 n. 68, 164

Leslie, Charles   81 n. 43

Liebing, Heinz   150 n. 45, 151 n. 49, 164

Lightfoot, John   222

Lincicum, David   129 n. 32

Luedemann, Gerd   68 n. 3, 90, 138 n. 2, 139 n. 6, 150 n. 46, 161, 164

Luomanen, Petri   68 n. 4

Lurbe, Pierre   62 n. 35, 66, 92 n. 5

MacKay, R. W.   145 n. 23, 164

Mainusch, H.   62 n. 35, 66

Mangey, Thomas 55, 55 n. 22, 56, 56 n. 28, 58, 58–60 nn. 30–33, 62–63 n. 37, 65, 97 n. 24, 100

Mannarino, Lia 45 n. 2, 65, 92 n. 5, 100

Maracci, Louis 195, 196, 200

Martin, Gregory 9–11, 10 nn. 16–18, 11 nn. 19–22, 12, 38

McGiffert, Michael 23 n. 65, 38

McLachlan, Herbert 38

Metzger, Bruce M. 99 n. 35, 100

Mimouni, Simon Claude 138 n. 2, 164

Moeller, Bernd 126 nn. 13–14, 135

Monnoye, Bertrand de la 52, 52 n. 18, 65, 175

More, Thomas 22, 38

Morgan, Robert 99 n. 36, 100, 145 n. 23, 151 n. 47, 164

Morgan, Thomas 3, 36, 36 n. 121, 38, **105–22**, 123 n. 2, 140–42, 140 n. 8, 141 nn. 10–11, 143 nn. 17 and 19–20, 144, 144 n. 21, 145 n. 23, 146, 160, 161, 164

Morton, Thomas 16, 16 n. 42, 38

Mosheim, Johann Lorenz **124–27**, 128 n. 28, 131 n. 51, 133, 135, 142, 142 n. 15, 164

Müller, Gotthold 151 n. 50, 164

Myllykoski, Matti 69 n. 7, 98 n. 30

Neander, August 129, 146, 146 nn. 26 and 29, 147, 147 nn. 31 and 33, 149, 164

Nicholl, H. F. 86 n. 57, 90

Nye, Stephen 27–28, 27–28 nn. 85–87, 38–39, 48 nn. 4–5, 65, 203

Ochino, Bernardino 22, 22 n. 58, 39

O'Neill, J. C. 130, 130 n. 46, 135

Orsi, Laura 62 n. 35, 66

Palmer, Claus-Michael 67 n. 1, 71 nn. 12–13, 90, 92 n. 5, 101, 140 nn. 8–9, 165

Palmer, Gesine 67 n. 1, 71 n. 14, 77 n. 31, 90, 101, 140 n. 8, 165

Parker, Samuel 39

Patrick, David 68 n. 5, 90, 105 n. 2, 106 nn. 3 and 5, 107 n. 9, 120–21 n. 72, 122, 123, 123 n. 3, 127 n. 20, 135, 140 n. 8, 141 nn. 10–11, 144, 144 n. 21, 145 n. 23, 165

Paulus, Heinrich Eberhard Gottlob 133 n. 65, 135, 145 nn. 24 and 26, 165

Penn, William 10 n. 15, 39

Penzel, Klaus 137 n. 1, 151 n. 47, 165

Perkins, William 12, 12 nn. 26–27, 39

Pétau, Denis 199

Pfleiderer, Otto 145 n. 23

Popkin, Richard 4 n. 3, 39

Poliakov, Léon 62 n. 36

Price, John Vladimir 105 nn. 1–2, 106 nn. 3–4, 122

Prideaux, Humphrey 175, 189

Prynne, William 6, 7 n. 10, 15–16, 16 n. 41, 39

Purchas, Samuel 6, 6 n. 8, 14, 14 n. 36, 19–20, 19 n. 51, 39

Rainoldes, John 19, 19 n. 50, 39

Reedy, Gerard 30 n. 97, 39

Reimarus, Hermann Samuel 125 n. 11, 135

Reland, Adrian 189, 193, 193 n. 11, 194, 196

Reventlow, Henning Graf 88 n. 60, 90, 125 n. 11, 126 nn. 12 and 14, 135, 140 n. 8, 165

Rhenferd, Jacob 211, 236

Richardson, John 48 nn. 4–5, 65

Ricuperati, Guiseppe 92 n. 5, 101

Riegel, Stanley K. 139, 139 n. 4, 165

Rosenblatt, Jason P. 30, 30 n. 98, 39

Rudolph, Anette 139 n. 6, 165

Saumaise, Claude 216

Schelling, F. W. J. 151–52, 151 n. 50, 152 nn. 51–52, 165

Schelstrate, Emmanuel 239

Schliemann, Adolph 96 n. 21, 101, 149 n. 38, 165

Schloemann, Martin 127 n. 22, 135

Schmidt, Francis 99 n. 35, 101

Schmidt, Johann Ernst Christian 145–46 n. 26, 148, 148 n. 34, 149, 165

Scholder, Klaus   151 n. 50, 153, 153 n. 58, 165

Schuffels, Klaus   137 n. 1, 165

Schwegler, Albert 123, 123 n. 2, 133, 133 nn. 63–64, 135, 141 n. 10

Schweitzer, Albert   112 n. 27, 122

Selden, John 30–34, 31–34 nn. 100–112, 35, 35 n. 118, 39–40, 203, 206

Semler, Johann Salomo   124, **127–32**, 134, 135–36, 144–45, 144 nn. 21–22, 145 nn. 23 and 25–26, 146, 147, 148, 148 n. 35, 161, 165–66

Sergeant, John 25–26, 25–26 nn. 74–82, 40

Sigonio, Carlo   175

Sike, Henry   200

Sionita, Gabriel   194–95, 194 n. 13

Skarsaune, Oskar   68 n. 2, 90

Smalbroke, Thomas   28–29, 28–29 nn. 89–92, 40

Smith, Jonathan Z.   107 n. 7, 122

Southgate, Beverley C.   23 n. 64, 40

South, Robert 72–73, 83 n. 49, 93, 93 n. 10, 101

Spanheim, Frederick   95, 95 nn. 19, 20, 101, 170–71

Stemberger, Günter   138 n. 2, 166

Stennett, Joseph   98, 221

Stephen, Leslie   40, 105 n. 2, 106 n. 6, 122

Stillingfleet, Edward   29–30, 29–30 nn. 93–96, 40

Stubbe, Henry   97, 97 nn. 24–25, 98, 98 n. 29, 99 n. 32, 101

Sullivan, Robert E.   92 n. 3, 101, 126 n. 14, 136

Taylor, Jeremy   13, 13 nn. 32–33, 40

Taylor, Joan E.   139, 139 n. 5, 166

Tholuck, August   125 n. 10, 128 n. 25, 136

Thorschmid, U. G.   142, 142 n. 16, 166

Toland, John 3, 4, 30, 35–36, 35–36 nn. 113–20, 40, **45–101**, 106–7, 106 nn. 5–6, 107, 120–21, 123–27, 123 n. 1, 125 nn. 10–11, 126 nn. 12 and 14, 128

n. 28, 129, 129 nn. 31–33, 131, 131 n. 51, 132, 133–34, 136, 140–42, 140 n. 89, 142 n. 16, 143 nn. 19–20, 144, 144 n. 21, 145 n. 23, 146, 147, 161, 166

Toomer, G. J.   31, 31 nn. 99, 101, 40

Traske, John   16, 16 n. 43, 40

Tremelius, John Emanuel   6

Twisse, William   15 n. 39, 40

Uhlhorn, Gerhard   130 n. 46, 136

Verheyden, Joseph   68 n. 4, 90

Voigt, Christoph   125 n. 11, 136, 142 n. 16, 143 n. 17, 166

Voltaire   127

Voss, Gerrit Janszoon   216

Wallis, John   13, 13–14 n. 34, 40

Ward, Samuel   6, 6 n. 7, 40

Warner, Levinus   194, 199–200

Wette, Wilhelm Martin Leberecht de 133 n. 65, 136, 145 n. 26

Wettstein, Johann Jakob   176

Whiston, William   127, 219, 233

Whichcote, Benjamin   230

Wiener, Max   140 n. 8, 166

Willet, Andrew   13, 13 n. 31, 40

Williams, Daniel   98

Wilson, Thomas   14, 14 n. 37, 40

Wither, George   11, 11 n. 25, 21, 21 n. 57, 41

Wolff, Christian   127

Zeller, Eduard 143 n. 19, 150, 150 n. 46, 151 nn. 48 and 50, 156, 156 n. 73, 166

Zwicker, Daniel   96 n. 21, 97 n. 27, 101

CPSIA information can be obtained at www.ICGtesting.com
Printed in the USA
BVOW020934030712

294187BV00001B/6/P